To Ron

Your work inspired
me greatly when planning
this volume.

Wolfgang

Sept. 94

The Future Population of the World

The International Institute for Applied Systems Analysis

is an interdisciplinary, nongovernmental research institution founded in 1972 by leading scientific organizations in 12 countries. Situated near Vienna, in the center of Europe, IIASA has been for more than two decades producing valuable scientific research on economic, technological, and environmental issues.

IIASA was one of the first international institutes to systematically study global issues of environment, technology, and development. IIASA's Governing Council states that the Institute's goal is: *to conduct international and interdisciplinary scientific studies to provide timely and relevant information and options, addressing critical issues of global environmental, economic, and social change, for the benefit of the public, the scientific community, and national and international institutions.* Research is organized around three central themes:

- Global Environmental Change;
- Global Economic and Technological Change;
- Systems Methods for the Analysis of Global Issues.

The Institute now has national member organizations in the following countries:

Austria
The Austrian Academy of Sciences

Bulgaria
The National Committee for Applied Systems Analysis and Management

Canada
The Canadian Committee for IIASA

Czech Republic
The Czech Committee for IIASA

Finland
The Finnish Committee for IIASA

Germany
The Association for the Advancement of IIASA

Hungary
The Hungarian Committee for Applied Systems Analysis

Italy
The National Research Council (CNR) and the National Commission for Nuclear and Alternative Energy Sources (ENEA)

Japan
The Japan Committee for IIASA

Netherlands
The Netherlands Organization for Scientific Research (NWO)

Poland
The Polish Academy of Sciences

Russia
The Russian Academy of Sciences

Slovak Republic
Membership under consideration

Sweden
The Swedish Council for Planning and Coordination of Research (FRN)

Ukraine
The Ukrainian Academy of Sciences

United States of America
The American Academy of Arts and Sciences

The Future Population of the World

What Can We Assume Today?

edited by **Wolfgang Lutz**

International Institute
for Applied Systems Analysis

EARTHSCAN
Earthscan Publications Ltd, London

First published in 1994 by
Earthscan Publications Ltd
120 Pentonville Road, London N1 9JN

A catalogue record for this book is available from the British Library

ISBN: 1 85383 239 1

Printed and bound by Biddles Limited, Guildford and King's Lynn

Earthscan Publications Ltd is an editorially independent subsidiary of Kogan Page
Ltd, and publishes in association with the International Institute for Environment
and Development and the World Wide Fund for Nature.

Contents

Illustrations

Figures

Tables

Foreword

Forecasting is one of the oldest of demographic activities, and yet it has never been fully integrated with the main body of demographic theory and data. The fact that the public regards it as our most important task finds no reflection in our research agenda; the amount of it done is out of all proportion to the fraction of space devoted to it in professional journals. The best demographers do it, but none would stake their reputation on the agreement of their forecasts with the subsequent realization – in fact some of the most eminent demographers have been the authors of the widest departures.

Demographers do not use the departures as data for learning how to improve their skills; in fact they rarely even look back at forecasts made 10 or 20 years earlier to note what the errors have been. Anyone who expects that after a census is taken there will be a flurry of articles recalling previous forecasts and congratulating or condemning will be disappointed. Writers merely go on to forecast the next following census, usually without even a glance at their past errors.

The present volume is designed to correct this unsatisfactory condition. Its writers include some of the best-known names in the profession, as well as younger people who in due course will succeed them as leaders. They systematically go through the components of future population – births, deaths, migration – that for any individual include all the possible ways of entering or leaving the world or any country in it. The chapters systemically explore the possibilities of bringing the best demographic methods to the improvement of our knowledge of future population. Few show any defensiveness in regard to their own earlier forecasts; the approach throughout is fresh and original.

By bringing to bear the best of demographic knowledge on an application whose importance has recently been accentuated by concern with environment, this book will provide a valuable contribution in its own right, and at the same time be a stimulus to further needed research.

Nathan Keyfitz
International Institute for
Applied Systems Analysis
November 1993

Introduction

Public and academic interest in population seems to follow a cyclical pattern of ups and downs that is much more pronounced than waves in demographic rates. Whereas the 1960s and early 1970s was a period of international upsurge in public population concern and demographic research, during the 1980s population hardly made it into the headlines. Presently, we are experiencing the onset of a new wave of public interest in world population growth which is largely fueled by ecological concerns. Population growth is mentioned repeatedly in international fora as one of the driving forces, if not the single most important factor, in global environmental change. But this time it is natural scientists rather than demographers who point at the importance of the issue.

Demographers remain conspicuously silent in the face of the attention suddenly given to an issue they have carefully studied for decades, while researchers in other disciplines attempt to occupy this territory. Demographers, who should have better knowledge of population dynamics and the determinants of fertility, mortality, and migration, tend to be embarrassed over frequent oversimplifications in the present debate, and also tend to be puzzled over how to approach the highly complex issue of population–environment interaction. Scientists from other disciplines are often less cautious in making statements about the role of population and do not always apply the same rules of scientific scrutiny that they are expected to apply in their own discipline. It is also problematic when scientific paradigms from the natural sciences and animal ecology are directly applied to complex social systems.

Without a doubt this new interest in population issues presents a positive challenge and opportunity for demographers and social scientists in general. Instead of retreating from this territory of increasingly interdisciplinary population analysis, the demographic community could show flexibility and directly address some of the well-justified questions asked by the outside world. These questions are discussed extensively in Chapter 2 of this volume. One central question in this context regards possible future population trends in the face of ecological constraints and new threats to human life. An increasing number of people want to know more about possible alternative population trends than the standard population projections provide. Such people include scholars in energy analysis who want long-range population scenarios as input to their models; regional planners, politicians, and business leaders who want to develop robust strategies that hold under different possible future population patterns; and an increasing number of individuals who are simply interested in the issue. These nondemographers often want to know more about the assumptions made, their justifications, and the range of uncertainty than has been given to them up to now by demographers.

This volume has been produced because of the belief that the demographic community can do more in terms of summarizing its knowledge about future population trends than has been done in the past. In this, the book attempts to serve a dual purpose: to respond to the challenge of increased outside interest in alternative future population trends; and to advance within the demographic community the discussion on the approaches and assumptions to be chosen for population projections.

In its approach the volume follows that of an earlier book, *Future Demographic Trends in Europe and North America: What Can We Assume Today?* (Lutz, ed., 1991, Academic Press, London, UK). The basic idea is to devote the bulk of space to substantive deliberations of experts with partly differing views about possible future trends in the three components of population change: fertility, mortality, and migration. In a final part the alternative views on future trends of each component are translated into a set of alternative scenarios. In this book the scenario approach is applied in a more systematic and elaborate way than in the 1991 book. Different sets of projections are presented until 2030 and 2100.

Part I of the volume addresses the question of what justifies another set of global population projections. It starts with a comprehensive survey of past long-range global population projections in Chapter 1 written by Tomas Frejka, who in the early 1970s produced the most influential set of long-range projections following Notestein's work of 1945 and introduced the concept of convergence toward replacement-level fertility. In his contribution, Frejka emphasizes the lessons learned from past projections and points at desirable features of new world population projections. In Chapter 2, Wolfgang Lutz, Joshua Goldstein, and Christopher Prinz discuss some basic questions in population projections which are rarely addressed in an explicit way. The chapter, entitled "Alternative Approaches to Population Projection," deals with such issues as who is interested in projections, what output parameters are desired, what should be the time horizon, and how can the issue of uncertainty be handled. Chapter 2 also presents and justifies the specific scenario approach chosen for this study and compares its features with previous population projections.

Part II is dedicated to future fertility in today's developing countries. It consists of four chapters dealing with different aspects of this issue which will dominate the extent of future world population growth. In Chapter 3, John Cleland gives a comprehensive survey of regional fertility trends between 1960 and 1990 and the factors behind these changes. This chapter serves as an important basis for our fertility assumptions. Chapter 4, by Charles Westoff, is more explicitly oriented toward the future; it summarizes the extensive empirical evidence on reproductive preferences and discusses their implications for the future course of fertility decline. From this analysis, powerful arguments can be derived for assuming fertility declines, at least in the near future. In Chapter 5, Mercedes Concepcion looks at another important factor in determining future fertility levels, namely, the role of population policies and family-planning programs. Based on the experience from Southeast Asia, she shows that such programs can make a big difference if certain preconditions are met. In Chapter 6, Griffith Feeney gives an account of the amazing fertility changes in China. Based on the analysis of parity progression ratios, he also derives some alternative scenarios for future fertility in that country, which currently is home to one-fifth of the world's population.

Part III of the volume looks at future mortality in developing countries. It also consists of four chapters. An introductory chapter by Birgitta Bucht (Chapter 7) provides a comprehensive analysis of recent mortality trends in the different developing regions. Michel Garenne in Chapter 8 focuses on mortality in sub-Saharan Africa, the world region with the greatest uncertainties. One of the uncertainties, the mortality impact of AIDS, is explicitly addressed in Chapter 9 by John Bongaarts. Although both chapters focus on Africa, many of the considerations also apply to other developing regions. Finally, Gerhard Heilig in Chapter 10 addresses a crucial question which is usually excluded from population projections, namely, whether there will be enough food to feed all the people projected or whether famine-related mortality is likely to increase at some point. His conclusion is that at least for the next decades, global food supplies should be sufficient under favorable political conditions.

Part IV considers fertility and mortality in today's industrialized countries. It has two chapters but, in the discussion, reference is also made to the 14 chapters on that topic included in Lutz (1991). Lutz in Chapter 11 considers various arguments that would suggest further fertility declines in today's low fertility countries opposed to some arguments implying higher fertility. James Vaupel and Hans Lundström in Chapter 12 focus on the controversial issue of future old-age mortality in developed societies. For making future mortality assumptions over many decades in countries that already have female life expectancies of around 80 years, the question of an upper limit to the human life span becomes decisive.

Part V of the volume considers migration between the world regions. International migration is a weak point in most population projections because of deficient data and the assumed volatility of future migration trends. For this reason it has sometimes been omitted altogether, which in fact means the assumption of zero migration. This volume makes an effort to deal with migration more explicitly. In Chapter 13, Hania Zlotnik presents a systematic analysis of past interregional migration flows with the best data available.

This is complemented by a very broad consideration of possible future migration patterns by Sture Öberg in Chapter 14. Taken together, these two chapters provide a basis for making alternative assumptions on future interregional migration flows which will have a status that is equal to fertility and mortality assumptions in the following scenario calculations.

Part VI presents the actual population projections for 12 world regions with assumptions based on the substantive considerations given in all previous chapters. Lutz, Prinz, and Jeannette Langgassner present two quite different sets of alternative population projections. The first, described in Chapter 15, is a set of systematic permutation scenarios defined until 2030. These are eight scenarios that result from all possible combinations of high and low values in fertility, mortality, and migration, plus a ninth central scenario combining the averages of these values. The second set, described in Chapter 16, gives long-range extensions for illustrative purposes to the year 2100. It presents extensions of the central scenario and high-fertility/high-mortality and low-fertility/low-mortality extensions, plus special scenarios that assume interdependence between the components and possible feedbacks from population size and age structures on the components. Extensive appendix tables document the results. These two chapters also contain sections comparing the IIASA scenarios to the UN and World Bank projections.

An epilogue by Lutz puts the results of the scenario calculations back into the broader perspective of global change and the contribution demographers can make to this important new field of studies. It also considers the necessary trade-off between curbing population growth and rapid population aging and discusses the importance of sensitivity analysis of alternative population trends for robust policies. The epilogue concludes by distinguishing between future population trends that are inevitable and those that can be influenced to a certain degree by human activities and changes in behavior. By 2030 the world population will almost certainly grow by between 50 percent and 100 percent. Where it will be within this range will crucially depend on choices made during the next decade.

Wolfgang Lutz
Leader, Population Project
IIASA

Contributors

John Bongaarts
The Population Council
New York, New York, USA

Birgitta Bucht
Population Division
United Nations
New York, New York, USA

John Cleland
Centre for Population Studies
London School of Hygiene and
 Tropical Medicine
London, UK

Mercedes B Concepcion
The Population Institute
University of Philippines
Diliman, Quezon City, Philippines

Griffith Feeney
Program on Population
East-West Center
Honolulu, Hawaii, USA

Tomas Frejka
United Nations
Economic Commission for Europe
Geneva, Switzerland

Michel Garenne
Harvard Center for Population
 and Development Studies
Cambridge, Massachusetts, USA

Joshua R Goldstein
Department of Demography
University of California
Berkeley, California, USA
and IIASA

Gerhard K Heilig
International Institute for
 Applied Systems Analysis
Laxenburg, Austria

Jeannette Langgassner
International Institute for
 Applied Systems Analysis
Laxenburg, Austria

Hans Lundström
Statistics Sweden
Stockholm, Sweden

Wolfgang Lutz
International Institute for
 Applied Systems Analysis
Laxenburg, Austria

Sture Öberg
Department of Social and
 Economic Geography
University of Uppsala, Sweden
and IIASA

Christopher Prinz
International Institute for
 Applied Systems Analysis
Laxenburg, Austria

James W Vaupel
Odense University Medical School
Odense, Denmark

Charles F Westoff
Office of Population Research
Princeton University
Princeton, New Jersey, USA

Hania Zlotnik
Population Division
United Nations
New York, New York, USA

Part I

Why Another Set of Global Population Projections?

Chapter 1

Long-range Global Population Projections: Lessons Learned

Tomas Frejka

Gregory King (1648–1712), the first known creator of long-range global population projections, wrote that "if the World should continue to A° Mundi [anno mundi] 20,000 [A.D. 16,052] it might then have 6,500 million" (King, 1696). In reality, the world's population will reach the number projected by King early in the next century, most likely in about 10 years from the writing of this chapter. In hindsight his projection left much to be desired. But did he provide knowledge and insights that were interesting and valuable to his contemporaries?

This chapter provides an overview of the leading long-term population projections that have been developed to date: their basic characteristics and an examination of this experience to extract the lessons learned and to attempt to formulate some general principles on what makes long-range projections interesting and useful and what kinds of circumstances justify the creation of a new set of projections. As a rule, to which there will be some exceptions,

---

This chapter uses a significant part of the work done in Frejka (1981a).

3

this chapter deals only with long-range population projections – i.e., those that span over a century or more.

Frejka (1981a) introduces a classification of global population projections which distinguishes between extrapolations of total numbers and global component projections. The latter are component projections in two senses: demographic components (fertility, mortality, and age structure) and country and region components that are aggregated into global projections. Progress from the former to the latter was historically the basic methodological innovation. In this chapter we briefly review other new ideas and methods as they are being applied in the preparation of long-range global population projections.

1.1   Early Global Projections: Extrapolations

The few global population projections made up to the mid-20th century tended to be long range and were based on extrapolations of total numbers (*Table 1.1*). The authors (King, 1696; Knibbs, 1928; Pearl, 1924; Pearl and Gould, 1936) based these projections on their respective observations of population growth rates and of mechanisms of population growth that were believed to regulate human population change. The reason for concern about future population growth was anxiety with regard to the world's carrying capacity. The method used by King and Knibbs was very simple. They applied the current estimated population growth rates to the estimated size of the population.

Pearl undertook extensive research which led him to believe that there is a law according to which growth of populations (not only human) takes place, that this law is in principle shaped by biological and environmental forces, and that the resulting trend can be expressed mathematically in various forms of the stretched out S-shaped logistic curve. In 1924 Pearl calculated the curve for the world population and subsequently, in 1936, together with Gould he revised the curve for the world population upward arguing that there is a "necessity for frequent revision of human population logistics as new data become available."

Table 1.1. Long-term global population projections.

Author	Year	Alternative	Population (in millions)					
			To 1950	1950	1970	2000	2050	2100
King	1696		630 (B=1695)				780 (2052)	
Pearl	1924		1649 (B=1914)	1832	1901	1963	2007	2020
Knibbs	1928		1950 (B=1928)			3900 (2008)		15600 (2169)
Pearl & Gould	1936		2073 (B=1931)	2153	2305	2459	2582	2625
Notestein	1945					3300		
Frejka	1973	NRR=1.0						
		2040				6670	13025	15102
		2020				6422	10473	11169
		2000			3645(B)	5923	8172	8389
		1980				5116	6286	6417
		1970				4746	5592	5691
UN	1974	Medium			3621(B)	6406	11163	12257
Littman & Keyfitz	1977				3968 (B=1975)	5882	8188	
UN	1978	High				6509	12076	14180
		Medium			4033	6199	9775	10525
		Low			(B=1975)	5856	8004	8029
Bogue & Tsui	1979	High				5972		
		Medium			B=1975	5883	8107	
		Low				5756	7816	
World Bank	1980				4416 (B=1980)	6015		9868 (stat.)
Frejka	1980	NRR=1.0						
		plausible high				6353	11015	12348
		2040				6357	11648	13427
		2020			4412	6234	9902	10639
		2000			(B=1980)	5930	8214	8539
		1980				5333	6743	6986
		plausible low				6046	8762	9208
UN	1982	Growth			4441	6337	11690	14927
		High			4441	6337	11629	14199
		Medium			4432	6119	9513	10185
		Low			4420	5837	7687	7524
		Decline			4420 (B=1980)	5837	7667	7247
World Bank	1985				4442 (B=1980)	6147	9496	10681 (stat.)
UN	1992	High			5327	6420	12506	19156
		Medium/High			5327	6420	12495	17592
		Medium			5292	6261	10019	11186
		Medium/Low			5262	6093	7817	6415
		Low			5262 (B=1990)	6093	7813	6009

B stands for base year of projection; NRR stands for net reproduction rate.
Sources: See references.

1.2   Modern Global Component Projections

The evolution of population theory and methods, as well as the
continuously greater availability of demographic data, has provided
the base for developing more sophisticated population projections.
The leading scholar who transformed the potentiality into reality
was Frank Notestein. The methodology of component population
projections was first applied in a study of Europe and the Soviet
Union commissioned by the League of Nations in the early 1940s
(Notestein *et al.*, 1944). This study was perceived as the first volume of a series of studies on world population trends and problems.
Soon thereafter, Notestein (1945) presented the first modern global
population projections. He reviewed past population trends of countries and continents; he discussed his understanding of the mechanisms of population change, distinguishing three main demographic
types of populations corresponding to different stages of the "demographic evolution" ("incipient decline," "transitional growth," and
"high growth potential"); and finally, he discussed prospects for
growth and provided projections separately by continent on the basis of which he concluded that "summing the hypothetical figures
for the year 2000, we have a world total of 3.3 billion people. On the
assumption of general order and the spread of modern techniques
of production the figure is probably conservative." Even though it
spanned only over a period of half a century, Notestein's projection of the world population is discussed in this chapter because of
its pioneering nature and because the applied ideas, approach, and
methods provided the base for a generation of world, regional, and
national projections to follow.

Notestein's projections permit the formulation of general characteristics and procedures that constitute the *basis* of long-range
population projections:

- An explicit or implicit *theoretical framework* of the mechanisms
  of population change, which guides the formulation of assumptions about future changes in demographic trends.
- A wealth of accumulated *demographic data* which serves as the
  empirical base for the framework, provides the input data for the
  benchmark year/period of the projections, and makes possible
  a disaggregated approach.

- A *methodology* which usually consists of (a) a separate assessment of an initial age structure and separate projection of the two motor forces of demographic dynamics in a closed population – mortality and fertility (the combination of these elements yields the so-called component projection of a population) – and (b) a separate assessment and projection of national and/or regional populations, which, when aggregated, yield global projections or which provide a check on separately computed global projections.
- Advances in any of these characteristics and procedures depend on advances of demographic and social science research as well as on advances in data collection.

Notestein's contribution was important not only because he applied and combined all of the above elements but critical also from a substantive perspective. His theoretical framework is based on the demographic transition theory labeled the "demographic evolution" in Notestein's 1945 piece. It is the demographic transition theory which – for the most part implicitly – is the theoretical base for the majority of the global long-range population projections that followed.

The sets of the United Nations population projections of the 1950s and 1960s followed Notestein's model, with refinements being introduced as methods of demographic analysis developed and new data became available. The time span of these projections was from 30 to 45 years. A particularly innovative set was prepared in 1957 (UN, 1958) which made considerable use of sophisticated methods in estimating demographic parameters and in the projection computations. For these projections the UN (1955) prepared a set of model life tables, as well as models of fertility trends. This was the first UN projection extended to the year 2000, for which time a global population ranging between 4.9 and 6.9 billion was projected. As we approach the year 2000 it now appears that the UN's 1957 medium projection will come remarkably close to what the actual figure for the year 2000 is likely to be, 6.3 billion. The central objective of the UN sets was defined as "an attempt to project population changes into the future as accurately as possible with available information to provide basic data on population size and characteristics for future planning" (UN, 1973). The focus of population projections up to this point in time was on providing the best possible, "as accurate as possible," projection, forecast, or even prediction.

1.3 Contemporary Long-range Projections

The first set of long-range projections to follow Notestein's work of 1945 was developed by Frejka (1973a) in the early 1970s (the ideas and methods applied were originally developed in a study of the US population in Frejka, 1968). These projections were meant to demonstrate the strength of the population growth momentum inherent in current demographic characteristics – age structure and levels as well as age-specific structures of fertility and mortality – and the strength of behavioral continuities. The principal innovation was to prepare *scenario projections* in contrast to projections that were aimed at projecting future demographic trends as accurately as possible. More specifically, these projections were designed:

- To map alternative scenarios of how the demographic transition could proceed toward an assumed low mortality–low fertility equilibrium expressed by a net reproduction rate of unity being reached at defined alternative future dates.
- To illustrate the long-range implications for population growth of specific demographic, mainly fertility, trends.
- To demonstrate the more likely alternatives of future population growth in the context of unrealistic/unlikely projections based on implausibly rapid or implausibly slow assumed trends of fertility decline.

The emphasis was on generating illustrative scenario projections, not on generating projections that would aim at depicting future trends as accurately as possible. At the same time, however, there was a clear intention to supply a good idea of likely future trends by providing the possibility of comparing more realistic alternatives with what appeared to be clearly unrealistic options. The projections were computed for a period of almost 200 years rather than the customary period of between 30 and 50 years (for instance, the UN projections).

The assumption that a low fertility–low mortality stationary population could be achieved and possibly maintained in the long run appeared quite plausible in light of the trends in the demographically mature countries through the late 1960s. There seemed to be a reasonable (tacit) consensus at the time that post-demographic transition societies would stabilize, with fertility and mortality being such that the long-term net reproduction rate average would be around unity. In hindsight, the experience of Western countries, particularly since the early 1970s, has not confirmed this assumption.

These projections provided a vivid illustration of the long-term consequences for population growth of demographic trends, mainly of fertility, of the foreseeable future, say of the 1970s and 1980s, which presumably could be modified by public policies. While the calculations of the global population for the year 2050, for example, ranged between 5.6 and 13.0 billion (see *Table 1.1*), it was argued that the alternative results yielding figures below 8 billion could be dismissed as unrealistic because the calculations were based on assumptions of unrealistically rapid fertility decline. With considerably less certainty the numbers at the upper limits of the range were cast in doubt, as historical experience seemed to indicate that fertility would be likely to decline faster than the defined assumptions for the high projection. Consequently, it was argued that the global population in the middle of the next century would probably be between 8 and 12 billion and that whether the actual population would be closer to the upper or lower limit would depend on how vigorously major factors shaping fertility decline, including public policies, would exert their impact.

During the 1970s and 1980s various institutions, in particular the UN (1975, 1981, 1982, 1992) but also the World Bank (Zachariah and Vu, 1978, 1980; Vu, 1985), the US Bureau of the Census (1979), and individuals (Littman and Keyfitz, 1977; Bogue and Tsui, 1979) prepared long-range projections. To a significant extent, these projections used a principle analogous to Frejka's projections, namely, that they were scenario projections aiming, sooner or later, for an eventual low mortality–low fertility equilibrium. Many did introduce additional ideas/arguments or methodological refinements.

In their projections of the early 1970s, the UN adjusted the models for the future course of fertility in both the developed and developing countries, and introduced the reverse logistic curve (a stretched-out reverse S) with specified time points at which replacement-level fertility will be reached and, beyond it, sustained.

A notable departure from the principle of aiming at eventual replacement-level fertility is contained in the UN 1992 projections where the experience of below replacement-level fertility in the Western countries is reflected. The idea of reaching and maintaining replacement-level fertility is assumed only for the medium variant and for an instant replacement-level fertility projection. Two variants assume reaching and maintaining below replacement-level fertility, two other projections assume a fertility decline that is above replacement-level fertility which when the defined level is reached it is maintained, and a fifth projection assumes constant fertility and mortality. Among the conclusions of these recent projections, the UN stresses that according to the medium projection the world population would be 11.2 billion in the year 2100 which is 1 billion, or 10 percent, larger than the UN 1982 projections. According to the UN, "upwardly revised estimated and projected average life expectancies at birth probably play the key role." Also, there is a much wider range between the lowest and highest results in the 1992 compared with the 1982 projections for the year 2100, namely, 6.0–19.2 compared with 7.2–14.9 billion. The authors emphasize "that there is a wide range of uncertainty regarding the future size of the world population."

Bogue and Tsui (1979) reached a very different conclusion, albeit over a decade earlier: "the magnitude and pace of the (1965–1975 fertility) decline is greater than many demographers had expected" and therefore

> this development makes it necessary for demographers to review and re-examine their projections for the future. We predict that by the year 2025 the world will have nearly achieved zero population growth. It is estimated that this equilibrium will be achieved with a world population of about 7.4 billion (8.1 in 2050)...primarily because of the worldwide drive by Third World countries to introduce family planning as part of their national social-development services.

In the early 1970s studies associated with the Club of Rome introduced ambitious methodological innovations. An attempt was made to link population projections more tightly to social, economic, environmental, resource consumption, and political trends. Mead-ows *et al.* (1972) and Mesarovic and Pestel (1974) defined global dy-namic systems analysis models that contained population as one of several basic components. Projections of these systems were carried into the 21st century to demonstrate possible disastrous or harmo-nious long-term consequences inherent in global societal trends. Ac-cording to these projections, the likely trends in population growth as well as in other societal trends will lead to a collapse of the world system. This will include an increase in mortality and a consequent rapid population decline. The studies conclude that if such a col-lapse is to be avoided, a rapid fertility decline, significantly faster than that of the low UN projection of that era, would have to be generated. These projections were indeed innovative in their com-prehensive approach, but numerous critics doubted the validity of employed assumptions and relationships (Ridker, 1973).

1.4 A Recent Critical Review of Long-run Global Projections

A critical review of long-run population projections has recently been undertaken by Lee (1991). He takes a substantive rather than a historic approach. Lee comprehensively analyzes important aspects of population projections: demography's contribution to forecasting, theories underlying projections, the degree of uncertainty of long-run population projections, and recent long-run projections of the global population. Among the numerous insightful observations and findings, many can be applied to future work.

One observation which appears to be a central concern to Lee and which deserves particular attention in the context of this chap-ter is that in a number of the above-discussed global projections a sufficiently explicit and systematic theoretical framework is lacking. Two views expressed in Lee's paper warrant a brief discussion at this point.

Lee eloquently challenges a central premise applied in the long-range global projections of the 1970s and the 1980s, namely, that the end point of most of these projections are stationary populations with a net reproduction rate of unity. He claims that he could not find any explanation of this in Frejka's 1973 book (see Frejka, 1973a, which according to Lee provides the origin of this idea; actually the origin of the idea is in Frejka, 1968) and criticizes the justification given in Frejka (1981b). Admittedly, the theoretical justification of using replacement-level fertility as an end point might not have been thorough enough, however, it was clear that Frejka's work in the late 1960s and early 1970s was conducted within the demographic transition theory framework as it was understood at that time. If nowhere else this was succinctly expressed in Frejka (1973b): "The experience of history suggests that the population of the world may eventually reach a state close to non-growth, that is, all countries will be in the third stage of the demographic transition."

The second issue relates to the content and purpose of the concept of projections. A basic premise of Lee's, which he states without providing arguments or justification, is that "almost all demographic projections are in fact forecasts, in that they present the author's best guess about the future." Therefore he uses forecasts throughout his piece. As has been discussed at length above, the distinction between *forecasts* – i.e., projections that attempt to depict future trends as accurately as possible at any given moment in time – and *scenario projections* – i.e., projections which introduce elements that aim to illustrate certain developments some of which might actually be intentionally unrealistic in order to demonstrate a particular outcome – is justified. That does not exclude the purpose of *also* attempting to provide a reasonable perception of realistic future population trends through scenario projections.

1.5   Conclusions

Contemporary long-range global population projections of the past 25 years are all constructed along the lines of the Notestein model. They are based on an explicit or implicit theoretical framework, using the best available data, and they are component projections. They are usually straightforward demographic projections where the possible impacts of changes in behavioral, social, economic, or political trends are introduced via the theoretical framework. A basic innovation was added by devising and using scenario projections in contrast to projections aiming at prediction. However, even when

using scenario-type projections the intention of more or less approx-
imating likely future demographic trends is almost always present.

The various projections briefly discussed above provide examples of justifications for new projections. At the most general level,
whenever a significant innovation can be introduced in any one of
the elements a new projection is justified. Thus, formulating a new
or different theoretical framework, the application of new data, or
the development of a new or different methodology provides such a
justification.

Each of the subsequent UN sets of projections used newly
collected or estimated base data. Some of these sets introduced
methodological advances, and in some the formulation of assumptions about demographic trends was modified based on the developments of actual trends. Bogue and Tsui (1979) based their projections on their interpretation of fertility trends between 1965 and
1975 and on their belief that policy measures in the form of strong
family-planning programs could and would modify fertility trends
more than experience to date indicated. Meadows *et al.* (1972) attempted to expand the theoretical framework by direct linkage to
social, economic, environmental, resource consumption, and political trends and applied a large number of assumptions about trends
and linkages. In addition to using new fertility and mortality data,
the most recent United Nations long-range global projections (1992)
assumed a variety of fertility trends: reaching and maintaining
replacement-level fertility, reaching and maintaining fertility levels
below and above replacement.

The purpose of long-range global population projections can be
more than attempting to predict total population numbers 50, 100,
or 150 years into the future. In addition, their purpose can be:

- To demonstrate shorter- and long-run implications of alternative
  fertility and mortality trends of the foreseeable future.
- To demonstrate what type of trends need to occur to achieve
  a population of a desirable size and with specific structural
  characteristics.
- To demonstrate various structural implications of certain fertility and mortality trends for major regions and functional age
  groups, for example.

- To demonstrate the consequences of intended policy interventions if they were to succeed.

Whatever the purpose of a single projection or a set of projections may be, for them to be meaningful and to provide new insights, a significant and well-justified *new* or *innovative element* has to be embedded in the projections.

References

Bogue, D.J., and Tsui, A.O., 1979, Zero world population growth? *The Public Interest* **55**(Spring):99–113.

Frejka, T., 1968, Reflections on the demographic conditions needed to establish a US stationary population growth, *Population Studies* **22**(3):379–397.

Frejka, T., 1973a, *The Future of Population Growth: Alternative Paths to Equilibrium*, John Wiley & Sons, New York, NY, USA.

Frejka, T., 1973b, The prospects for a stationary world population, *Scientific American* **228**(3):15–23.

Frejka, T., 1981a, World population projections: A concise history, in *International Population Conference*, Vol. 3, IUSSP, Manila, Philippines.

Frejka, T., 1981b, Long-term prospects for world population growth, *Population and Development Review* **7**(3):489–511.

King, G., 1696 [1973], 17th Century Manuscript Book of Gregory King, *The Earliest Classics: Graunt and King*, Gregg International, Germany.

Knibbs, G.H., 1928 [1976], *The Shadow of the World's Future*, Reprint Edition, Arno Press, New York, NY, USA.

Lee, R.D., 1991, Long-run global population forecasts: A critical appraisal, in K. Davis and M.S. Bernstam, eds., *Resources, Environment, and Population: Present Knowledge, Future Options*, Oxford University Press, New York, NY, USA.

Littman, G., and Keyfitz, N., 1977, The Next Hundred Years, Working Paper No. 101, Harvard University Center for Population Studies, Cambridge, MA, USA.

Meadows, D.H., Meadows, D.L., Randers, J., and Behrens III, W.W., 1972, *The Limits to Growth*, Universe Books, New York, NY, USA.

Mesarovic, M., and Pestel, E., 1974, *Mankind at the Turning Point*, E.P. Dutton, New York, NY, USA.

Notestein, F.W., 1945, Population: The long view, in T.W. Schultz, ed., *Food for the World*, University of Chicago Press, Chicago, IL, USA.

Notestein, F.W., Taeuber, I.B., Kirk, D., Coale, A.J., and Kiser, L.K., 1944, *The Future Population of Europe and the Soviet Union: Population Projections 1940–1970*, League of Nations, Geneva, Switzerland.

Pearl, R., 1924, *Studies in Human Biology*, Williams and Wilkins, Baltimore, MD, USA.

Pearl, R., and Gould, S., 1936, World population growth, *Human Biology* 8(3):399–419.

Ridker, R.G., 1973, To grow or not to grow: That is not the relevant question, *Science* 128(December):1315–1318.

UN, 1955, Age and sex patterns of mortality: Model life tables for underdeveloped countries, *Population Studies* 2.

UN, 1958, The future growth of world population, *Population Studies* 28.

UN, 1973, *World Population Prospects as Assessed in 1968*, Population Studies, No. 53, Sales No. E.72.XIII.4, United Nations, New York, NY, USA.

UN, 1975, *Concise Report on the World Population Situation in 1970–1975 and its Long-range Implications*, Population Studies, No. 56, United Nations, NY, USA.

UN, 1981, *Long-range Global Population Projections, Based on Data As Assessed in 1978*, Population Division Working Paper, ESA/P/WP.75, United Nations, New York, NY, USA.

UN, 1982, Long-range global population projections, as assessed in 1980, *Population Bulletin of the United Nations*, 14.

UN, 1992, *Long-Range World Population Projections: Two Centuries of Population Growth 1950–2150*, ST/ESA/SER.A/125, United Nations, New York, NY, USA.

US Bureau of the Census, 1979, Illustrative projections of world populations to the 21st century, *Current Population Reports: Special Studies*, Series P-23, No. 79, Washington, DC, USA.

Vu, M.T., 1985, *World Population Projections 1985*, World Bank/Johns Hopkins University Press, Baltimore, MD, USA.

Zachariah, K.C., and Mi Thi Vu, 1978, *Population Projections: 1975–2000*, World Bank, Washington, DC, USA.

Zachariah, K.C., and Mi Thi Vu, 1980, *Population Projections, 1980–2000 and Long-Term (Stationary Population)*, World Bank, Washington, DC, USA.

Chapter 2

Alternative Approaches to Population Projection

Wolfgang Lutz, Joshua R. Goldstein, and Christopher Prinz

Future demographic trends are inherently uncertain, and the further one goes into the future, the greater the uncertainty. On the other hand, few social and economic trends are as stable as population trends. No social scientist would challenge the statement that the percentage increase of the world population over the next five years can be more accurately projected than changes in unemployment rates, trade balances, or stock markets. Because of the great inertia of population trends, long term and short term mean different things for demographic and economic forecasts, but in all forecasts uncertainty is assumed to increase with the time horizon because of the greater probability of structural changes.

Summarizing the limits of population forecasting, Nathan Keyfitz (1981:583) states: "The practical conclusion, then, is that relatively short-term forecasts, say up to ten or 20 years, do tell us something, but that beyond a quarter-century or so we simply do not know what the population will be." Such a statement still seems to reflect the consensus of most demographers today, including the group of experts invited to contribute to this book, which defines assumptions only up to the year 2030. But the question of what we can know today about the future goes beyond the issue of the time horizon which is discussed later in this chapter.

First we need to ask what kind of knowledge of the future do we want to have? Do we want to have one single number, a certain range, or a probability distribution? Do we want total population size alone or for age-structural information as well? Who is interested in these numbers and for what reason? And what is the motivation of those who prepare population projections? These questions all affect the approach taken to population forecasting and the methods and assumptions chosen.

This chapter on alternative approaches to population projection gives a broad and nontechnical exposition of some fundamental questions involved in population projection. These kinds of questions are usually not addressed in more technical scientific papers or in the publication of projection results because certain choices are taken for granted. This broader perspective is necessary, however, to answer the question which forms the title of Part I: Why another set of global population projections? Several fundamental issues in population projection are addressed in the following eight sections. The approach chosen in this book is described and justified against the background of the possible approaches. The concluding section gives a concise summary of our choice.

2.1   Who Wants Population Projections?

What motivates demographers to prepare population projections, and for whom are they preparing them? There seem to be three major groups of people that have interest in population projections and are willing to pay demographers to do this job: other scientists, politicians, and the general public, including business.

There is increasing demand from a large number of natural and social scientists for information about future population size and structure. The recent upsurge of environmental and global change research has only heightened this demand. A major reason for this demand lies in the fact that a large number of the indicators used in such studies are on a per capita basis, i.e., by definition require a population figure in the denominator. Most explicitly this is the case in studies on CO_2 emissions such as Bongaarts (1992), Birdsall

(1992), and Bartiaux and van Ypersele (1993). All these studies combine future population trends with assumed future per capita CO_2 emissions. Lutz (1993) has also demonstrated that the level of regional aggregation is decisive for the results obtained. The time horizon of these studies is typically long (at least to 2030–2050) because global-warming is a long-term phenomenon.

Related to global warming issues is the large group of energy demand models which is probably the greatest scientific consumer of population projection data. A minority of forecasters (e.g., Odell and Rosing, 1980) omits the explicit consideration of population, and instead projects total energy demand. Most, however, combine scenarios about the evolution of energy demand with population forecasts (Gouse *et al.*, 1992; Leontief and Sohn, 1984; WECCC, 1983). The time horizons of these studies range from 2020 to 2100.

Another field of studies which routinely includes population projections is the analysis of world food consumption. The Food and Agriculture Organization (FAO, 1988) has produced forecasts of demand to 2000 and will include projections through 2010 in a forthcoming volume. The approach taken by Mellor and Paulino (1986), for example, is to produce two scenarios: the first is based on present per capita calorie consumption and the second includes increased calorie consumption arising from assumed economic growth. Many more fields, such as economic forecasting, epidemiological studies, and insurance mathematics, demand population projections as input.

In the past non-demographic scientific studies requiring population forecasts tended to consider only one variant of future population trends. Increasingly, however, the further sophistication of scenario approaches in many of these disciplines suggests also the consideration of alternative population scenarios. There clearly is a demand not only for one best guess of the future population but also for information concerning the degree of uncertainty and more extreme scenarios for sensitivity analysis. So far demographers have not done much to satisfy this demand.

Politicians, including public administrators, need population projections largely for planning purposes. Especially in the health, education, and social-security sectors, medium- and long-term planning includes demographic variables as crucial components.

Typically, politicians and administrators would like to receive one likely variant of future population size and structure that they can input into their own models of where new hospitals and schools should be constructed and how the legal system of pension payments should be organized to accommodate changes in the age composition of the population.

Unlike the scientific community, public administrators and political planners hardly ever ask for alternative variants, and generally have little appreciation of methods dealing with uncertainty in population projections, despite the fact that policies should be robust and hold under varying conditions. They typically want to be given one most likely figure.

Despite the tradition of government planners to use only a single central forecast, the design of policies that hold under uncertain future conditions should be a main concern of good politics. For instance, a restructuring of the pension scheme as currently being done by many European countries should by no means consider only one assumed future mortality trend. Since national population projections tend to assume very low future mortality improvements, even a continuation of past increases in life expectancy results in a much faster increase of the old age dependency ratio, and might bring about painful if not disastrous surprises to the new system. In this situation demographers have a responsibility to communicate their knowledge about uncertainty.

The third group of users of population projections is by far the largest and most heterogeneous. Many individuals, organizations, and enterprises in the general public have specific interests in population projections. Aside from individual curiosity, this interest is related to the planning of future activities and the estimation of the expected returns from such activities, ranging from the individual decision of buying real estate in an area with future increase in population density to marketing strategies for certain commercial products, such as baby food or special products for the elderly.

Generally the expectations of this group toward population projections can be assumed to be similar to that of the group of politicians and administrators. The interest tends to focus on one most likely variant. Considerations of uncertainty may play a role in corporate planning, but generally the planning horizon of companies is too short for alternative population trends to make a difference. An exception may be companies in the field of energy supply that tend to have very long time horizons.

In addition to these three major groups interested in population projections there is one very specific group that explicitly wants to use population projections for educational and illustrative purposes. The most vocal of these are advocacy groups in the field of environment or family planning that want to illustrate to the public and political circles what would happen in the more distant future if policies aiming at a reduction of population growth were not implemented. Such people are not as much interested in one medium population projection as they are in the calculation of extreme alternatives to demonstrate the longer-term impacts of today's choices.

Another special group are students in the social sciences who should understand the basic functioning of population dynamics. For them phenomena such as the momentum of population growth could best be illustrated through comparisons of alternative long-term population projections.

In summary the different groups interested in population projections seem to expect two different things from the demographers preparing such projections: one most likely variant that can be used without further thinking about the problem of uncertainty and information about less likely but still possible trends that can be used for sensitivity analysis, i.e., for understanding how the systems studied or any planned policy or individual action would perform under different possible demographic futures. Although most of the users of projections are satisfied with a 30- to 40-year time horizon, some clearly want a longer time horizon.

2.2   Time Horizon

Technically, it is a simple matter to continue a population projection one hundred, or even one million years into the future. The choice of a projection horizon therefore represents a compromise between the advantages of providing more information and the dangers of making false forecasts. Beyond a certain point in time, we feel too unsure about the state of the family, health, and the world to specify rates of fertility, mortality, and migration. In this section we explore the possible reasons demographers could have for seeing 30 to 40 years as a threshold beyond which projections become less reliable. We also address the question of whether uncertainty increases monotonically with time or whether there are thresholds and discontinuities suggesting a certain cutoff point.

The time scale of population projections is of distinctly human dimensions. This is because not only do the human life span and the gap between generations have important demographic consequences, but also because forecasters' judgments about the speed of social change depend on their own personal experience.

From a psychological perspective, there may be reasons for discomfort involving forecasts of longer than 40 or 50 years, a little less than two generations into the future.[1] During our lifetimes, most of us get to know our grandparents, but not our great-grandparents. Consequently, we have first-hand experience of the amount of social change that can occur over two generations of time. When we specify demographic rates beyond this, not only must we forecast the behavior of individuals whom we will probably never meet, but we are dealing with individuals that are more distant, in generational terms, than anyone we have met in our own lives. In addition to this subjective reason for setting a threshold of increased uncertainty, we can point to other, less personal, justifications for a particular time horizon.

Forty years is roughly the average age in developed countries. As such, it marks the period of time beyond which a population will consist of a majority of people not yet born. The wholly individual psychological perspective just mentioned thus corresponds also to the experience of the entire population, the timing of which might mark a rupture in social change.

In addition to uncertainty in the inputs of population projection, the demographic rates that reflect individual behavior, we must also consider the size of the population at risk. The number of births in the future is a function not only of birth rates but also of the number of potential mothers and fathers in the population, itself a function of past demographic rates. This feedback property is well known in the case of the echoes of a baby boom (or bust). The time it takes for a boom to echo is approximately the mean age of childbearing, which ranges between 25 and 30 in almost all populations. Beyond this time horizon, therefore, we add to our uncertainty about birth rates the uncertainty of how many potential mothers will be in the population.

The number of deaths in a population is also a function of the number of past births and deaths, but since the mean age at death (in a stationary population, equal to life expectancy) is about three-quarters of a century, the lagged mortality effect will be of relatively minor importance in developed countries. In developing countries, however, a rapid improvement in infant mortality might increase the number of potential mothers in as little as 15 to 20 years.

Migration levels, while not subject to uncertainties about cohort size, are subject to perhaps a more arbitrary type of change – the change in government policy. Annual migration trends are largely determined by government policy. If we asked, for instance, how many immigrants will Western Europe admit, most analysts would feel reluctant to predict more than a few years into the future. And indeed we have seen tremendous ups and downs in migration flows over the past few years. When migration plays a major role in determining the demography of a region, it would seem that 5 to 10 years might mark the point beyond which any projection would become quite speculative.

If we ask why, for example, 10,000 years is too long to perform a projection, we discover a further constraint on forecast horizons. In addition to the fact that we are in no position to specify demographic rates for such a long period, the meaningfulness of the projection models used applies only to certain time scales. With an ageless population growing at a constant exponential rate, the only possible average growth rate in the very long term that would avoid extinction or inconceivable explosion is zero. The dynamics of an age-structured population are of interest only for as long as one century. After this time, no traces of the starting age structure of the starting population remain visible in the age pyramid. A projection that continues far into the future first loses its connection to its starting age structure and eventually bears little relation even to its initial size as zero growth rates become the only possibility in the very long run.

Figure 2.1 summarizes the possible thresholds of increasing uncertainty. The times shown are of an extremely stylized form and are

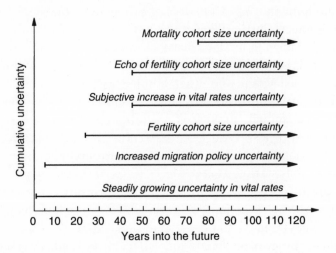

Figure 2.1. Different components of uncertainty entering the population projection over time.

meant to summarize the arguments given above. The second-wave of fertility cohort size uncertainty is added to indicate that the baby boom (bust) resulting from the cohort size uncertainty after about 25 years will have echoes in the following generation also, although of lesser amplitude. Cohort size is also determined by migration, so we might want to add additional uncertainty 25, 50, and 75 years after the migration uncertainty begins.

Despite its speculative nature, we can draw several lessons from *Figure 2.1.* First, no single clear threshold of uncertainty emerges. Instead, there are arguments for stopping the forecast at many different times. Second, the commonly accepted threshold of a little less than half a century emerges not so much as a clear demographic threshold (which might dictate a choice closer to the mean age of childbearing), but rather from the timing of the increased subjective uncertainty in demographic rates. Last, the timing of the demographic thresholds, particularly the delayed effect of births on the future number of deaths, may vary according to the population under consideration. The average age at death in a population with high infant mortality might be considerably less than 75 years.

Equally important is perhaps what this schematic figure leaves out, namely, the relative size of the different sources of uncertainty.

For some countries, like Canada, migration levels may be the largest source of uncertainty, while for others, like many African countries, structural change in birth or death rates might play the largest role.

The risk of projecting too far into the future is the loss of legitimacy ("believability") either because assumptions seem to lack foundation or because the projected populations violate constraints, such as an assumed carrying capacity of the globe. On the other hand, the fact that several features of population dynamics, such as growth momentum and echoes, do persist strongly for at least one or two generations means that projections of less than 50 years probably do not reveal all the information already present in even today's age structure. This offers an argument for a minimum length of projection.

The reluctance of demographers to go beyond a certain time horizon is in conflict with some of the expectations of potential users as described in Section 2.1. Some users clearly want population figures for the year 2100 and beyond. Should the demographer disappoint such expectations and leave it to others with less expertise to produce them? The answer we found for this study is no. But as discussed below, we make a clear distinction between what we call projections up to 2030 and everything beyond that time, which we term extensions for illustrative purposes.

2.3 Spatial Resolution and Heterogeneity

Because of the great heterogeneity of the world population it clearly does not make sense to treat the whole world as one region in a population projection. Users of projections mostly want to have information by countries or at least major world regions that are different not only in demographic but also in socioeconomic and cultural terms. If the output parameters are to be regional, clearly the projection needs to be done on a regional basis. But even if one is only interested in aggregate global results, assumptions on future fertility and mortality cannot meaningfully be made for all the different regions together for two reasons.

First, different parts of the world are at very different stages of the process of demographic transition, which in most projections is the basic underlying paradigm on which assumptions about future fertility are founded. Aggregating these different parts obscures the picture and makes the reasoning behind assumptions more difficult.

Second, because of much higher rates of population growth in the South than in the North, the weights of the two hemispheres will change significantly in the future, which by itself leads to a change in aggregate rates even if the rates per hemisphere remain constant. This can be quantitatively illustrated by a simple calculation, recently done by Lutz and Prinz (1991). In the purely hypothetical case that all vital rates stay constant at their present levels, the projection carried out on the basis of six world regions yields a 50 percent higher total population than the projection treating the world as one region. These results are based on the identical assumption of constant rates, and the amazing difference is simply due to that today the low fertility regions are still a larger proportion of the world population than they will be in the future. With this change in weights constant fertility in the main world regions results in increasing fertility of the world total and hence in a larger total population than in the case of constant global fertility.

While the above example makes it clear that heterogeneity of the population can have a strong effect, it is not clear how much one must disaggregate to avoid this problem. Even within nations there may be subpopulations with very different demographic regimes. In some of the South American countries, such as Bolivia, national fertility rates have been stagnant at a rather high level which can be explained by the bifurcation of society into a group that is well advanced in its demographic transition and by the Indian population which has not yet fully entered the fertility decline and is gaining weight through more rapid growth. In addition to the observable heterogeneity in the population, Vaupel and Yashin (1983) have demonstrated the significance of unobserved heterogeneity.

For our global population projections a basic question was, how far should one go in disaggregating the world population? Theoretically, disaggregations need not follow territorial or national boundaries but should follow the most strongly discriminating variables. In practice, however, data are most readily available by countries and groups of countries. The United Nations and the World Bank produce their population projections at the level of individual countries. Under this approach the 1.2 billion Chinese get as much attention as the 72,000 inhabitants of the Seychelles. This is due to the national constituencies of these organizations and convenience of data availability rather than questions of demographic heterogeneity.

With 150 or more countries, however, simultaneous projections become awkward especially with respect to the migration matrix to be assumed among all these states. It is perhaps for this reason that migration is not a major emphasis of the UN and World Bank projections. An alternative, which has been chosen for the present study, is to limit the number of populations projected simultaneously to subcontinental regions. As discussed extensively in Part V on migration and in the concluding chapter of this book, 12 world regions have been defined according to criteria of geographic proximity and socioeconomic, as well as demographic, similarity. These 12 regions are projected simultaneously by a multistate model assuming region-specific future paths of age-specific fertility and mortality rates and full matrices of interregional migratory streams.

These regional assumptions have to be considered aggregate future paths of fertility, mortality, and migration that reflect not only changing behavior within the subpopulations of the region but also the compositional effect of changing weights. This is the only way to deal with the bothersome issue of population heterogeneity.

2.4 Expected Output Parameters

The methodology to be chosen for population projection crucially depends on the choice of population characteristics. If one is only interested in total population size, methods such as simple exponential growth models may be used that are not sufficient if one is also interested in the future age and sex composition of the population. But many other population characteristics, such as urban/rural residence, marital status composition, and educational or labor force composition, may be of considerable interest for the user of projections and require specific methodologies.

The questions of desired output parameters together with the above-discussed issues of time horizon and of the desirability of a range of projections need to be discussed before the question of appropriate methodologies. Introductions to population forecasting usually do not address these issues explicitly, but rather group projection methods by the statistical models on which they are based (e.g., time-series models, structural equation models) as is done in the introduction to a recent comprehensive volume on population forecasting (Ahlburg and Land, 1992). Because the proper evaluation of different methods requires the systematic consideration of objectives, in this section we distinguish between forecasts aiming only at total population size, projections on the age and sex compositions of the population and projections on characteristics other than age and sex.

2.4.1 Projections of total population size

For projections of total population size alone a basic choice is between methods that consider the age structure of the population and those that do not. When advocates of the projections of population totals through various time-series models (e.g., Pflaumer, 1992) stress that such models may be more reliable than cohort-component models, which project the population by age groups, it is important to keep in mind that this debate only concerns the aggregate totals – figures that from a substantive point of view have rather limited value. Most of the economic and social issues for which the population variable is considered important heavily depend on the age profile of the population, ranging from social-security considerations to marketing, from health expenditures to education, from the size of the labor force to internal migration. Even in the recent discussion on population–environment and carrying capacity, the population composition seems to make a big difference (see Lutz, 1994) because of varying age-specific impacts.

But let us assume, for the time being, that the number of total population size in a territory at some point in the future has a meaning and value in itself. To derive such a figure we have the choice between simple and sophisticated guesses. The most simple would be a guess of a number of future population size without any formal model. If some sort of a formal model is desired, we might consider basing the method on past experience or just consider the population in the starting year together with assumptions on the future.

Probably the simplest model of population growth over time is that of an exponential growth model with a constant rate of growth. In practice, however, growth rates have never been constant over long periods. Through the millennia of early human history, birth and death rates fluctuated widely due to weather, war, food shortages, and diseases. Typically birth rates were high when death rates were low and vice versa, resulting in even wider fluctuations in the growth rates of the population. Although during the 20th century the curve of world population growth has resembled the typical exponential growth curve, growth rates have been far from constant. The growth rate was about 0.5 percent during the first half of this century, increased to a peak of 2.06 percent in 1965–1970, and slowly declined thereafter. The appealing feature of an exponential growth model as opposed to more sophisticated ones is that one has to make assumptions only for one parameter – the growth rate.

Several important deficiencies of the exponential growth model result from the fact that it does not consider the age structure of the population. The most important is that it cannot capture the momentum of population growth, a phenomenon caused by the fact that only women aged 15–49 have children and in the case of a very young age distribution more and more women enter this age group and hence the population would grow significantly even with a constant fertility at replacement level. Another aspect of this deficiency relates to countries with very irregular age pyramids, such as some European countries where irregularities in births due to world wars, the baby boom, and the baby bust resulted in great fluctuations in cohort size. Here some changes in the population growth rate are pre-programmed by the population age structures that do not reflect any change in fertility, mortality, and migration. For instance, a phenomenon such as the echo of the baby boom – the larger number of babies borne by the large baby boom cohorts– could never be captured by a model that considers only total population size.

For these reasons it is generally advisable to use projection models such as the cohort-component method which explicitly consider age and sex, even if one is only interested in total population size. However, in these models one has to make assumptions on a much larger number of parameters, which raises the danger of losing sight of the behavior of the total system while giving great attention to specific issues such as period-cohort translation in fertility. In this respect the suggestion made by Pflaumer (1992), that time-series methods applied to population totals should be used as a baseline against which the results of more complex models should be assessed, seems to be worth considering. Ideally the analyst could then identify the sources of difference between the two approaches.

2.4.2   Projecting the age and sex composition

As mentioned above people are interested in population projections because they want to understand population changes that go beyond projecting total population size. This knowledge is used in a variety of ways, ranging from aging and social-security considerations to labor market questions, educational issues, and even marketing in private business. For all these considerations one needs to have estimates of future population structure at least in broad age groups. Few users would demand projections in single-year age groups. Projection of five-year age groups in five-year steps of historical time has become popular, mostly for convenience.

A projection of the population by age and sex requires first the age and sex composition of the population in the starting year. Next one must assume age-specific fertility, mortality, and migration rates for each five-year period to be projected. For this age-group projection of the population, the so-called cohort-component method has become standard. This method was introduced by Whelpton in 1936 and formalized by Leslie (1945). Notestein (1945) first applied it to project the world population. The basic method has not changed since that time. In short, cohorts are groups of men and women born in the same time interval and representing a specific age group at any later point in time. Their sizes can only change through mortality and migration. The size of the youngest age group is determined by age-specific fertility levels applied to the corresponding female age groups. Hence the projected size and age structure of the population at any point in the future depends exclusively on the size and age structure in the starting year and on assumed age-specific fertility, mortality, and migration over the projection period.

The cohort-component method tells us what to do with the assumptions on future fertility, mortality, and migration, but not how to derive them. And it is in this all-deciding question of the choice of assumptions and structuring of sets of alternative assumptions where controversy exists and continuous improvement of population projection methodologies is possible and indeed necessary. Alternative approaches to deriving assumptions on future fertility, mortality, and migration are discussed in the following sections of this chapter.

In the context of the cohort-component method, one unresolved question is whether assumptions should be made in terms of period or cohort fertility. Technically, the Leslie matrix requires age-specific period rates. But these period rates could be either assumed directly or derived from assumptions on future cohort fertility behavior. This decision goes essentially back to the rather philosophical controversy of whether the cohort approach is more appropriate in fertility analysis. In practical terms the cohort fertility approach requires assumptions on both the level of cohort fertility and the timing of births over the reproductive life span. If the age pattern is assumed to be constant and the level assumed to approach a certain constant value, cohort and period fertility assumptions turn out to be very similar. Theoretically the same cohort-period arguments could be made for mortality and migration, but they are rarely ever discussed.

2.4.3   Multistate models for additional characteristics

Usually populations are defined in terms of a territory in which they live. But as mentioned earlier, populations may also be defined as subgroups of the population in a given territory, such as ethnic groups, marital status groups, or educational groups. These groups can be treated as independent populations that may interact with each other, i.e., people leave one group and join another. The traditional cohort-component method can only consider one population and needs to be expanded to simultaneously project several populations which are interacting with one another. Such expansions are called multistate models as developed by Rogers (1975) and others during the 1970s. The original applications of multistate models were in the field of multiregional demography and migration.

No global population projection has gone beyond projecting the age and sex distribution by regions or countries. But on a smaller scale many multistate projections have been produced, mostly with respect to marital status or household characteristics (for example, Gonnot *et al.*, 1994). Assumptions on fertility, mortality, and transitions between the states have to be state specific in addition to age and sex specific, e.g., in case of a marital status projection the age-specific mortality of married men must be assumed independently of that of divorced men. This multistate approach can be applied to any other breakdown of the population (socioeconomic, ethnic, etc.) as long as the categories are clearly defined and sufficient empirical information on transition intensities is given. Such population projections that also provide estimates of future distributions of socioeconomic variables other than age and sex may be more interesting for many users, and may become more popular as methodologies and computer programs disseminate further.

At the global level, however, a difficulty to applying multistate models, including additional not strictly demographic variables, is the availability of relevant empirical data. Hence the projections presented in this book are based on alternative projections of only the age and sex distribution for the 12 world regions specified.

2.5   Different Uses of Past Experience to Derive Assumptions for the Future

The real challenge in population projection is not the method itself but the generation of one set or several sets of assumptions on age-specific fertility and age- and sex-specific mortality and migration. In this context there are two basic questions. The first question relates to the way in which past experience is used to derive assumptions on the future. The second concerns the strategy one takes to deal with uncertainty, whether a range of possible assumptions based on some distribution or individual point scenarios will be considered. We can distinguish between three levels drawing from past experience.

The Future as a Continuation of the Past Trend

This is the strongest possible way in which the past can enter. A simple trend extrapolation can be performed without any additional input about likely future conditions. It can be blind and mechanical after one has chosen the indicator to be extrapolated, the length of the period to be considered, and the information to be derived from the time series. It can take the form of simple linear trend extrapolation, other functional forms of extrapolation, or, if periodicity is assumed, a combined trend with superimposed cycles.

The blind continuation of past trends seems appropriate only when absolutely no information is available about likely future trends. In the context of fertility assumptions it would mean completely disregarding considerations derived from demographic transition theories, information about desired family size, and surveys on family-planning demands. But even this simple method does not save the forecaster from making choices. The indicator, the length of the past period, and the structure of the process need to be defined.

Variance from History

If one is willing to incorporate into one's assumptions external substantive information about likely future trends, one possibility of combining this with information from the past is to determine the average level externally and to derive only the likely variance from the past. In the context of a probabilistic model this would mean, for instance, setting future upper and lower bounds to the level of fertility but deriving from history the percentage by which fertility rates change from one period to another (see Goldstein *et al.*, 1994). Also into this category falls the work by Keyfitz (1981) and Stoto (1983) who estimate future errors in population projections from past errors.

Structure and Understanding from History

Under this approach it is not the past time series itself which is used to derive assumptions on the future evolution, but the substantive knowledge about the process and its structure. Taking mortality as an example, this approach goes beyond the analysis of past trends in integrating knowledge from medicine and biology and addressing questions such as that of a genetically determined limits to human life. Naturally this understanding is also informed by the analysis of past trends but goes further, integrating outside knowledge derived from other sources. Under this approach historical information enters only indirectly into the formulation of assumptions about the future. This third approach is the one chosen for our study. It is the reason why large parts of this volume consist of substantive papers about our understanding of the processes of fertility, mortality, and migration in the different world regions. A group of experts was asked to write about alternative possible future paths of fertility, mortality, and migration and produce assumptions of a most likely central value as well as high and low extreme values for the various indicators by the year 2030, based on their substantive understanding of the processes. The strategy of the chosen scenario approach is described in more detail in Section 2.7.

2.6   Different Probabilistic Approaches to Deal with Uncertainty

The future evolution of the world's population will almost surely differ from the central scenario as described in this volume. This is unavoidable, for there is inherent uncertainty in the future. Wars will break out; some societies will modernize more quickly than we expect while others will develop more slowly; new diseases may break out, old ones may be cured; childbearing might become more fashionable in the developed world, or, quite the contrary, less so; the industrialized countries may close themselves to immigration, or might even become more open. All these factors are of crucial importance to the demographic future, but are uncertain.

What does a forecaster do in the face of such uncertainty? A first approach is to freeze all demographic rates at their current level. Rates will almost certainly not remain unchanged as the future unfolds, but this approach enables the forecaster to avoid making statements about the direction of demographic trends, and at the same time makes absolutely clear the hypothetical nature of the projection. This was the approach followed by early demographic projectionists/forecasters of the 1920s, 1930s, and 1940s.

A second approach, the one used by this volume's projections, is to create extreme case scenarios. This enables one to make statements about how far off the future population could be from the expected evolution. The effectiveness of this approach, of course, depends on the thoroughness of the scenarios. On the one hand, there is a danger that the interval between the high and low scenarios might be so large that it is uninformative. On the other hand, when the scenarios become more plausible, and thus more likely, one begins to ask what the probability of a given scenario in fact is.

The third approach, explicit quantification of uncertainty, is designed to incorporate information about vital rate variability and the success of past forecasts into statements about the certainty with which present forecasts are made. It is evident that both forecasters and users would like to know what confidence to place in projections, but as yet no single technique to do this unambiguously has gained currency. As the most recent US Bureau of the Census (1989) forecast notes: "Many problems remain before a method can be developed for placing reliable confidence intervals around population projections." This lack of success is not for want of trying, but rather because of the inherent difficulties in modeling uncertainty.

How can the future population differ from that which is projected? The compendium of possible mistakes is long (Keilman, 1990), but we can schematize the sources of error into three types:

1. Measurement and calculation errors. These can take the form of mistaken input data (for example, starting the projection with a population based on an incorrect census count) or a simple calculation mistake.
2. Incorrect specification of vital rates. One can predict that life expectancy will continue to rise at the same rate as the past 20 years, but instead it might well increase at twice that rate. A second baby boom could occur. Or, less spectacularly, the seemingly random "natural" variation (see Brillinger 1986) might cause fertility, mortality, and migration rates to vary from year to year.
3. Unexpected events. The unexpected could cause large structural changes: the outbreak of war, a sudden cure for AIDS, an economic boom in Africa. Any number of ruptures with current trends is imaginable, any of which might render extrapolated visions of the future irrelevant. To these structural changes we could also add errors resulting from aggregation of heterogeneous groups.

We can call these, respectively, measurement error, parameter specification error, and model specification error. The sum of all forms of error is called total error.

On first glance, only the second source of error – the variation in vital rates – seems a likely candidate for the application of probabilistic thinking, and, indeed, most attempts to incorporate randomness into population forecasting have chosen this as their focus. Before examining these techniques, however, one technique for quantifying the total error deserves mention. The empirical evaluation of the success and failures of past forecasts, developed by Keyfitz and Stoto in the early 1980s, consists simply of gathering a large number of past forecasts and evaluating what the average error has been. The most noteworthy conclusion of these studies, both of which focused only on error in total population size, was that the traditional high and low variants offered by population projections corresponded to approximately a two-thirds confidence interval. In other words, the population grew at rates outside of those predicted by the high and low variants about one-third of the time (Keyfitz, 1981; Stoto, 1983).

This empirical method of estimating uncertainty clearly takes into account all three types of error.[2] In order to apply it to current forecasts, however, a very strong assumption needs to be made: that the errors in future forecasts are of the same magnitude as in the past. This assumption is of particular concern since the most recent forecasts are least represented in the sample of empirical forecasts because their accuracy has yet to be seen. This is problematic because not only do methods of choosing high, low, and medium variants change, but so also does the potential variability of vital rates. Unless both the variability of vital rates and the methodology of projection together with the degree of care used in making the assumptions stay the same, it is unclear how good an indicator past errors are of future uncertainty.

While an application of the results from Keyfitz and Stoto to future population projections extrapolates in forecasting, the direct analysis of population trends themselves offers a distinct alternative. It is here that time-series analysts have plied their trade. Starting with the Lee (1974) analysis of US fertility rates until today, time-series methods aim to assign a structure to the process of changing rates, for example, a random walk with drift, or an ARIMA. Time-series methods produce not only a central forecast, but also the entire probability distribution, showing where fertility and mortality rates are likely to be at any future specified date contingent on a normal distribution of errors.

The principal drawback of time-series methods has been the dependence of the results on the choice of a model structure – particularly for fertility, the demographic component which not only has the largest effect on the evolution of populations but also is the most variable (Lee, 1974; Ahlburg and Land, 1992). Mortality, on the other hand, appears to offer much better hopes of forecasting, at least in the most developed countries. In particular, both the Lee–Carter (1992) and McNown–Rogers (1989) methods offer means of producing trends based on large matrices of age-specific mortality rates. These techniques have large data requirements and have been criticized for producing overly narrow confidence intervals. They are clear in their aim, however, only to provide estimates of parameter variation, providing minimum error ranges.

An alternative method for obtaining probability distributions is to simulate the evolution of demographic rates using Monte Carlo simulation methods. Random draws of past levels (Keyfitz, 1989) or of past variation (Goldstein *et al.*, 1994) are made and applied to the evolving population. A large number, say 10,000, of sample populations are projected forward, and the resulting empirical distribution of population size and age structure is used to estimate the theoretical probability range. These simulations allow one to analyze the combined effect of uncertainty in mortality, fertility, and migration; this last component has not been included in time-series models.

Both the simulation and the time-series techniques are means to address only the second type of parameter uncertainty. They answer the question of how much uncertainty would there be if past levels of variation continue into the future. They explicitly do not include the possibility of structural change. Questions such as will their be another baby boom in Western Europe, when will sub-Saharan Africa experience a fertility transition, what the chances are of an AIDS cure or of a war or revolution cannot be addressed without probability models of the likelihood for each of these unexpected events. The scenario approach, focusing as it does on the hypothetical effect rather than on likelihood, offers the chance to see the hypothesized impact of unpredictable events, and seems the best means for analyzing structural change.

While much work is being devoted to probabilistic models of population projection, no method has emerged. For the moment, large data requirements combine with a tremendous sensitivity of techniques to assumptions about the form of the probability model. One clear advantage of scenarios is that although it may be difficult for users to assess the likelihood of the scenario, it is quite easy for them to understand what is being assumed. Probabilistic forecasts, thus far, do not seem to offer this advantage, for it is difficult for most users to understand the assumptions of the different probability models, let alone to say which set of assumptions is the most sensible.

There is no need for an either/or approach to scenario and probabilistic projections. Ideally, projections would include both an estimate of "natural variability" as well as the implications of possible structural changes.

2.7   Non-probabilistic Approaches: Single Projections, Variants, Scenarios

In practice, both national statistics departments and international agencies have taken non-probabilistic approaches to forecasting. Until recently, it was still the practice for some agencies to offer only one set of rate trajectories. Thus, it was possible to speak of "the" future population. Today, however, the uncertainties of future population growth are better recognized, and it is quite rare to find a projection without at least one alternative set of assumptions.

Both variants and scenarios offer alternative sets of assumptions. The difference between the two is to some extent only a difference in detail, but this is also reflected in the intended use. The variant approach usually offers three alternatives: high, medium, and low. The high and low scenarios are typically defined in terms of the resulting population size, and not in terms of their components. Therefore, the larger population can come from increased migration, lower mortality, higher fertility, or a combination of any of these.

The *World Population Prospects* produced by the United Nations Population Division (UN, 1993), the most commonly used set of world projections, currently offers four variants to 2025: high, medium, low, and constant fertility, the last being for illustrative purposes. Fertility is allowed to vary, but only one set of mortality and migration assumptions are used throughout.

In their recently published long-range world population projections, the UN (1992) gives projections until 2150 for nine world regions. Seven different fertility extensions are considered, but mortality and migration assumptions also remain invariant.

The World Bank (1992) offers only one central set of projections. Birdsall (1992), however, offers a set of alternative projections resulting from faster than expected fertility decline in the developing world.

Sometimes the selection of inputs for high and low variants is directly influenced by the interests of the agency producing the forecasts. For example, the US Social Security Administration, whose principal interest lies in the age structure of the population, combines high fertility and high mortality for its high variant, and low fertility with low mortality for its low variant, giving the two most extreme values for the old age dependency ratio. The US Bureau of the Census, on the other hand, combines low fertility with high mortality and vice versa in order to get the most extreme values for the total population size.

Recently an increasing number of authors (Lutz, 1991; Ahlburg and Vaupel, 1990; Cliquet, 1993) and agencies (EUROSTAT, UN) have chosen to speak of population scenarios instead of the more traditional variants. Substantively, a scenario approach to population projection may be defined through several characteristics: more emphasis is put on the if-then nature of the calculation as opposed to a likely prediction; a scenario approach is expected to make all assumptions very explicit and to offer a sensitivity analysis over the assumptions chosen; all three components of change are addressed separately, and if one is chosen to remain invariant (such as mortality and migration in the 1992 UN long-term projections) this needs to be justified; finally, a scenario approach has the connotation of a somewhat larger number of different outputs – for instance, the decision of EUROSTAT (1991) to present just two scenarios including different fertility, mortality, and migration assumptions does not allow the analysis of the effects of individual components.

The disadvantage of the scenario approach is that it calls upon users to exercise judgment in the choice of scenarios they wish to consider and the relative likelihood of the different scenarios. The advantage is that a user can get a comprehensive sense of how changeable different population output variables are and what conditions would have to arise for large changes to take place. For those unconcerned with variation, less may be better, and the middle variant or central scenario may be the only relevant set of projections.

2.8   Interactions among Components and Possible Feedbacks from Results

In Chapter 15, two extreme scenarios (rather than probabilistic distributions) are defined for each component based on the substantive analysis described in Chapters 3 to 14. Combining two extremes each in fertility, mortality, and migration results in eight different combinations. This systematic permutation of alternative scenario assumptions is a prerequisite for careful sensitivity analysis. In addition, a central scenario is defined by combining the arithmetic means of the fertility, mortality, and migration assumptions. This central scenario attempts to satisfy the demand for one main projection for orientation.

The systematic permutation scenario approach is based on the assumption of independence between demographic components. The level of one demographic rate is unaffected by the level of the others. Thus, for example, high mortality from AIDS in Africa has no effect on fertility levels. Similarly, high migration rates from high fertility regions to low fertility regions do not affect fertility of the receiving region. However unrealistic this assumption may be, it best serves the purpose of a thorough sensitivity analysis: how robust are certain policies under alternative population futures? For testing robustness, extremes have to be considered. Also, systematic permutations help to explain the relative impacts of the individual components under given age structures.

But the basic assumption of independence is very strong. In particular in the long run it can lead to unreasonable results. In a world of dependencies, independence is rarely observed. The problem is to capture and specify the nature of these dependencies. Because of this lack of solid empirical information about the structure and degree of such interdependencies, most forecasters choose to remain on safer grounds by not specifying any. But at least for illustrative purposes population projections should also explicitly focus on possible dependencies. The development of fertility, mortality, and migration rates is influenced by a number of determinants. At least three different levels of interactions can be distinguished:

- Interaction between demographic components.
- Feedbacks from other demographic variables, in particular population size or age structure.
- Feedbacks from non-demographic variables, such as economic development, education, or environmental factors.

Interaction between demographic components is incorporated relatively easily. For example, high migration to low fertility countries may have an impact on fertility rates in the receiving countries. Such dependencies can be taken into account by adjusting some of the systematic permutation scenarios from above, e.g., increase the fertility level in Western Europe in the case of high immigration.

Feedbacks from other demographic variables, such as population size or age structure, are more debatable and hence more difficult to be included. There is full consensus that the world population cannot grow indefinitely, but no agreement exists on the levels at which some sort of collapse might happen. The (land) carrying capacity concept is accepted in the natural sciences, but less so among social scientists. Collapses, if they happen at all, will probably occur suddenly and with large regional differences. As to possible reactions of fertility, mortality, or migration to negative effects of population aging, little consensus is found. Very rapid aging will certainly create problems, in particular when countries are not well prepared, e.g., with regard to social security. But, as is shown by the example of today's industrialized world, populations can adapt to gradual changes in the age structure. Because of the possible discrepancy between individual desired family sizes and societal goals, it is unclear whether, for example, extreme aging will result in higher fertility.

For any type of dependence, feedbacks for the most part work indirectly via such complex matters as levels of education, status of health care, economic development, or environmental pollution. Only a comprehensive multisector system would be able to track such feedbacks. However, the strength – and sometimes even the direction – of such multifarious feedbacks is largely unknown, or at least highly uncertain. As a consequence, multisector systems models tend to create dependencies and future paths far different from reality, a world in itself driven by rather vague feedback loops. While conceptually such multisector models are desirable, they are usually not suited for the purpose of population projections. By inclusion of multiple feedbacks from non-population variables in such models, a great potential exists of introducing more errors than one resolves.

A well-known example of such a multisector system is the World3 model developed by the Forrester–Meadows group during the 1970s – an economic, demographic, and environmental model of the world taken as a whole (Forrester, 1971; Meadows *et al.*, 1972, 1974, 1992; Meadows and Meadows, 1973). The population segment of World3 includes 48 equations, and keeps track of the population in four broad age groups, 0–14, 15–44, 45–64, and 65 and above. Population growth is determined by the difference between the crude birth rate and the crude death rate. These two crude rates are changed internally through a number of feedbacks. In particular, the crude birth rate declines with increases in food intake, increases in pollution, improvements in material standard of living, and population crowding (which results from industrialization). The crude death rate decreases with increasing food intake and improvements in the material standard of living, and increases with increasing pollution and (to a much lesser extent) population crowding. Some of the effects are ambiguous – for example, an increase in agricultural production increases pollution and at the same time increases food availability per capita, making its effect on death rates and hence on the population growth rate unclear. A major shortcoming of World3 is that education is not included.

During the 1970s, motivated by the World3 model, a number of global models were developed. Among those, the Bariloche model (Bariloche Group, 1976; Herrera *et al.*, 1976) is worthy of mention as it has a relatively large number of feedbacks to the population submodel. For example, among other things, the crude birth rate is influenced by school enrollment, calorie intake, housing availability, and the life expectancy at birth. The modelers circumspectly emphasized that their interrelations are based on descriptive statistical analysis and "should not be confused with causal relationships." However, in their judgment, "the results are very satisfactory, from the point of view of the precision achieved, and make it possible to predict population changes resulting from the socioeconomic variables considered in the model" (Herrera *et al.*, 1976:51).

A different approach was used 20 years later by researchers working at the International Institute for Applied Systems Analysis (Lutz, 1994). They studied population–development–environment interactions in a specific setting on the island of Mauritius.[3] The Mauritius modeling team avoided the ambiguous relationships found in other multisector systems, put substantial emphasis on common property problems (in particular water and land), and chose a decentralized modular approach. This helped to avoid black box relationships in which the effects of certain parameter changes cannot be understood by the user. A strength of the Mauritius model is its population module, which – using a multistate cohort-component model – produces projections of the population by age, sex, labor force status, and educational attainment. Education is explicitly incorporated. Education increases the productivity of labor, but costs money. A main feature of the model is that it is extraordinarily open. Since the nature and the strength of most of the feedbacks included in previous models are subject to much debate among scientists, most of those feedbacks are not hard-wired in the model. The feedbacks need to be defined by the scenario maker. The disadvantage of this is that the use of the model can be daunting at first. On the other hand, experienced users have at their disposal a flexible tool for the study of population–development–environment interactions in a specific setting.

Feedbacks from non-demographic variables cannot be captured by the multiregional cohort-component approach chosen in Chapter 15. Such feedbacks go beyond the scope of this volume. But both feedbacks from population size and age structure on demographic components and dependencies on demographic components themselves are explicitly dealt with in a separate chapter on special long-term scenarios (Chapter 16).

2.9   Summary: The Approach We Chose

In this chapter we have addressed the question "Why another set of global population projections?" We have considered who wants projections and for what reasons, what should be the time horizon and spatial resolution, what output parameters are expected, and what are the alternative approaches to address the issue of uncertainty in population projections. Throughout the chapter we contrasted our choice of approach to that of others. Issues have been listed in which progress is possible and desirable, and where alternative new strategies promise new insights. *Table 2.1* summarizes some of the key issues in population projection on the left-hand side and specifies the approach we have chosen on the right-hand side.

There seems to be little disagreement on the projection methodology to be used for (global) population projections. Our projections are carried out using a multiregional cohort-component model, with five-year age groups. In contrast to global projections produced by the UN and the World Bank, which are based on individual country estimates, we have disaggregated the globe into 12 major world regions. By doing so, much of the world's heterogeneity is taken into account, and one need not bother with national particularities, especially with respect to migration.

The crucial difference with respect to existing global population projections lies in the specification, justification, and combination of alternative scenario assumptions. The approach chosen involves a number of steps. First, selected experts with different backgrounds in the fields of fertility, mortality, and migration analysis are asked to think about the future of the three demographic components. If necessary, different experts are invited for different regions. The experts are asked to suggest possible high and low assumptions for future fertility, mortality, and migration levels up to the year 2030. The experts have to substantively argue for their points and justify their views. These elements are documented in Chapters 3 to 14. Next, those alternative views expressed on future levels of fertility, mortality, and migration, which are sometimes only of a qualitative

Table 2.1. Major characteristics of our projection approach.

Issue	Our choice
Projection methodology	Multiregional cohort-component model with 5-year projection intervals; based on 12 major world regions
Uncertainty	Alternative scenarios combining extreme fertility, mortality, and migration assumptions (uncertainty ranges)
Variability of components	Fertility, mortality, and migration are given equal importance; high and low values and their arithmetic mean for each component are specified
Basis of assumptions	Expert judgment on low and high values in fertility, mortality, and migration based on understanding of underlying processes plus outside knowledge
Justification of assumptions	Scientific chapters by experts in the fields of fertility, mortality, and migration; for developed and developing areas separately
Scenario combinations	Systematic permutation of high and low scenario assumptions (8 alternative combinations) as a basis for sensitivity analysis; plus 1 central scenario for orientation resulting from combination of means
Time horizon	Both medium-term projections until 2030 and long-term extensions for illustrative purpose until 2100
Interactions	Special scenarios assuming dependence of levels of fertility and mortality in the long run and increases in fertility in industrialized countries as a consequence of immigration
Feedbacks	Special scenarios assuming a food crisis in certain high fertility regions (feedback from population size on mortality) and a social crisis in certain low fertility regions (feedback from population aging on fertility)

nature, are transformed into alternative quantitative assumptions on different future paths in each region considered. These future demographic trends are thought to be extreme, but certainly not impossible. The high and low assumptions should somehow correspond to a 80–90 percent confidence interval of an intuitive probability

distribution. In other words, on each side only about 5–10 percent
of all possible cases, depending on the region considered, should lie
outside the values considered. Assuming a symmetric distribution,
the assumed central value should be both the most likely case and
the mean of the high and low values. Finally, a systematic permutation of the high and low scenario assumptions in each of the three
components resulted in eight scenario combinations. This provides
the basis for sensitivity analysis. Systematic permutations also help
to explain the relative impacts of changes in individual components
under given age structures. Fertility, mortality, and migration are
explicitly assumed to be independent. In addition to the eight combinations, a central scenario obtained by combining the arithmetic
means of the low and high fertility, mortality, and migration assumptions are defined for orientation.

This expert opinion-based scenario approach with systematic
permutations of high and low values for each component together
with a central scenario in each of the 12 world regions is, in our view,
the most appropriate for meeting the expectations of the users of
projections while giving maximum justice to scientific criteria and
minimizing computational efforts and input data requirements. This
was our choice for alternative projections up to 2030 (see Chapter 15).

Beyond 2030, as described above, expert judgments are considered less reliable, and many experts indeed refuse to specify assumptions for longer-term demographic trends. Also, in the long run
independence of components is implausible. Therefore, a slightly
different approach is taken for the long-term extensions until 2100
which serve as purely illustrative purposes in this book (see Chapter 16). Beyond 2030 scenarios are defined which demonstrate the
effects of various forms of dependency between demographic components and possible feedbacks from population size/density and
population aging on demographic rates. Those exercises are quite
speculative and serve to illustrate certain features of population dynamics rather than giving likely long-term projections.

Notes

[1] The word projection, of course, carries psychological connotations. As
Webster's defines the word: "projection. 6b: the attribution of one's

own ideas, feelings, or attitudes to other people or to objects ... 8: an estimate of future possibilities based on a current trend" *(Webster's New Collegiate Dictionary,* 1974, Springfield, MA: G. & C. Merriam Company). These two meanings are not wholly separable, for, in imagining individual behavior in the future, we cannot but include our own perspectives.

[2] There does exist the possibility of mistaken counts of the achieved population that would give false estimates of empirical error. These could result in either overestimates or underestimates of error size.

[3] The last two decades produced a lively and rapidly growing literature on the interrelationships between economic, demographic, and environmental variables, but the development of simulation models that included these three factors almost came to a complete halt after the burst of activity in the early 1970s.

References

Ahlburg, D.A., and Land, K.C., 1992, Population forecasting: Guest editors' introduction, *International Journal of Forecasting* **8**(3):289–299.

Ahlburg, D.A., and Vaupel, J., 1990, Alternative projections of the US population, *Demography* **27**:639–652.

Bariloche Group, 1976, The Latin American world model, in G. Bruckmann, ed., *Proceedings of the Second IIASA Conference on Global Modeling,* CP-76-8, International Institute for Applied Systems Analysis, Laxenburg, Austria.

Bartiaux, F., and van Ypersele, J.-F., 1993, The role of population growth in global warming, in *IUSSP International Population Conference: Montreal,* Vol. 4, International Union for the Scientific Study of Population, Liège, Belgium.

Birdsall, N., 1992, Another Look at Population and Global Warming, Policy Research Working Paper WPS 1020, November, World Bank, Country Economics Department, Washington, DC, USA.

Bongaarts, J., 1992, Population growth and global warming, *Population and Development Review* **18**(2):299–319.

Brillinger, D.R., 1986, The natural variability of vital rates and associated statistics, *Biometrics* **42**(4):693–734.

Cliquet, R., ed., 1993, *The Future of Europe's Population: A Scenario Approach,* Council of Europe, European Population Committee, Strasbourg, France.

EUROSTAT, 1991, Two Long-Term Population Scenarios for the European Community, Scenarios prepared for the International Conference on Human Resources in Europe at the Dawn of the 21st Century, November 27–29, Luxembourg.

FAO (Food and Agriculture Organization), 1988, *World Agriculture: Towards 2000: An FAO Study*, edited by N. Alexandratos, New York University Press, New York, NY, USA.

Forrester, J.W., 1971, *World Dynamics*, Wright-Allen Press, Cambridge, MA, USA.

Goldstein, J.R., Lutz, W., Pflug, G., 1994, Constant Variance Forecasting, unpublished manuscript, International Institute for Applied Systems Analysis, Laxenburg, Austria.

Gonnot, J.-P., Keilman, N., and Prinz, C., eds., 1994, *Social Security, Household and Family Dynamics in Aging Societies*, Swets & Zeitlinger, Amsterdam, Netherlands.

Gouse, S.W., Gray, D., Tomlinson, G.C., and Morrison, D.L., 1992, Potential world development through 2100: The impacts on energy demand, resources, and the environment, *World Energy Council Journal* December:18–32.

Herrera, A.D., Scolnik, H.D. *et al.*, 1976, *Catastrophe or New Society? A Latin American World Model*, International Development Research Centre, Ottawa, Canada.

Keilman, N.W., 1990, *Uncertainty in National Population Forecasting: Issues, Backgrounds, Analyses, Recommendations*, Swets & Zeitlinger, Amsterdam, Netherlands.

Keyfitz, N., 1981, The limits of population forecasting, *Population and Development Review* 7(4):579–593.

Keyfitz, N., 1989, Measuring in Advance the Accuracy of Population Forecasts, WP-89-72, International Institute for Applied Systems Analysis, Laxenburg, Austria.

Lee, R.D., 1974, Forecasting births in post-transitional populations: Stochastic renewal with serially correlated fertility, *Journal of the American Statistical Association* 69(247):607–617.

Lee, R.D., and Carter, L., 1992, Modeling and forecasting the time series of US mortality, *Journal of the American Statistical Association* 87(September):659–675.

Leontief, W., and Sohn, I., 1984, Population, food, and energy: The prospects for worldwide economic growth to the year 2030, in B.N. Kursunoglu *et al.*, eds., *Global Energy Assessment and Outlook: Proceedings of the International Scientific Forum on Changes in Energy*, November 9–13, Mexico City, Harwood, London, UK.

Leslie, P.H., 1945, On the use of matrices in certain population mathematics, *Biometrika* 33:183–212.

Lutz, W., ed., 1991, *Future Demographic Trends in Europe and North America: What Can We Assume Today?* Academic Press, London, UK.

Lutz, W., 1993, Population and environment, what do we need more urgently: Better data, better models, or better questions? in J. Clarke and B. Zaba, eds., *Environment and Population Change,* Ordina Editions, Liège, Belgium.

Lutz, W., ed., 1994, *Population–Development–Environment: Understanding Interactions in Mauritius,* Springer-Verlag, Berlin, Germany.

Lutz, W., and Prinz, Ch., 1991, Scenarios for the World Population in the Next Century: Excessive Growth or Extreme Aging, WP-91-22, International Institute for Applied Systems Analysis, Laxenburg, Austria.

McNown, R., and Rogers, A., 1989, Forecasting mortality: A parameterized time series approach, *Demography* **26**:645–660.

Meadows, D.L., and Meadows, D.H., eds., 1973, *Toward Global Equilibrium: Collected Papers,* MIT Press, Cambridge, MA, USA.

Meadows, D.H., Meadows, D.L., Randers, J., and Behrens III, W.W., 1972, *The Limits to Growth,* Universe Books, New York, NY, USA.

Meadows, D.L., Behrens III, W.W., Meadows, D.H., Naill, R.F., Randers, J., and Zahn, E.K.O., 1974, *Dynamics of Growth in a Finite World,* MIT Press, Cambridge, MA, USA.

Meadows, D.H., Meadows, D.L., and Randers, J., 1992, *Beyond the Limits: Confronting Global Collapse, Envisioning a Sustainable Future,* Chelsea Green Publishing Company, Post Mills, VT, USA.

Mellor, J.W., and Paulino, L., 1986, Food production needs in a consumption perspective, in M.S. Swaminathan and S.K. Sinha, eds., *Global Aspects of Food Production,* Tycooly International, Oxford, UK.

Notestein, F.W., 1945, Population: The long view, in T.W. Schultz, ed., *Food for the World,* University of Chicago Press, Chicago, IL, USA.

Odell, P.R., and Rosing, K.E., 1980, *The Future of Oil: A Simulation Study of the Inter-Relationships of Resources, Reserves and Use, 1980–2080,* Kogan Page, London, UK.

Pflaumer, P., 1992, Forecasting US population totals with the Box–Jenkins approach, *International Journal of Forecasting* **8**(3):329–338.

Rogers, A., 1975, *Introduction to Multiregional Mathematical Demography,* John Wiley & Sons, New York, NY, USA.

Stoto, M., 1983, The accuracy of population projections, *Journal of the American Statistical Association* **78**(381):13–20.

UN, 1992, *Long-Range World Population Projections: Two Centuries of Population Growth: 1950–2150,* ST/ESA/SER.A/125, United Nations, New York, NY, USA.

UN, 1993, *World Population Prospects,* United Nations, New York, NY, USA.

US Bureau of the Census, 1989, *Projections of the Population of the United States, by Age, Sex, and Race: 1988 to 2080,* Current Population Reports, Series P-25, No. 1018, Washington, DC, USA.

Vaupel, J.W., and Yashin, A.I., 1983, *The Deviant Dynamics of Death in Heterogeneous Populations,* RR-83-1, International Institute for Applied Systems Analysis, Laxenburg, Austria.

WECCC (World Energy Conference Conservation Commission), 1983, *Energy 2000–2020: World Prospects and Regional Stresses,* edited by J.R. Frisch, Graham and Trotman, London, UK.

Whelpton, P.K., 1936, An empirical method of calculating future population, *Journal of the American Statistical Association* **31**:457–473.

World Bank, 1992, *World Population Projections,* 1992–1993 Edition, Johns Hopkins University Press, Baltimore, MD, USA.

Editor's Note for Part I

The two contributions in Part I provide a framework for the projections carried out in Part VI. They clearly indicate that new, world population projections are useful if they (a) consider a broader range of possible future trends in all three components (fertility, mortality, and migration), (b) leave room for substantive considerations on the state of knowledge about the determinants of possible future trends in these three components, and (c) explicitly include analyses beyond the field of demography on factors (such as food supply and AIDS) that may impact future fertility, mortality, and migration rates. For this reason, Parts II through V of this volume are devoted to substantive considerations in demography and related disciplines.

Users of world population projections seem to expect two different aspects: (a) one most likely projection that can be used as a guideline and (b) information about a plausible range of uncertainty and sensitivity analyses for testing the robustness of certain strategies or policies. The most appropriate and practically feasible response to these expectations is that of systematic permutation scenarios where high, central, and low future values are assumed separately for fertility, mortality, and migration, which are then combined in a systematic manner. With respect to the time horizon of projections, experts feel that defendable assumptions can only be made up to 2025–2030. For this reason the scenarios presented in Chapter 15 have been defined up to this threshold. But several users – especially environmental modelers – demand projections until the end of the 21st century. Therefore, some clearly more speculative scenario calculations up to 2100 are presented in Chapter 16.

Part II

Future Fertility
in Developing Countries

Chapter 3

A Regional Review of Fertility Trends in Developing Countries: 1960 to 1990

John Cleland

This chapter contains a review of fertility trends in developing countries over the period 1960 to 1990. The choice of starting date is simple to justify. Before 1960, fertility decline was very rare in developing countries. Indeed, there is evidence that levels of childbearing in many countries increased in the 15 years following World War II. In this period, substantial improvements in life expectancy were achieved and thus rates of growth of Third World populations accelerated. Concerns about the effects of rapid population growth arose, and the 1960s saw the first examples of a unique and new form of social engineering: state-sponsored family-planning programs. These programs originated in Asia before spreading to other regions. As we shall see, any account of fertility trends has to address the centrally important issue of the contribution made to fertility decline by government interventions.

A broad-ranging review such as ·that contained in this chapter has to make explicit choices about the framework within which to present the demographic data. The goal is to choose a framework that will clarify the underlying forces of change. In this instance, a regional grouping of data has been chosen, rather than one based on development indicators. There are several reasons for this choice. First, one clear lesson from the past 30 years is that simple mono-causal explanations of fertility decline totally fail to capture the complex interplay of factors that influence the onset and speed of fertility decline. Thus fertility trends cannot be illuminated adequately by a straightforward ordering of nations in terms of their stage of socioeconomic development. This is not to deny that development, particularly in the social sector, has an influence on childbearing. Rather it is to assert that this influence is strongly conditioned by cultural factors and government policies.

A second reason for choosing a regional framework is the existence of a pronounced regional imprint on fertility transition. The clearest example is the European fertility transition that was distinct in its timing from that in other regions. As will be demonstrated later in this chapter, there is also an undeniable element of synchronicity in the onset of fertility transition in other major regions, such as Latin America and East Asia.

The importance of a region lies less in the implied geographical contiguity of constituent states than in the fact that it represents a surrogate for shared cultural values and features of social organization. A major advance in our understanding of fertility transition has been the realization that cultural factors, as denoted by religious, ethnic, or linguistic markers, may have a decisive impact on fertility, independently of economic and other types of influence.

The statistical underpinning for this review is the fertility rates collated and published by the United Nations Population Division. Specifically, the 1992 edition of *World Population Prospects* is the source of information on trends since the quinquennium 1960 to 1965. For some countries, UN fertility estimates are little more than guesswork; in other cases, they are based on poor data and may be incorrect. Nevertheless they represent the most carefully compiled and adjusted set of figures in existence and carry a corresponding authority. In the account that follows, major uncertainties about the rates for specific important countries are noted, but no attempt is made to amend UN estimates.

Throughout the chapter, levels of fertility are represented in the form of period total fertility rates (TFRs): the single most useful and widely used indicator. As is well known, period fertility rates are sensitive to variations in the tempo of childbearing as well as to the numbers of births that any cohort will achieve. Thus a period TFR can provide misleading impressions of the underlying level of cohort fertility. With the main exception of China, however, there is little evidence that TFRs in developing countries have been heavily influenced by large, reversible changes in the speed of childbearing. Insofar as this assertion is correct, period TFRs provide a valid indication of what age-specific fertility rates in a particular calendar period imply in terms of ultimate family size.

With these introductory remarks, the groundwork has been laid for the main part of the chapter: an essentially descriptive review of the course of fertility in the main regions of the developing world. Following this, an attempt is made to distill the main lessons that have been learned and what may lie ahead.

3.1   The Course of Fertility in Major Regions

3.1.1   East and Southeast Asia

East and Southeast Asia, excluding Japan, accounts for nearly one-third of the world's population, with China alone comprising about one-fifth of the total. Global population trends are thus largely determined by the course of events in this region. In contrast to South Asia, economic growth has been rapid: China, Indonesia, Thailand, Malaysia, Republic of Korea, Taiwan, Hong Kong, and Singapore have all achieved annual rates of growth in GDP per head between 1965 and 1988 of 4 percent or more. (The equivalent figure for India is 2.5 percent.) As a consequence, an increasing number of states in the region are now classified as upper-middle or high income countries; they are included in this review only because incomes per head were low at the start of the 30-year period.

As shown in *Table 3.1*, several countries (Taiwan, Republic of Korea, Hong Kong, and Singapore) now have period fertility that is below replacement level. In all cases, decline started in the late

Table 3.1. Fertility trends in East and Southeast Asia.

	1960–65	1965–70	1970–75	1975–80	1980–85	1985–90
Laos	6.15	6.15	6.15	6.69	6.69	6.69
Cambodia	6.29	6.22	5.53	4.10	4.80	4.60
Myanmar	6.00	6.00	5.75	5.30	4.90	4.50
Philippines	6.61	6.04	5.50	4.96	4.74	4.30
Vietnam	6.05	5.94	5.85	5.59	4.69	4.22
Malaysia	6.72	5.94	5.15	4.16	4.24	4.00
Indonesia	5.42	5.57	5.10	4.68	4.05	3.48
Thailand	5.42	5.14	5.01	4.27	2.96	2.57
Korea (North)	5.75	7.00	5.70	3.46	2.77	2.50
China	5.93	5.99	4.76	2.90	2.52	2.38
Taiwan	5.46	4.46	3.47	2.80	2.30	1.76
Korea (South)	5.40	4.52	4.11	2.80	2.40	1.73
Singapore	4.93	3.46	2.63	1.87	1.69	1.69
Hong Kong	5.30	4.01	2.89	2.31	1.80	1.36

1950s or 1960s in response to rising age at marriage as well as increasing use of birth control. Careful analyses for Korea (Park, 1992) and for Taiwan (Feeney, 1991) suggest that current period fertility may be depressed by postponement of marriage and births and that the underlying cohort level may be slightly above two births. This interpretation is of considerable policy importance because there is growing concern among several governments about the implications of very low fertility. Singapore has already adopted explicitly pronatalist policies, and it is possible that Taiwan and South Korea will follow this lead, unless they can be reassured that period rates are likely to rise.

Two other countries may join the below-replacement group before the end of the century: Thailand and North Korea. Thailand's decline started in the late 1960s and has proceeded rapidly ever since. Fertility is approaching replacement level with no sign thus far of stabilization. Much less is known about the demography of North Korea, and the government, unlike that of South Korea, has been hostile or indifferent to the promotion of family planning. Nevertheless, there is evidence that fertility has fallen steeply: a vivid demonstration that transition is not necessarily dependent on strong government support. Another country of the region, Myanmar, appears also to have experienced fertility decline, despite government indifference to family planning and isolation from the rest of the world.

Fertility trends in urban China closely parallel those in the city states of Hong Kong and Singapore. Decline started in the early 1960s from a level of about 5.0 births. By 1980, fertility in all three settings had fallen below or close to replacement level. While the major mechanism was increased birth control within marriage, age at marriage for women also rose sharply from about 20 years in 1960 to about 25 years in the early 1980s.

Of course, fertility in China as a whole is determined by rural trends. As in India, traditional fertility levels in China appear to have been modest, within the range of five to six births. Also like India, there is some evidence that natural fertility increased initially under the impact of modernization. Marital fertility rates in the mid-1950s appear to have been about 15 percent higher than rates recorded in the 1930s (Coale and Freedman, 1993). The first major destabilization of rural fertility was the disastrous Great Leap Forward in the late 1950s. Mortality rose sharply and period fertility plummeted to a little above three births before rebounding to over seven in 1963. There followed a period of vacillation in fertility rates during the Cultural Revolution. The dramatic decline in rural fertility started in about 1970, coinciding with the introduction of a forceful family-planning program. Between 1970 and 1980, the TFR for the whole country fell from about 6.0 to 2.4 births. This decline of nearly 60 percent in 10 years represents the single most important contribution to the fall in global fertility over the last 30 years. However, the emergence of pronounced regional variations during this period is often overlooked (Peng, 1981). By the end of the decade, TFRs in more remote provinces of China, such as Tibet, Guizhou, and Ningxia, was still over 4.0.

In 1979, the Chinese government announced the one-child policy, and in the following year passed a marriage law that was widely interpreted as a relaxation of the previous strong discouragement of early marriage. Both measures had profound but partially offsetting effects on the course of fertility in the 1980s. The one-child policy was enforced with considerable success in urban areas. By 1985–1987, urban fertility was well below 2.0 in all provinces of China. Indeed in most of the larger cities, second- and higher-order births almost disappeared. In the rural areas, however, the policy encountered strong resistance. The majority was not prepared to sign the one-child pledge, and period fertility in nearly all provinces remained well above 2.0.

For the whole country, the period TFR has fluctuated through-out the 1980s around a level of 2.4 births per woman, with no clear evidence of a continuation of the decline of the 1970s. Many commentators assumed that the economic reforms of the 1980s made it increasingly difficult for central and local officials to enforce an unpopular policy. However, in 1989 population policy was again strengthened and responsibility for enforcement transferred to local civilian authorities. Preliminary results from a 1992 survey conducted by the State Family Planning Commission suggest that fertility fell sharply in the period 1989 to 1992.

Fertility transition in Indonesia shares several characteristics with that in China. In both countries, levels of socioeconomic development were low at the onset of decline and, in both cases, couples were subjected to very strong official pressure to adopt birth control. The Indonesian government initially focused its attention on densely settled Java, which comprises just 6 percent of the country's land area but over 60 percent of the population. Fertility started to decline there (and in Bali) in the early 1970s. By 1976, fertility in Java was actually lower among the least-educated rural population than among the urban, more-educated sectors: a highly unusual situation that undoubtedly reflected the impact of the government program (Freedman *et al.*, 1981).

Between the late 1960s and the late 1980s, fertility in the whole country fell from 5.7 to 3.5 births, a decline of nearly 40 percent. In Java, the current level is below 3.0 births per woman but in Sumatra, the second most populous island, fertility remains much higher.

The neighboring countries of the Philippines and Malaysia contrast in numerous and fascinating ways with Indonesia. In the 1960s, economic and educational standards were higher than in Indonesia and fertility began to decline earlier. But the pace of decline has been much more gradual. Total fertility rates in Malaysia and the Philippines – estimated by the UN to be 4.0 and 4.3 over the period 1985–1990 – are now markedly higher than in Indonesia.

The stalling of fertility decline in Malaysia dates from the late 1970s and appears to originate with a resurgence in Islamic values and shifts in government policy. While fertility among the Chinese and Indian minorities continued to decline, and is now little above replacement level, that of the majority Malay population actually rose in the 1980s, in response to a decline in the use of contraception (Leete and Tan, 1993). In 1984, the government announced a new population policy which set a target of 70 million inhabitants by the year 2100. It was widely perceived to be a pronatalist measure, and a national survey conducted shortly afterward indicated that a significant fraction of Malay women had revised their family-size expectations upward in response (Arshat *et al.*, 1988).

In the Philippines, there was no radical change in population policy but official support for family planning has always been relatively weak because of the opposition of the Roman Catholic church. Although President Marcos created in 1969 a Commission on Population to coordinate family-planning activities, it failed to secure consensus support or widespread coverage of services. Between 1976 and 1987, the level of contraceptive practice among married women rose only from 38 to 46 percent; and slightly over half of users at both points in time relied on less effective traditional methods.

In summary, the fertility transition in East and Southeast Asia is varied and complex. Variability is evident in the starting level of fertility; the timing of the onset of decline and level of socioeconomic development at the time; the speed of decline; and the role of government policy. Anyone who still believes that the level of reproduction is a predictable outcome of education, urbanization, and living standards should pause to ponder the difference in fertility transition between Indonesia and Thailand, on the one hand, and Malaysia and the Philippines, on the other.

3.1.2 South Asia

For present purposes, this region is defined as the Indian subcontinent, extending west to include Iran. It accounts for about 20 percent of the world's population and represents the largest numerical concentration of poverty. Bangladesh and Nepal, with GDPs per head of US $170–$180, are among the poorest countries of the

Table 3.2. Fertility trends in continental South Asia.

	1960–65	1965–70	1970–75	1975–80	1980–85	1985–90
Afghanistan	7.01	7.13	7.14	7.21	6.90	6.90
Pakistan	7.00	7.00	7.00	7.00	7.00	6.75
Iran	7.26	6.97	6.54	6.50	6.50	6.50
Nepal	5.86	6.17	6.52	6.54	6.25	5.95
Bhutan	5.95	5.95	5.95	5.95	5.89	5.89
Bangladesh	6.68	6.91	7.02	6.66	6.15	5.10
India	5.81	5.69	5.43	4.83	4.73	4.20

world, while India and Pakistan, with per caput GDPs of $350, rank twenty-second and twenty-third in the world of poverty.

In the region as a whole, fertility has declined modestly from a level of about 6.0 in the early 1960s to a little over 4.5 births in the late 1980s, a fall of some 25 percent. However, there is considerable uncertainty about South Asian demographic trends. For three countries – Iran, Afghanistan, and Bhutan – recent fertility trends are essentially unknown. For three other countries (Bangladesh, Pakistan, and Nepal) they are a matter of controversy, leaving only India for which vital rates are clearly established.

United Nations estimates for Afghanistan, Iran, and Bhutan show high fertility rates in the 1960s of about seven births per woman and very modest declines in the last 20 years (*Table 3.2*). For Afghanistan, a verdict of unchanging high fertility seems entirely reasonable, though the military disruptions of recent years may well have caused a temporary drop. The UN scenario for Iran is more doubtful. Before the revolution, the country had a vigorous family-planning program that claimed a considerable impact. After the fall of the Shah, the program was discredited, but in recent years the government has reaffirmed the need to moderate the population growth rate and is again promoting family planning. The degree of success achieved remains uncertain but fertility may have declined, rather than remaining at the constant level of 6.5 births, as suggested by the UN

By contrast, Bangladesh, Pakistan, and Nepal generate a relative abundance of demographic data. All three countries have conducted regular censuses; all have conducted a number of detailed fertility surveys, supplemented by contraceptive prevalence surveys;

and Bangladesh and Pakistan have sample registration systems that publish vital rates. Yet demographic trends remain in dispute. The reason for this uncertainty lies in the poor quality of the data. Surveys, in particular, tend to suffer from the pernicious problem of backward displacement of dates of recent births, leading to an underestimation of the current level of fertility. Claims of fertility decline are often made but these are equally often shown to be false by the next survey.

Accordingly, the results of the 1991 Demographic and Health Survey (DHS) in Pakistan, which indicates a big decline in fertility to about 5.5 births, should be regarded with great skepticism. Reliance on the sample registration system, run by the Federal Bureau of Statistics in Karachi, is more prudent. This system portrays a constant total fertility of about 7.0 births until 1988, when a drop to 6.5 is recorded. The preliminary results of 1989 show a level of 6.4. Falls in lower birth order-specific rates tend to be more pronounced than in higher-order births; thus it remains unclear whether marital fertility decline (which normally affects higher-order births at the initial stages) has really started. Certainly the level of contraceptive practice reported in the 1991 DHS (12 percent) is too low to make an appreciable impact on fertility. To conclude, the level of fertility in Pakistan remained high and constant until the late 1980s but has probably fallen slightly in the period 1988–1990. The UN estimates in *Table 3.2* are essentially correct.

The 1991 Fertility, Family Planning, and Health Survey yielded an unadjusted TFR of 5.1. The level of contraceptive use rose from 5 percent in 1976 to 23 percent in 1991, and age at marriage for women also increased over this period. Thus fertility transition in Nepal has almost certainly started.

In Bangladesh the pace of change is more rapid and pronounced than in Pakistan and Nepal. It is increasingly apparent that fertility decline started in the late 1970s and gathered pace in the 1980s. Between 1975 and 1990, the TFR fell from about 7.0 to about 4.5. Evidence for these assertions comes largely from a 1989 fertility survey and from two contraceptive prevalence surveys in 1989 and 1991, both of which collected truncated birth histories. The consistency of the three data sets is striking. Detailed analysis of the 1989 fertility survey shows that the main change has taken the form of a reduction in higher-order births; for instance, the percent decline in age-order specific rates (cumulated to age 40) between the period 1974–1978 and 1984–1986 was 10 percent for second births but 38 percent for fifth births. This evidence of increasing marital fertility control is confirmed by the rising level of reported contraceptive use, from 7 percent in 1975 to 40 percent in 1991. Age at marriage for women has also increased but the antinatal effect is modest and offset by a decline in widowhood and in the length of the first-birth interval.

In broad terms, the remarkable transition in Bangladesh, the fifth poorest country in the world, has affected all socioeconomic strata equally. Thus fertility decline is as pronounced among illiterate, landless laborers as among the slightly more affluent cultivators. The experience of Bangladesh proves beyond doubt that extreme poverty and low literacy do not represent absolute barriers to fertility decline.

Like Nepal, but in contrast to its Islamic neighbors, the traditional level of fertility in India was low, fluctuating between 1880 and 1960 between five and six births per woman (Bhat, 1989). One possible reason for the slow pace of fertility decline in India is that modernization acted to increase natural fertility through changes in lactational and sexual behavior. There is evidence that marital fertility in the rural areas of many states actually increased during the 1960s, despite the existence of a family-planning program and a gradual rise in reported contraceptive practice (Srinivasan, 1989). The onset of decline in total fertility occurred in the late 1960s and continued for almost a decade; it then stalled before resuming its downward path in the mid-1980s. The most obvious explanation for this sequence concerns the politics of population control. In the 1960s under Indira Ghandi, the family-planning program became increasingly coercive and, when she fell from power in 1977, its credibility also fell and recovered only gradually. Over the entire period from the early 1960s to the late 1980s, total fertility in India fell by only 28 percent, from 5.8 to 4.2 births. Various decompositions (e.g., Srikantan and Balasubramanian, 1989; Chaudhry, 1989) indicate that one-fifth of this decline is attributable to rising age at marriage and the rest to marital fertility.

Some of the reasons for the slow pace of change in India – the possible relaxation of traditional restraints on fertility and the checkered history of the family-planning program – have already been mentioned. However, no account of Indian transition can fail to note the immense cultural and economic diversity of the country and its relevance to demographic trends. Transition is most advanced in the southern states, notably Kerala and Tamil Nadu with TFRs of 2.2 and 2.6, respectively. In most of the northern states such as Rajasthan, Uttar Pradesh, and Bihar, fertility and childhood mortality remain high with TFRs ranging between 4.8 and 5.5. Many (e.g., Dyson and Moore, 1983) attribute this north–south divide to fundamental cultural differences that affect the status of women. In Kerala, for instance, 87 percent of women are literate, compared to 20–30 percent in the high fertility, more northern states.

3.1.3 Latin America

Latin America is defined here to include all states of continental South America and Central America, except Guyana and Suriname. In contrast to other major developing regions, Latin America experienced large-scale and permanent settlement of European populations, and this legacy is evident in certain features of the economy and fertility transition. Two countries, Argentina and Uruguay, were once among the wealthiest in the world and are still ranked in the upper-middle income category. Both had completed their fertility transition by 1950, with TFRs of 3.2 and 2.7, respectively, at that time. In the past 40 years, fertility in both countries has changed little, remaining well above replacement level (*Table 3.3*). This stabilization at levels ranging between 2.5 and 3.5 births per woman appears to be characteristic of the region. In Chile, as in Argentina and Uruguay, the era of rapid decline is over but period fertility remains within this range. However, there is no good reason for believing that Latin American culture possesses features that will sustain moderate fertility indefinitely. The majorities of the populations of these three countries are of Spanish and Italian extraction. Fertility levels in the countries of origin, Spain and Italy, are now among the lowest in the world. If Latin America experiences the socioeconomic transformation – particularly with regard to the position of women in society – that has characterized Southern Europe, it is probable that Latin American fertility will fall to replacement level or below.

Table 3.3. Fertility trends in Latin America.

	1960–65	1965–70	1970–75	1975–80	1980–85	1985–90
Guatemala	6.85	6.60	6.45	6.40	6.12	5.77
Honduras	7.36	7.42	7.38	6.58	6.16	5.55
Nicaragua	7.37	7.17	6.79	6.40	6.00	5.55
Bolivia	6.63	6.56	6.50	6.15	5.50	5.00
Paraguay	6.80	6.40	5.65	5.05	4.82	4.58
El Salvador	6.85	6.62	6.10	5.70	5.00	4.52
Ecuador	6.90	6.70	6.05	5.40	4.70	4.10
Peru	6.85	6.56	6.00	5.38	4.65	4.00
Mexico	6.75	6.70	6.37	5.03	4.29	3.60
Venezuela	6.46	5.89	4.96	4.44	3.90	3.45
Costa Rica	6.95	5.80	4.33	3.89	3.50	3.36
Brazil	6.15	5.31	4.70	4.21	3.81	3.20
Panama	5.92	5.62	4.94	4.06	3.46	3.14
Argentina	3.09	3.05	3.15	3.36	3.15	2.96
Colombia	6.76	6.28	4.66	4.14	3.51	2.90
Chile	5.28	4.44	3.63	2.90	2.80	2.73
Uruguay	2.90	2.80	3.00	2.89	2.57	2.43

From speculations about the future, let us return to a consideration of the past. Because the demography of Latin America is rather well documented, it is possible to extend the historical description of fertility trends back to the 1950s. Between the early 1950s and the early 1960s, there is little evidence of any fertility decline. Indeed, in some countries such as Costa Rica, El Salvador, and Panama, a slight increase is registered, perhaps in response to declines in widowhood (Dyson and Murphy, 1985). In this regard, Latin America is very different from Asia, where rising age at marriage for women heralded and then accompanied declines in marital fertility. For most countries, the early 1960s represent the last quinquennium prior to the fertility transition. TFRs are typically close to seven births per woman, though lower in Brazil, Chile, Panama, and Venezuela.

The synchronicity of the onset of fertility decline in Latin America is its most remarkable feature. Leaving aside Argentina and Uruguay, which belong to the earlier European transition, all but two countries (Mexico and Bolivia) started their declines in the 1960s. However, the speed of change varied widely. Guzman's (1991) calculations of the year of onset of decline and the percent

Table 3.4. Year of onset of decline and percent decline in following decade: Latin America.

	Year	Percentage decline
Brazil	1960	8.3
Guatemala	1960	9.6
Venezuela	1960	15.6
Costa Rica	1961	37.5
Colombia	1962	34.3
Chile	1962	28.7
El Salvador	1962	10.8
Nicaragua	1962	8.5
Panama	1962	20.0
Paraguay	1963	19.7
Ecuador	1965	20.0
Peru	1965	16.8
Honduras	1966	11.5
Bolivia	1972	13.8
Mexico	1972	36.4

Source: Guzman, 1991.

decline in the following decade are shown in *Table 3.4*. Declines of over 30 percent are registered on Colombia, Costa Rica, and Mexico. At the other extreme are Brazil, Guatemala, and Nicaragua which experienced declines of less than 10 percent. Interpretation of these figures is difficult, because of the somewhat arbitrary definition of the onset of decline. For instance, it is perfectly correct to characterize the transition in Mexico as both late to start but extremely rapid once under way; but it would be misleading to claim that fertility decline in Brazil has been slow but steady. Over the whole period from 1960 to 1990, the pace of change in Brazil has been as great as in Costa Rica and Colombia.

In terms of their current situation, Latin American states fall into four groups. The first group consists of Argentina, Chile, and Uruguay where fertility is low and stable. A large second group follows where total fertility is now in the range of three to four births and where there is some sign of incipient stabilization, particularly in Costa Rica. The three most populous countries of the region – Brazil, Mexico, and Colombia – fall into this group. It should be noted that fertility in Colombia is now slightly lower than in Argentina. The third group comprises four countries which are in

the midst of transition with recent fertility rates of four to five births
per woman. Finally, there is a cluster of four high fertility countries,
three of which are in Central America.

While the simultaneity of the onset of decline is the most remarkable feature of Latin American transition, a further distinguishing feature is the emergence of very pronounced but temporary urban–rural, socioeconomic, and regional differentials during
the period of decline. In most countries of the region, decline started
among the more educated and metropolitan sectors and spread gradually to less educated, rural sectors. The typical process is well illustrated by Rodriguez and Hobcraft (1984) in an analysis of Colom-
bian data. They were able to identify the beginnings of decline in
the 1960s for women with complete primary or higher education, in
the late 1960s for women with incomplete primary schooling, and
in the late 1970s for those with no formal schooling. Furthermore,
they demonstrated that, within each educational stratum, decline
was initially restricted to a reduction in higher-order births and only
subsequently affected earlier stages of family formation.

This sequence suggests strongly that fertility decline in Colombia has taken the form of social diffusion of a new form of behavior,
birth control. A more recent analysis by Rodriguez (1990) supports
this view. He examined subgroup changes in fertility behavior, using
World Fertility Survey (WFS) and Demographic and Health Survey
(DHS) data for five Latin American countries. Remarkable regularities in the spacing and limitation components of marital fertility
were observed. Specifically, the strata with the least evidence of
fertility control at the start tended to experience the greatest pro-
portional change. Within strata, transition followed a self-sustaining
course that is consistent with a basic diffusion process. To the extent that Rodriguez's analysis and interpretation are correct, it is
inevitable that fertility in all strata will converge at a modest level.
Thus the prospects for a continuation of fertility decline in the region
as a whole appear good.

3.1.4   The Arab states

The Arab states constitute a linguistic and cultural rather than a
compact geographical entity. Most have small populations: Egypt,
with over 50 million inhabitants, followed by Sudan, Morocco, and

Algeria, with about 25 million each, are the main exceptions. There is a very wide spread in living standards. At one extreme are the United Arab Emirates, Kuwait, and Saudi Arabia, classified as high income countries. At the other end of the spectrum are Sudan, Mauritania, and Yemen with per caput GDPs of less than $500.

Information on the demography of the Arab world is patchy. For Libya, Lebanon, Syria, and some of the Gulf states, there is little recent evidence concerning fertility levels. In other countries of the region – for instance, Sudan and Mauritania – recent survey information is available, but, as in South Asia, data quality is poor and estimation of trends correspondingly difficult.

Nevertheless, several features of Arab fertility have clearly been established. At the start of the period under discussion, the early 1960s, levels of fertility were universally very high, with TFRs ranging between 6.5 and 8.0. This exceptionally high level is the result of an unusual combination of early marriage ages, relatively short periods of breast-feeding, and little practice of birth control. It is clear from *Table 3.5* that fertility remains high in this region. Only one country, Lebanon, records a rate decisively below 4.0.

For the entire region, total fertility has fallen from about 7.0 in the early 1960s to about 5.0 in the late 1980s, a drop of 28 percent. This average conceals very large differences in trends and current levels and an equally large divergence in government policies toward population and family planning. Apart from Lebanon, whose ethnic and religious diversity sets it apart from the rest of the Arab world, the Egyptian and Tunisian governments were the first to provide public sector family-planning services and associated publicity, and were among the few Arab states to experience fertility decline in the 1960s. Tunisian fertility dropped steadily, and this country now records one of the lowest TFRs in the region with 3.9 births per woman. For reasons that are not fully understood, Egyptian fertility plateaued in the 1970s, before resuming a downward path in the 1980s to reach a TFR of 4.5 in the period from 1985 to 1990.

In the 1970s, declines in Arab fertility became more widespread with well-documented falls in Jordan, Morocco, and a number of the small Gulf states. By the late 1980s, fertility decline had started throughout most of the Arab world, though the change was often modest. The main exceptions include two of the poorest countries,

Table 3.5. Fertility trends in the Arab states.

	1960–65	1965–70	1970–75	1975–80	1980–85	1985–90
Yemen	7.61	7.77	7.77	7.77	7.71	7.69
Oman	7.17	7.17	7.17	7.17	7.17	7.17
Libya	7.17	7.48	7.58	7.38	7.17	6.87
Saudi Arabia	7.26	7.26	7.30	7.28	7.28	6.80
Syria	7.46	7.79	7.69	7.44	7.38	6.66
Mauritania	6.50	6.50	6.50	6.50	6.50	6.50
Sudan	6.67	6.67	6.67	6.67	6.58	6.44
Jordan	7.99	7.99	7.79	7.38	6.76	6.15
Iraq	7.17	7.17	7.11	6.56	6.35	6.15
Algeria	7.38	7.48	7.38	7.17	6.35	5.43
Morocco	7.15	7.09	6.89	5.90	5.43	4.82
UAE	6.87	6.76	6.35	5.66	5.23	4.82
Qatar	6.97	6.97	6.76	6.00	5.00	4.80
Egypt	7.07	6.56	5.53	5.27	5.06	4.53
Bahrain	7.17	6.97	5.94	5.23	4.63	4.08
Tunisia	7.17	6.83	6.15	5.66	4.88	3.94
Kuwait	7.31	7.41	6.90	5.89	4.87	3.94
Lebanon	6.35	6.05	4.92	4.30	3.79	3.42

Yemen and Mauritania, but may also include some of the richest
states, such as Libya, and Oman. Little is known about fertility in
Libya but it is thought that any decline is recent and modest. In
Oman, fertility in 1987 was estimated from the Gulf Child Health
Survey to be 7.8 with only 9 percent of currently married women
reporting use of contraception. According to the results of the Gulf
Child Health Survey Program, fertility in the late 1980s also remained high in several other Gulf states: 6.5 among the indigenous
populations of Kuwait and of Saudi Arabia, 5.9 in the United Arab
Emirates, and 5.3 in Iraq (Farid, 1993). However, fertility had fallen
more steeply in Bahrain and Qatar.

Fertility transition in this region shares some features of both
the Asian and the Latin American transitions. As in Asia, rising
age at marriage for women has made an important contribution to
fertility decline, and, as in Latin America, huge differences in fertility
have arisen between urban and rural strata and between educational
strata. This differentiation, in both Latin America and the Arab
states, may reflect the rather weak nature or nonexistence of many

government family-planning services; under such circumstances, the poor and less-educated have limited access to modern birth control.

In general, levels of Arab fertility remain much higher than might be expected from consideration of living standards and urbanization. This resilience is sometimes attributed to low levels of female autonomy and education. While it is true that female labor force participation remains low, educational standards for women are rising rapidly in many Arab countries. But even among educated women, fertility is remarkably high. For instance, the 1990 Jordanian Demographic and Health Survey records the following TFRs by educational status of women: no schooling, 6.92; primary, 6.00; secondary, 5.39; and postsecondary, 4.10. There are few highly urbanized countries with reasonable access to family-planning services where fertility levels, even among educated couples, remain as buoyant as in Jordan. It seems reasonable to conclude that replacement-level fertility is a more distant prospect for the Arab world than for some other regions.

3.1.5 Sub-Saharan Africa

Sub-Saharan Africa comprises only 10 percent of the population of the Third World but accounts for a disproportionately large number of the least developed countries. The economic plight of the region deteriorated further in the 1980s, with declines in income per head in many countries. Although it possesses more cultural diversity than most of the other regions considered in this chapter, sub-Saharan Africa exhibits features of social organization and cultural values that distinguish it from other major regions: traditions of postnatal abstinence, polygyny, and the importance of lineage are the best known of these.

The first comprehensive account of Africa's demography had little direct information on fertility at its disposal and had to rely heavily on stable population analysis (Brass *et al.*, 1968). Since that time, data availability has improved steadily. Large sums were invested in censuses, and in the 1970s an increasing number of countries undertook more specialized demographic surveys. The World Fertility Survey represented the next step forward with the participation of 10 African countries. Under the successor to this program

Table 3.6. Fertility levels in sub-Saharan Africa: 1985–1990.

East Africa		*Southern Africa*	
Rwanda	8.49	Namibia	6.00
Malawi	7.60	Botswana	5.50
Uganda	7.30	Swaziland	5.25
Ethiopia	7.00	Lesotho	5.00
Somalia	7.00	South Africa	4.38
Burundi	6.80		
Kenya	6.80	*West Africa*	
Zambia	6.75	Côte d'Ivoire	7.41
Djibouti	6.60	Benin	7.10
Zimbabwe	5.79	Mali	7.10
		Niger	7.10
Central Africa		Guinea	7.00
Angola	7.20	Nigeria	6.90
Zaire	6.70	Togo	6.58
Congo	6.29	Burkina Faso	6.50
Central African Republic	6.20	Gambia	6.50
Cameroon	6.10	Senegal	6.50
Equatorial Guinea	5.89	Sierra Leone	6.50
Chad	5.89	Ghana	6.39
Gabon	4.99	Guinea-Bissau	5.79

(the Demographic and Health Survey Project) national surveys have been conducted in a further 12 countries.

Despite this improvement, knowledge of fertility levels in Africa remains uneven. Out of 35 continental states with a population of 1 million or more, direct information on fertility in the period 1985 to 1990 is available for only 17. Moreover, the reliability of estimates is lower than in South Asia. Hence *Table 3.6* is restricted to current levels and no attempt is made to depict trends as for other regions.

However, the evidence strongly suggests that, prior to 1980, fertility in Africa remained constant at a high level and even recorded increases in some countries. Between the early 1960s and the 1980s, UN statistics show increases of 0.5 births or more for Rwanda, Angola, Zaire, Central African Republic, Gabon, and Guinea-Bissau. In some cases, the most plausible explanation is a decline in pathological sterility. In other cases, it may be attributed to an attenuation of traditional birth-spacing mechanisms. Indeed it is probable that prior to 1960, fertility increase was more widespread. Feeney's analysis of Kenyan census data, for instance, suggests that fertility rose substantially prior to 1960 (Feeney, 1988). Unfortunately few countries have a record of census taking as good as Kenya's to allow a similar historical depth of analysis.

The persistence of high fertility in Africa gave rise to a prevailing view that this situation would continue for some time to come. It was argued that Africa possessed unique cultural and economic characteristics that would render reproductive behavior unusually impervious to the forces of change (e.g., Caldwell and Caldwell, 1990). The high desired family sizes reported in surveys further strengthened this prognosis.

Events of the last decade have transformed perceptions about the stability of African reproductive regimes. First, an appreciable shift in population policies has occurred, with governments increasingly expressing concern about population growth and support for family-planning services. According to Mauldin and Ross (1991), sub-Saharan Africa recorded greater increases in the strength of family-planning programs than any other region. There are also signs of change in reproductive behavior. Nearly all Demographic and Health Surveys have recorded appreciable increases in median ages at first birth. For instance, the differences between cohorts aged 30 to 34 and 20 to 24 amount to 1.0, 0.9, 0.8, and 0.8 years in Kenya, Zambia, Burundi, and Togo, respectively. Improvements in the educational attainment of young African women may be one reason for this change. It is also possible that economic stress has acted to delay the formation of stable partnerships and the onset of childbearing.

Postponement of childbearing may be a temporary phenomenon. But there is evidence in an increasing number of East and Southern African states that fertility decline, fueled by contraceptive use, has started. Such a trend is much more likely to mark the onset of a sustained transition than to represent a transitory response to economic hardship. At the forefront of this movement is the Republic of South Africa. By the late 1980s, the level of contraceptive practice among the black population was estimated to be about 50 percent and total fertility at about 4.5 births (Mostert, 1991). Moderate levels of use among married women have also been recorded in Zimbabwe (43 percent), Botswana (33 percent), Kenya

(27 percent), Namibia (23 percent), and Swaziland (21 percent). In all these countries there is parallel evidence of declining fertility. In South Africa and Zimbabwe, the decline has amounted to about 2.0 births, in Kenya and Botswana to about 1.5 births, and in Namibia and Swaziland to less than 1.0 birth per woman.

Successive surveys in Kenya show how rapidly the climate of reproductive opinion and behavior can change. The Kenya Fertility Survey of 1977–1978 portrayed a very pronatalist society. Total fertility was about 8.0; desired family size averaged 7.2 children; only 7 percent of couples reported contraceptive use; and only 16 percent of women said that they wanted no more children. There was little ground for believing that fertility transition was about to start. Yet a mere decade later, desired family size had dropped to 4.4 children, 49 percent of women expressed a wish to have no more, contraceptive use had risen to 27 percent, and fertility had fallen to 6.5 births. This radical change had affected women of all educational backgrounds and ages.

This impression of change in the subregion should be balanced by data from other countries. Recent Demographic and Health Surveys provide no convincing evidence of appreciable decline in Burundi, Uganda, Zambia, or Tanzania. Nor is it reasonable to expect any decline in Angola or Mozambique because of prolonged civil unrest.

In West and Central Africa, fertility shows fewer signs of actual or incipient decline, though it is probable that fertility decline has started among younger women in Senegal and in Southwest and Southeast Nigeria (Cleland *et al.*, 1993). Elsewhere, however, there is no strong evidence of fertility decline. This stability is particularly puzzling in a country such as Ghana. Ghana has long had a rather well-educated and urbanized population, where women possess considerable autonomy and indeed dominate trading. Moreover, there has been some attempt, since the late 1960s, to promote family planning, albeit on a limited scale. Despite the severe economic recession of the late 1970s and early 1980s which threatened living standards of the urban middle classes, fertility has remained more or less constant over the past 15 years (Onuoha, 1993). The experience

Table 3.7. Fertility trends in island states.

	1960–65	1965–70	1970–75	1975–80	1980–85	1985–90
Comoros	6.91	7.05	7.05	7.05	7.05	7.05
Madagascar	6.60	6.60	6.60	6.60	6.60	6.60
Maldives	7.00	7.00	7.00	7.00	6.75	6.50
Melanesia	6.24	6.01	5.80	5.59	5.31	4.95
Cape Verde	7.00	7.00	7.00	6.70	6.29	4.83
Micronesia	6.21	5.92	5.49	5.30	5.00	4.70
Polynesia	7.30	6.80	6.30	5.80	5.20	4.50
Caribbean	5.46	5.01	4.37	3.49	3.18	2.96
Sri Lanka	5.16	4.68	4.00	3.83	3.26	2.67
Réunion	5.65	4.82	3.93	3.28	2.90	2.54
Mauritius	5.73	4.25	3.25	3.07	2.46	2.10

suggests that Ghanaian society and perhaps other West African societies present obstacles to fertility decline and mass adoption of contraception that are absent in East and Southern Africa. While the prospects are good for widespread fertility decline in the East and South, the prognosis for West and Central Africa is uncertain.

3.1.6 Island states

To complete this geographic account of fertility trends, *Table 3.7* depicts relevant data for the main islands and island groups. Their contribution to global population trends is minimal. Yet the demography of islands is of special interest, and several have been at the forefront of fertility transition.

In the 1960s, for instance, Fiji, Mauritius, and Sri Lanka were among the very few developing countries to have started fertility transition. This evidence gave rise to speculations that Malthusian constraints on population growth may take a particularly visible form in islands where territorial expansion is precluded.

Table 3.7 shows that such simple generalizations are unjustified. In the period 1985 to 1990, fertility in island states ranged from close to replacement level in Mauritius to about to seven births per woman in Comoros and Madagascar.

3.2   Synthesis and Implications
for the Future

Several lessons can be drawn from this regional review of fertility
trends in the period 1960 to 1990. The first provides grounds for optimism about the economic and environmental future of the planet.
During the past 30 years, fertility transition has spread throughout
the developing world with a speed that has dazzled demographers
and confounded many experts. It is easy to forget the profound pessimism about the prospects for fertility decline that prevailed in the
1960s and much of the 1970s. In particular, it was doubted that the
mere promotion of birth control services could have an impact on the
birth rate of largely agricultural, low income, and poorly educated
nations. As a consequence, there was intense interest in so-called
beyond family-planning measures that included, *inter alia*, the use
of financial payments to induce couples to accept contraception or
to have fewer children.

The turning point in popular perceptions came in the mid-1970s
with convincing signs that fertility decline was under way in Thailand and Indonesia, both largely agricultural countries with low incomes at that time. Hitherto, fertility decline had been confined
to countries with atypically favorable conditions: rapid economic
transformation in the case of Taiwan and South Korea; a metropolitan environment as in Hong Kong and Singapore; and the idiosyn-
crasies of an insular status such as Fiji, Mauritius, and parts of the
Caribbean.

As we have seen, fertility decline in the Third World is now
the norm rather than the exception. In Asia, the main exceptions
are Pakistan, Afghanistan, and some of the small countries of Indo-
China. In Central and South America, fertility decline is already
completed or under way in all countries. Among the Arab states of
North Africa and the Middle East, most countries have experienced
falls in fertility though decline is not yet ubiquitous. Finally in
sub-Saharan Africa, fertility transition is clearly starting in East
and Southern Africa, leaving Central and West Africa as the main
areas where fertility remains largely unchanged. Such widespread
transformations of reproductive behavior have come as a surprise
and their existence is not yet fully appreciated outside the specialist

domain of demography. The rates of population growth in most developing countries remain high because of the continued decline in mortality and because crude birth rates are buoyed by increases in the relative and absolute numbers of couples in the reproductive ages. Thus, the impact of declining fertility is offset by these other demographic forces and, in many countries, will not be felt until the next century.

A major generalization of demographic transition theory is that once fertility decline, fueled by birth control within marriage, is under way, the trend is irreversible and sustained until fertility reaches replacement level or thereabouts. Like most simple generalizations, this one has to be qualified. Reversals have occurred, most notably the post–World War II baby boom in Western Europe and North America. More commonly, fertility may plateau before resuming a downward path, as has been the case in Egypt and Malaysia. Moreover, the speed of decline has varied from the near-precipitous drops in China and Mexico to a slow pace of change, as, for instance, in the Philippines or Jordan. A much more profound uncertainty exists about the proposition that fertility will continue to fall until the replacement level of a little over two births per woman is reached. In the aggregate, there is a logic in this ultimate destination for levels of human reproduction because it implies long-term stability of population sizes and, in the very long term, no animal population can continue to grow or decline indefinitely. But, at the level of families and individuals, such aggregate considerations may hold little force. It has already been noted that family sizes appear to have stabilized in some Latin American countries at a level that is well above replacement. In other regions, most notably sub-Saharan Africa and the Arab states, it is difficult to imagine the achievement of replacement-level fertility under existing socioeconomic and cultural conditions. Fertility aspirations, as recorded in surveys, remain much higher. In Zimbabwe, for instance, which is at the forefront of fertility transition in Africa, the 1988 Demographic and Health Survey indicates a mean ideal family size of 5.4 children among currently married women; and nearly half of women who already have 4 or more living children want additional children.

Of course, societal conditions do not remain stable. Indeed one of the biggest mistakes of demographers has been to underestimate the rapidity with which societies change. Nevertheless, the prospects for the attainment of replacement-level fertility within the next 40 years remain doubtful in some parts of the developing world.

The second major lesson from this review concerns the need for humility on the part of scientists. Despite a huge volume of new empirical evidence concerning fertility transition that has accumulated in the past 30 years, our understanding of the underlying causes remains rudimentary. Nor is there any sign of a growing consensus among population scientists regarding fertility theories or the relative importance of specific causes. The gulf remains wide between the two dominant schools of thought – one placing emphasis on economic determinism and the other on culture and the diffusion of ideas.

At the start of this chapter, the inadequacy of simple mono-causal explanations of fertility decline was noted. This point is vividly illustrated by recent reviews of the socioeconomic status of Asian and Latin American countries at the onset of fertility decline (Casterline, 1991; Guzman, 1991). For every indicator (life expectancy, infant mortality, urbanization, adult literacy, income per head, percent engaged in agriculture), there was a very wide spread among countries. To take but two examples from Latin America, infant mortality ranged from 62 per 1,000 births in Paraguay to 151 in Bolivia, and adult literacy from 84 percent in Costa Rica to 34 percent in Guatemala. This huge disparity in the stage of socioeconomic development reinforces similar conclusions from studies of the European transition, where birth control spread across a region with little regard for socioeconomic differences between counties, bringing lower fertility in its wake.

With the steady increase in the number of countries where fertility transition has already started, research priorities will shift from the study of the determinants of the onset of decline to the study of factors that influence speed of decline and point of stabilization. Here again though it is unlikely that very strong links will be found between speed of transition and socioeconomic indicators. The earlier comparison between Indonesia, Malaysia, and the Philippines is a pertinent example. Even more striking is the rapid fertility decline that has taken place in Bangladesh, one of the poorest countries in the world.

The reason for this complexity is that both culture and government policies exert strong independent influences on fertility. It is appropriate to end this chapter with a brief consideration of one of these factors, government policies, because of its practical relevance. To the extent that state-sponsored initiatives to promote birth control and the acceptability of smaller families can be effective, the future course of human fertility depends, at least in part, on government policies and the availability of funds to implement them. Conversely, if the influence of such interventions is minor, then future fertility trends will be determined by broader forces of cultural and socioeconomic change that are less amenable to governmental and international decisions.

The effectiveness of family-planning programs has been high on the demographic research agenda for the past 20 years. The most influential body of work comprises statistical estimations of the relationship between the strength of family-planning programs and the demographic outcomes such as level of fertility, percent decline in fertility, and contraceptive use, using countries as units of analysis (e.g., Mauldin and Berelson, 1978; Mauldin and Ross, 1991). The general finding is that strong programs do reduce fertility, though this effect is conditioned by, and subordinate to, the effect of socioeconomic development. It is also clear from these analyses that the creation of family-planning programs cannot be divorced easily from general development. Few of the least developed countries have birth control services, education, and publicity that are rated as strong. Conversely, few of the more developed countries have programs that are rated as nonexistent or weak. This correlation obviously complicates the task of isolating the effect of programs from effects of broader development.

One major limitation of this type of study is that program strength is taken as an exogenous factor. The analytic design is vulnerable to the criticism that serious programs are most likely to arise in response to spontaneous expressions of need and prior fertility decline, and only grow in strength (i.e., political commitment and resource allocation) when success is already visible. Programs can thus be seen as a consequence as well as a potential cause of demographic change. This weakness severely limits the validity of results.

Perhaps a more convincing approach to an assessment of program impact would be to compare fertility trends in countries that are broadly similar in cultural characteristics and stage of development but where population policies have diverged, perhaps because of the convictions of political leadership. Algeria and Tunisia, Pakistan and Bangladesh, Mexico and Colombia, North Korea and South Korea, Zambia and Zimbabwe are possible candidates for such a study. In each pair, the first country was much slower than the second country to adopt and implement policies and programs to reduce fertility. And in each case, the timing of the start of fertility decline appears to reflect the policy divergence. Thus it is hard to resist the inference that Mexico's very late fertility transition is connected to the government's hostility to provision of family-planning services until the dramatic change in 1972. Similarly, the persistence of high fertility in Algeria until the early 1980s is surely related to the low priority attached to birth control, which shifted only in the 1980s.

Such a comparative case study approach shows that government policies can have and have had appreciable demographic impacts by changing reproductive attitudes, by legitimizing birth control, and by enhancing access to family-planning services. To the extent that this verdict is valid, the future course of fertility in regions where it is still high depends to some extent on political leadership. As a consequence, demographic forecasting becomes more uncertain but the politics of population and birth control become more important and exciting.

References

Arshat, H., Tan, B.A., Tey, N.P., and Subbiah, M., 1988, *Marriage and Family Formation in Peninsular Malaysia: Analytic Report on the 1984/85 Malaysian Population and Family Survey,* National Population and Family Development Board, Kuala Lumpur, Malaysia.

Bhat, P.N. Mari, 1989, Mortality and fertility in India, 1881–1961: A reassessment, in T. Dyson, ed., *India's Historical Demography,* Curzon Press, London, UK.

Brass, W., Coale, A.J., Demeny, P., Heisel, D.F., Lorimer, F., Romaniuk, A., and Van de Walle, E., 1968, *The Demography of Tropical Africa,* Princeton University Press, Princeton, NJ, USA.

Caldwell, J.C., and Caldwell, P., 1990, High fertility in sub-Saharan Africa, *Scientific American* May:118–125.

Casterline, J., 1991, Fertility Transition in Asia, Paper presented at International Union for Scientific Study of Population Seminar, Harare, Zimbabwe.

Chaudhry, M.D., 1989, Fertility behavior in India, 1961–1986: The stalled decline in the crude birth rate, in S.N. Singh, M.K. Premi, P.S. Bhatia, and A. Bose, eds., *Population Transition in India*, Vol. 2, B.R. Publishing Corp., Delhi, India.

Cleland, J., Onuoha, N., and Timæus, I., 1993, Fertility change in sub-Saharan Africa: A review of the evidence, in T. Locoh, ed., *The Course of Fertility Transition in Sub-Saharan Africa,* International Union for the Scientific Study of Population, Liège, Belgium.

Coale, A.J., and Freedman, R., 1993, Similarities in the fertility transition in China and three other East Asian populations, in R. Leete and I. Alam, eds., *The Revolution in Asian Fertility,* Oxford University Press, Oxford, UK.

Dyson, T., and Moore, M., 1983, Kinship structure, female autonomy and demographic behavior in India, *Population and Development Review* 9:35–60.

Dyson, T., and Murphy, M., 1985, The onset of the fertility transition, *Population and Development Review* 11:399–440.

Family Planning and Maternal and Child Health Project, 1987, *Nepal Fertility and Family Planning Survey Report 1986,* Central Bureau of Statistics, Kathmandu, Nepal.

Farid, S., 1993, Family Planning, Health and Family Well-Being in the Arab World, Paper presented at Arab Population Conference, Ammon.

Feeney, G., 1988, The use of parity progression ratios in evaluating family planning programs, in *Proceedings of African Population Conference, Dakar,* International Union for the Scientific Study of Population, Liège, Belgium.

Feeney, G., 1991, Fertility decline in Taiwan: A study using parity progression ratios, *Demography* 28:467–480.

Freedman, R., Khoo, S., and Supraptilah, D., 1981, *Modern Contraceptive Use in Indonesia: A Challenge to Conventional Wisdom,* WFS Scientific Report No. 20, International Statistical Institute, Voorburg, Netherlands.

Guzman, J.M., 1991, The Onset of Fertility Decline in Latin America, Paper presented at International Union for the Scientific Study of Population Seminar, Harare, Zimbabwe.

Leete, R., and Tan Boon An, 1993, Contrasting fertility trends among ethnic groups in Malaysia, in R. Leete and I. Alam, eds., *The Revolution in Asian Fertility,* Oxford University Press, Oxford, UK.

Mauldin, W.P., and Berelson, B., 1978, Conditions of fertility decline in developing countries, 1964–1975, *Studies in Family Planning* **9**(5).

Mauldin, W.P., and Ross, J., 1991, Family planning programs: Efforts and results, 1982–1989, *Studies in Family Planning* **22**:350–367.

Mostert, W., 1991, Recent fertility trends in South Africa, in W. Mostert and J. Lötter, eds., *South African Demographic Future,* Human Science Research Council, Pretoria, South Africa.

Onuoha, N., 1993, Changing Patterns of Reproduction and Social Organization in West Africa, Unpublished report, Centre for Population Studies, London School of Hygiene and Tropical Medicine, London, UK.

Park, Chai-Bin, 1992, Family building in the Republic of Korea: Recent trends, in *Impact of Fertility Decline on Population Policies and Program Strategies,* Korean Institute for Health and Social Affairs, Seoul, South Korea.

Peng, Xizhe, 1981, *Demographic Transition in China,* Oxford University Press, Oxford, UK.

Rodriguez, G., 1990, The Spacing and Limiting Components of the Fertility Transition in Latin America, Paper presented at International Union for Scientific Study of Population Seminar, Buenos Aires, Argentina.

Rodriguez, G., and Hobcraft, J.N., 1984, *Illustrative Analysis: Life Table Analysis of Birth Intervals in Colombia,* WFS Scientific Report No. 16, International Statistical Institute, Voorburg, Netherlands.

Srikantan, K.S., and Balasubramanian, K., 1989, Stalling of fertility decline in India, in S.N. Singh, M.K. Premi, P.S. Bhatia, and A. Bose, eds., *Population Transition in India,* Vol. 2, B.R. Publishing Corp., Delhi, India.

Srinivasan, K., 1989, Natural fertility and nuptiality patterns in India: Historical levels and recent changes, in S.N. Singh, M.K. Premi, P.S. Bhatia, and A. Bose, eds., *Population Transition in India,* Vol. 1, B.R. Publishing Corp., Delhi, India.

Chapter 4

Reproductive Preferences and Future Fertility in Developing Countries

Charles F. Westoff

The classical paradigm of the demographic transition features a decline in the rate of reproduction from the conditions of natural fertility at high levels to a regimen in which fertility is highly controlled and has declined to replacement or lower levels. In many of the developing countries that have entered this transitional stage, increases in age at marriage have played an important role. But the principal mechanism driving this transition is birth control, mainly in the form of contraception, though abortion has made significant impacts at different times and in different places.

In Asia and in Latin America, the use of contraception has typically been adopted at higher parities after couples have achieved the number of children desired; its use at lower parities for the regulation of spacing has appeared later in the fertility transition. In contrast, in Africa, especially in sub-Saharan Africa, a demand for spacing evidently has emerged before a demand for limiting fertility. Currently, in the nine sub-Saharan African countries included in the first phase of the Demographic and Health Surveys (1986-1990), the average percentage of married women using contraception for

spacing purposes was 10 percent compared with 8 percent for limiting fertility. In the 16 other developing countries (including those
in North Africa), the corresponding percentages were 12 and 36
percent, respectively, a dramatically different ratio (calculated from
data presented in Westoff and Ochoa, 1991:7).

Whether contraception is employed for purposes of spacing or
for purposes of limiting fertility, it reduces the likelihood of pregnancy and thus has an impact on the period rate of fertility. There
is evidence that contraceptive failure rates are greater when methods are used for spacing rather than for limiting births, but, even
with such higher failure rates, fertility is reduced far below that implied in the natural fertility model (especially considering the higher
fecundability at the younger ages, where spacing behavior is more
common). In any event, a full appraisal of the subject of reproductive preferences should ideally include both preferences to postpone
the next birth and preferences to terminate fertility. Data on spacing
preferences are not as widely available, however, as data on preferences to terminate fertility. The World Fertility Survey included no
direct questions on the subject, and the DHS-I questionnaire did not
include the questions necessary to estimate preferred lengths of birth
intervals for all women. Therefore, the emphasis in this chapter is
on the number of children desired and the intention to terminate fertility. These measures are particularly relevant for Asian and Latin
American populations where the contraceptive prevalence level is
determined largely by such limiting practice. As noted above, the
use of contraception for birth spacing dominates in the sub-Saharan
African countries and thus makes more of a contribution to the prediction of fertility in that part of the world.

4.1   Desired Number of Children

The most common measure of reproductive preferences is the number of children desired. The basic question included in all DHS
interviews was "If you could go back to the time you did not have
any children and could choose exactly the number of children to
have in your whole life, how many would that be?"

The mean number of children desired is shown in the first column of *Table 4.1* for currently married women in all of the countries

Table 4.1. Indices of reproductive preferences.

	Mean desired number of children (currently married)	Percent who have more than desired	TFR	DTFR	Percent want no more
Sub-Saharan Africa					
Botswana	5.4	14	5.0	4.1	38
Burundi	5.5	12	6.7	5.7	24
Ghana	5.5	13	6.4	5.3	23
Kenya	4.8	30	6.4	4.5	49
Liberia	6.5	6	6.9	6.3	17
Mali	6.9	5	7.6	7.1	16
Ondo State	6.1	5	6.1	5.8	23
Senegal	7.2	9	6.6	5.6	19
Sudan	5.9	8	5.0	4.2	25
Togo	5.6	18	6.6	5.1	25
Uganda	6.8	9	7.5	6.5	23
Zimbabwe	5.4	15	5.2	4.3	33
North Africa					
Egypt	2.9	37	4.4	2.8	60
Morocco	3.7	27	4.6	3.3	47
Tunisia	3.5	34	4.1	2.9	58
Asia					
Indonesia	3.2	19	2.9	2.4	51
Sri Lanka	3.1	21	2.6	2.2	64
Thailand	2.8	21	2.2	1.8	66
Latin America					
Bolivia	2.8	42	5.1	2.8	68
Brazil	3.0	35	3.3	2.2	64
Colombia	3.0	31	3.1	2.1	69
Dominican Rep.	3.7	28	3.6	2.6	63
Ecuador	3.4	30	4.3	2.9	65
Guatemala	4.2	18	5.5	4.5	47
Mexico	3.3	29	4.0	2.9	65
Peru	2.9	44	4.0	2.3	75
Trinidad/Tobago	3.1	24	3.0	2.2	54

included in DHS-I. The range of these preferences varies widely, from as high as seven children in a few countries in sub-Saharan Africa to under three children in a few countries elsewhere.

One well-known difficulty with this measure is that it is influenced by the number of children already born (and surviving), some of whom may not have been wanted at the time. The second column of *Table 4.1* shows, for each country, the percent of currently married women whose number of living children exceeds their desired number. Even considering the likely tendency for women to rationalize unwanted births as wanted, this statistic indicates significant proportions of women who prefer fewer children than they have. In sub-Saharan Africa, this measure shows the lowest levels of excess fertility, ranging between 5 and 18 percent except in Kenya, where 30 percent of women are classified as preferring fewer children than they have. The percentages with unwanted fertility are much higher elsewhere, involving roughly between one-fifth and two-fifths of married women. It is clear, even from this simple measure, that fertility is significantly higher in many countries of the Third World than it would be if women's preferences prevailed.

What do these levels of unwanted births imply for the rates of reproduction? In column 3 of *Table 4.1*, the total fertility rate (TFR) is shown for each country. These rates have been calculated from the birth histories of all women based on person-months of experience up to 24 months before the survey. A desired total fertility rate (DTFR) has been derived by confining the numerator for each age-specific category to those births classified as desired or, conversely, by deleting those births in excess of the number preferred. The DTFR (in column 4) is intended as an estimate of what the TFR would be if only wanted births prevailed.

In sub-Saharan Africa (including Sudan), the DTFR averages about 15 percent below the TFR. The greatest differences are in North Africa and in Latin America, where the DTFR averages 31 and 32 percent, respectively, below their TFRs. The levels of fertility implied by women's preferences are quite low. The lowest level is for Thailand, where the DTFR reaches 1.8, some 18 percent below the TFR of 2.2. In Latin America, all of the values of the DTFR except for Guatemala fall below three births per woman.

In sum, the evidence implies a potential for further major declines in fertility in North Africa and in most of Latin America; for moderate further declines approaching replacement levels in Thailand, Sri Lanka, and Indonesia; and for smaller declines in sub-Saharan Africa. Section 4.2 presents some short-term forecasts of the TFR and evaluates the extent to which the DTFRs are likely to be approximated.

4.2   Fertility Forecasts

The TFR can be forecast (with considerable accuracy, judging from eight DHS-II surveys recently completed) by taking advantage of the strong interrelationships among fertility, reproductive intentions, and contraceptive prevalence. We know (Westoff, 1990; Mauldin and Segal, 1988) that there is a very high correlation between the TFR and the percentage of married women currently practicing contraception – an R^2 of 0.91, based on a large number (84) of national fertility surveys. We also now know that contraceptive prevalence has a strong association with reproductive intentions, i.e., the percentage of married women who want no more births. In a recent analysis (Westoff, 1990) of data from these same countries, the R^2 between these two variables was estimated at 0.78. We also know that the same strong associations exist not only across countries at a given time but also between successive surveys in the same countries observed at five-year intervals. In developing forecasts based on these associations, we relied upon the association between reproductive intentions and contraceptive prevalence measured in those countries where surveys have been repeated. The procedure first estimated the future proportion of women who want no more births based on the regression equation connecting this variable at two points in time. The predicted value for each country is then included in a second equation to forecast the contraceptive prevalence. To improve this fit, the regression is expanded to include the earlier contraceptive prevalence. Finally, the TFR is forecast from the predicted prevalence and, to improve the fit, from the earlier TFR. In short, the model relies upon estimates of the regressions between t_1 and t_2 to predict the values at t_3, incorporating an additional predictor at each stage (Westoff, 1991). The results are shown in *Table 4.2*.

Let us examine the end product first – the forecasts of the TFR – and then return to the foundation of reproductive intentions. The forecasts of the TFR indicate an average decline over the next five years or so of close to 10 percent in sub-Saharan African and range

Table 4.2. Forecasts of reproductive preferences, contraceptive prevalence, and fertility.

	Percent want no more		Contraceptive prevalence		TFR		
	Current	Fore-cast	Current	Fore-cast	Current	Fore-cast	DTFR
Sub-Saharan Africa							
Botswana	38	45	33	37	5.0	4.5	4.1
Burundi	24	34	9	14	6.7	6.1	5.7
Ghana	23	33	13	18	6.4	5.8	5.3
Kenya	49	54	27	34	6.4	5.3	4.5
Liberia	17	28	7	11	6.9	6.3	6.3
Mali	16	27	5	10	7.6	6.8	7.1
Ondo State	23	33	6	12	6.1	5.7	5.8
Senegal	19	30	11	15	6.6	6.0	5.6
Sudan	25	35	9	15	5.0	4.8	4.2
Togo	25	34	12	17	6.6	6.0	5.1
Uganda	23	33	5	11	7.5	6.7	6.5
Zimbabwe	33	41	43	45	5.2	4.5	4.3
North Africa							
Egypt	60	63	38	45	4.4	3.9	2.8
Morocco	47	52	36	41	4.6	4.1	3.3
Tunisia	58	61	50	55	4.1	3.5	2.9
Asia							
Indonesia	51	55	48	52	2.9	2.7	2.4
Sri Lanka	64	66	62	66	2.6	2.3	2.2
Thailand	66	67	66	70	2.2	1.9	1.8
Latin America							
Bolivia	68	69	30	39	5.1	4.5	2.8
Brazil	64	66	66	69	3.3	2.7	2.2
Colombia	69	70	63	68	3.1	2.6	2.1
Dominican Rep.	63	65	50	55	3.6	3.2	2.6
Ecuador	65	67	44	51	4.3	3.7	2.9
Guatemala	47	52	23	30	5.5	5.0	4.5
Mexico	65	67	53	58	4.0	3.4	2.9
Peru	75	75	46	54	4.0	3.5	2.3
Trinidad/Tobago	54	58	53	57	3.0	2.7	2.2

to an average of 13 percent in Latin America. How close are these forecasts to the DTFR? A comparison of the values in the last two columns of *Table 4.2* reveals considerable variation across these countries. In most of the sub-Saharan African countries, the DTFR is modestly lower than the forecasts. Kenya and Togo show the largest differences, indicating that women's reproductive preferences are declining more rapidly than the likelihood of such preferences being realized. In a few countries, there is hardly any difference – Liberia, Ondo State in Nigeria, and Uganda. Zimbabwe is also in this category, with a forecast TFR of 4.5 and a DTFR, for example, of 4.3.

The differences between these rates are much greater in North Africa, with the DTFR considerably lower than the expected TFR. In Egypt, the forecast shows a TFR of 3.9 with the DTFR at 2.8. The three Asian countries have already gone through most of the fertility transition; although the forecast TFRs show some continued decline, they are very close to the DTFRs. In contrast, Latin America is more like the three countries in North Africa. Wide differences remain between the forecast values and the desired levels, especially in Bolivia and Peru, where the DTFR is around one-third lower than the TFR forecast. In the other seven Latin American countries, the DTFR is an average of one-sixth below the average forecast value.

One of the intrinsically unsatisfactory features of the forecasting procedure described here is its essential bootstrap nature, in particular, the initial forecast of the proportion of (married) women wanting no more children from the regression equation connecting this variable at two points in time. It is not unlike forecasting tomorrow's weather from today's weather in an area of the country that typically sends its weather systems in one direction. The underlying theory in this case is a knowledge of the prevailing wind direction and the pace of its movement. Our procedure is even less theoretically grounded. It recognizes that a population's reproductive preferences at t_1 are highly correlated with those at t_2 and that the sign of the regression coefficient indicates a decline.[1] It then uses this relationship to predict the proportion wanting no more births at t_3. The next step, which relies upon the regression of contraceptive prevalence on reproductive intentions, is less unsatisfactory because it identifies a causal antecedent in substantive terms,[2] whereas the forecast of reproductive intentions relies only on the association between these intentions over time.

The actual forecasts of reproductive intentions (columns 1 and 2 of *Table 4.2*) appear reasonable enough. The forecast for the sub-Saharan African populations show a rise from an average of 27 percent to an average of 36 percent of women who want no more children. The projected increases elsewhere in the percent who want no more are less dramatic: in North Africa from 55 to 59 percent; in Asia from 60 to 63 percent; and in Latin America from 63 to 65 percent.

4.3   Determinants of Reproductive Preferences

The main reason that the forecast of reproductive intentions relies on the same variable at an earlier time is simply that we have little else to use. In a broad sense, the determinants of reproductive intentions or preferences in developing countries cover the whole range of social changes included in the concept of modernization. These determinants are only partially represented in the WFS and DHS; e.g., economic status is inadequately measured. We do know that the desired number of children has been declining in many, probably in most, developing countries. The mechanics of this process are less well known. The conventional explanations focus on the changes in the economic value of children; recent speculation minimizes the importance of structural economic changes and emphasizes the role of Western or modern ideas about the control of reproduction and small family norms (Cleland and Wilson, 1987). There is probably a time lag in the process of change in reproductive norms. The most likely process is one that first witnesses an increase in the proportion of women who want no more children without a commensurate decline in ideal or desired family size. In turn, this leads to a demand for and the use of contraception and an ensuing decline in fertility. Eventually the number of children desired begins its decline as smaller family norms develop. The urban and middle-class populations typically lead the transition.

In sub-Saharan Africa, the marital fertility transition may follow a different path. As noted earlier, the primary stage may be the adoption of fertility control to increase birth intervals, a motivation derived from health rather than from socioeconomic considerations. Kenya is a major exception to this generalization; over the decade from 1978 to 1988, the proportion of women wanting no more children increased from 17 to 49 percent.

Analysis of the determinants of reproductive preferences can be approached at two levels: the macro-demographic level, in which the statistical units of observations are the provinces or regions of countries, and the micro or individual woman level.

4.4 Regional-level Analysis

Analysis of the determinants of reproductive preferences at the provincial or regional level focuses on the question of what characteristics of these areas are associated with the mean number of children desired or the proportion of married women who want no more children. The areas assembled for this purpose are the 302 provinces or regions of the 51 countries that participated in the WFS or in the first stage of the DHS. Although this is a relatively large number of areas for analysis, it should be kept in mind that it is not a representative sample of the developing world; China and India, for example, are not included.

Since the object of interest is the number of children desired rather than fertility and because there is some tendency to rationalize as desired children that may have been unwanted at the time of conception, we have tried to eliminate the life-cycle effects by singling out a particular age group. Women aged 25–29 were selected because most would be married by that age (removing the censoring by age at marriage) and the experience of unwanted fertility would be still largely in the future, thus minimizing the factor of rationalization. The mean number of children desired for this age group across the 302 regions is 4.6, with a range from 2.3 to 8.5. For the proportion who want no more children a similar logic was followed by confining the analysis to married women with four or five children. The mean percentage of women at this parity who want no more children is 58.0, with a range from 0 to 98.1. Because there is a high correlation between these two measures (−0.92), the same covariates are observed. Areas with women wanting no more children or desiring smaller families are those with high proportions of their population classified as urban, high proportions of husbands

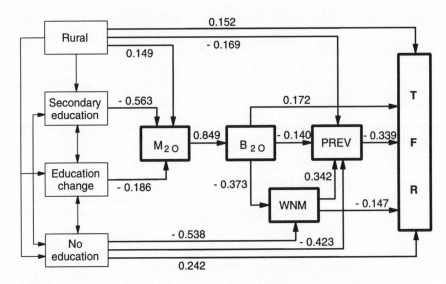

Figure 4.1. The nuptiality–fertility model for 216 regions.

in professional occupations, low proportions of women with no education, lower proportions of women 15–19 currently married, lower proportions having a birth before age 20, and are areas with lower rates of infant mortality. This constellation of correlates is a familiar package of variables associated with development. There is considerable overlap in these predictors that collectively account for 60 to 70 percent of the variance of reproductive preferences across regions. The unexplained variance is partly error of measurement, but also reflects the absence of other relevant explanatory variables, perhaps measures of income or wealth.

The complete picture of the paths through which reproductive intentions affect fertility and are determined by different variables is shown in *Figure 4.1*. In this analysis, which shows imputed causal directions and the path (standardized) regression coefficients, the role of reproductive intentions is interconnected in various ways. (The analysis is confined to a subset of 216 regions for which information on all variables is available.) The variable WNM is the proportion of married women with 4–5 children who report that they want no more children. This variable is directly influenced by the percentage of women with no education and is indirectly influenced by the proportion who have had a birth by exact age 20

(B_{20}). In turn, the latter variable is determined by the proportions first married by age 20 (M_{20}), which is seen to be a function of residence (the percent rural), the proportion that attended secondary school, and a measure of educational change that reflects the generational decline in the proportion of women with no education. The influence of reproductive intentions on the TFR, in turn, is seen to operate indirectly through the prevalence of contraception and directly, presumably through unmeasured non-contraceptive paths such as abortion.

4.5   Individual-level Analysis

We have also explored the determinants of reproductive preferences at the level of individual women in several countries, partly to validate the aggregate analysis but also to exploit some economic and media exposure data that have not been collected by many of the surveys included in the regional-level analysis. Several countries were selected from different areas that represent various stages in the fertility transition: Colombia, Ghana, Kenya, Guatemala, Peru, Thailand, Tunisia, and Indonesia. The surveys in these countries were all part of the DHS-I project.

In none of these countries are we able to account for much of the individual variance of the desired number of children. The regression equations for each country are shown in *Table 4.3*; the R^2s range in value from only 0.065 to 0.314. We have confined the examination to women 25–29 years of age as a life-cycle control, and our multivariate exploration has excluded measures of fertility that would add to the explained variance. We have concentrated instead on social and economic measures and have added only age at marriage and/or age at first birth in order to parallel the aggregate analysis.

A similar set of determinants of reproductive norms operates across these countries. Several variables stand out prominently in all six countries. One is the importance of region of residence. In all of these countries, region exerts a strong influence on the number of children desired. It is a surrogate for many other variables: region frequently reflects language, ethnic origin, or religion as well as the stage of economic development. In principle, region could be further disaggregated to seek explanations at these compositional levels.

Table 4.3. Linear regression equations for variables related to number of children desired[a] by women 25–29 years of age.

	Regression coefficients[b]							
	Colombia	Ghana	Guatemala	Indonesia	Kenya	Peru	Thailand	Tunisia
Urban–rural[c]			0.586		0.692		0.237	0.462
Region[d]								
1			-1.170	-1.100			-0.246	-0.604
2	-0.365		-0.989		-0.457			-0.834
3					0.892	-0.240		-1.020
4					-0.758		0.346	
5		-0.538	-0.890					-0.360
6		-0.651	-1.159					
7								
8		3.176						
Ethnicity[e]			-1.224					
Education (wife)[f]		-0.895	-0.431	-0.209	-0.531		-0.124	-0.175
Education (husband)[f]		-0.443	-0.476	-0.169		-0.266		
Age at marriage[g]				-0.065	-0.052	-0.030	-0.045	-0.053
Age at first birth[g]	-0.050							
Watch TV[h]	-0.669			-0.340		-0.266	-0.154	-0.473
Listen to radio[h]				-0.234	-0.299			
Electricity[i]	-0.607		-0.733				-0.199	
Constant	4.835	6.655	8.016	6.247	5.317	4.000	3.495	4.970
R^2	0.123	0.314	0.223	0.108	0.146	0.065	0.085	0.164
Number of women[j]	566	745	781	2448	1126	546	1252	836
Mean number desired	2.74	5.73	5.36	3.61	4.74	2.69	2.54	3.51
Standard deviation	1.38	2.66	3.56	2.16	1.99	1.21	1.08	1.52

[a]Non-numeric responses of the type "as many as God sends" or "as many as come" were usually recoded in category 12+ or with the highest numerical response if less than 12.

[b]All of the regression coefficients shown in the table were significant at least at the 0.05 level, mostly $p < 0.001$.

[c]Urban–rural residence scored as 0 and 1.

[d]Regions were defined as dummy variables. Those with the highest significant coefficients recorded here are Pacifica in Colombia; Volta, Ashanti, and upper and northern regions in Ghana; Guatemala City, Central, Norte, and Norte Oriental in Guatemala; Java–Bali in Indonesia; central, coast, and eastern regions in Kenya; Selva in Peru; north and south in Thailand; and Tunis, north–east, north–west, and Sahel in Tunisia.

[e]Ethnicity in Guatemala is coded as Indigina or Ladino.

[f]Education of wife and husband are coded here in terms of the categories: no education, primary, secondary, higher. Single years of schooling were not used because of significant numbers of missing cases.

[g]Age at first marriage and age at first birth were coded in units of single years.

[h]Watching TV and listening to the radio coded as 0 for no and 1 for yes.

[i]Electricity coded as 0 for no and 1 for yes.

[j]These are the unweighted numbers. Missing information cases are assigned to the modal frequency category.

Where such requisite data are available, the variable still retains its power, although sometimes it obliterates rural–urban differences as well. Of course, the importance of region in the study of differences in fertility has been underscored in many other studies, including the well-known 19th-century European fertility study (Coale and Watkins, 1986). Urban–rural residence also features in half of the countries in the multivariate analysis.

One variable that holds up consistently is education of women, which is inversely related to preferences for fewer children, a pattern that persists in the presence of all other variables. In a few countries, the husband's education makes a similar and additive contribution (in Peru, it overshadows women's education). Education has been demonstrated to be probably the most dependable and predictable determinant of fertility and fertility regulation behavior among all of the socioeconomic measures examined in hundreds of studies.

Several other determinants operate in some countries but not in others. Age at marriage or age at first birth is a factor in all of these countries except Ghana and Guatemala: the later the age of the event, the fewer the number of children desired. How often the woman reports listening to the radio or watching television has an effect in all but these two countries as well. In all likelihood, the mass media transmit outside values and ideas. In other research, we have demonstrated a powerful association with reproductive attitudes and behavior of media messages on family planning, including soap operas that extol the advantages of smaller families (Westoff and Rodríguez, forthcoming).

One of the more surprising findings is a negative one, *viz.*, that various measures of economic status either singly or in combination fail to disclose any significant associations with the number of children desired. Admittedly, the availability of economic data in these surveys is less than ideal. Nonetheless, there is a variety of items including ownership of bicycles, cars, radios, televisions, refrigerators, kinds of toilet facilities, source of drinking water, electricity, and different country-specific information on ownership of homes, land, livestock, and so on. In only a few countries do any of these measures seem to play any direct role in the determination of reproductive preferences. Only in Colombia, Guatemala, and Thailand does one of these economic variables hold up – the presence of electricity in the household. The economic variables frequently show the expected negative associations with reproductive preferences at the zero-order level, but their influence is absorbed or dominated by the regional and educational factors. It seems implausible that economic status would be totally irrelevant to the number of children women desire. However, there is simply no empirical support from the data for the hypothesis that smaller or larger families are viewed as inconsistent with economic resources, or more precisely, that any such inconsistency persists in the presence of these other variables. One might of course reason that economic resources play an earlier role in facilitating education, but this notion is not testable with these data.

4.6   Conclusions

So what do we know about reproductive preferences and the dynamics of fertility change in the developing world? A fair summary would be as follows:

1. Whether measured by the average desired number of children or by the proportion of married women who want no more children, dramatic changes toward the small family norm are under way in Latin America, much of Asia, and North Africa, but only in a few sub-Saharan African countries (where spacing rather than limiting preferences and behavior predominate).
2. Reproductive preferences are highly correlated (in the aggregate) with the fertility rate, operating mainly, though not exclusively, through contraceptive prevalence.
3. At the regional or provincial level, the main determinants of reproductive preferences are those typically associated with modernization: residence in cities or in rural areas, education of women, occupational status of men, and age at marriage and at first birth.
4. Our knowledge of determinants at the level of the individual woman remains very limited: region, rural–urban residence, education of women, age at marriage, and exposure to mass media dominate the picture rather than individual economic variables. However, the amount of variation explained is very small.

Notes

[1] Unlike the direction of the wind in the weather analogy, the direction of reproductive preferences cannot remain pointed in the same way indefinitely. At the end of the fertility transition, reproductive preferences stabilize and may even change directions for periods of time, as has been observed in some developed countries.

[2] Operationally, it is also corrupted by this bootstrapping quality in that the actual forecasting equation adds the earlier prevalence value. The redeeming feature here is that at least it does not depend exclusively on the forecast value of intentions that is based on its own earlier values.

References

Cleland, J., and Wilson, C., 1987, Demand theories of the fertility transition: An iconoclastic view, *Population Studies* **41**(1):5–30 (March).

Coale, A.J., and Watkins, S.C., eds., 1986, *The Decline of Fertility in Europe,* Princeton University Press, Princeton, NJ, USA.

Mauldin, W.P., and Segal, S.J., 1988, Prevalence of contraceptive use: Trends and issues, *Studies in Family Planning* **19**:335–353.

Westoff, Ch.F., 1990, Reproductive intentions and fertility rates, *International Family Planning Perspectives* **16**(3):84–89 (September).

Westoff, Ch.F., 1991, Reproductive preferences: A comparative view, *Comparative Studies* **3**:19–20, Institute for Resources Development, Columbia, MD, USA.

Westoff, Ch.F., and Ochoa, L.H., 1991, *Unmet Need and the Demand for Family Planning,* DHS Comparative Studies No. 5, Institute for Resource Development, Columbia, MD, USA.

Westoff, Ch.F., and Rodríguez, G., forthcoming, *Mass Media and Reproductive Behavior in Kenya: An Illustrative Analysis* (in preparation).

Chapter 5

Population Policies and Family-Planning in Southeast Asia

Mercedes B. Concepcion

Impressive gains in the control of fertility and in the reduction of population growth rates have been observed in many countries within the purview of the Economic and Social Commission for Asia and the Pacific (ESCAP). Family-planning (FP) and maternal and child health (MCH) programs have played an important role in reducing population growth, improving the quality of life, and developing human resources in the region. The success of FP and MCH programs is closely associated with the enhanced role and status of women, lower infant, child, and maternal mortality rates, better birth-spacing and breast-feeding practices, and the delivery of services by trained personnel. Nevertheless, the population as a whole continues to grow by more than 50 million yearly. Moreover, progress in lessening population growth rates has been uneven and has generally widened the gap between countries with continued high growth rates and those which have succeeded in moderating or lowering their growth rates.

In Southeast Asia, three of the region's 10 component countries are expected to grow at rates of 1.8 percent or less per annum during the 1990–1995 quinquennium while the rest are expected to increase annually by at least 2.1 percent. By the beginning of the 21st century, all but one of the countries in Southeast Asia are projected to grow no faster than 1.7 percent yearly. Total fertility rates (TFRs) during the early 1990s are also expected to range from Singapore's reported low 1.7 children to the estimated 6.4 children per woman in the Lao People's Democratic Republic. These rates are foreseen by the United Nations to drop to about 3 children or fewer at the start of the next century (UN, 1991). The exceptions are Cambodia and the Lao People's Democratic Republic.

Governments in 5 of the 10 Southeast Asian countries perceive their current fertility levels as unsatisfactory and have ongoing programs to lower such rates. Three others – Brunei Darussalam, Lao People's Democratic Republic, and Myanmar – are satisfied with their present fertility levels. Brunei Darussalam and Myanmar do not report any direct intervention, while the Lao People's Democratic Republic is intervening to maintain current rates. Cambodia and Singapore consider their fertility rates too low. The former restricts access to contraception, while the latter has been offering tax rebates to couples having a third or fourth child.

This chapter examines the population policies and FP programs in selected Southeast Asian countries (Indonesia, Malaysia, the Philippines, Singapore, Thailand, and Vietnam) and attempts to draw from their experience the critical preconditions for family-planning program success. Such experiences have been gleaned from the country statements provided by participants of the 4th Asian and Pacific Population Conference (APPC) held in Bali, Indonesia, on 19–27 August 1992.

5.1 Demographic Situation

During the 4th APPC, which was entitled Population and Sustainable Development: Goals and Strategies into the 21st Century, the present population situation and future outlook were reviewed in the light of the 1982 APPC Asia–Pacific Call for Action on Population and Development. The participants noted that while substantial progress had been achieved by the ESCAP region in responding to the Asia–Pacific Call for Action, population issues continue to pose

a most critical challenge. The conference adopted the Bali Declaration on Population and Sustainable Development, which set goals
and made recommendations for population and sustainable development into the next century.

One of the population goals included in the Bali Declaration
enjoined countries and areas to adopt suitable strategies to attain
replacement-level fertility, equivalent to a TFR of around 2.2 children per woman, by the year 2010 or earlier. In addition, member
countries were also urged to reduce the level of infant mortality to
no more than 40 infant deaths per 1,000 live births during the same
period. Countries and areas where maternal mortality remains high
were called upon to effect a 50 percent reduction by the year 2010.

The Bali Declaration recommended that priority be given to
strengthening policy development and related processes in those
countries where the MCH and FP programs have not yet achieved
desired objectives. Furthermore, such countries were urged to
expand and streamline MCH and FP delivery systems within
the primary health-care framework, adopt innovative management
and multi-sectoral approaches, and encourage wider community
and inter-sectoral participation in program implementation efforts.
Countries which have already reduced their fertility to low or acceptable levels were prompted to devise program strategies aimed
at achieving self-sustainability.

5.2 Family-planning Policies and Programs

The country statements circulated during the 4th APPC contained
a section on the policy and objectives of national FP/family health
and welfare programs.

5.2.1 Indonesia

The state policy guidelines, issued by the 1973 People's Consultative
Assembly, declared that the objective of the national FP program
during the second five-year development plan period (1974–1978)
was to improve maternal and child health in order to create a small,
happy, and prosperous family. The guidelines also stated that economic and social welfare development can be implemented rapidly,

together with population growth control, through a properly administered national FP program. The most recent guidelines, issued in 1988, added that the Indonesian FP program should also be directed at reducing mortality rates. At the same time, the need for successful implementation without endangering future generations was emphasized. In addition, a policy to enhance support to FP acceptors through improvements in the quality of available contraceptives and services was outlined. As a general course of action, FP acceptors are encouraged to use more effective contraceptives, thus ensuring better protection against pregnancy and accelerating fertility reduction.

The Indonesian FP program has three broad objectives: expansion of contraceptive coverage in accordance with government targets; promotion of continued contraceptive use; and institutionalization of FP and small family norm concepts by shifting responsibility for FP decisions to the individual, the family, and the community.

Nine important program strategy elements have been taken into account in the Indonesian FP program: integration of an array of governmental, nongovernmental, private, and community agencies; decentralization of responsibility and authority; commitment to meet targets at every program level; provision of FP services combined with medical advice; National Family Planning Coordinating Board (BKKBN) cooperation with the Ministry of Health in health services beyond FP in order to improve FP outreach; development of a climate of community support for FP through the cooperation of community and religious leaders; support for activities which raise women's social and economic status; emphasis on reaching the rapidly increasing numbers of youth; and encouragement of self-reliance, the newest strategy element involving the private sector.

The Indonesian Country Report (1992) stated that the TFR which was 5.6 children between 1965 and 1969 fell to 3.0 by 1992. The corresponding decrease for the crude birth rate (CBR) was from 42.6 to 25.2 births per 1,000. By 1990, the crude death rate (CDR) was estimated to be 9.7 deaths, down from 21 deaths per 1,000 over the period 1961–1971. The CDR is projected to reach 8.5 deaths per 1,000 at the start of 1993, declining to around 7 per 1,000 by the year 2020. The infant mortality rate (IMR), currently estimated at 65 infant deaths per 1,000 live births, is expected to drop to 28 by the year 2020. The life expectancy at birth, now reported to be around 60 years for both sexes, is forecast to lengthen by 10 years during the next quarter of a century. Maternal mortality is predicted to fall from a level of 450 deaths per 100,000 live births in 1986 to 200 by 2020.

The Indonesians foresee a likely deceleration in the future rate of fertility decline. The reasons given in the Country Report were that the desired family size of some couples is unlikely to decrease further; those who most want to avail themselves of family planning as well as those for whom the services are most accessible have already been covered by the program; and the couples who still need to be brought into the program express larger family-size preferences and are more difficult to reach. Among these are the urban poor, those living in outlying areas, those with low educational levels as well as those who find it difficult to use contraceptives correctly. Therefore, further mortality and fertility reductions will entail considerably greater efforts. For example, the family-planning program will have to reach unprecedented numbers of contraceptive acceptors and motivate couples with high fertility preferences, people who are less likely to know about health and family-planning programs and are less disposed to seek services.

5.2.2 Malaysia

Given the rapid economic growth and the prospect of a further decline in fertility, the Malaysian government changed its official stance in 1984 and promulgated a national population policy. As expressed in the Malaysian Country Report (1992), a long-term target of 70 million people by the year 2100 is to be achieved through decelerating the TFR decline. The plan is to reduce the TFR by 0.1 point over five-year periods until a level of 2.05 children is reached in the year 2070. The TFR in peninsular Malaysia had fallen from a high 6.8 children in 1957 to about 3.3 children in 1990. At this pace, a TFR of 2.1 could be reached by 2010. The average age at marriage for females had risen from 22.1 in 1970 to 24.6 years in 1990. The IMR was recorded at 13.3 infant deaths per 1,000 live births in 1990. The life expectancy at birth of Malaysian males was lengthened from 55.8 years in 1957 to 69.1 years in 1990. The corresponding rates for females were 58.2 and 73.3 years, respectively. Given current trends, the most probable outlook during the next three decades is for small nuclear families with the couples participating actively in the labor force.

Since its inception in 1966, the Malaysian FP program has undergone several phases of development, each involving expansion in terms of the approach used, the area covered, or the number of agencies involved in the provision of contraceptive services. The spread of FP services to the rural areas as part of an integrated MCH/FP program was initiated in the early 1970s and led to FP services being integrated in the MCH services provided by the Health Ministry. The blending of FP with health and other social programs not only aided in overcoming the resource constraints but also in contributing to wider FP acceptance and a heightened contraceptive prevalence rate.

In line with the national objective of improving the quality of life, a comprehensive family development program has been developed and is now being implemented. It emphasizes the improvement of family health and welfare through family-life education, parenting courses, and marriage and family counseling. The stress is now on improving infrastructure in underserved and remote areas, on enhancing coverage and quality of care in designated areas of low coverage, and on program consolidation. The implementation of the risk approach in MCH/FP care has for its ultimate objective the availability and accessibility of a range of services, including FP, to all women and families for their better health and well-being.

5.2.3 The Philippines

Since 1970, the Philippine FP program as described in the Country Report (1992) has been a social development initiative aimed at diminishing the country's fertility level for the benefit of family and national welfare. Over the course of its history, the program has adopted varying approaches and strategies to suit the changing needs and conditions of the time. There have been modest increases in contraceptive prevalence rate coupled with moderate declines in total fertility. Program efforts have contributed substantially to this decline. However, the gains made did not approximate those of neighboring countries owing to problems besetting policy and program implementation.

In response to the difficulties experienced in relying on static clinics, the Outreach Project was implemented in 1976 to expand the availability and accessibility of services. The Outreach Project viewed FP not only as a means to reduce fertility but, more importantly, as advancing family welfare. Furthermore, a closer integration of broader population concerns into the country's development plans, policies, and programs was sought. The Outreach Project also paved the way for strengthening and deepening local government involvement in, and support for, FP.

In 1987, a new population policy statement was formulated, taking into account relevant provisions of the 1987 constitution. The new policy broadened program concern beyond that of fertility reduction. Consequently, the 1989–1993 five-year population program directional plan was drawn up focusing on two components, namely, responsible parenthood/FP and population and development. The program's institutional arrangement was altered along with the policy and the program. The Department of Health was designated as the implementing agency for the FP program with jurisdiction over the activities of all FP service delivery agencies. The Commission on Population, on the other hand, remained as the overall planning, policy-making, coordinating, and monitoring body of the entire program with specific responsibility for coordinating the population and development integration thrust.

The new FP program uses a health-oriented, demand-driven approach, anchored on safe motherhood and child survival. Its primary objective is to reduce the level of unmet needs for FP, particularly among poor families. The population and development thrust is one of systematically incorporating population matters into the development efforts of concerned agencies.

Whether the program will be able to make a more significant contribution toward development goals depends on its ability to align policies and operational aspects to individual and societal needs. Some considerations include expanding and intensifying the provision of women's health and family-planning services; integrating FP in other health programs, particularly MCH; strengthening the capacity of agencies to manage the services; promoting collaboration among the governments, nongovernmental organizations (NGOs), and other private organizations and local communities to improve access to these services; and shortening the gestation period for an effective program implementation by local government units, including appropriating local funds for the program.

As stated earlier, the slow pace of decline in Philippine population growth is the consequence of a moderately decreasing fertility and a decelerating mortality decline. The CBR fell from a level of 46 births per 1,000 in 1969 to about 30 in 1990. The CDR dropped from 32 deaths per 1,000 in 1940 to around 7.2 in 1990. Further pronounced decreases are not expected as the pace of decline has slackened significantly. The IMR has fluctuated around 61 infant deaths per 1,000 live births since the 1960s. The estimate for 1990 was 57. Communicable diseases still account for the majority of morbidity and mortality cases. Since 1970, the TFR has been slowly but steadily declining and was estimated to be around 4 children per woman in 1990. This gradual descent can be attributed to four causes: the continued expansion in the number of women of reproductive age as an outcome of past high fertility; shrinkage in the prevalence and duration of breast-feeding; low-level use of the more effective contraceptive methods; and the Roman Catholic hierarchy's open and active opposition to the government's FP program, thus affecting its political support.

5.2.4   Singapore

The country's FP and population program was initiated in 1966, soon after independence. Ambitious FP targets were set for each five-year plan (1966–1970, 1971–1975, and 1976–1980), and social disincentives were introduced. The government actively promoted the two-child family norm. Contraceptives were made easily available, and abortion and sterilization were legalized. With the attainment of replacement-level fertility in 1975, the government started to emphasize child spacing as the main policy orientation. The program impact on population growth was significant. According to the Country Report, Singapore's fertility fell by almost 70 percent within a span of two decades (Ministry of Health, 1992). The TFR dropped from 4.7 children in 1965 to a historic low of 1.4 in 1986.

With the continued decline in fertility rates in the early 1980s, population projections indicated that if below-replacement fertility were to continue, the country would experience negative population growth within the next 30 years. A new population policy was promulgated in 1987 in response to the prospect of a decline in numbers. The new policy thrust encourages marriage and childbearing. A new slogan, "Have three or more if you can afford it," was adopted reflecting the new direction. Generous incentives are being provided such as income tax rebates, subsidies for child-care centers and for delivery fees, and special leave schemes. In addition, two programs – Strengthening the Marriage Program and Family Life Education Program – have been implemented.

Since the adoption of the new policy, TFRs have inched upward. The rate rose to 1.9 in 1988, but is now about 1.7 children. Since the tax incentives were announced, the number of third- and fourth-order births have gone up. However, marriage trends have not manifested significant improvements. The critical issue on population and development facing policy makers is one of ensuring replacement-level fertility to achieve the optimum population size and a balanced age structure.

5.2.5 Thailand

In 1970, the government officially launched the National Family Planning Program (NFPP) aimed at further reducing the population growth rate. According to targets set by successive five-year plans in the last two decades, the program succeeded in decreasing the growth rate through quantitative target-oriented strategies. The provision of an extensive contraceptive distribution system and the efforts to legitimize the preference for fewer children and to increase awareness of the possibility of controlling family size through effective and acceptable means contributed to the program's success. Past successes, however, do not imply that there are no longer any unmet needs or new and more difficult challenges ahead. The seventh plan (1992–1996) has renewed the emphasis on human resource development, thus posing new challenges to the health sector. The strategy for MCH/FP over the next five years will be to maintain the program momentum to raise contraceptive prevalence rates in the face of a 10 percent rise in the number of women of childbearing age; provide effective follow-up for couples who are already using contraceptives; meet more effectively the special needs of adolescents and ethnic minorities; and improve the management, training, and information systems, particularly at the regional level. Since health is a national responsibility, the strategy calls for providing MCH/FP services within a national and inter-sectoral framework.

Thailand's fairly well-developed and extensive health infrastructure has brought about a significant improvement in the health status of mothers and children. The NFPP is well integrated in the tasks of the Ministry of Public Health's Family Health Division. The NFPP has effectively utilized the wide primary health care network to make contraceptive services available throughout the country. However, equal attention needs be given to both the quality of services and the achievement of the plan's targets. This action entails strong collaboration with other government agencies, with the private sector and with NGOs, all of whom have important roles to play in supplementing government activities.

The population growth rate decreased from 3.0–3.3 percent in the 1960s to about 1.4 percent in 1991, as stated in the Thailand Country Statement (1992). The seventh plan has targeted the reduction of the growth rate to 1.2 percent by the end of the plan period. The TFR has dropped from about 6.1 during the period 1968–1969 to less than 2.5 children per woman today. In 1990, the CDR was estimated at about 5 to 6 deaths per 1,000 population, with the IMR at approximately 34.5 infant deaths per 1,000 live births a year later. Currently, life expectancy is estimated to be 66 years for males and 71 years for females. Recently, married couples whether rural- or urban-based, lesser or better educated, have overwhelmingly expressed a desire for a family size of some two children.

5.2.6   Vietnam

As recorded in the Country Report (1992), decision number 29 of the Council of Ministers of the Socialist Republic of Vietnam, issued on 12 August 1981, contained the following objectives for the national population and FP program: married women should be prompted to have their first birth after age 22; each couple should be persuaded to have only one or two children; and a spacing of five years should be encouraged between the first and second birth.

According to the country's 1989 population census, there were 64.4 million people in Vietnam. The intercensal growth rate for the period 1979–1989 was 2.1 percent. The population in 1991 was estimated at 67.7 million. The CBR recorded for the 12-month period preceding the 1989 census was 31 births per 1,000, with urban and rural areas reporting 23 and 34 births per 1,000, respectively. The CDR was 8.4 deaths per 1,000, while the IMR was 49 infant deaths per 1,000 live births. The average life expectancy at birth was 63 years for men and 67.5 years for women.

On 18 October 1988, the Council of Ministers' Decree on Population and Family Planning Policies was promulgated (Vietnam, 1989). The stated goal is to reinforce and strengthen measures to lower population growth and to ensure that adequate family-planning methods are readily available and utilized by the population. Norms were set for the minimum age at first birth (at least 22 years for urban women, 19 for rural women), for the number of children (no more than two for most families), and for birth spacing (three to five years after the first).

A national health law passed by the National Assembly on 30 June 1989 legalized some of the above-mentioned measures. In addition, the law gives legal force to the individual's right to choose to limit births and provides for recourse to the judicial system should this right be violated (Allman *et al.*, 1991).

The population of Vietnam is projected to reach 87 million by the period 2005–2010 with a growth rate of 1.4 percent, a CBR of 22.2 births per 1,000 population, and a CDR of 7.9 deaths per 1,000. In projecting the future population, the National Committee for Population and Family Planning (NCPFP) took into account the over 17 million women currently of reproductive age who comprise nearly half of the country's total female population. Moreover, past high fertility rates are obviously affecting the replacement capacities of future generations. Starting in the year 2000, half a million women, on the average, will be added yearly to the cohort of reproductive age. This poses additional constraints on the achievement of an annual decrease in the TFR of 0.11 in the 1990s and of 0.6 in the first decade of the 21st century.

To achieve the immediate as well as long-term objectives set forth in the national population program, Vietnam will endeavor to improve the quality and effectiveness of FP activities by utilizing a network of intercommunal FP centers and communal health clinics; make a wider choice of contraceptives available; integrate FP activities in other MCH, nutrition, rural development, income generation, and women's status improvement programs; train FP staff at the grass-roots level; and support studies on impacts of FP programs and contraceptive methods as a basis for the formulation of a more effective and practical FP program.

5.3   Family-Planning Program Effectiveness

Family-planning programs have a long tradition in the Asian region, and are firmly established there. Various countries in the region have conceived novel approaches and have devised new strategies to reduce fertility. In this section an attempt is made to extract the most important factors contributing to family-planning program effectiveness from the experiences of the countries considered in this chapter.

In common with other Asian countries, Indonesia, Malaysia, the Philippines, Singapore, and Thailand boast of a relatively longer experience with intervention schemes to modify reproductive behavior. All these countries directly support family-planning programs and provide unlimited access to modern contraceptives. As a whole, the most common approaches in these countries consist of integrating family-planning services in the health care system at the community level or in rural development schemes. Incentives and disincentives have been introduced to discourage large families.

Singapore, which achieved replacement fertility in 1975, introduced a comprehensive package of incentives and disincentives in 1969 which was further intensified in 1972 to exert pressure on couples to limit their family size. In addition, sterilization was promoted as the best contraceptive method for those who had completed their families. Abortion became available on demand for a small fee in government facilities. There were graduated charges for delivery in government hospitals, paid maternity leaves covering the first two children only, preferential treatment in choice of primary school for the first three children in a family, and no priority for public housing for large families. An additional policy which was made known to the public in 1976 was designed to encourage later marriage and wider birth spacing.

The high commitment of President Soeharto, reflected in the above-mentioned state policy guidelines, represents one of the keys to the success of the Indonesian family-planning program. This commitment is not merely a personal one but is institutionalized in the existing systems, both in the People's Consultative Assembly and in Parliament and other executive systems. The program strengthened its links with rural communities by recruiting acceptors by means of a village-based delivery system. Acceptors in the program are maintained through various measures extending beyond family planning. To enhance family planning within the framework of institutionalizing the small family-size norm, the BKKBN developed a system of nonmonetary rewards for individual or group acceptors. A system was introduced in 1989 whereby a community with high contraceptive prevalence rates receives a deep well. The reward can also be in the form of scholarships for children of low income families that have been resorting to contraception for at least a decade. Moreover, some private Indonesian firms give discount cards to certain acceptor groups in major cities for the purchase of selected items.

The success of Thailand's family-planning program, as stated in the preceding section, can be traced to both the provision of an extensive system of contraceptive distribution and the efforts to legitimize the preference for fewer children and increase awareness of the possibility of controlling family size through effective and acceptable means.

The Philippines has tried a variety of schemes intended to induce couples to have fewer children. Among these are income tax deductions limited to four dependents, abolition of paid maternity leaves after the fourth child, and payment of lower interest rates for rural bank loans by couples using contraceptives. However, the coverage of these schemes was limited and therefore of little value in motivating couples to limit their family size. Malaysia also introduced tax deductions and maternity benefits but limited them to the first three children.

In Vietnam the rewards that had been implemented since 1982 included monetary bonuses and exemption from the required month per year of corvée labor for sterilization, IUD insertion, or agreeing not to have another child (Banister, 1989). Violations of family-planning policy resulted in loss of bonuses, benefits, and family allowances. The Council of Ministers' Decision in October 1988 limited couples in cities, deltas, or lowlands to a maximum of two children. Those couples having more than the allowed number are made to pay extra for housing or land space, education, and health care. Such couples are prohibited to move to urban areas and are required to perform more corvée work.

There is still considerable uncertainty concerning the processes and factors that motivate couples to limit the number of the children and account for the adoption of contraception in various societies at different periods of time. There is general agreement that socioeconomic development and organized family-planning programs play prominent roles in altering reproductive behavior. According to Bongaarts *et al.* (1990), socioeconomic development and family-planning programs operate synergistically, with one reinforcing the other.

The family-planning program experience of the selected Southeast Asian countries demonstrates that by making contraceptives easily available and by encouraging smaller families through a variety of measures, public and private sector family-planning programs have heightened contraceptive use. In turn, fertility and population growth rates have been reduced. The key to effective programs is to emphasize integrated high-quality outreach services and to take into account the traditional social structure and norms where the delivery system is to be introduced. Moreover, careful trial and phased development of alternative approaches to service delivery systems are critical to the success of a program. Finally, political support for family planning is often essential for the establishment of strong program effort.

References

Allman, J., Vu, Q.N., Nguyen, M.T., Pham, B.S., and Vu, D.M., 1991, Fertility and family planning in Vietnam, *Studies in Family Planning* **22**(5):308–317.

Banister, J., 1989, Vietnam's evolving population policies, *International Population Conference* **1**:155–168.

Bongaarts, J., Mauldin, W.P., and Phillips, J.E., 1990, The demographic impact of family planning programs, *Studies in Family Planning* **21**(6):299–310.

Country Report, 1992, Population and Sustainable Development: The Challenges of Vietnam, Paper circulated during the 4th Asian and Pacific Population Conference, Bali, Indonesia, 19–27 August.

Country Report: Indonesia, 1992, Paper circulated during the 4th Asian and Pacific Population Conference, Bali, Indonesia, 19–27 August.

Country Report: Malaysia, 1992, Paper circulated during the 4th Asian and Pacific Population Conference, Bali, Indonesia, 19–27 August.

Country Report: Philippines, 1992, Paper circulated during the 4th Asian and Pacific Population Conference, Bali, Indonesia, 19–27 August.

Country Statement: Thailand, 1992, Paper circulated during the 4th Asian and Pacific Population Conference, Bali, Indonesia, 19–27 August.

Ministry of Health, 1992, Population and Development in Singapore, Country Report circulated during the 4th Asian and Pacific Population Conference, Bali, Indonesia, 19–27 August.

UN, 1991, *1990 Assessment of the World Population*, United Nations, New York, NY, USA.

Vietnam, 1989, Vietnam's new fertility policy, *Population and Development Review* **15**(1):169–172.

Chapter 6

Fertility in China: Past, Present, Prospects

Griffith Feeney

Future population growth in any population is determined by the current age distribution and by future trends in fertility, mortality, and migration. The influence of the current age distribution is governed by purely formal demographic considerations that are the same for every population. The role of mortality depends crucially on its current level. Under conditions of high mortality, rapid declines are possible, and the normal interaction of mortality and age structure may lead to rapid population increase even in the face of substantial fertility decline. Once mortality has declined to the levels now observed in much of the world, however, mortality is relatively stable, largely because the features relevant to future population growth reflect biology more than social circumstance. Under current world demographic conditions, then, appropriate consideration of mortality and age distribution may be given without close attention to social structure or to policy issues that vary widely from one country to another.

The assessment of future levels and trends in fertility and migration is a different matter altogether. Circumstances influencing fertility, and even more so circumstances influencing migration, vary widely from one country to another, and all but the most superficial consideration of possible future trends requires study of particular circumstances. International migration may be an important influence of future population growth for particular countries, large as well as small. Immigration and emigration cancel out for the world as a whole, however, whence a global perspective renders the assessment of migration trends relatively unimportant.

Fertility behavior is heavily conditioned by both biology and society. Social influences may be roughly classified into the direct and intended consequences of national government policy and all other influences. The distinction is relevant to consideration of future fertility levels because it focuses attention in different directions: to broad social and economic conditions thought to influence fertility in the population at large, on the one hand, and to the minds of a relatively small number of policy makers, on the other. It should hardly be necessary to point out that the existence of policies to limit fertility and/or population growth does not imply the effectiveness of such policies. This is an issue to be decided by empirical analysis in each case.

The argument for country-specific consideration of influences on future fertility is particularly compelling for China, which is unique both in the nature and in the impacts of governmental population policies. This chapter aims to give a reasonably comprehensive treatment of China's fertility decline at the national level, with emphasis on those factors relevant to a consideration of the future trajectory of fertility. The qualifying clause is important, for there is now such a quantity of demographic data available for China that it is difficult to conceive, much less write in the space of one book chapter, anything that might reasonably be called definitive.

6.1 China's Fertility Decline in International Perspective

That fertility declined rapidly in China is well known, but the speed of the decline can be appreciated only when China's experience is systematically compared with that of other countries. This section compares Chinese experience with that of the rest of the developing world. The analysis relies primarily on the historical estimates

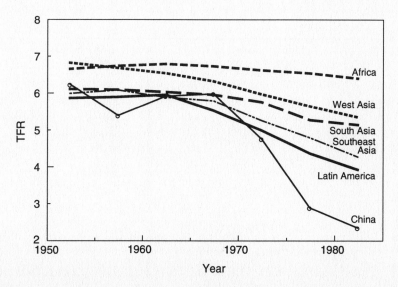

Figure 6.1. Fertility decline in China compared with fertility decline in other areas in the developing world. Source: *Table 6.1.*

developed by the United Nations (1991). These estimates share the weakness of all secondary compilations, most importantly the spurious impression of the uniformity of information available for various countries. An independent familiarity with demographic data sources in the various countries mitigates serious misunderstanding, however, and the United Nations estimates render a valuable service in making possible an international comparison that would otherwise be impossible.

Figure 6.1 compares fertility decline in China with fertility decline in the major regions of the developing world. In each case we plot the total fertility rates for quinquennial periods from 1950 through 1985, shown in *Table 6.1.* During the 1950s and 1960s, the level of fertility in China was similar to that of the developing countries generally. Beginning in the 1970s, however, China's total fertility rate fell from around six children per woman to slightly over two children per woman in the space of 15 years. Fertility in the rest of the developing world declined also, but at a much slower rate. Thus at the end of the period shown, total fertility for other areas ranged from a high of over six children per woman in Africa

Table 6.1. Total fertility rates in China and in other major areas in the developing world.

	1950–1954	1955–1959	1960–1964	1965–1969	1970–1974	1975–1979	1980–1984
China	6.24	5.40	5.93	5.99	4.76	2.90	2.36
Africa	6.65	6.74	6.79	6.73	6.62	6.54	6.40
West Asia	6.82	6.68	6.54	6.32	5.97	5.64	5.35
South Asia	6.11	6.09	6.03	5.96	5.76	5.27	5.14
Southeast Asia	5.99	6.08	5.89	5.79	5.26	4.79	4.27
Latin America	5.87	5.90	5.96	5.53	4.99	4.36	3.93

Source: UN, 1991:354, 232, 262, 260, 258, 244, respectively, for the six regions shown.

to slightly under four children per woman in Latin America, all far above the level in China.

There may be considerable variation in fertility trends between different countries in the same region. This is particularly true within Asia, which contains many countries that have experienced rapid fertility decline, as well as a few that have experienced little or none. To make country comparisons it is desirable to summarize the information contained in the time series of total fertility rates, and a natural way to do this is to calculate a rate of decline. In the case of China, for example, we see from *Figure 6.1* that the total fertility rate declined after 1970, with two rapid drops followed by a more modest fall. Consulting *Table 6.1*, we see that the total fertility rate for 1965–1969, before the decline, was 5.99 children per woman, that the two sharp drops brought it down to 2.90 children per woman for 1975–1979, and that it fell further to 2.36 children per woman for 1980–1985. To calculate a rate of decline we begin with the 5.99 children per woman in 1965–1969, the last point before the decline begins, but we may end either with the 2.90 children per women for 1975–1979, which will give a higher rate, or with the 2.36 children per woman for 1980–1984, which will give a lower rate. To make a conservative comparison, we take the latter rate. This gives a decline of 3.63 children per woman over 15 years, for a rate of decline of 0.24 children per woman per year.

Similar calculations have been made for 20 other Asian countries and for Taiwan, yielding the results shown in *Table 6.2*.[1] The median rate of decline for the 22 populations shown in *Table 6.2* is

Table 6.2. Comparative data on fertility decline in the developing world.

Country	Period Begin	End	TFR Begin	End	Yrs.	Decl.	Rate
1. China	1965–69	1980–84	5.99	2.36	15	3.63	0.24
2. Taiwan	1955	1986	6.53	1.68	31	4.85	0.16
3. Hong Kong	1960–64	1980–84	5.30	1.80	20	3.50	0.18
4. Japan	1933	1953	4.42	2.26	20	2.16	0.11
5. Korea (S)	1955–59	1980–84	6.07	2.40	25	3.67	0.15
6. Korea (N)	1965–69	1980–84	6.97	2.76	15	4.21	0.29
7. Mongolia	1970–74	1980–84	5.80	5.25	10	0.55	0.06
8. Indonesia	1965–69	1980–84	5.57	4.05	15	1.52	0.10
9. Lao (PDR)	1970–74	1975–79	6.15	6.69	5	−0.54	−0.11
10. Malaysia	1960–64	1975–79	6.72	4.16	15	2.56	0.17
11. Myanmar	1965–69	1980–84	5.74	4.61	15	1.13	0.08
12. Philippines	1950–54	1980–84	7.29	4.74	30	2.55	0.09
13. Singapore	1955–59	1980–84	6.41	1.87	25	4.54	0.18
14. Thailand	1965–69	1980–84	6.14	3.52	15	2.62	0.17
15. Vietnam	1968–72	1983–88	5.90	3.98	15	1.92	0.13
16. Afghanistan	1975–79	1980–84	7.21	6.90	5	0.31	0.06
17. Bangladesh	1970–74	1980–84	7.02	6.15	10	0.87	0.09
18. India	1965–69	1975–79	5.69	4.83	10	0.86	0.09
19. Iran	1960–64	1980–84	7.26	5.64	20	1.62	0.08
20. Nepal	1975–79	1980–84	6.54	6.25	5	0.29	0.06
21. Pakistan	1960–65	1980–84	7.00	7.00	20	0.00	0.00
22. Sri Lanka	1950–54	1980–84	5.74	3.25	30	2.49	0.08

Stem and leaf →	0	0
(excl. Lao)	*	666888999
	1	013
Median=0.10	*	567788
	2	4
	*	9

Sources: Table 46 of UN, 1991, except for Japan and Taiwan. Data for Taiwan from *Taiwan Demographic Yearbook,* various years. Data for Japan from Feeney, 1990, time/TFR as follows: 1933.5/4.42 (Table 11:32), 1938.5/3.84 (Table 12:33), 1943.5/3.17, 1948.5/2.66, and 1953.5/2.26 (Table 13:34).

0.10 child per woman per year, or one child per woman per decade. At this rate, decline from a roughly typical premodern fertility level of six children per woman to an equally roughly typical modern level of two children per woman would take 40 years. China, with a rate of decline of 0.24 children per woman per year, experienced a decline nearly this large in only 15 years.

The range of values in *Table 6.2* illustrates the difficulties of international comparisons. Neither of the extreme values, for example, −0.11 for Lao People's Democratic Republic and 0.29 for Democratic People's Republic of Korea, should be given much weight. The demographic data necessary for calculating total fertility rates for Lao People's Democratic Republic over this period do not exist, and even casual scrutiny of the estimates given in the United Nations source will raise suspicion that the numbers are little more than rough guesses. Little is known of data sources for Democratic People's Republic of Korea, for they are almost without exception not public, and here again scrutiny of the values shown in the source places their accuracy in doubt. For most of the other countries, however, sources are plentiful and public, and while accuracy varies from one country to another, the estimates of rate of decline may be regarded as reasonably sound.

China's rapid fertility decline is more surprising and significant for having occurred in the largest country in the world. It is more surprising because, insofar as fertility decline reflects government policy initiatives, it is a reasonable hypothesis that larger countries pose greater challenges. It is more significant because an interest in world population growth will weigh larger populations more heavily than smaller ones. The rates of fertility decline shown in *Table 6.2* are therefore displayed together with population size in *Figure 6.2*, which compares size and rate of fertility decline in China with that for 20 other Asian populations. Because of the great range in population sizes, from under 2 million for Mongolia to over 1 billion for China, we use the logarithm of population size, rather than size as such, as the indicator. Thus the vertical axis shows the logarithm of population size, and the horizontal axis the rate of decline in the total fertility rate.

We see at once how far removed China is from the experience of other countries. Only one other country in the world, Democratic People's Republic of Korea, has a rate of fertility decline exceeding that of China, and we have just noted that these data are suspect. The highest rate of decline for all other countries is 0.18, shared by

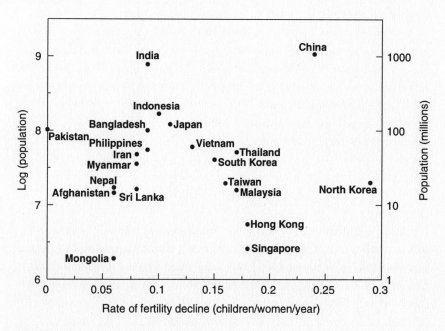

Figure 6.2. Rate of fertility decline and log population size for 21 Asian countries. Source: *Table 6.2.*

Hong Kong and Singapore. Pakistan, one of the largest countries in the world, shows no decline whatever, though also no increase. This is the extreme low value for the populations shown in *Figure 6.2*, from which Lao People's Democratic Republic has been excluded.

It is interesting to note the level and distribution of rates of decline among countries. Until rather recently, Japan was generally considered to have experienced the most rapid fertility decline in the world. Yet the rate of decline shown here for Japan is only 0.11 children per woman per year, just over the median value for the 21 populations displayed in *Figure 6.2*. It is notable, moreover, that with the exceptions of the Philippines and Myanmar, every country in East and Southeast Asia had a rate of decline higher than Japan, and every country in South and West Asia a lower rate of decline than Japan. It is significant that the higher rates of decline are observed not only in the small city-states of Hong Kong and Singapore, but also in the large nations of Malaysia, Vietnam and Thailand.

The inverted V pattern in the plot is particularly notable. Smaller countries tend to have either relatively high or relatively low rates of fertility decline, with a convergence toward the median as size increases. Perhaps this reflects the possibility that, in the diffusion of modernization, small countries may be bypassed altogether for a time, but may also modernize rapidly once the process begins, whereas larger countries cannot escape modernizing influences, but tend to react more slowly to them.

6.2   China's Fertility Decline: A Closer Look

Looking at total fertility rates for quinquennial periods obscures important details of China's fertility decline. In this section we examine several single-year time series to provide a more precise picture of fertility decline, a picture that may then be compared with government population policy initiatives. Incidentally, we present evidence of the accuracy of the data from which these fertility statistics are calculated. While certainly not perfect, the Chinese data are superior to that available for most countries in the world, developed as well as developing.

Figure 6.3 shows conventional total fertility rates (TFR) for China from 1965 through mid-1987.[2] We are in fact looking at two different series here, shown in the first two columns in *Table 6.3*. The first, plotted with solid dots, is calculated from age-specific birth rates (ASBR) derived from the birth histories collected in the 1982 One-per-Thousand Fertility Survey conducted by the State Family Planning Commission (see China Population Information Center 1984; Coale 1984; Coale and Chen 1987). The values shown are those given in Coale and Chen (1987), though these hardly differ from those reported in the first survey (China Population Information Center 1984). These values are for calendar years.

The second series in *Figure 6.3*, plotted with small circles, is calculated from age-specific birth rates derived from birth histories reconstructed from a 10 percent sample of the 1987 One-per-Hundred Survey carried out by the State Statistical Bureau. The reconstruction procedure, developed by Luther, is described in Luther and Cho (1988). An extension of the own-children method (Cho *et al.*,

Table 6.3. Total fertility rates and mean age at marriage for China, various sources and calculations: 1965–1987.

Year	ASBR TFR (1)	(2)	Mean age at marriage (3)	(4)	(5)	PPPR TFR (6)	(7)	(8)
1987	–	2.46	–	21.8	22.0	–	2.33	2.26
1986	–	2.33	–	21.8	21.8	–	2.17	2.11
1985	–	2.27	–	21.7	22.0	–	2.07	1.97
1984	–	2.35	–	21.7	22.1	–	2.06	1.99
1983	–	2.53	–	21.8	22.1	–	2.32	2.10
1982	–	2.83	–	22.1	21.9	–	2.63	2.58
1981	2.71	2.41	22.8	22.6	22.0	2.65	2.61	2.56
1980	2.32	2.55	23.0	22.8	22.4	2.70	2.90	2.58
1979	2.80	2.77	23.1	23.0	23.0	3.20	3.14	3.20
1978	2.75	2.72	22.8	22.8	23.2	3.16	3.14	3.16
1977	2.87	3.09	22.5	22.6	23.4	3.23	3.40	3.14
1976	3.25	3.30	22.3	22.3	23.1	3.47	3.52	3.48
1975	3.58	3.80	21.7	22.0	23.2	3.73	3.93	3.75
1974	4.15	4.24	21.4	21.5	22.8	4.14	4.33	4.33
1973	4.51	4.72	21.0	21.1	22.5	4.37	4.69	–
1972	4.92	–	20.6	20.7	22.2	4.73	4.85	–
1971	5.40	–	20.3	20.4	21.9	5.08	–	–
1970	5.75	–	20.2	20.3	21.1	5.43	–	–
1969	5.67	–	20.3	20.4	20.8	5.41	–	–
1968	6.37	–	20.1	20.2	20.6	5.68	–	–
1967	5.25	–	20.0	20.2	21.0	4.98	–	–
1966	6.21	–	19.8	–	–	5.75	–	–
1965	6.02	–	19.7	–	–	5.96	–	–

Values in columns 2 and 7 refer to years ending June 30 of each year. Other values refer to calendar years.

Sources: column 1 from Coale and Chen (1987, Basic Table 1.A.:25); column 2 from Luther *et al.* (1990, Table 4:350); column 3 from Banister (1987, Table 6.1:156); column 4 from unpublished computer printouts of the 1988 Two-per-Thousand Survey; column 5 from Feeney and Wang (1993, Table 2:69); column 6 from Feeney and Yu (1987, Table 1:81); column 7 from Luther *et al.* (1990, Table 5:353); column 8 from Feeney and Wang (1993, Table 2:69).

1986), it begins with the "own-children histories" generated by that method and imputes deceased and non-own children to each woman based on reported numbers of children ever born and surviving and on the standard own-children estimates of age-specific birth rates.

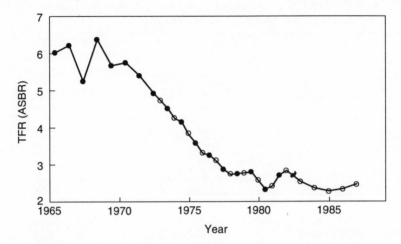

Figure 6.3. Conventional total fertility rates for China: 1965–1987.
Source: *Table 6.3*, columns 1 and 2.

The consistency of the two series shown in *Figure 6.3* testifies
to the exceptional accuracy of these Chinese data. These two series
are derived from different survey operations, conducted by different
organizations, using different methods applied to different questionnaire items. Given these differences, the consistency displayed in
Figure 6.3 is most unlikely to be the result of common errors, and
of course the likelihood of chance agreement over this long time
series is negligible.

The total fertility rates plotted in *Figure 6.3* decline nearly linearly from 5.75 children per woman in calendar year 1970 to 2.72
children per woman for the year ending June 30, 1978. This represents a decline of 3.03 children per woman over a period of seven
and one-half years for a rate of decline of 0.40 children per woman
per year. This is much higher than the 0.24 children per woman
per year based on the last three points shown in *Figure 6.1*. It is
also substantially higher than the rate of decline indicated in *Figure
6.1* if we leave off the last point and calculate the decline between
1965–1969 and 1975–1979, which works out to be 0.31 children per
woman per year. In short, the speed and timing of China's fertility
decline are such that the use of quinquennial periods substantially
underestimates the speed of the decline.

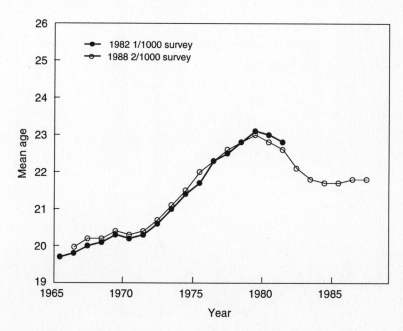

Figure 6.4. Mean age at first marriage in China: 1965–1987.
Source: *Table 6.3*, columns 3 and 4.

In reading the record of fertility change shown in *Figure 6.3*, however, there is a confounding factor that must be taken into account. *Figure 6.4* shows mean age at marriage in China for the period in question (data from columns 3 and 4 of *Table 6.3*), defined as the mean of all marriages occurring in each year. As in previous figures, we have statistics from two data sources, in this case the 1982 One-per-Thousand Survey and the 1988 Two-per-Thousand Survey, both taken by the State Family Planning Commission. The consistency between the two series gives an indication of their remarkably high accuracy.

Mean age at marriage rose rapidly during most of the 1970s. The mean age at first marriage series shown in column 4 of *Table 6.3* rose from 20.3 years in 1970 to a high of 23.1 years in 1979, a rate of 0.4 years per year.[3] If this rate of increase translated into a corresponding rate of increase in mean age at childbearing, and if the increase were observed over a sufficiently long period of time, it would have increased period total fertility rates by approximately 40

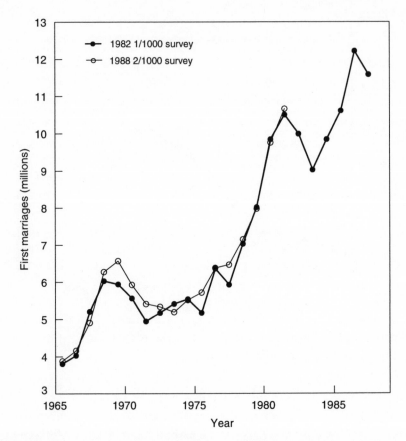

Figure 6.5. Approximate annual numbers of first marriages in China: 1965–1987. Source: Appendix *Table 6.1*.

percent over corresponding cohort levels (Ryder, 1983:741). These conditions do not hold, and the actual effect is less than this, but it is nonetheless substantial.

Figure 6.5 shows numbers of first marriages in China during 1965–1987, based on the 1982 and 1988 surveys. Since we are looking at numbers here, there is a bias due both to mortality and to the upper age limit in the surveys.[4] The comparison of the series from the two surveys shows that this bias is not serious during the period in question.

The striking feature of *Figure 6.5* is the extraordinary rise in numbers of marriages between the late 1970s and the early 1980s.

During the late 1960s and mid- to late 1970s, we observe 5 to 6 million first marriages per year. During the 1980s the numbers range from slightly under 10 million in 1984 to over 12 million in 1986, fully twice the level of the 1970s.

This jump in marriages exerts a powerful upward influence on birth rates. Since virtually all Chinese women have a first birth within a few years of first marriage,[5] the increases in numbers of first marriages translate almost directly into a slightly lagged increase in numbers of first births. Thus in Appendix *Tables 6.1* and *6.2* we see that annual numbers of first births rise from about 5 million during the mid-1970s to about 10 million during the mid-1980s. This increase is due not to any change in the childbearing behavior of Chinese women, but to the rapidly increasing numbers of recently married women. If we choose to interpret the total fertility rates shown in *Figure 6.3* merely as indicators of numbers of births, these observations are irrelevant. If we wish to interpret them as indicators of childbearing behavior, however, it is necessary to recognize that they are distorted by the rapid changes in age at marriage and numbers of marriages during the period in question.

6.3 Period Parity Progression Measures of Fertility

The simplest approach to dealing with the effects of changing marriage patterns on the conventional fertility measures presented in the preceding section is to use alternative measures that are less sensitive to changing marriage patterns. Period parity progression ratios (PPPRs) calculated from birth probabilities specific for parity and birth interval provide an effective way to do this. In the calculation of probabilities of progression from marriage to first birth, for example, numbers of women marrying each year and the corresponding numbers of married women remaining in parity zero appear in the denominator of each birth probability, whence an increase in numbers of marriages from one year to the next does not imply any increase in the proportion of women progressing to first birth.

The parity progression approach to fertility measurement asks what proportions of women move from one childbearing event to the next. Of all women born, what proportion ever have a first

birth? Of all women who have a first birth, what proportion go
on (progress) to have a second, and so on? The answers to these
questions are *parity progression ratios,* and, like other demographic
measures, they may be calculated on a period as well as on a cohort
basis. (For a general discussion of period parity progression ratio
measures of fertility, see Feeney and Lutz, 1991. For applications
to China, see Feeney and Yu, 1987; Feeney *et al.*, 1989; Luther
et al., 1990; Feeney and Wang, 1993.) For populations in which
fertility is restricted to married couples, as in China, it is useful to
break down the proportion of women ever having a first birth into
two multiplicative components: the proportion of women who ever
marry and the proportion of women marrying who ever have a first
birth.

Total fertility rates may be calculated from period parity progression ratios as well as from age-specific birth rates, and the logic
of the calculation is parallel. We ask what average number of children would be born to a hypothetical cohort of women that experience the parity progression ratios observed during a given time
period. The formula is easily shown to be (see, for example, Feeney
and Yu, 1987)

$$TFR = p_0 + p_0p_1 + p_0p_1p_2 + \cdots .$$

A convenient approximation for use with incomplete series of
parity progression ratios is given by replacing the last term in the
series by itself divided by $1-p_n$, where p_n is the last available ratio.[6]

Period parity progression ratios are unusual fertility measures,
even within the field of demography, and it will be useful to provide some examples of their values for different countries.[7] *Table
6.4* assembles schedules of parity progression ratios for a variety of
high and low fertility countries. Progression to marriage and first
and second births is generally high for both high and low fertility
countries. Among the high fertility Hutterites, some 97 percent of
all married women have at least one child. In China, virtually all
women married and had a first birth, both before fertility began to
decline (1965) and after it had declined nearly to replacement level
(1982).[8] The lowest levels of progression from marriage to first
birth occur in low fertility countries, to be sure, but even here it is
unusual for less than 80 percent of women who have a first birth to
go on to have a second.

Table 6.4. Parity progression ratios for selected populations, per 1,000.

Population	Progression									
	B→M	M→1	0→1	1→2	2→3	3→4	4→5	5→6	6→7	7→8
Hutterites	–	971	–	988	972	968	967	953	929	905
China 1965	990	982	972	979	964	929	886	845	786	720
China 1979	994	991	985	959	700	539	431	414	322	309
Rural	997	992	989	978	759	572	448	422	328	310
Urban	981	979	960	799	259	168	131	185	44	373
Taiwan 1986	992	959	951	782	428	212	170	185	198	216
Thailand										
1960–1964	–	–	948	966	951	925	918	890	859	800
1975–1979	–	–	813	917	771	681	646	610	580	548
Japan 1982	925	916	847	856	320	137	221[a]	–	–	–
USA										
1941	–	–	779	745	628	639	651	670	666	635[a]
1960	–	–	923	922	746	645	619	650	682	689[a]
1984	–	–	802	789	488	386	382	419	439	456[a]
Canada 1985	–	–	–	793	423	301	287	370	412	430[a]
Netherlands 1985	–	–	–	835	382	298	363	483	555	562[a]
East Germany 1985	–	–	–	688	274	300	366	427	443	422[a]
Hungary 1984	–	–	–	750	242	249	377	414	470	458[a]
Yugoslavia 1982	–	–	–	815	318	416	518	567	547	464[a]
France 1976	891	939	837	645	325	267	277[a]	–	–	–
Italy 1978	926	861	797	739	345	280	287[a]	–	–	–
England & Wales 1977	–	829	–	855	347	267	241[a]	–	–	–

[a]Values are aggregates for progression from *i*-th or higher order to (*i*+1)st or higher-order births.

Sources: Cohort data for Hutterites calculated from Eaton and Mayer (1954:20, Table 10). All remaining figures are period data. China from Feeney and Yu (1987:81). Thailand from Luther and Pejaranondam (1991:Tables B1 and B2). Japan from Feeney (1986:20). USA from Feeney (1988:Table 1). East Germany from Feeney and Lutz (1991). Values for Canada, the Netherlands, East Germany, Hungary, and Yugoslavia estimated by the indirect procedure described in the text from time series of registered births by order from United Nations *Demographic Yearbooks*. Values for France, Italy, and England and Wales from Penhale (1984:Tables 12–14).

The difference between high and low fertility populations is most pronounced in the higher-order parity progression ratios, and most importantly in the proportion of women progressing from second to third birth. In a high fertility population – for the high fertility Hutterites, for China in 1965, and for Thailand in 1960–1964 – parity progression ratios decline slowly with increasing parity, remaining in the 70 to 90 percent range even for progression from seventh to eighth birth. In a low fertility population, however, progression from second to third birth is sharply lower than progression to first or from first to second. The values shown in *Table 6.4* range from a low of 24 percent for Hungary to a high of 75 percent for the United States near the height of the baby boom, but this last value is atypically high. The normal range for progression from second to third birth in low fertility populations is 25 to 50 percent.

Higher-order parity progression ratios in low fertility populations are surprisingly high – the median value for progression from seventh to ninth birth for the low fertility countries in *Table 6.4* is 44 percent. There can be little doubt that this reflects a selection effect. In a low fertility population, the only women who reach high parities are necessarily highly fecund, regularly exposed to the risk of conception, and either nonusers or inept users of contraception. These relatively high parity progression ratios have little effect on the overall level of fertility, however, since only a small fraction of women reach high parities.

6.4   Period Parity Progression Measures of Fertility in China

Total fertility rates calculated from period parity progression ratios are plotted in *Figure 6.6*. Here as in *Figure 6.3* we have values both from the 1982 One-per-Thousand Fertility Survey conducted by the State Family Planning Commission and from the 1987 One-per-Hundred Survey conducted by the State Statistical Bureau, and the consistency of the two series attests to their accuracy.

The total fertility rates in *Figure 6.6* decline irregularly along a linear trend from 5.43 children per woman for calendar year 1970 to 2.06 children per woman for the year ending June 30, 1984. This is a decline of 3.37 children per woman in 13.5 years, for a rate of

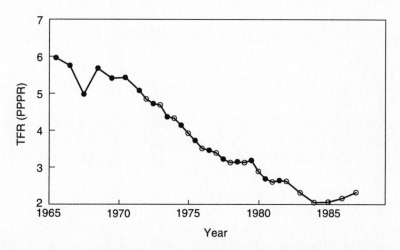

Figure 6.6. Total fertility rates calculated from period parity progression ratios for China: 1965–1987. Source: *Table 6.3*, columns 6 and 7.

0.25 children per woman per year – remarkably close, though only by coincidence, to the 0.24 children per woman per year indicated by the quinquennial data shown in *Figure 6.1* and *Table 6.1*.

The contrast between this picture and that shown by the conventional total fertility rates plotted in *Figure 6.3* illustrates the distorting effects of changing marriage patterns. There are two main differences. First, the rate of decline shown by the conventional total fertility rates is much more rapid, 0.40 as compared with 0.25 children per woman per year, because rapidly rising age at marriage during the 1980s caused a decline beyond that due to declining childbearing within marriage. Second, and more importantly, the conventional total fertility rates indicate a decline ending in 1978, whereas the total fertility rates calculated from period parity progression ratios continue until 1984, a full six years later.

The parity progression ratio total fertility rates show that the level of fertility implicit in the childbearing behavior of Chinese women continued to decline until the mid-1980s. Because of the tremendous surge of marriages beginning in the late 1970s, this continuing behavioral change is completely obscured by the conventional total fertility rates. The conventional total fertility rates suggest that fertility decline in China ended, at least temporarily,

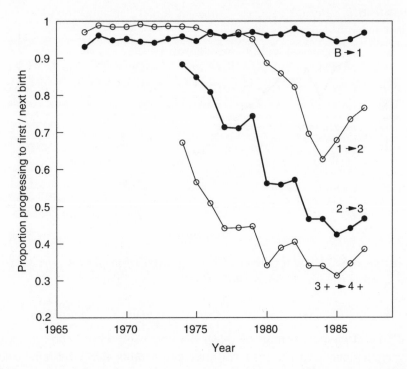

Figure 6.7. Period parity progression ratios for China: 1967–1987.
Source: *Table 6.5.*

in 1979. This was precisely the year in which a major new policy
initiative, the one-child family program, was taken. The time series of conventional total fertility rates suggest that the new policy
was unsuccessful. In fact, as we see below, it achieved considerable
success.

One advantage of total fertility rates calculated from period parity progression ratios is superior control for the distorting effects of
changing marriage patterns. A second advantage, and one particularly important in the Chinese context, is the correspondence established with the period parity progression ratios themselves. The
level of progression from first to second birth, in particular, reflects
the demographic impact of the one-child family policy.

Table 6.5 and *Figure 6.7* show period parity progression ratios and the corresponding total fertility rates for the years 1967–
1987 calculated from the 1988 Two-per-Thousand Fertility Survey

Table 6.5. Period progression ratios and PPR total fertility rates for China: 1967–1987.

| Year | Progression and progression ratio | | | | | |
	B→M	M→1	1→2	2→3	$3^+ \to 4^+$	TFR
1987	995	968	765	466	384	2.26
1986	997	950	734	440	345	2.11
1985	996	944	678	423	312	1.97
1984	999	961	626	465	338	1.99
1983	997	963	695	465	339	2.10
1982	1000	979	821	571	404	2.58
1981	998	963	858	558	388	2.56
1980	999	960	886	562	340	2.58
1979	999	970	951	743	446	3.20
1978	996	963	969	710	442	3.16
1977	996	958	958	713	441	3.14
1976	983	970	964	808	508	3.48
1975	992	946	982	848	565	3.75
1974	992	958	985	883	672	4.33
1973	993	952	986	–	–	–
1972	973	941	984	–	–	–
1971	994	944	991	–	–	–
1970	999	952	984	–	–	–
1969	997	948	984	–	–	–
1968	998	961	988	–	–	–
1967	999	930	970	–	–	–

Calculated from birth histories collected in the National Fertility and Birth Control Survey of 1988. TFR values calculated from parity progression ratio schedule extending to progression from seventh to eighth birth. Progression from third and higher to fourth and higher is the aggregate of progression from third to fourth through progression from seventh to eighth. So few women reach these high parities, however, that the difference is entirely negligible.
Source: Feeney and Wang (1993:Tables 3, 5, 7, 9, and 16) and unpublished computer printouts for annual values in first column.

conducted by the State Family Planning Commission (Feeney and Wang, 1993; see also Lavely, 1991). Because progression to first marriage is virtually constant at close to one throughout the period shown, *Figure 6.7* shows proportions of women progressing to first birth (B→1), the product of women progressing to first marriage (B→M) and women progressing from first marriage to first birth (M→1), rather than showing these two series separately.

Figure 6.7 shows that proportions of women ever having a first birth have been high, around 95 percent, throughout the period considered. Fertility decline has resulted entirely from declines in progression to higher-order births. Progression from first to second birth, in particular, shows the impact of the one-child family program. In 1979, the year the program was introduced, 95 percent of all women were progressing from first to second birth. By 1984, after the policy had been in effect for only five years, progression to second birth had been reduced to 63 percent. That year, however, marked a relaxation in the policy, and progression to second birth rose continuously through 1987, the last year of the series, at which point it stood at 76 percent.

Progression to both first and second births was essentially constant through 1979, whence the great fertility decline of the 1970s was due entirely to declines in third- and higher-order births. Progression from second to third birth declined by more than half between 1974 (88 percent) and 1985 (42 percent), and progression from third- and higher-order births to fourth- and higher-order births declined from 67 to 31 percent over the same period.

6.5   Scenarios for Future Fertility Change

The foregoing analysis of fertility decline in China indicates that government policy and programs played a major role in these trends. (For a more detailed assessment see Feeney and Wang, 1993:92–95. On population policy in China, see Chen and Kols, 1982; Tuan, 1982; Greenhalgh, 1986, 1990, 1993; Hardee-Cleaveland and Banister, 1988; Zeng, 1989; and Kaufman *et al.*, 1989. See also the ethnographic accounts of Huang, 1989; Moser, 1983; and Potter and Potter, 1990.) The rapidity of the fall in age at marriage following the relaxation of administrative controls *circa* 1980 strongly suggests that the earlier rise in age at marriage was in substantial part due to explicit government policy, specifically to the later *(wan)* marriage component of the *wan-shi-shao* policy. The sudden decline in progression from first to second birth following the introduction of the one-child family program in 1979 and the subsequent rise following the relaxation of 1984 are even stronger evidence that this particular component of fertility decline was due largely to government policy.

The structure of China's birth-planning efforts and the attention and resources allocated to them make this remarkable effectiveness more plausible than it might otherwise be. Government policy was effective despite imperfect implementation. Substantial proportions of men and women married beneath the prescribed ages in the 1970s, for example, but the encouragement to later marriage did result in a very substantial increase in mean age at marriage. Even at the peak of its effectiveness to date, the one-child family program saw well over half of all Chinese women having two or more children, but the program nonetheless had a substantial and continuing effect on fertility levels.

In considering future fertility trends, then, it makes sense to emphasize the role of government policy. The centerpiece of China's current birth-planning efforts is still the one-child family policy introduced in 1979, but this simple statement conceals a more complicated demographic reality. One-child families have been realized among most of the urban population, with progression from first to second birth in recent years between 10 and 20 percent (Feeney and Wang, 1993:Table 6.5). The one-child family remains the official population policy in rural areas as well, but numerous adaptations belie the "one-child" label, and progression from first to second birth in recent years has been around 85 percent. At the national level, progression from first to second birth in rural areas rose from a low of 63 percent in 1984 to 76 percent in 1987 (*Figure 6.7*), with a continued increase indicated.

This discussion of scenarios is limited to high and low extremes for the next two decades. A high trajectory is obtained by assuming a continued relaxation of the one-child family policy, with progression from first to second birth rising to about 95 percent, the level observed before the introduction of the policy in 1979; and with progression from second to third birth rising modestly from 47 to 62 percent, both plausible extrapolations of recent experience. This yields total fertility rates rising from 2.3 in 1987 to 2.5 in 1990, to 2.7 in 1995 and 2000, and finally to 2.8 in 2005.

A low trajectory is obtained by assuming implementation of the one-child policy in rural as well as urban areas, but assuming both a somewhat higher level of progression from first to second birth than has been achieved in cities (30 percent as opposed to about 15 percent recently) and a slower rate of decline (15 years for rural areas as compared with only four years for cities). Progression from second to third birth is assumed to decline as well, though the very low values of progression from first to second birth make this relatively unimportant. This yields total fertility rates falling from 2.3 in 1987 to 2.2 in 1990, to 1.7 in 1995, to 1.5 in 2000, and finally to 1.4 in 2005.

Between now and the beginning of the next century, we expect fertility in China not to exceed 2.7 children per woman or to fall below 1.5 children per woman.[9]

6.6   Conclusion

For most countries in the world, consideration of future fertility levels focuses on how rapidly fertility will decline. The success of China's birth-planning policies urges us to consider the possibility of rising fertility, for to say that government policies have been successful is to say that fertility under less restrictive policies would be higher. Our analysis of the Chinese situation suggests that fertility might rise as high as 3 children per woman over the next 20 years, an eventuality that could occur if the one-child family policy were relaxed to the point of allowing second children in essentially all families that wanted them. At the other extreme, a relatively successful implementation of the one-child policy in rural as well as urban areas might bring fertility down to between 1 and 1.5 children per woman. It should be emphasized that these are both improbable extremes. We would be very surprised to see fertility go outside of this range, and not at all surprised to see it fluctuate modestly around levels of 2 to 2.5 children per woman.

There is very little basis for speculation about the longer-term future of fertility. The only thing that can be said with any semblance of scientific support is that world demographic trends to date suggest that a plausible range is between 1.5 and 3 children per woman. It is a reasonable supposition that levels and trends of fertility over the past few decades contain information about the likely trends over the next few decades, and that is the basis of our conclusions about fertility in China through the early years of the next century. Recent levels and trends cannot plausibly be expected to contain any information about detailed levels 50 or 100 years into the future, however. Assumptions about these more distant levels must either be regarded as purely formal or be made on some basis other than a study of recent levels and trends.

Notes

[1] Since fertility decline occurs during different periods in different countries, it makes little sense to compute rates of decline for the same period for all countries. At the same time, choosing a suitable time period over which to compute a rate of decline involves an element of judgment, if not of arbitrariness. The periods shown in *Table 6.1* have been selected by examining the plot of the TFR trend in each country. Because we are interested in showing how different China is from other countries, we have chosen periods to give larger rather than smaller rates of declines for all other countries.

[2] "Conventional" total fertility rates means rates calculated from age-specific birth rates. These are to be distinguished from total fertility rates calculated from period parity progression ratios, discussed in Section 6.3.

[3] Columns 3 and 4 of *Table 6.3* show mean age at first marriage calculated directly as the mean of all first marriages occurring during the indicated year. Column 5 shows mean age at first marriage calculated from first marriage probabilities, i.e., for the period nuptiality table, for the given year. The former statistic is more readily computed and more common. The latter has the advantage of being uninfluenced by changing age distribution. All three series show a sharp rise in mean age at marriage. Comparing the plot of the nuptiality table values (not shown) with *Figure 6.4* shows sharp divergences between the two types of means. See Feeney and Wang (1993:70–71) for discussion of these differences and their significance.

[4] The 1982 survey included women less than exact age 68 years; the 1988 survey, women less than exact age 58 years.

[5] The evidence of this is given below in the form of period parity progression ratios for progression from marriage to first birth. See *Table 6.5* and the corresponding text discussion.

[6] The approximation assumes that parity progression ratios beyond p_n are identically equal to p_n. Although not in the least realistic, the approximation is very good as long as p_n is not too large, which in practice means not much over one-half. The $1-p_n$ arises from a geometric series, as a little algebra readily shows.

[7] The reasons for this are beyond the scope of the present discussion; for more information see Feeney and Lutz (1991:186–187).

[8] The value shown for the proportion of married women having a first birth is probably too high, one of the relatively few imperfections in the data from the 1982 One-per-Thousand Survey. See Feeney and Wang (1993:71) for a discussion of evidence.

[9] Since this was written, 1990 census data have become available. The analysis given in Feeney *et al.* (1992) indicates that fertility decline resumed after 1987, falling to 2.02 children per woman (period parity progression ratio TFR) for the year ending June 30, 1990.

References

Banister, J., 1987, *China's Changing Population*, Stanford University Press, Stanford, CA, USA.

Chen, Pi-chao, and Kols, A., 1982, Population and birth planning in the People's Republic of China, *Population Reports*, Series J, Number 25, Family Planning Programs, Population Information Program, Johns Hopkins University, Baltimore, MD, USA.

China Population Information Center, 1984, *Analysis on China's National One-per-Thousand Population Fertility Sampling Survey*, China Population Information Center, PO Box 2444, Beijing, China.

Cho, Lee-Jay, Retherford, R.D., and Minja Kim Choe, 1986, *The Own-Children Method of Fertility Estimation*, East–West Center, University of Hawaii Press, Honolulu, HI, USA.

Coale, A.J., 1984, *Rapid Population Change in China, 1952–1982*, Committee on Population and Demography, Report No. 27, National Academy Press, Washington, DC, USA.

Coale, A.J., and Sheng Li Chen, 1987, *Basic Data on Fertility in the Provinces of China, 1940–1982*, Papers of the East–West Population Institute, Number 104, East–West Center, Honolulu, HI, USA.

Eaton, J.W., and Mayer, A.J., 1954, *Man's Capacity to Reproduce: The Demography of a Unique Population*, The Free Press, New York, NY, USA.

Feeney, G., 1986, *Period Parity Progression Ratios of Fertility in Japan*, NUPRI Research Paper Series No. 35 (December), Nihon University Population Research Institute, Tokyo, Japan.

Feeney, G., 1988, Comparative Structure of Low Fertility in Japan and the United States, Paper presented to the Conference on Future Changes in Population Age Structure, Sopron, Hungary, 18–21 October 1988, organized by the International Institute for Applied Systems Analysis, Laxenburg, Austria.

Feeney, G., 1990, *The Demography of Aging in Japan: 1950–2025*, NUPRI Research Paper Series No. 55, Nihon University Population Research Institute, Tokyo, Japan.

Feeney, G., and Jingyuan Yu, 1987, Period parity progression measures of fertility in China, *Population Studies* **41**(1):77–102.

Feeney, G., and Lutz, W., 1991, Distributional analysis of period fertility, in W. Lutz, ed., *Future Demographic Trends in Europe and North America: What Can We Assume Today?* Academic Press, London, UK.

Feeney, G., and Wang, F., 1993, Parity progression and birth intervals in China: The influence of policy in hastening fertility decline, *Population and Development Review* **19**(1):61–101.

Feeney, G., Wang, F., Zhou, M., and Xiao, B., 1989, Recent fertility decline in China: Results from the 1987 one percent population survey, *Population and Development Review* **15**(2):297–322.

Feeney, G., Luther, N.Y., Meng, Q.P., and Sun, Y., 1992, Recent Fertility Trends in China: Results from the 1990 Census, Paper prepared for the International Seminar on China's 1990 Population Census, 19–23 October, Beijing, China.

Greenhalgh, S., 1986, Shifts in China's population policy, 1984–1986: Views from the central, provincial, and local levels, *Population and Development Review* **12**(3):491–515.

Greenhalgh, S., 1990, The Peasantization of Population Policy in Shaanxi: Cadre Mediation of State-Society Conflict, Working Paper No. 21, The Population Council, New York, NY, USA.

Greenhalgh, S., 1993, The peasantization of the one-child policy in Shaanxi, in D. Davis and S. Harrell, eds., *Chinese Family in the Post-Mao Era*, Harvard University Press, Cambridge, MA, USA.

Hardee-Cleaveland, K., and Banisterm J., 1988, Fertility policy and implementation in China, 1986–1988, *Population and Development Review* **14**(2):245–286.

Huang, Shu-min, 1989, *The Spiral Road: Change in a Chinese Village Through the Eyes of a Communist Party Leader*, Westview Press, Boulder, CO, USA.

Kaufman, J., Zhirong Zhang, Sinjian Qiao, and Yang Zhang, 1989, Family planning policy and practice in China: A study of four rural counties, *Population and Development Review* **15**(4):707–729.

Lavely, W.R., 1991, China unveils its monumental Two-per-Thousand Fertility Survey, *Asian and Pacific Population Forum* **5**(4):89–92, 116.

Luther, N.Y., and Lee-Jay Cho, 1988, Reconstruction of birth histories from census and household survey data, *Population Studies* **42**(3):451–472.

Luther, N.Y., and Pejaranondam, C., 1991, The parity structure of fertility decline in Thailand, 1953–1979, *Genus* **47**(1–2):63–88.

Luther, N.Y., Feeney, G., and Weimin Zhang, 1990, One-child families of a baby-boom? Evidence from China's 1987 one-per-hundred survey, *Population Studies* **44**(2):341–357.

Moser, S.W., 1983, *Broken Earth: The Rural Chinese,* The Free Press, New York, NY, USA.

Penhale, B., 1984, The Course of Fertility in France, Italy and England and Wales since 1955, Msc. Thesis, Centre for Population Studies, London School of Hygiene and Tropical Medicine, London, UK.

Potter, S.H., and Potter, H.M., 1990, *China's Peasants: The Anthropology of a Revolution,* Cambridge University Press, Cambridge, UK.

Ryder, N.B., 1983, Cohort and period measures of changing fertility, in R.A. Buletao and R.D. Lee, eds., *Determinants of Fertility in Developing Countries,* Vol. 2, Academic Press, New York, NY, USA.

Tuan, Chi-hsien, 1982, China's population in perspective, in H. Brown, ed., *China Among the Nations of the Pacific,* Westview Press, Boulder, CO, USA.

UN, 1991, *World Population Prospects: 1990,* Population Studies, No. 120, Publication No. ST/ESA/SER.A/120, Department of International Economic and Social Affairs, United Nations, New York, NY, USA.

Zeng, Yi, 1989, Is the Chinese family planning program "tightening up"? *Population and Development Review* **15**(2):333–337.

Fertility in China: Past, Present, Prospects   141

Appendix Table 6.1. Annual first marriages and births by order.

Year	M	Birth order							
		1	2	3	4	5	6	7	8
1987	11,605	11,951	7,283	2,619	1,022	321	145	107	55
1986	12,237	10,055	6,624	2,319	897	418	193	95	59
1985	10,624	8,937	5,416	2,151	754	298	275	143	48
1984	9,851	9,147	5,056	2,325	975	442	290	89	59
1983	9,044	9,161	5,060	2,148	923	547	348	113	59
1982	10,001	10,459	5,491	2,702	1,391	663	398	223	53
1981	10,516	9,332	4,097	2,607	1,406	842	357	285	94
1980	9,850	7,289	4,662	2,395	1,369	674	328	219	61
1979	8,036	6,923	5,365	3,564	1,874	1,080	649	266	183
1978	7,048	6,256	4,935	3,218	2,111	1,014	580	416	216
1977	5,947	5,596	4,661	3,276	1,904	1,252	676	389	234
1976	6,376	5,948	4,719	3,995	2,122	1,435	894	628	334
1975	5,191	5,117	4,975	3,785	2,594	1,650	1,156	533	365
1974	5,559	5,643	5,459	4,058	2,896	2,140	1,378	909	425
1973	5,430	5,288	5,213	4,161	3,164	2,366	1,524	1,004	510
1972	5,193	4,985	4,824	4,046	3,332	2,512	1,699	1,029	560
1971	4,964	5,193	5,383	4,151	3,832	2,609	1,616	971	530
1970	5,586	5,680	4,568	3,841	3,882	2,527	1,809	852	479
1969	5,956	5,141	4,150	4,384	3,129	2,186	1,548	826	407
1968	6,047	5,298	4,761	5,109	3,645	2,512	1,459	829	382
1967	5,226	3,781	4,020	4,030	2,592	2,077	1,001	547	191
1966	4,047	4,225	5,425	3,869	2,689	1,912	1,107	448	193
1965	3,827	4,241	4,836	3,285	2,650	1,707	821	351	143

Source: 1988 Two-per-Thousand National Fertility and Birth Control Survey.

Appendix Table 6.2. Annual first marriages and births by order.

Year	M	Birth order						
		1	2	3	4	5	6	7
1981	10,673	9,912	5,486	2,971	1,498	779	461	233
1980	9,779	7,504	4,858	2,699	1,482	690	389	222
1979	7,993	7,542	5,704	3,470	2,025	1,061	688	340
1978	7,166	6,713	5,178	3,459	1,980	1,220	671	431
1977	6,489	6,178	4,892	3,575	2,108	1,323	835	527
1976	6,399	6,004	5,224	3,837	2,468	1,565	1,058	709
1975	5,731	5,572	5,132	4,097	2,742	1,924	1,270	835
1974	5,530	5,834	5,579	4,374	3,117	2,271	1,597	1,056
1973	5,213	5,389	5,628	4,294	3,415	2,606	1,841	1,186
1972	5,350	5,500	5,488	4,195	3,702	2,914	2,119	1,356
1971	5,435	5,891	5,343	4,449	4,126	3,245	2,208	1,480
1970	5,942	6,092	5,029	4,713	4,285	3,187	2,459	1,580
1969	6,583	5,643	4,447	4,927	4,130	3,121	2,262	1,493
1968	6,293	5,618	5,319	5,586	4,400	3,276	2,522	1,729
1967	4,929	4,007	4,758	4,571	3,403	2,706	2,028	1,302
1966	4,172	4,689	5,864	4,730	3,798	3,121	2,445	1,551
1965	3,896	4,687	5,579	4,197	3,601	3,062	2,316	1,494

Source: 1982 National One-per-Thousand Population Fertility Sampling Survey.

Editor's Note for Part II

The material presented in Part II shows that fertility has started to decline in virtually all countries of the world. Even countries that until recently showed very high fertility levels seem to have entered the fertility transition toward low average fertility. The majority of developing countries are in the middle of this transition process. China is most advanced, followed by Latin America and Southeast Asia; Africa is least advanced in this process. Research on desired family sizes, as stated in surveys, also suggests further fertility declines as do Asian success stories in government population policy and family planning.

Fertility is assumed to decline further in the future in all regions except in China, where fertility has already reached such a low level that one could even infer a slight increase if the one-child policy is relaxed in the future. In all other developing regions, differences between high- and low-fertility scenarios mostly reflect different assumed speeds of decline. But the ultimate fertility level to be reached at the end of the transition process is also an open question. There seems to be little substantive justification to assume that eventually fertility will stay at the replacement level of two surviving children per woman. Accordingly the low-fertility scenarios assume below-replacement fertility by 2030 in all regions except in sub-Saharan Africa, where fertility was still above six children per woman in 1990; the high scenarios assume a retardation of decline and fertility around three children in 2030.

A more detailed justification of the numerical assumptions is given in Chapter 15.

Part III

Future Mortality
in Developing Countries

Chapter 7

Mortality Trends in Developing Countries: A Survey

Birgitta Bucht

In preparing population projections for low mortality developed countries with good statistics, mortality assumptions are considered the least problematic, at least for short-term projections, because mortality rates tend to change slowly. In developing countries, assumptions about future mortality trends are much less certain, even for short-term projections, because of the inadequacy of reliable information on past levels and trends.

This chapter reviews past levels and trends of mortality in developing countries, makes assumptions about future trends made by the United Nations, compares past assumptions with actual performance, and concludes with a review of recent and possible future changes in the pace of mortality decline. Mortality assumptions made more recently by the World Bank are also reviewed.

The review of past levels and trends is based on mortality estimates prepared for the *World Population Monitoring, 1993* (UN, 1994) as well as the latest United Nations population estimates and

The views and opinions expressed in this paper are those of the author and do not necessarily reflect those of the United Nations.

projections, *World Population Prospects: The 1992 Revision* (UN, 1993).

7.1   Levels and Trends of Mortality Since 1950

Considerable progress has been made in reducing mortality in the less developed regions in recent decades. Over a period of 35 years from the early 1950s to the late 1980s, the average expectation of life at birth in the less developed regions is estimated to have increased 20 years, from about 40.7 in 1950–1955 to 60.7 in 1985–1990 according to the United Nations latest world population estimates and projections (*Table 7.1*). The difference between the more and the less developed regions narrowed during this period, from 25 years in the early 1950s to 13 years in 1985–1990. Life expectancy is projected to further increase to 71.2 in 2020–2025, and the difference between the more and the less developed regions is expected to reduce to seven years. There is a considerable degree of heterogeneity, however, at the regional and subregional levels and differences among countries are even larger as will be discussed below. Progress has been slowest in Africa and life expectancy is still estimated at only about 50 years in East, Central, and West Africa. Mortality is somewhat lower in North and Southern Africa where life expectancy is estimated at 59 and 60 years, respectively, in 1985–1990. In Asia, estimates of life expectancies at birth in 1985–1990 are generally higher and range from 57 in South Asia to 70 in East Asia. (It should be noted that the latter region includes Japan, which is a developed country.) There was little regional diversity in Asia in the early 1950s, with life expectancy estimated at 39 in South Asia, 41 in Southeast Asia, and 43 in East and West Asia. The estimates for the Latin American regions are still higher on the average and fall within a narrow range: 66 in South America and 68 years in the Caribbean and Central America. Among the developing regions of Oceania, life expectancy ranges from 57 years in Melanesia to 69 years in Polynesia.

It should also be noted that the estimates shown in *Table 7.1*, in particular those for the 1980s, are a mixture of estimates and projections and may be revised as more recent data become available.

Table 7.1. Estimated and projected life expectancy at birth, world and major areas and regions: 1950–2025.

Major area and region	Life expectancy (years) 1950-1955	1960-1965	1970-1975	1980-1985	1990-1995	2000-2005	2010-2015	2020-2025
World	46.4	52.4	57.9	61.4	64.7	67.5	70.2	72.5
More developed regions[a]	66.0	69.8	71.1	72.7	74.6	76.2	77.5	78.6
Less developed regions[b]	40.7	47.4	54.5	58.6	62.4	65.5	68.6	71.2
Africa	37.7	41.9	46.1	49.6	53.0	56.2	61.1	65.6
East Africa	36.2	40.7	44.8	46.8	49.0	51.6	58.0	63.6
Central Africa	36.0	39.6	43.9	47.9	51.0	53.3	59.3	65.4
North Africa	41.7	46.2	51.1	56.2	61.0	65.2	68.4	71.1
Southern Africa	44.2	49.2	53.4	57.5	62.5	66.9	70.1	72.5
West Africa	35.6	39.4	43.3	47.3	51.1	54.8	59.1	63.4
Asia	41.0	48.1	56.1	60.5	64.8	68.1	71.1	73.4
East Asia	42.9	51.4	64.1	68.8	71.7	73.9	75.1	77.3
Southeast Asia	40.6	46.4	51.9	58.0	63.3	67.3	70.4	72.9
South Asia	38.8	44.9	49.5	54.4	59.4	63.9	67.7	70.5
West Asia	43.2	50.3	56.5	61.7	66.4	69.6	72.1	74.3
Europe	65.7	69.9	71.5	73.4	75.2	76.8	78.0	79.1
Eastern Europe	62.7	68.6	70.1	70.5	71.3	73.3	74.8	76.3
North Europe	69.2	71.2	72.3	74.0	76.0	77.5	78.6	79.6
South Europe	63.4	68.6	71.4	74.1	76.1	77.5	78.6	79.5
Western Europe	67.6	70.8	71.8	74.3	76.4	77.8	78.9	79.9
Latin America	51.4	56.9	61.1	65.0	68.0	70.3	72.0	73.3
Caribbean	52.0	58.4	63.1	66.2	68.8	70.8	72.5	73.7
Central America	49.3	56.6	61.5	65.5	69.4	71.9	73.6	74.8
South America	52.0	56.8	60.7	64.6	67.4	69.6	71.4	72.7
North America	69.0	70.1	71.5	74.7	76.1	77.5	78.8	79.8
Oceania	61.1	64.8	66.8	70.4	72.6	74.6	76.4	77.9
Australia–New Zealand	69.5	70.9	71.7	75.0	76.7	78.0	79.0	80.0
Melanesia	37.5	45.1	50.4	54.8	58.5	62.3	66.1	69.4
Micronesia	47.5	52.6	57.5	62.6	67.3	71.0	73.7	75.9
Polynesia	55.9	59.9	63.9	68.0	70.8	73.0	74.9	76.5
USSR (former)[c]	64.1	69.2	68.6	67.9	70.4	72.4	74.1	75.5

[a]More developed regions comprise North America, Japan, Europe, Australia–New Zealand, and the former USSR.
[b]Less developed regions comprise all regions of Africa, Latin America, Asia (excluding Japan), and Melanesia, Micronesia, and Polynesia.
[c]Including Armenia, Azerbaijan, Belarus, Georgia, Moldova, Russia, Ukraine, Kazakhstan, Kyrgyzstan, Tajikistan, Turkmenistan, and Uzbekistan. Estonia, Latvia, and Lithuania are included in North Europe.
Source: UN, 1993:Table A.15.

Table 7.2. Distribution of developing countries[a] with relatively reliable data according to the reference period of latest estimate, since 1970.

Region	Number of countries in region	Number of countries				
		Total	Prior to 1975	1975–1979	1980–1984	1985 and later
With estimates of life expectancy at birth						
Africa	51	16	3	4	7	2
Asia and Oceania	42	23	–	5	5	13
Latin America	27	23	5	3	9	6
Total	120	62	8	12	21	21
With estimates of infant and child mortality						
Africa	51	36	2	9	12	13
Asia and Oceania	42	31	–	3	5	23
Latin America	27	27	–	–	5	22
Total	120	94	2	12	22	58

[a]Countries with an estimated population of 300,000 or more in 1990.
Source: UN, 1994.

The availability of data on mortality in developing countries has improved considerably during the past two decades. Vital registration is gradually becoming more complete, particularly in Latin America and East Asia. Data that permit estimation of infant and child mortality have been widely collected in censuses and surveys, in particular those conducted by the World Fertility Survey program (WFS) and more recently by the Demographic and Health Surveys (DHS). Despite these improvements, lack of reliable data continues to be a serious handicap in the analysis of mortality in developing countries. *Table 7.2* shows the distribution of countries with relatively reliable data since 1970 together with the reference period of the latest estimate. With regard to recency of data, less than half of the countries have any data referring to 1985 and later. This is because the results of the 1990 censuses have not yet been analyzed. However, estimates for the second half of the 1980s have successfully been provided by DHS for countries covered by that survey. Twenty-six countries have no mortality data since 1970. Obviously, countries for which data on mortality are available may not necessarily be representative of other countries since mortality conditions are likely to be worse in countries lacking data. There are no recent surveys or registration data, for example, in countries affected by war or civil strife. The countries without any national-level data, however, form only about 4 percent of the total population of the less developed regions, so that even large errors in the country estimates will not affect the regional totals very much.

Although the data situation has improved in Africa, it is still more problematic there than in other less developed regions to estimate levels and trends. The only countries in sub-Saharan Africa with reliable systems of vital registration from which life tables can be derived are three small island countries in the Indian Ocean: Mauritius, Réunion, and the Seychelles. All three countries have reached low levels of mortality with life expectancies now above 69 years. Most of the available information in mainland sub-Saharan Africa refers to child mortality. Few countries have adequate data on adult mortality.

Mortality is high throughout most of sub-Saharan Africa, but there is variation among countries in terms of both levels and trends. Child mortality has generally been most severe in West Africa, a fact attributed both to the level of socioeconomic development and to environmental factors (Blacker, 1991). Although differences with the other regions have narrowed, West Africa as a whole still has the highest child mortality on the continent. Sierra Leone, a West African country, exhibits the highest mortality ever measured in a contemporary country: a probability of dying by age 5 of 364 per 1,000 in 1971, declining to 334 per 1,000 in 1981 according to the 1974 and 1985 censuses. Gambia and Mali in West Africa and Malawi in East Africa which had similarly high levels of child mortality in the 1970s have experienced larger improvements, but the latest estimates of mortality under the age of 5 for these countries are still above 240 per 1,000. The lowest mortality in mainland sub-Saharan Africa has been achieved by Kenya and Zimbabwe in East Africa and Botswana in Southern Africa. The low child mortality in Botswana (65 per 1,000 in 1984) may be explained, in addition to its impressive economic growth during the 1970s and 1980s, by the high proportion of women receiving prenatal care and immunization with tetanus toxoid, the high proportion of births delivered by trained health personnel, and the high immunization coverage of children (Lesetedi *et al.*, 1989; World Bank, 1992). Immunization coverage and proportions of women receiving prenatal care are also high in Kenya and Zimbabwe (Kenya, 1989; Zimbabwe, 1989).

The countries of North Africa have experienced more rapid mortality declines with an acceleration in the decline since the mid-1970s or late 1970s. In Algeria, the only country in the region with a series of life tables derived from vital registration, life expectancy increased slowly from 53 in 1970 to 57 in 1978 and then to 64 in 1985, an annual increase of one year. Life tables after 1985 are not yet available, but later data on infants show that mortality has continued to decline. The latest official life table for Egypt refers to 1975–1977, when life expectancy at birth was estimated at 53 years. Later data on infant and child mortality show that mortality has declined rapidly since then: mortality fell by more than half between 1976 and 1986. In Tunisia, which currently has the lowest infant and child mortality rates in North Africa, the decline has been equally impressive, from an under-five mortality of 204 per 1,000 in 1968–1969 to 65 per 1,000 in 1983–1987 according to a 1968–1969 demographic survey, the 1975 census, and the 1988 DHS.

Asia presents the most varied picture among the developing regions, both in terms of levels and trends in mortality and in terms of availability and quality of data, reflecting very diverse histories and levels of development.

East Asia has achieved the lowest mortality levels in the region. The main reason here is obviously the remarkable progress achieved by China. Life expectancy in China was estimated at 41 in 1950–1955, reached 68 in 1981 and despite the high level continued to increase to 72 in 1986, an annual increase of almost a year; infant mortality was estimated at 195 per 1,000 in 1950–1955, reached 35 in 1981 and 22 in 1986. The other countries of the region with available data, Hong Kong and the Republic of Korea, have also successfully reduced their mortality levels. According to its civil registration data, Hong Kong now has the lowest mortality among all developing countries with a life expectancy in 1987–1989 of 77 years (80 for females and 74 for males) and an infant and under-five mortality of 7 and 9 per 1,000, respectively.

Southeast Asia is characterized by a wide disparity of mortality levels and trends. Brunei Darussalam, peninsular Malaysia, and Singapore have achieved mortality levels comparable to those of developed countries with life-expectancy estimates above 70. Progress has also been made in other countries of the region, particularly in Thailand where expectation of life at birth reached 66 in 1985–1986 and in the Philippines where it reached 64 in 1987–1989. On the other hand, the region includes countries such as East Timor, Cambodia, and Lao People's Democratic Republic where mortality is believed to be high and life expectancy estimated to be below 50 years.

South Asia exhibits the highest mortality levels and has experienced the slowest decline in Asia, although one country in that region, Sri Lanka, has attained relatively low mortality: life expectancy was 69 in 1980–1981, and is now estimated to exceed 70. Afghanistan has the highest mortality in the region which is not surprising in view of the social and political circumstances of that country. Although mortality is still high in the three largest countries of the Indian subcontinent – Bangladesh, India, and Pakistan – the levels have been declining. In Bangladesh, life expectancy increased from 48 in the late 1970s to 56 in 1987. In India, life expectancy was estimated at 53 in 1981–1983. More recent data from the Sample Registration System show that infant mortality has continued to decline, from 107 per 1,000 in 1981–1983 to 94 per 1,000 in 1988. The latest data for Pakistan give a life expectancy of 60 in 1984–1988, an increase from 53 in 1972–1981.

In West Asia, several countries have experienced very rapid declines, not only the small oil-producing countries of the region, but also countries such as Jordan, the Syrian Arab Republic, and Turkey. Cyprus and Israel have the lowest mortality in the region with life expectancies above 75, followed by Kuwait where life expectancy was estimated at 72 in 1984–1986. The only country with high mortality in the region is Yemen, where infant and under-five mortality were 162 and 237 per 1,000, respectively, according to the 1979 WFS.

As mentioned earlier, Latin America has achieved lower mortality levels than Africa and Asia. The mortality decline in the Caribbean Islands is particularly impressive with levels of life expectancy reaching those of the developed countries despite lower levels of economic development. Life expectancy at birth is estimated to be above 70 in all islands except the Dominican Republic and Haiti. In Cuba and Puerto Rico life expectancy was 75 in

1985–1986 and 1986–1988, respectively, the highest in Latin America. To give an example of the mortality decline that has occurred in some of those countries, life expectancy at birth in Barbados increased from 57 in 1950–1955 to 72 in 1980. Infant mortality declined from 132 per 1,000 in the early 1950s to 13 per 1,000 in the late 1980s, or by over 90 percent. On the other hand, the decline has been slow in the Dominican Republic and Haiti. Under-five mortality in Haiti was still estimated at 193 per 1,000 in 1983, higher than in many African countries.

Two countries in Central America – Costa Rica and Panama – have also achieved very low levels of mortality with life expectancies above 70. In Mexico, the largest country of the region, life expectancy at birth increased from 61 in 1970 to 66 in 1980 and is now believed to be close to 70.

In South America, the lowest mortality levels are observed in Argentina, Chile, Uruguay, and Venezuela. In Chile, life expectancy at birth increased from 62 to 71 during the 12-year period between 1970 and 1982, and infant and child mortality declined by almost 70 percent during the same period. Recent data show a continuing but slower decline during the 1980s. Bolivia and Peru, on the other hand, have the highest mortality in the region, but like all South American countries, have experienced substantial mortality reductions. In Bolivia, for example, the probability of dying by age 5 declined by almost half between 1972 and 1988, from 254 to 130 per 1,000. In Brazil, the largest country of the region, with half its population, the mortality decline has been moderate. Life expectancy at birth increased from 58 in 1970 to 62 in 1976–1980 and may be above 65 at present.

Mortality has also declined steadily in the developing countries of Oceania, and some countries have achieved low levels of mortality. In Guam, Micronesia, life expectancy was estimated at 73 in 1979–1981 and infant mortality at 11 per 1,000 in 1985–1987. The only countries where mortality is still high is Kiribati, a small island in Micronesia, where under-five mortality was estimated at 123 in 1981 according to the 1985 census and in Papua New Guinea, Melanesia, where under-five mortality was estimated at 96 in 1976.

The United Nations has recently completed a review of child mortality since the 1960s in developing countries with an estimated

1990 population of 1 million or more (UN, 1992). Among the countries with adequate estimates of the probability of dying by age 5 for two points in time between 1960 and 1985, altogether 79 observations, child mortality declined by about 3 percent per annum. Asia and Latin America both experienced rates slightly above this average, whereas the rate of decline in Africa was only about 2 percent per annum. These figures may be somewhat different, however, if data for all countries were available. In sub-Saharan Africa, there are a few countries where available data show that child mortality declines may have stalled or even increased, although the observed trend could be due to poor data quality. Data are so defective in some countries, not only in Africa, that it is not really possible to tell how mortality has evolved. In many countries outside sub-Saharan Africa with sufficient data to indicate a change in trends, child mortality decline appears to have accelerated in the late 1970s and in the 1980s.

7.2 Assumptions about Future Trends in Mortality

The United Nations has prepared global population projections since the 1950s. The details of the projections have expanded over time with improvements in data and methods of analysis and with the utilization of computer technology. Detailed mortality assumptions by country were first made in 1968. The assumptions are formulated in terms of life expectancy at birth and age and sex patterns of probabilities of surviving, corresponding to the different levels of life expectancy at birth. The age-specific survival ratios needed for the projections are derived from appropriate model life tables. For countries with reliable data on mortality by age and sex, that information is used to complement the derivation of the required survival ratios. A national life table for a given date is used as a base for the projections, and, as mortality is projected to decline, it is assumed that the mortality rates of the national life table will gradually approach those of a model life table. This procedure has been referred to as the "modified method" of mortality projection (UN, 1977a). For countries without reliable mortality data by age and sex, the mortality rates are taken directly from

the model life tables selected for the projections. The Coale and
Demeny regional model life tables (Coale and Demeny, 1966, 1983)
and, since the 1988 assessment, the United Nations model life tables for developing countries (UN, 1982) are used in preparing the
United Nations projections.

One of the roles of the United Nations projections is to produce comparable global and interregional prospects of population.
To maintain comparability in the assumptions of mortality between
regions and among countries within regions, a uniform procedure
is used for all countries. The assumptions about life expectancy at
birth are made to follow models of mortality improvement. These
models have been developed on the basis of data from countries
with reliable death statistics and have been revised and modified
as new data have become available, reflecting the most recent observations about mortality decline. It has generally been assumed
that life expectancy at birth would increase by half a year annually until life expectancy for females reaches 55, 62.5, or 65 years,
followed by a slowdown in the gain thereafter. In countries where
evidence suggests that the mortality decline has been faster or slower
than the model implies, the assumptions have been adjusted. The
most recent working model, which was developed for the 1988 assessment and summarized in *Table 7.3*, introduces three variations
in the speed of improvement and labels them fast, middle, and slow
models.

In the model developed for the 1973 assessment, it was assumed
that the highest female life expectancy that could be attained would
be 77.5 years, the value given as maximum in the Coale–Demeny regional model life tables, and the highest male life expectancy, 72.6
years, the value given as maximum in the first United Nations model
life tables (*Table 7.4*). In the 1978 assessment, the maximum life
expectancies were raised to 80 for females and 73.5 for males. In
the 1982 assessment, the maxima were further raised to 82.5 years
for females and 75 for males. The Coale–Demeny regional model
life tables were extrapolated to incorporate survival ratios corresponding to these higher levels of life expectancies. The most recent
model, developed for the 1988 assessment, represents a major revision in terms of long-range mortality assumptions. The highest life
expectancies at birth were extended to 87.5 for females and 82.5 for

Table 7.3. Working model for mortality improvement, quinquennial gains (in years) in life expectancy at birth ($^o e_o$) according to initial level of mortality.

Initial mortality level	Fast Male	Female	Middle Male	Female	Slow Male	Female
55.0–57.5	2.5	2.5	2.5	2.5	2.0	2.0
57.5–60.0	2.5	2.5	2.5	2.5	2.0	2.0
60.0–62.5	2.5	2.5	2.3	2.5	2.0	2.0
62.5–65.0	2.3	2.5	2.0	2.5	2.0	2.0
65.0–67.5	2.0	2.5	1.5	2.3	1.5	2.0
67.5–70.0	1.5	2.3	1.2	2.0	1.0	1.5
70.0–72.5	1.2	2.0	1.0	1.5	0.8	1.2
72.5–75.0	1.0	1.5	0.8	1.2	0.5	1.0
75.0–77.5	0.8	1.2	0.5	1.0	0.3	0.8
77.5–80.0	0.5	1.0	0.4	0.8	0.3	0.5
80.0–82.5	0.5	0.8	0.4	0.5	0.3	0.3
82.5–85.0	–	0.5	–	0.4	–	0.3
85.0–87.5	–	0.5	–	0.4	–	0.3

Source: UN, 1989:Table 1.4.

Table 7.4. Limit life expectancies in United Nations working models of mortality decline.

Assessment year	Male	Female
1973	72.6	77.5
1978	73.5	80.0
1982	75.0	82.5
1988	82.5	87.5

Sources: UN, 1977b:11; 1981:3; 1985:10; and 1989:15.

males. In order to extend the model life tables to the new maximum life expectancies, working life tables with life expectancies of 87.5 for females and 82.5 for males were constructed by using the reduced values of age-specific probabilities of dying (qx) available from countries that now have the lowest mortality rates. The highest levels of survival of each of the nine model life tables (West, North, South, and East model of the Coale and Demeny regional model life tables and General, Latin American, Chilean, Far Eastern, and South Asian model life tables of the United Nations) were linked individually with the age-specific survival ratios derived from the working life table so that survival ratios of other intermediate mortality levels could be obtained through interpolation (UN, 1989). These survival ratios have been used in the 1988, 1990, and 1992 revisions of the population projections.

Several developing countries have now surpassed the maximum life expectancy for females of 77.5 assumed in 1973. Only one country, Hong Kong, is currently estimated to have a life expectancy above 80 for females, the maximum assumed in 1980, although several other countries, mainly small island countries, have reached life expectancies close to that level. No country has yet reached the limit for females set in 1982, but two developed countries – Japan and Sweden – have surpassed the limit assumed for males, 75 years.

The most recent United Nations projections have taken into account the effects of the acquired immunodeficiency syndrome (AIDS) pandemic for 15 high prevalence countries in sub-Saharan Africa. The number of deaths related to AIDS is estimated and projected using an epidemiological model developed by the World Health Organization (Chin and Lwanga, 1991). In applying the model at the United Nations, it is assumed that there are no new adult human immunodeficiency virus (HIV) infections after 2005; mother-to-child infections do continue to occur after this date and AIDS deaths follow for many years thereafter due to the long latency period between HIV and AIDS. This assumption has little effect on projected AIDS mortality until after 2015. The estimates of deaths due to AIDS by age and sex, for each five-year period, are then integrated into the existing (non-AIDS) model life tables, producing a set of life tables which incorporates the risk of dying from AIDS and which are used for the projections.

The World Bank has published projections in recent years; the first results were published in *World Development Report 1978* (World Bank, 1978). Detailed results of the projections have only been published since 1984 in *World Population Projections,* various years. The base-year mortality estimates used in the World Bank projections are mainly obtained from the United Nations, but methods used to prepare assumptions about future trends are different. In the 1984 to 1987–1988 assessments, life expectancy at birth was projected with a model using past patterns of relationships between the change in life expectancy, the level of life expectancy, and the female primary school enrollment ratio. Two different schedules of annual increments in female life expectancy were developed: one for countries with female primary school enrollment less than 70 percent and another for those where the enrollment is 70 percent or more. For a given expectation of life at birth, survival ratios for males and females were derived from the Coale and Demeny regional model life tables. In the more recent projections, a different procedure has been used to project mortality (Bulatao and Bos, 1989). Life expectancy and infant mortality are projected separately using logistic functions, taking into account past trends and socioeconomic factors. The logistic function is determined so that life expectancy rises most rapidly from a level of 50 years and increasingly slowly at higher levels. Rates of change are estimated from past rates of change and from the female secondary school enrollment ratio or, in a few cases where data on school enrollment are not available, from the percent urban. Maximum life expectancies were assumed to be 90 for females and 83.3 for males. Life tables are selected from the Coale–Demeny regional model life tables combining different levels to give exactly the desired infant mortality rate and life expectancy. Coale and Guo's (1989) new extended model life tables are used at low levels of mortality. The most recent World Bank projections have also taken into account the effects of AIDS, applying an epidemiological model developed by Bulatao (1991) and Bos *et al.* (1992).

The World Bank assumptions show more variation among individual countries than do those assumed by the United Nations, and indicate, on average, slightly faster decline at lower levels of life expectancy and slower decline at higher levels. Mortality assumptions for the less developed regions according to different United Nations and World Bank assessments are shown in *Tables 7.5* and *7.6*.

7.3 Comparison of Past Assumptions with Actual Performance

Since the United Nations has a long series of population estimates and projections, assumptions made in past projections can be compared to more recent assumptions and to actual performance. *Table 7.5* shows estimated and projected life expectancies at birth for the less developed regions for different periods available from the

160   *Birgitta Bucht*

Table 7.5. Estimated and projected life expectancy at birth for less developed regions, both sexes, according to different United Nations assessments.

Year	1980–1985	1985–1990	1990–1995	2020–2025
1968	58.0	60.6	63.0	–
1973	56.7	58.7	60.7	–
1978	57.1	59.2	61.1	–
1980	57.0	58.9	60.7	69.6
1982	56.6	58.2	60.0	68.9
1984	57.3	59.1	60.8	69.5
1988	57.6	59.7	61.5	70.4
1990	59.4	61.4	63.3	71.6
1992	58.6	60.7	62.4	71.2

Sources: UN, 1973:Table A.2.1; 1977b:Table 41; 1979; 1981:Table A-15; 1985:Table A-15; 1986:Table A-15; 1989:Table 15; 1991:Table 44; and 1993:Table A-15.

Table 7.6. Estimated and projected life expectancy at birth for less developed regions, both sexes, according to different World Bank assessments.

Year	1980–1985	1985–1990	1990–1995	2020–2025
1984	59.5	61.2	62.8	70.7
1985	59.4	61.1	62.8	70.8
1987–1988	–	61.4	62.9	70.3
1989–1990	–	62.1	63.6	69.3
1992–1993	–	61.9	63.2	71.1

Sources: Vu, 1984, 1985; Zachariah and Vu, 1988; Bulatao *et al.*, 1990; and Bos *et al.*, 1992.

different series of United Nations projections prepared between 1968 and 1992. The projected life expectancy at birth for the less developed regions as a whole has turned out to be reasonably accurate in each revision carried out over a quarter of a century. In 1968, when detailed projections were first performed for each country, life expectancy at birth was projected to be 60.6 in 1985–1990 for the less developed regions. In 1992, it was estimated at 60.7 for the same period. The long-range projections show a small and gradual improvement in assumed mortality levels over time. In 1980, life expectancy at birth was projected to be 69.6 in 2020–2025. In 1992, it was projected to be 71.2 in the same period.

It is remarkable that the projected life expectancy for the less developed regions has changed so little despite large revisions for individual countries. Country estimates have been raised or lowered as new data have become available and with new and better methods of estimating mortality. Several countries have experienced unforeseen and almost spectacular gains in the life expectancy at birth, most notably China, the most populous country in the world. The 1968 mortality assumption for China, a life expectancy of 62 years in 1985–1990, was surpassed by 10 years. The mortality decline has been slower than projected in a sufficient number of countries, however, to offset the more rapid decline in others so that the regional averages have not changed much. For the more developed regions, in contrast, the projected life expectancies have gradually been revised upward.

It should be noted that the sudden increase in life expectancy at birth between the 1988 and the 1990 revisions is partly the result of a new method of calculating life expectancy at the regional and global levels from country-specific figures. In the earlier revisions, regional and global life expectancies were estimated by weighing the country-specific life expectancy figures by the number of births. This method provided unbiased estimates only when countries within the region had similar age structures and similar levels of fertility. Beginning with the 1990 revision, the method was changed to exactly calculate survival ratios (and hence life expectancies) at the regional and country levels by aggregating deaths and population by age and sex at the country level (UN, 1991:91).

7.4 Possible Changes in the Pace of Future Mortality Decline

There has been some concern that the deteriorating economic conditions since the mid-1970s in many developing countries would lead to a slowdown or stagnation in the mortality decline because of a reduction in expenditures on social services implemented to cope with the economic crisis. There is no evidence yet of such a change except possibly for a few countries in sub-Saharan Africa where the mortality trends are difficult to interpret. In countries with negative growth of GDP per capita from 1965–1980 or 1980–1990 (World

Bank, 1992) and with sufficient data to estimate mortality trends, for example, Senegal in sub-Saharan Africa and several countries in Latin America, mortality has continued to decline without change. However, one cannot rule out the possibility that the deterioration in economic conditions and reduced spending on health could have a delayed effect on mortality in some countries.

A most important measure that is likely to have a substantial effect on mortality trends in the near future is the child survival programs that have been implemented during the 1980s by governments and international organizations. These programs have consisted mainly in making a few simple and low-cost technologies widely available, in particular immunization and oral rehydration therapy (ORT). When the World Health Organization launched its Expanded Programme on Immunization in 1974, it was estimated that less than 5 percent of children in the developing world were immunized (UNICEF, 1989). In 1985, the coverage had increased to around 30 percent for measles and 40 percent for the other targeted diseases. Since then, many countries have sharply increased their coverage, and it is estimated that by 1990 between 79 and 90 percent of infants were vaccinated against the target diseases. Immunization of women against tetanus still lags behind at about 56 percent (UNICEF, 1992). Awareness and use of oral rehydration therapy have also increased substantially. These efforts should have an important impact on child mortality, and favorable results have already been reported in a number of countries. However, since the programs have only recently gained momentum in many countries and since data for the late 1980s are still not available in many countries, the full impact of these programs cannot yet be measured.

Other factors that will affect child survival in the future are increasing education of women and declines in fertility, with a reduction in high-risk births. Reduced fertility is also likely to have indirect positive effects on a child's survival chances because a family with fewer children can allocate more resources per child, including parental care and attention, food, schooling, and access to health services. There is also a reduced risk of infection of children in smaller, less-crowded households. Maternal mortality which is high in many developing countries is also lowered with fertility declines.

In the near future, the outlook in general indicates a continuation of the mortality decline. Among the helpful factors will be, in addition to those mentioned above, further improvements in education, medical research, training of health personnel, and the spread of democracy which will enable people to put pressure on governments to improve health services.

Several developing countries have reached mortality levels comparable to those in the developed countries, even in countries where the levels of economic development are far behind those of the developed countries. There is no reason that the mortality declines will not continue and that other countries will follow, barring of course wars, famines, and other catastrophes.

This does not mean that it is going to be easy to achieve continued impressive improvements. The progress in sub-Saharan Africa is likely to still lag behind that of the other developing regions. Apart from the droughts and famines that are plaguing substantial parts of Africa at the present time and the civil strife that exists not only in Africa but also in Asia, there are two important concerns: the AIDS epidemic and the spread of chloroquine-resistant malaria. Both are likely to have a particularly devastating effect in sub-Saharan Africa. Environmental problems of various kinds aggravated by population growth, such as water scarcity and loss of agricultural land and cutbacks in food production, could also lead to increased risks to health.

References

Blacker, J.G.C., 1991, Infant and child mortality: Development, environment, and custom, in R.G. Feachem and D.T. Jamison, eds., *Disease and Mortality in Sub-Saharan Africa,* World Bank/Oxford University Press, New York, NY, USA.

Bos, E., My T. Vu, Levin, A., and Bulatao, R.A., 1992, *World Population Projections 1992–1993 Edition: Estimates and Projections with Related Demographic Statistics,* World Bank/Johns Hopkins University Press, Baltimore, MD, USA.

Bulatao, R.A., 1991, The Bulatao approach: Projecting the demographic impact of the HIV epidemic using standard parameters, in *The AIDS Epidemic and Its Demographic Consequences,* Sales No. E.91.XIII.5, United Nations, New York, NY, USA.

Bulatao, R.A., and Bos, E. (with P.W. Stephens and My T. Vu), 1989, Projecting Mortality for All Countries, Policy, Planning, and Population Research Working Paper Series 337, World Bank, Population and Human Resources Department, Washington, DC, USA.

Bulatao, R.A., Bos, E., Stephens, P.W., and My T. Vu, 1990, *World Population Projections 1989–1990 Edition: Short- and Long-Term Estimates*, World Bank/Johns Hopkins University Press, Baltimore, MD, USA.

Chin, J., and Lwanga, S.K., 1991, The World Health Organization approach: Projections of non-paediatric HIV infection and AIDS in pattern II areas, in *The AIDS Epidemic and Its Demographic Consequences*, Sales No. E.91.XIII.5, United Nations, New York, NY, USA.

Coale, A.J., and Demeny, P., 1966, *Regional Model Life Tables and Stable Populations*, Princeton University Press, Princeton, NJ, USA.

Coale, A.J., and Demeny, P. (with B. Vaughan), 1983, *Regional Model Life Tables and Stable Populations*, 2nd Edition, Academic Press, New York, NY, USA.

Coale, A.J., and Guang Guo, 1989, Revised model life tables at very low levels of mortality, *Population Index* **55**(4).

Kenya, 1989, *Kenya Demographic and Health Survey, 1989*, Ministry of Home Affairs and National Heritage, National Council for Population and Development, Nairobi, Kenya; and Institute for Resource Development/Macro Systems, Inc., Columbia, MD, USA.

Lesetedi, L.T., Mompati, G.D., Khulumani, P., Lesetedi, G.N., and Rutenberg, N., 1989, *Botswana Family Health Survey II, 1988*, Ministry of Finance and Development Planning, Gaborone, Botswana; and Institute for Resource Development/Macro Systems, Inc., Columbia, MD, USA.

UN, 1973, *World Population Prospects as Assessed in 1968*, Population Studies, No. 53, Sales No. E.72.XIII.4, United Nations, New York, NY, USA.

UN, 1977a, *A Modified Method Estimating Age-Specific Survival Ratios*, ESA/P/WP.61, United Nations, New York, NY, USA.

UN, 1977b, *World Population Prospects as Assessed in 1973*, Population Studies, No. 60, Sales No. E.76.XIII.4, United Nations, New York, NY, USA.

UN, 1979, *World Population Trends and Prospects by Country, 1950–2000: Summary Report of the 1978 Assessment*, ST/ESA/SER.R/33, United Nations, New York, NY, USA.

UN, 1981, *World Population Prospects as Assessed in 1980*, Population Studies, No. 78, Sales No. E.81.XIII.8, United Nations, New York, NY, USA.

UN, 1982, *Model Life Tables for Developing Countries*, Population Studies, No. 77, Sales No. E.81.XIII.7, United Nations, New York, NY, USA.

UN, 1985, *World Population Prospects, Estimates and Projections as Assessed in 1982,* Population Studies, No. 86, Sales No. E.83.XIII.5, United Nations, New York, NY, USA.

UN, 1986, *World Population Prospects, Estimates and Projections as Assessed in 1984,* Population Studies, No. 98, Sales No. E.86.XIII.3, United Nations, New York, NY, USA.

UN, 1989, *World Population Prospects 1988,* Population Studies, No. 106, Sales No. E.88.XIII.7, United Nations, New York, NY, USA.

UN, 1991, *World Population Prospects: 1990,* Population Studies, No. 120, Publication No. ST/ESA/SER.A/120, Department of International and Social Affairs, United Nations, New York, NY, USA.

UN, 1992, *Child Mortality Since the 1960s: A Database for Developing Countries,* Sales No. E.92.XIII.10, United Nations, New York, NY, USA.

UN, 1993, *World Population Prospects: The 1992 Revision,* United Nations, New York, NY, USA.

UN, 1994, *World Population Monitoring, 1993,* ESA/P/WP.121, United Nations, New York, NY, USA.

UNICEF, 1989, *The State of the World's Children 1989,* United Nations Children's Fund/Oxford University Press, New York, NY, USA.

UNICEF, 1992, *The State of the World's Children 1992,* United Nations Children's Fund/Oxford University Press, New York, NY, USA.

Vu, My T., 1984, *World Population Projections 1984: Short- and Long-Term Estimates by Age and Sex with Related Demographic Statistics,* World Bank, Washington, DC, USA.

Vu, My T., 1985, *World Population Projections 1985: Short- and Long-Term Estimates by Age and Sex with Related Demographic Statistics,* World Bank/Johns Hopkins University Press, Baltimore, MD, USA.

World Bank, 1978, *World Development Report 1978,* Washington, DC, USA.

World Bank, 1992, *World Development Report 1992,* World Bank/Oxford University Press, New York, NY, USA.

Zachariah, K.C., and Vu, My T., 1988, *World Population Projections 1987–1988 Edition: Short- and Long-Term Estimates,* World Bank/Johns Hopkins University Press, Baltimore, MD, USA.

Zimbabwe, 1989, *Zimbabwe Demographic and Health Survey, 1988,* Ministry of Finance, Economic Planning, and Development, Central Statistical Office, Harare, Zimbabwe; and Institute for Resource Development/Macro Systems, Inc., Columbia, MD, USA.

Chapter 8

Mortality in Sub-Saharan Africa: Trends and Prospects

Michel Garenne

Interest in the population growth of the Third World began after World War II, owing mostly to the growing concern for *population pressure* and its possible effects upon the world economy, ecology, and political balance. The sources of the high rate of population growth were the fast-declining mortality and to a lesser extent the increasing natality. The primary concern was with Asia, in particular China and the Indian subcontinent, and with Latin America, in particular Central America. Somewhat later, the demography of sub-Saharan Africa became a subject for research.

The first systematic studies of African populations took place in the early 1960s. A team of researchers working at Princeton University published the first comprehensive account of African demography in 1968 (Brass, 1968). At about the same time, a group of French demographers published a summary of their experiences and findings on tropical Africa, with emphasis on the sample surveys conducted by the French National Statistical Office (INSEE) beginning in 1954 (GDA, 1967). Since this pioneer period, only a few syntheses on the population dynamics of the region have been published. Mandjale (1985) analyzes infant and child mortality. Van de Walle *et al.*, (1988) review the state of African demography. The collection of work edited by Feachem and Jamison (1991) focuses on morbidity and mortality.

Fertility in Africa experienced minimal fluctuations over the past 50 years, whereas mortality underwent a major decline, creating considerable potential for population growth. The decline in mortality has been documented only recently in a systematic way (Hill and Hill, 1988; Hill, 1991; Timaeus, 1991). However, there is a growing concern that the mortality decline will not continue, and may even be reversed under new conditions such as the AIDS epidemic.

This chapter reviews the available evidence of mortality decline, before and after independence, and discusses the future of mortality. It focuses on the countries of continental sub-Saharan Africa listed in *Table 8.1*. The islands such as Cape Verde, Sao Tome and Principe, Mauritius, and the Seychelles have very different population dynamics, and data from Madagascar are too poor to be used.

8.1   The Colonial Period: 1920–1959

8.1.1   Mortality trends

Data from the end of the colonial period (1920–1959) are very scarce, and there is virtually no data available on tropical Africa prior to 1915. The only long-term series available come from Dakar and Saint-Louis, two cities in Senegal, where a high-quality vital registration system has been maintained. The vital registration data from Saint-Louis were analyzed in a PhD dissertation (Diop, 1990), and the vital data from Dakar were discussed in a recent paper (Garenne *et al.*, 1993). In Dakar, there was clear evidence of a decline in mortality since at least 1920, the 1915–1919 period being seriously disturbed by the 1918 influenza world epidemic as well as by a local plague epidemic. In Saint-Louis, mortality has been declining steadily since 1930, the earliest date for which data were analyzed (*Figure 8.1*). In both cases, the crude death rates at the beginning of the series were among the highest recorded, and were only slightly lower than the crude birth rate: CDR = 35/1000 in Dakar during the 1920–1924 period, and CDR = 36/1000 in Saint-Louis

Table 8.1. Reconstructed levels and trends in child mortality in continental sub-Saharan Africa, by country and period: probability of dying before age 5, $q(5)$, per 1,000.

Country	<1960	1960	1965	1970	1975	1980	1985
Angola	360	–	–	–	–	–	–
Benin	360	–	–	255	240	200	–
Botswana	–	175	160	140	120	90	60
Burkina Faso	420	315	295	275	255	220	215
Burundi	–	270	240	220	220	210	175
Cameroon	290	–	235	220	185	–	–
Central Afr. Rep.	–	325	295	245	–	–	–
Chad	340	310	–	–	–	–	–
Congo, People's Rep.	290	200	165	140	–	–	–
Côte d'Ivoire	–	–	265	245	210	165	140
Equatorial Guinea	–	–	–	–	–	–	–
Ethiopia	–	235	230	225	220	–	–
Gabon	350	250	–	–	–	–	–
Gambia	–	350	345	310	275	240	–
Ghana	370	220	210	185	170	155	160
Guinea (Conakry)	380	–	–	–	–	–	–
Guinea-Bissau	300	–	–	–	–	–	–
Kenya	260	210	185	165	145	125	100
Lesotho	–	200	195	185	175	–	–
Liberia	–	280	270	255	245	235	220
Malawi	–	360	345	335	320	285	–
Mali	385	–	–	–	360	310	250
Mozambique	260	–	280	280	280	–	–
Namibia	–	–	–	–	–	–	–
Niger	300	–	–	–	–	–	–
Nigeria	–	–	–	–	–	195	190
Rwanda	–	240	220	220	220	220	–
Senegal	375	300	295	285	265	220	190
Sierra Leone	–	400	385	365	–	–	–
Somalia	–	–	240	225	210	–	–
South Africa	–	–	–	–	–	–	–
Sudan	–	220	205	170	150	145	135
Swaziland	240	230	220	215	–	–	–
Tanzania	260	240	235	225	215	–	–
Togo	350	300	245	220	200	180	160
Uganda	245	225	195	180	175	185	185
Zaire	285	–	–	–	235	210	200
Zambia	–	220	190	180	165	150	–
Zimbabwe	–	160	155	145	140	135	95

Source: Adapted from Hill, 1992.

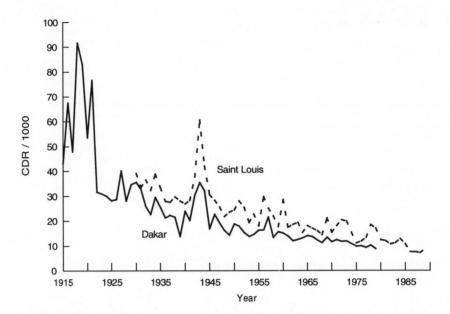

Figure 8.1. Crude death rates in Dakar and Saint-Louis (Senegal): vital registration 1915–1989. Source: Garenne *et al.*, 1993.

in 1930–1934. It is reasonable to conclude that mortality began to decline dramatically during the period just following World War I. This finding is confirmed by the fact that the population increased significantly between 1920 and 1960, as shown by the series of administrative censuses in Senegal (Becker and Martin, 1983).

Other evidence is available in early censuses and from the retrospective questioning of mothers. In Ghana, the probability of dying before the fifth birthday, $q(5)$, was estimated at 380/1000 in 1933 and has been declining since then. In Angola, $q(5)$ was estimated at 356 in 1926 (Hill, 1991). Again, these values are very high, and they probably no longer exist in any country of the continent.

By 1960, when most countries obtained independence, major differences in infant and child mortality already existed among countries. The quotient $q(5)$ ranged from 160/1000 in Zimbabwe to 400/1000 in Sierra Leone (*Table 8.1*). These large differences among countries were attributed primarily to the level of development (for instance, Zimbabwe and Botswana were countries much wealthier than the average) and to a certain extent to the environment: the highland countries of East Africa were reputed to have fewer cases of malaria and therefore a lower mortality rate (Blacker, 1991). The classic exception to this pattern was Malawi, a country known to have a high prevalence of malnutrition and vitamin-A deficiency (Feachem and Jamison, 1991).

8.1.2 Socioeconomic change

Reasons for the mortality decline during the 40 years following World War I are poorly understood. Colonial powers opened roads in most of Africa, sometimes railways, which have drawn most of the villages out of their isolation. One noticeable consequence of improving communications, well documented in the past in Europe and also in the 20th century in India (Davis, 1951), is the drastic reduction in the number of famines. In northern Senegal in the 19th century, there were famines every three to four years (Chastanet, 1982). Severe famines virtually disappeared after World War I, with the exception of the year 1942, and, although food shortages continued to occur with the same frequency, they became far less acute. Colonization also brought to Africa the monetary economy, in particular the following cash crops – peanuts, coffee, cocoa, rubber – which gave the peasants the power to purchase what they needed.

Cities were rare and small in Africa prior to 1900. However, they developed rapidly thereafter, which subsequently provided for the opening of schools and the creation of an elite branch of Africans who had a modern education. The level of modern education has been shown to be closely associated with mortality decline throughout the world (Caldwell, 1986).

8.1.3 Public health

In addition to improving socioeconomic conditions, considerable efforts were made to improve public health. Health programs focused on diseases affecting the expatriate community, especially adults, but they were directed to the whole population as well. Modern hospitals were built at the turn of the century. Local dispensaries soon followed in the secondary towns. The water supply was treated in cities at about the same period (1928 in Dakar).

Newly developed vaccines against tuberculosis (BCG), yellow fever, smallpox, and the plague became available and widely used, even in the most remote villages. As a consequence, the last three of these deadly diseases were under control by 1960. Tuberculosis was more difficult to control, mostly because the BCG has a low efficacy but also because the disease has a more complex epidemiology. Major efforts were also made to control syphilis and yaws, as well as trypanosomiasis. The control of syphilis and other infectious diseases reached a new dimension with the marketing of antibiotics just after World War II. Synthetic antimalarial drugs became available in 1945 in most of tropical Africa. Malaria control programs started also after World War II, and, although they failed to achieve their goals, they certainly contributed to mortality decline and perhaps to an increase in fertility.

8.2   Evolution since Independence: 1960–1992

8.2.1   Recent trends in mortality

After 1960, a relatively large amount of data concerning mortality became available: censuses with retrospective questions, sample surveys (prospective or retrospective), maternity histories in the World Fertility Survey (WFS), and the Demographic and Health Surveys (DHS). These surveys provide levels and trends in child mortality at various points in time from which a history of mortality decline can be reconstructed (Hill, 1989, 1991; Cantrelle *et al.*, 1986; Garenne *et al.*, 1985). Results of this reconstruction are shown in *Table 8.1*.

Among the countries listed in *Table 8.1*, data are satisfactory in more than half of the cases and indicate a 40 percent decline in $q(5)$ between 1960 and 1985, from an average of 275 in 1960 to an average of 165 in 1985. This represents a rapid decline in mortality. In England and Wales, it took about 85 years to achieve the same decline.

Some countries did not seem to enjoy the favorable evolution of the majority. For instance, Uganda was rather advanced in 1960, but failed to continue along its path; mortality trends may have even been reversed after 1975. Although less dramatic a case, mortality

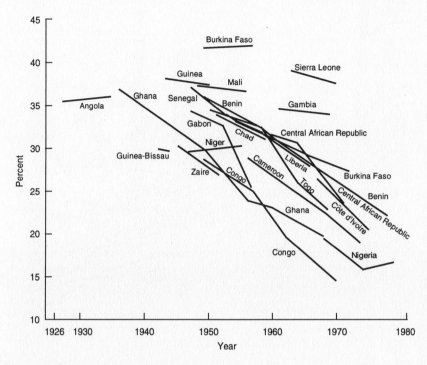

Figure 8.2. Under-five mortality risk, West Africa: 1926–1980. Source: Hill, 1991.

decline seems to have stopped in Ghana after 1980. Ghana had virtually the same mortality as Kenya in 1960, but had a 60 percent higher mortality in 1985 (see *Figures 8.2* and *8.3*).

Adult mortality has also been studied, from retrospective questions and from direct estimates from sample surveys (Timaeus, 1991). Adult mortality data are available in 21 countries, but only a few provide trends over time. Convincing evidence exists of an increase in adult survival in Benin (1967–1978), Congo (1962–1971), Cameroon (1945–1976), Sudan (1960–1974), Kenya (1955–1975), Uganda (1955–1965), Tanzania (1958–1968), Zimbabwe (1973–1979), and Swaziland (1960–1974). For those countries on the average, life expectancy at age 15 increased by about 10 years between 1960 and 1980, from around 45 years to approximately 55 years. The only two exceptions in this study were Lesotho

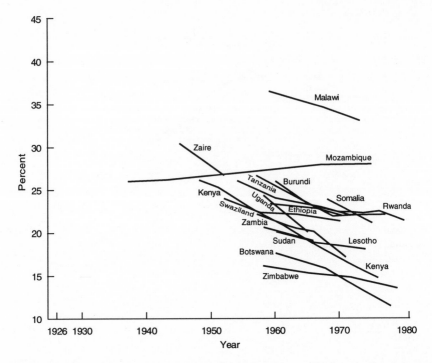

Figure 8.3. Under-five mortality risk, East Africa: 1926–1980. Source: Hill, 1991.

and Botswana, for which no change was visible during the period studied, which is surprising.

8.2.2 Socioeconomic correlates

Despite the poor quality of both demographic and socioeconomic data and the numerous missing values, various socioeconomic variables appear to be significant correlates of child survival. Feachem and Jamison (1991) found a significant correlation between the level of infant and child mortality and income, measured by the GNP per capita in 1987, as well as with secondary school enrollment. A systematic review of these correlations was undertaken by Trani (1992), using all the available evidence from socioeconomic data published by the World Bank (*Tables 8.2, 8.3*, and *8.4*).

In the linear simple regressions, seven variables appear significant: two measures of income (index of GDP/capita and

Table 8.2. Values of socioeconomic indicators: 1984–1990.

Country	Pop	Urb	GNP	FLFP	Lit	Phys	Nurse	Cal	Prim	Sec	IGDP	$q(5)$
Benin	4.741	37.7	390	47.4	74	15940	1750	2145	63	16	5.0	187
Botswana	1.254	27.5	2040	34.9	29	6900	700	2269	116	33	19.3	59
Burkina Faso	9.016	9.0	330	46.2	87	265250	1680	2061	32	6		199
Burundi	5.470	5.5	210	47.3	66	21030	4380	2253	70	4		151
Cameroon	11.941	41.2	940	33.3	44			2161	111	27	10.0	123
Centr.Afr.R.	3.036	46.7	390	45.7	60			1980	67	11		156
Chad	5.679	29.5	190	21.1	75	38360	3390	1852	51	6		223
Congo, PR	2.277	40.5	1010	38.8	37			2512			12.8	
Côte d'Ivoire	12.233	40.4	730	34.2	57			2365		19	8.2	140
Eq. Guinea	0.417	28.7	330	39.9								
Ethiopia	51.183	12.9	120	37.4	38	78770	5390	1658	36	15	1.6	216
Gabon	1.135	45.7	3220	37.3	38	2790	270	2396			0.0	
Gambia	0.875	23.2	260	40.3								206
Ghana	14.870	33.0	390	39.7	40	20460	1670	2209	73	39		153
Guinea-Bissau	0.981	19.9	180	40.8								
Kenya	24.368	23.6	370	39.9	41	10050		1973	93	23	5.2	87
Lesotho	1.771	20.3	470	43.4	26	18610		2307	112	25		165
Liberia	2.560	45.9	450	30.2	65	9350	1380	2270	35			215
Madagascar	11.620	25.0	230	39.3	33	9780		2101	97	19	3.4	
Malawi	8.504	11.8	200	41.2	59	11340		2009	72	4	3.2	211
Mali	8.461	19.2	270	16.2	83	25390	1350	2181	23	6	2.5	248
Mauritania	1.969	46.8	500	22.2		11900	1180	2528	52	16		
Mozambique	15.784	26.8	80	47.4	62			1632	68	5		291
Namibia	1.780	27.8		23.8				1889				
Niger	7.666	19.5	310	46.7	86	39670	460	2340	30	7		
Nigeria	117.510	35.2	270	34.8	58	6440	900	2039	62	16	6.2	193
Rwanda	7.113	7.7	310	47.7	53	35090	3690	1786	64	6	3.0	204
Senegal	7.428	38.4	710	39.3	72		2030	1989	59	16	6.5	186
Sierra Leone	4.137	32.2	240	32.7	71	13620	1090	1806	53	18	2.6	
Somalia	6.284	36.4	150	38.7	88	16080	1530	1736				169
Sudan	25.191	22.0	520	21.9		10190	1260	1996	49	20		130
Swaziland	0.789	33.1	840	38.8								199
Tanzania	24.518	32.8	120	47.9		24980	5490	2151	66	4	2.3	199
Togo	3.638	25.7	410	36.4	59	8700	1240	2133	101	24		164
Uganda	17.358	10.4	220	41.1	43			2013	77	8		183
Zaire	35.564	39.5	230	35.5	39	12940	1800	2034	76	22		
Zambia	8.122	49.9	480	29.0	24	7150	740	2026	97		4.3	117
Zimbabwe	9.809	27.6	640	34.6	26	6700	1000	2232	128	51	8.8	79

Pop = population (million), Urb = percent urban, GNP = GNP/capita (US$), FLFP = female labor force participation, Lit = percent adult illiterate, Phys = number of people/physician, Nurse = number of people/nurse, Cal = caloric consumption/capita (cal), Prim = primary school enrollment, Sec = secondary school enrollment, IGDP = index of GDP/capita (USA=100), $q(5)$ = mortality age 0-4 per 1000 live births.
Source: Hill, 1992, and World Development Indicators.

Table 8.3. Mean annual changes in socioeconomic indicators during the 1970–1990 period, per 1,000 people per year.

Country	Pop	Urb	GNP	Phys	Nurse	Cal	Prim	Sec	$q(5)$
Benin	29	36	63	37	20	03	26	72	40.6
Botswana	35	59	137	73	170	06	25	104	65.7
Burkina Faso	24	23	70	−67	48	05	42	77	46.9
Burundi	25	41	54	51	27	−02	43	60	41.2
Cameroon	30	35	82			03	7	73	53.9
Centr. Afr. R.	24	21	63			−01	7	74	47.7
Chad	22	48	32	33	73	−10	17	77	27.8
Congo, PR	32	11	71			05			
Côte d'Ivoire	40	19	49			01		50	55.1
Eq. Guinea	19	4	−						
Ethiopia	29	20	34	−06	5	−03	51	87	8.1
Gabon	41	29	79		54	12			
Gambia	32	22	47						41.6
Ghana	27	6	22	−21	42	06	2	47	33.8
Guinea-Bissau	31	14	6						
Kenya	38	41	52	15		−04	23	76	58.8
Lesotho	25	43	77	4		05	7	79	18.3
Liberia	30	28	23	16	28	03	−06		30.9
Madagascar	27	29	15	4		−05	17	37	
Malawi	32	34	60	75		−04	21	30	40.7
Mali	23	15	67	37	48	07	−01	17	29.3
Mauritania	24	61	51	59		14	60	120	
Mozambique	26	77	−			−02	26	22	−5.1
Namibia	28	20	−			00			
Niger	31	42	33	26	137	08	43	84	
Nigeria	29	28	29	80	101	−03	28	50	2.0
Rwanda	33	44	82	38	37	03	8	47	21.5
Senegal	29	07	58		10	−09	16	35	38.6
Sierra Leone	22	29	20	11	74	−04	26	55	
Somalia	28	24	25	44	50	09			38.3
Sudan	28	15	77	44	52	03	22	69	35.0
Swaziland	32	61	56						11.6
Tanzania	30	79	09	−07	−51	07	31	30	17.1
Togo	29	34	53	52	73	−04	26	68	47.4
Uganda	29	13	7			−06	6	30	22.1
Zaire	29	13	−04	52		−02	3	64	
Zambia	33	25	4	24	109	−00	26		43.8
Zimbabwe	31	25	36	9	−1	04	6	93	48.7

Pop = population, Urb = percent urban, GNP = GNP/capita, Phys = number of physician/capita, Nurse = number of nurse/capita, Cal = caloric consumption/capita, Prim = primary school enrollment, Sec = secondary school enrollment.
Source: World Development Indicators.

Table 8.4. Elasticities of $q(5)$ with respect to various socioeconomic indicators, in 36 countries of continental tropical Africa: 1980–1990.

	Standardized coefficient	P	R^2
Index of GDP/capita (US=100)	−0.745	0.002[a]	0.556
Secondary school enrollment	−0.734	0.000[a]	0.539
Primary school enrollment	−0.711	0.000[a]	0.506
% Adult illiterate	0.590	0.002[a]	0.348
GNP/capita	−0.517	0.006[a]	0.267
Population/physician	0.499	0.030[a]	0.249
Mean caloric consumption	−0.460	0.018[a]	0.211
Population/nurse	0.524	0.080	0.179
Export of agricultural products	0.287	0.155	0.082
% Urban population	−0.201	0.306	0.040
Exports of fuel, minerals, and metals	−0.138	0.586	0.019
% Female in labor force	0.091	0.645	0.008

[a] $P < 0.05$.
Source: Trani, 1992.

GNP/capita), three measures of education (literacy and primary and secondary school enrollment), one measure of public health (the number of physicians), and one measure of nutrition (caloric consumption). Owing to the poor quality of the data, no further analysis could be done. However, these correlations indicate that the mortality decline is part of the whole development process, and that countries doing well in economic and social terms are also doing well in mortality terms. There were, however, a number of outliers in the regression analysis. Countries such as Sierra Leone, Gambia, and Malawi have a mortality higher than expected; this was the case already in 1960. Countries such as Kenya, Botswana, and Zimbabwe have a lower than expected mortality, and they were among the lowest mortality countries in 1960 (see *Figures 8.4* and *8.5*).

8.2.3 Public health and primary health care

Modern health infrastructures developed significantly after 1960 and the number of health personnel per capita also increased. In particular the number of physicians per capita increased by about 100 percent during the 1960–1985 period and the number of nurses per capita, by 373 percent. In Botswana, the number of physicians

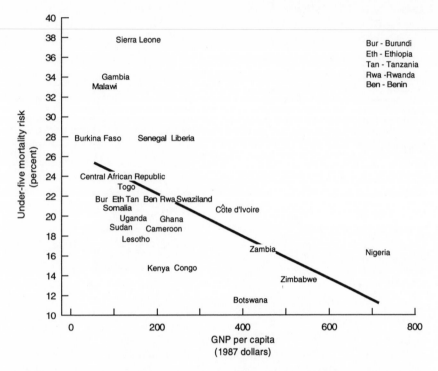

Figure 8.4. Under-five mortality risk and GNP per capita in 27 countries of sub-Saharan Africa, 1964–1979. Source: Feachem and Jamison, 1991.

per capita has multiplied by 6.2 and the number of nurses by 70. Botswana has 38 times more physicians per capita than Burkina Faso. Hence, there is little wonder why Botswana has the lowest mortality.

Major health programs were also implemented in Africa after 1960. The interest of the health authorities and of donor agencies shifted from tropical diseases affecting adult mortality toward maternal and pediatric care. Major efforts were made to provide new vaccines, in particular vaccines against measles and poliomyelitis. After 1978, selective primary health care strategies were implemented throughout the continent. Emphasis was on the treatment of diarrhea, using oral rehydration therapy, and to a certain extent on growth monitoring. More recent efforts focused on increasing vaccination coverage, on the treatment of acute respiratory

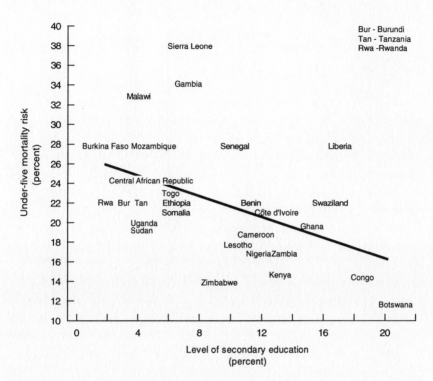

Figure 8.5. Under-five mortality risk and secondary schooling in 28 countries of sub-Saharan Africa, 1964–1979. Source: Feachem and Jamison, 1991.

infections (ARI), on the use of antibiotics, on essential drugs, and on the financing and management of the primary health care systems. Little is known yet about the exact impact of these strategies. However, it is certain that, when well implemented, they can have a dramatic effect on a child's survival, as exemplified in a number of small-scale case studies (Lamb *et al.*, 1984; Garenne *et al.*, 1991).

8.3   Prospects

The recent history of sub-Saharan Africa indicates a major mortality decline, virtually universal, which began probably as early as 1920 in the most advanced countries. The decline was faster in certain countries than in others. A clear association exists between the pace of the mortality decline, the general level of socioeconomic development, and the intensity of public-health efforts.

8.3.1 Sociopolitical factors

There are documented examples of countries experiencing a stagnant or even reverse mortality trend. These countries went through major political turmoil, and usually the changes in the trends are seen 5 to 10 years after the political crisis erupted. The level of sociopolitical organization seems therefore to be the most crucial determinant of mortality trends. It also determines the economic performances and the level of social investments.

Our picture of African mortality may even be optimistically biased, since the demographic situations of the most critical cases are not documented. For instance, recent reports of a major famine in Somalia claim that the life of one-third of the population is threatened. The demographic effect of the recurrent famines in Ethiopia has been poorly documented, and the little we do know leads to serious worries (Seaman, 1987). Relatively little is known about the situation in southern Sudan, which has been under the pressure of a civil war for more than three decades. The recent Sudanese data cover only the northern part of the country. The same is true for Angola and Mozambique, also amid the turmoil of civil wars. Griffiths (1988) displays a striking map of Africa: famines, political unrest, and civil wars occur simultaneously in the same countries and in the same regions. The future of African mortality may be divided into two categories: countries which do well and continue on their rapid trend toward low mortality situations, and countries which are so disturbed politically and economically that any improvements in the mortality situation will be postponed to an unforeseeable future (see *Figure 8.6*). International aid seems to reinforce this dichotomy rather than to diminish it. For instance, USAID, the most active agency for child survival programs, has a red list of countries for which it will not intervene. They are often the poorest and the most desperate of all. On the other hand, countries which are *democratic*, and in general are developing more rapidly, receive more international support than the others.

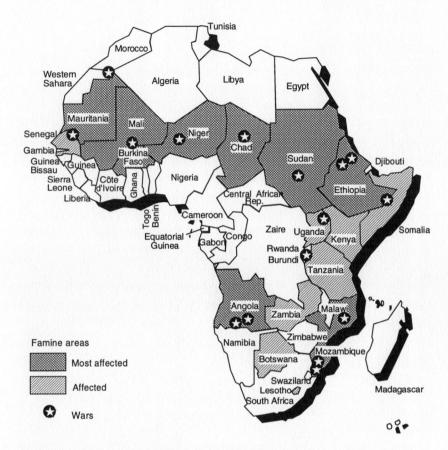

Figure 8.6. Famine areas and location of major wars in Africa. Source: Griffiths and Binns, 1988:49.

8.3.2 Epidemiological factors

Tropical Africa is also experiencing a profound sociological and epidemiological transition. The emergence of the modern economy destroyed most of the traditional agricultural and economic systems and perturbated the ecological balance between population and resources. It led to massive migration flows and to a very rapid urbanization. In Senegal, more than half of the population now lives in cities or large towns, whereas at the turn of the century 99 percent of the population was rural and no city accounted for more than 5000 inhabitants. In Mauritania, 80 percent of the population became urban in less than one generation.

This pattern of migration has been favorable to the rapid spread of communicable diseases, in particular sexually transmitted diseases, as happened with syphilis at the onset of economic development in Europe, and for the same reasons (Shorter, 1990). The AIDS epidemic is the leading source of concern in this respect. The dynamics of the AIDS epidemic has been affected by the existence of the network of international truck drivers (in Tanzania–Kenya–Uganda), by the emergence of urban commercial sex workers, and by the appearance of large communities of single male migrants in cities, like in Abidjan. The spread of AIDS is probably the most important negative factor affecting the future of mortality decline in sub-Saharan Africa. Projections made of the mortality of future generations are alarming: up to 50 percent of the population of certain countries or regions may have AIDS as a cause of death. The death rates may even exceed the birth rates in the most extreme situations, reversing the pattern of population growth (Anderson, 1991). The AIDS epidemic has another major consequence: the disruption of families, by the death of one or both parents, exposing new orphans to the multiple risks of infection, malnutrition, and accidents. Closely related to AIDS, there is also a risk of increasing mortality from tuberculosis, as already shown in developed countries (Murray *et al.*, 1990).

The massive implementation of modern medicine has also affected the ecology of certain diseases. This is the case for malaria, as more and more cases of strains resistant to chloroquine are documented (Bradley, 1991). Malaria has always been a leading cause of death in Africa. Although there is no documented evidence on increasing malaria mortality, resistant malaria strains may lead in the future toward an increase in deaths attributed to this disease. Furthermore, the wide-scale use of antimalarial drugs may have led to a decline in natural immunity. This in turn may make certain populations vulnerable to major outbreaks of malaria, such as what happened in Madagascar in 1988.

Cholera came back in 1971 to Africa, after some 80 years of absence. The index case was brought by plane to Conakry, Guinea, an example of a new pattern of spread of communicable diseases.

Since then, cholera has become endemic in most of tropical Africa, and seems also to have become a leading cause of death, at least in the Sahel of West Africa.

The vaccination coverage against yellow fever has dropped markedly in many countries. Recent outbreaks have taken place in Nigeria, and will occur again unless vaccination coverage increases dramatically. Although rare, the plague still exists in Madagascar and occurs occasionally on the east coast of Africa.

With changing lifestyles and urbanization, new diseases will also emerge or develop from increasing risk factors or changing ecological conditions. Smoking habits are increasing in Africa, with the help of the massive commercial campaigns by tobacco companies. Obesity, rare in the villages, has become prevalent in cities, and may be linked with a probable increase in the prevalence of diabetes. Car accidents are also becoming a significant cause of death, and African roads are among the most dangerous in the world.

8.4   Discussion

The past trends of mortality in Africa have been induced by transfers of technology from the West, which have affected virtually all countries in the continent in a short period of time. Public health, nutrition, economic development, and modern education seem to have been the key determinants in mortality change. However, the future of mortality in Africa is hard to determine and even harder to quantify. There are reasons for believing that the major mortality decline of the past 30 years will not be followed by a comparable decline in the next 30 years in all the countries of continental sub-Saharan Africa. Most likely, the major differences that already exist between countries will prevail, and may even increase. Some will continue along their successful routes to low mortality and others will see their health transition stop or even be reversed for some period of time. Besides the sociopolitical conditions, a critical factor will be the spread of the HIV virus in the general population.

The control that the countries have over the health of their population is also a function of their research capacity to identify new problems and to choose the most appropriate solutions in time. Essential national health research has been seen recently as one of the top priorities for developing countries (ENHR Report, 1990, 1991). Data information systems to identify and tackle new diseases and new health problems may be an important component of the success of health policies in the future. The AIDS epidemics could have been smaller in size if similar and appropriate steps had been taken at its onset.

Acknowledgments

I would like to thank warmly Jean-François Trani for his contribution to the statistical analysis and Meg Tyler for editorial comments.

References

Anderson, R.M., 1991, AIDS and its demographic impact, in R. Feachem and D. Jamison, eds., *Disease and Mortality in sub-Saharan Africa*, World Bank/Oxford University Press, New York, NY, USA.

Becker, C., and Martin, V., 1983, *Les premiers recensements au Sénégal, et l'évolution démographique*, ORSTOM, Dakar, Senegal.

Blacker, J.G.C., 1991, Infant and child mortality: Development, environment and custom, in R. Feachem and D. Jamison, eds., *Disease and Mortality in sub-Saharan Africa*, World Bank/Oxford University Press, New York, NY, USA.

Bradley, D.J., 1991, Malaria, in R. Feachem and D. Jamison, eds., *Disease and Mortality in sub-Saharan Africa*, World Bank/Oxford University Press, New York, NY, USA.

Brass, W., 1968, *The Demography of Tropical Africa*, Princeton University Press, Princeton, NJ, USA.

Caldwell, J.G.C., 1986, Routes to low mortality in poor countries, *Population and Development Review* **12**(2):171–220.

Cantrelle, P., Diop, I.L., Garenne, M., Gueye, M., and Sadio, A., 1986, The profile of mortality and its determinants in Senegal, 1960–1980, in *Determinants of Mortality Change and Differentials in Developing Countries: The Five-Country Case Study Project*, Population Studies, No. 94, United Nations, New York, NY, USA.

Chastanet, M., 1982, Les crises de subsistances dans les villages Soninke du cercle de Bakel de 1858 à 1945, *Problèmes méthodologiques et perspectives de recherches*, ORSTOM, Dakar, Senegal.

Davis, K., 1951, *The Population of India and Pakistan*, Princeton University Press, Princeton, NJ, USA.

Diop, I.L., 1990, Etude de la mortalité à Saint-Louis du Sénégal à partir des données d'état civil, Thèse de doctorat de 3ème cycle, Université de Paris I, Panthéon-Sorbonne, Paris, France.

ENHR Report, 1990, *Volume 1, Health Research: Essential Link to Equity in Development*, Report from the Commission on Health Research for Development, Oxford University Press, New York, NY, USA.

ENHR Report, 1991, *Volume 2, Essential National Health Research: A Strategy for Action in Health and Human Development*, Report from the Task Force on Health Research for Development, UNDO, Geneva, Switzerland.

Feachem, R., and Jamison, D., eds., 1991, *Disease and Mortality in sub-Saharan Africa*, World Bank/Oxford University Press, New York, NY, USA.

Garenne, M., Cantrelle, P., and Diop, I.L., 1985, Senegal, in J. Vallin and A. Lopez, eds., *Health Policy, Social Policy and Mortality Prospects*, Ordina, Liège, Belgium.

Garenne, M., Leroy, O., Beau, J.P., Sene, I., Whittle, H., and Sow, A.R., 1991, *Efficacy, Safety and Immunogenicity of Two High Titer Measles Vaccines: A Study in Niakhar*, Final Report, ORSTOM, Dakar, Senegal.

Garenne, M., Cantrelle, P., Sarr, I., Diop, I.L., and Becker, C., 1993, Estimation of Mortality Trends in Urban and Rural Senegal, Working Paper Series, Harvard Center for Population and Development Studies, Cambridge, MA, USA.

GDA, 1967, *Manuel de démographie africaine*, Groupe de Démographie Africaine, Paris, France.

Griffiths, I.L., 1988, Famine and war in Africa, *Geography* **73**(1):59–61.

Griffiths, I.L., and Binns, J.A., 1988, Hunger, help and hypocrisy: Crisis and response to crisis in Africa, *Geography* **73**(1):48–54.

Hill, A., 1989, La mortalité des enfants: niveau actuel et évolution depuis 1945, in *Mortalité et société en Afrique: Cahier de l'INED*, No. 124.

Hill, A., 1991, Infant and child mortality: Levels, trends and data deficiencies, in R. Feachem and D. Jamison, eds., *Disease and Mortality in sub-Saharan Africa*, World Bank/Oxford University Press, New York, NY, USA.

Hill, A., 1992, Trends in Childhood Mortality in sub-Saharan Africa in the 1970s and 1980s, Draft paper, World Bank, Population, Health and Nutrition Division, Washington, DC, USA.

Hill, A., and Hill, K., 1988, Mortality in Africa: Levels, trends, differentials and prospects, in E. van de Walle, P.O. Ohadike, and M.D. Sala-Diakanda, eds., *The State of African Demography*, IUSSP-Derouaux, Liège, Belgium.

Lamb, W.H., Foord, F.A., Lamb, C.M.B., and Whitehead, R.G., 1984, Changes in maternal and child mortality rates in three isolated Gambian villages over ten years, *The Lancet* 8408 (October 20):912–913.

Mandjale, A.E., 1985, *Mortalité infantile et juvénile en Afrique: niveaux et caractérisitiques, causes et déterminants,* CIACO, Louvain la Neuve, Belgium.

Murray, C.J.L., Styblo, K., and Rouillon, A., 1990, Tuberculosis in developing countries: Burden, intervention and cost, *Bulletin of the International Union Against Tuberculosis and Lung Disease* 65(1):2-20 (March).

Seaman, J., 1987, Famine mortality in Ethiopia and Sudan, in *Proceedings of the IUSSP Seminar on Comparative Mortality Changes,* Younde, Cameroon, 19-23 October, Oxford University Press, London, UK.

Shorter, E., 1990, What can two historical examples of sexually-transmitted diseases teach us about AIDS? in *Proceedings of the IUSSP Seminar on Anthropological Studies Relevant to the Sexual Transmission of HIV,* 19-22 November, Sonderborg, Denmark.

Timaeus, I.M., 1991, Adult mortality: Levels, trends, and data sources, in R. Feachem and D. Jamison, eds., *Disease and Mortality in Sub-Saharan Africa,* World Bank/Oxford University Press, New York, NY, USA.

Trani, J.F., 1992, Mémoire de DEA, Institut des Etudes Politiques de Paris. September, Paris, France.

van de Walle, E., Ohadike, P.O., and Sala-Diakanda, M.D., eds., 1988, *The State of African Demography,* IUSSP-Derouaux, Liège, Belgium.

∴

Chapter 9

Projection of the Mortality Impact of AIDS in Africa

John Bongaarts

The human immunodeficiency virus (HIV) began spreading widely around 1980, and it has now reached every corner of the world. This rapidly growing epidemic is considered an unprecedented health threat because AIDS, which follows HIV infection, results always in fatal illness, and the prospects for a cure or a vaccine in the near future are not good (Anderson and May, 1992). The speed with which the epidemic has spread is particularly disturbing. The number of reported AIDS cases worldwide doubled annually for most of the 1980s. By early 1991 more than 1 million AIDS cases had occurred among adults (WHO, 1991). Further large increases in the epidemic are essentially inevitable because millions more are already infected with HIV and the large majority of these individuals are expected to develop AIDS eventually. Moreover, new infections continue to occur. WHO expects the total number of AIDS cases to rise to 9–10 million among adults and 4–8 million among infants by the end of the century.

The African continent is more severely affected by this epidemic than any other major part of the world. More than two out of three adult AIDS cases and more than nine out of ten pediatric cases have occurred in Africa (WHO, 1991). In some urban areas of Central Africa more than 20 percent of the general adult population is already infected. A large proportion of all sexually active adults in Africa and elsewhere must be considered at risk of infection with HIV.

The future course of the epidemic is highly uncertain and the subject of considerable controversy. A variety of computerized mathematical models have been developed to project the future course of the AIDS epidemic and its demographic impact (UN, 1991a). A review of these different approaches is not attempted here, but it should be noted that the range of projections is very wide. Some investigators (e.g., Anderson *et al.*, 1991) conclude that the epidemic will be sufficiently severe in a few decades to cause a decline in population size in parts of Africa. Results obtained by others (e.g., Bos and Bulatao, forthcoming) indicate that even in the countries with the highest infection levels, the annual population growth rate will be reduced by only a fraction of 1 percent.

The overall objective of this chapter is to obtain estimates of plausible upper and lower boundaries of the mortality impact of the AIDS epidemic in Africa by the end of this century. A brief review of recent trends in the epidemic and the causes of intra-country variation is presented first. This is followed by an application of a computer simulation model to project alternative scenarios for the future HIV epidemic and its mortality impact in Africa.

9.1 Recent Trends in HIV Infections and AIDS Cases Worldwide

The number of AIDS cases reported to WHO is the most widely available statistic used for monitoring the evolution of the epidemic. Although some conclusions can be drawn from levels and trends in the number of AIDS cases, this indicator can be highly misleading for two reasons. First, underreporting is a serious problem in some countries, particularly in Africa, due to the unwillingness to recognize this disease, lack of diagnostic facilities, and a reluctance on the part of medical personnel and governments to report the full extent of the epidemic. According to WHO (1991) only about one out of every ten AIDS cases in Africa has been reported. Second, the interval between infection with HIV and the onset of AIDS is long – nearly a decade on average. As a result, trends in AIDS cases can be very different from trends in HIV infections and one cannot draw firm conclusions about the former from the latter. The epidemic in the USA provides an example of this problem. The number of new AIDS cases (which are fairly completely reported in the USA) rose steadily during the early 1980s suggesting a continuous spread of the disease. However, since the mid-1980s, HIV seroprevalence rates among homosexuals as well as in sentinel groups representative of the general population have shown little increase, thus suggesting that the incidence of HIV infections has been declining and that the epidemic has not been spreading rapidly in recent years except in certain high risk populations such as IV drug users and their partners (Brookmeyer, 1991; Centers for Disease Control, 1987). This conclusion is consistent with a leveling off in the annual number of new AIDS cases in the early 1990s. To assess future trends in an AIDS epidemic it is clearly preferable to monitor HIV infection rates rather than to rely on extrapolation of reported AIDS cases.

Unfortunately, reliable HIV seroprevalence estimates based on national samples of the general population are virtually nonexistent in Africa (Uganda is the only exception). Seroprevalence data are often only available for specific subpopulations (e.g., prostitutes or pregnant women). Many surveys are taken in settings such as hospitals and clinics where blood samples can be obtained relatively easily. Estimates of HIV prevalence in the general population are therefore typically based on data from pregnant women or blood donors. While certainly subject to error, this procedure gives reasonable approximations in most countries. Another problem with existing seroprevalence data is the focus on urban populations, which are definitely not representative of a country as a whole. In most countries where both rural and urban estimates are available, the former is only a fraction of the latter.

Estimates of seroprevalence are available from the HIV/AIDS Surveillance Data Base maintained by the Center for International Research at the US Bureau of the Census (1991). The distribution of countries by level of infection is given in *Table 9.1*.

Table 9.1. Urban HIV seroprevalence in African countries.

Percent of low-risk adult population	Countries
> 10%	Burundi, Malawi, Rwanda, Côte d'Ivoire, Uganda, Zambia
5–10%	Central African Republic, Congo, Kenya, Tanzania, Zaire
2–5%	Ethiopia, Gabon, Ghana, Namibia, Sierra Leone, Zimbabwe
< 2%	40 other countries

Seroprevalence rates of over 10 percent in urban areas of a few countries are extremely high and not found anywhere else in the world. On the other hand, in 40 African countries the epidemic has thus far affected less than 2 percent of the adult population. It should be emphasized that these are urban estimates. Countrywide data are rarely available, but they should be much lower because the large majority of Africans live in rural areas. For Africa as a whole WHO (1991) estimates a total of 6 million infected individuals. With an adult population of 353 million, in mid-1990 (UN, 1991b) the average seroprevalence among adults in the continent is therefore 1.7 percent.

Figure 9.1 plots trends in a few capital cities where repeated measurements have been made since 1985. In most cases the trend is firmly upward, indicating a continuing spread of HIV. Interestingly, in one instance, Kinshasa, seroprevalence has stabilized and in three other cities, Kampala, Nairobi, and Abidjan, prevalence rates among pregnant women appear to be growing slower in recent years than in the mid-1980s. Given the unreliability of some estimates it would be inappropriate to conclude that epidemics in these cities are approaching a plateau, but the absence of continued explosive growth is somewhat encouraging.

9.2   Determinants of Geographic Variation in the Spread of HIV

Available HIV seroprevalence data demonstrate clearly that the AIDS virus has spread rapidly in some African countries, while in

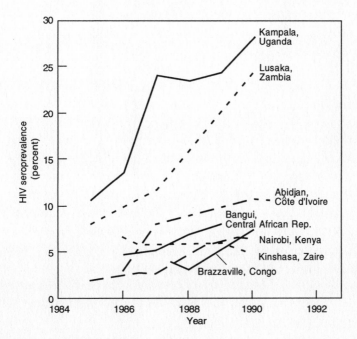

Figure 9.1. Trends in HIV seroprevalence among pregnant women in selected capital cities in Africa.

other parts of Africa HIV seroprevalence is still low or negligible. The causes of these geographic differences are not well understood, but they are probably due to variations in the following factors:

- *The timing of the onset of the epidemic.* In the unlikely case that all African populations are equally susceptible to an HIV epidemic, differences in HIV seroprevalence at one point in time could be due to the later introduction of HIV in the countries with low current levels of infection. However, all populations would then eventually be expected to experience similar epidemics.
- *Sexual behavior.* Sexual mobility is necessary for the spread of HIV because an HIV epidemic cannot occur in a population in which all or nearly all sexually active adults live in monogamous unions. The frequency of sexual contact with individuals other than a permanent partner and the frequency of change in partners are therefore important determinants of the size of the

epidemic. Although data on sexual behavior are often lacking or unreliable, it appears likely that there are substantial differences in sexual behavior between countries and between urban and rural areas within countries.

- *The prevalence of infectious agents.* Infections with viruses and parasites (e.g., hepatitis, cytomegalovirus, herpes simplex, toxoplasmosis) are common in Africa. Quinn *et al.* (1986, 1987) suggest that exposure to these agents results in a chronic activation of the immune system, which in turn may lead to greater susceptibility to HIV infection.

- *Sexually transmitted diseases (STDs) that cause genital ulcers.* In African case-control studies, the presence of genital ulcers in both men and women is correlated with the rate of infection with HIV (Simonson *et al.*, 1988; Plummer *et al.*, 1987, 1991). Substantial variation in the prevalence of STDs and hence in the presence of genital ulcers may be inferred from demographic evidence on variation in the levels of infertility among African populations (Frank, 1983).

- *The absence of male circumcision.* A case-control study of men attending a clinic for sexually transmitted diseases in Nairobi found that uncircumcised males were significantly more likely to be infected with HIV than circumcised controls (Simonson *et al.*, 1988). Supporting evidence for this possibly crucial role of circumcision is provided by Bongaarts *et al.* (1989). In this study a review of the anthropological literature yielded estimates on circumcision practices for 409 African ethnic groups from which corresponding national estimates were derived. A strong correlation ($r = 0.9$) was found between the estimated national proportion of males who were not circumcised and the HIV prevalence in capital cities. Enhanced viral survival under the foreskin and the more frequent occurrence of balanitis (inflammation of the glans of the penis) may be responsible for the increased susceptibility to HIV among uncircumcised males (Piot *et al.*, 1988; Fink, 1986).

- *Gender differences in sexual activity.* While premarital or extramarital sexual mobility of males is socially acceptable in most African populations, this behavior is much less tolerated among women. Moreover, important differences exist among societies in sexual permissiveness for girls and women. In much of Africa, women enter a permanent marital union at an early age and, once married, are expected to remain faithful. The implication of this behavior pattern is that males engage in premarital and extramarital sex with relatively few promiscuous women, mostly prostitutes. Seroprevalence in this small group of women with high sexual activity rates therefore rises quickly to a high level in the early years of the epidemic. This in turn leads to higher rates of HIV infection among their male partners than would have been the case had sexual activity been less concentrated among these females. In contrast, in a few other societies – e.g., cities of Zaire and Tanzania – women are permitted greater sexual freedom and the pool of potential female sexual partners is relatively larger. Paradoxically, the more equal levels of extramarital sexual activity of males and females in these cities could, other things being equal, produce lower rates of infection with HIV.

Although a lack of detailed measurements prevents a quantitative assessment of the roles played by these explanatory variables, it is likely that all have contributed to current differences in the severity of the epidemic. Differences in these behavioral and epidemiological factors (usually referred to as cofactors) need not be large to cause epidemics of widely varying sizes. In fact, relatively modest differences in transmission risks or sexual behavior can make the difference between epidemics that are self-sustaining and those that are not. The former are referred to as epidemics with a reproductive rate above 1.0 while the latter have reproductive rates below 1.0. (The reproductive rate, R, is defined as the number of new infections caused by one infected individual over his or her lifetime.) In populations in which R exceeds 1, epidemics grow exponentially once the virus has been introduced. Examples of such epidemics are found among homosexuals and IV drug users in the USA and among heterosexuals in many African cities. In contrast, no such epidemics occur in populations with reproductive rates below 1. This is true even if the virus is introduced repeatedly. The AIDS epidemic is apparently not self-sustaining among US heterosexuals who are not IV drug users because HIV seroprevalence in this group has remained stable at a fraction of 1 percent despite the presence of highly infected core groups of homosexuals and IV drug users (Centers for Disease Control, 1987). Similarly, it is quite possible, indeed probable, that substantial parts of rural Africa still have reproductive rates below 1. In areas where this is the case, infections can occur through contacts with infected individuals from nearby cities or countries, but HIV seroprevalence can be expected to remain at a low and relatively stable level. An illustration of this phenomenon may be found in Rwanda. Kigali is experiencing one of the most severe epidemics found anywhere in Africa, but in rural Rwanda (which is close to the capital in this small country) HIV seroprevalence is only 2 percent (Godefroid *et al.*, 1988). A large difference between the reproductive rates of urban and rural Rwanda is the most likely explanation for this contrast in HIV seroprevalence levels.

Important policy implications follow if these untested hypotheses for the causes of the geographic variation in the size of epidemics prove to be largely correct. At present much of the effort to control the spread of AIDS is focused on high-risk groups in urban areas, i.e., on prostitutes and their clients. Where the reproductive rate in these groups is large (e.g., over 10), even a successful intervention program that cuts the rate in half (e.g., by promoting widespread use of condoms) would only put a small dent in the epidemic. On the other hand, if one could identify populations with a reproductive rate just above 1 (which implies that they are at risk of experiencing substantial future epidemics), then a successful intervention program might reduce the reproductive rate below 1, thus preventing the occurrence of an epidemic. Intervention strategies aimed at changing sexual behavior or cofactors among all sexually active males and females in both rural and urban areas may therefore be more effective in the long run than highly targeted control efforts.

As demonstrated in Section 9.3, the future course of an AIDS epidemic depends to a large extent on which of the above causes of the geographic variation in epidemic sizes predominates.

9.3 A Summary of the Projection Model

The objective of the AIDS simulation model discussed in this section is to make long-range projections of the annual incidence and the prevalence of HIV infection and AIDS, as well as of the number of AIDS deaths in a population with given epidemiological, behavioral, and demographic characteristics. In addition, projections provide estimates of the impact of AIDS on a variety of demographic variables, including the population size and growth rate, age and sex structure, and birth and death rates. The model is highly complex and only a few key features can be described here (see Bongaarts, 1989, for further details).

The overall model is based on a demographic framework into which a number of epidemiological submodels are integrated. This framework consists essentially of a standard cohort-component projection model that uses single-year cohorts and single-year projection increments instead of the more conventional five-year intervals.

With this conventional demographic structure as a basis, the population is then stratified into different sexual behavior groups. Sexual behavior, and hence the risk of HIV infection, varies widely among subgroups within a population. To take into account this heterogeneity in sexual activity, each cohort is divided into the following strata:

- *Males.* Heterosexuals with high sexual mobility (e.g., clients of prostitutes); partners in monogamous unions; and sexually inactive males.
- *Females.* Prostitutes and other females with high sexual mobility; monogamous partners of sexually mobile males; partners in monogamous unions; and sexually inactive females.

Homosexuality and IV drug use, which apparently do not contribute significantly to the spread of the epidemic in Africa, are not considered. Heterosexual contact is therefore the main route of HIV transmission. At the core of the epidemic are prostitutes (or other females with high sexual mobility) and their male clients. These two groups infect one another, thus producing a self-sustaining epidemic. From these core groups infection spreads to others, primarily because male clients of prostitutes usually also have sexual contact with their spouses or other females (polygamy is common in parts of Africa). These females, in turn, can infect their newborns either *in utero* or at birth and perhaps through breast-feeding as well.

The distribution of individuals among the different sexual behavior groups changes as each cohort ages. After being sexually inactive until early adulthood, cohort members enter one of the sexual behavior groups and over time may switch between them. In addition to keeping track of the distribution of individuals among these groups, the model allows the rate of sexual activity to change as the cohort ages.

The model is completed by adding the epidemiological components. This requires a further stratification of each cohort and each sexual behavior stratum into subgroups with different infection/disease states. Three such states are included in the model: uninfected, infected, and AIDS. Sets of differential equations describe the rates at which the numbers of individuals in these states change over time. The key events associated with transfers between infection/disease states are:

- *HIV infection.* The probability of infection in a given period is assumed to depend on the frequency of sexual contact, the prevalence of infection in and the infectiousness of the contact group (having sex with a prostitute is more risky than having sex with one's spouse), and the rate of partner change (for example, marital disruption and remarriage). The infectiousness of a partner is a function of gender (male-to-female transmission is apparently more efficient than the reverse), cofactors, stage of disease (individuals with AIDS or symptomatic HIV diseases such as ARC are most infectious), and the use of condoms.
- *AIDS onset.* The incubation period – i.e., the interval between infection with HIV and the onset of AIDS – is a key determinant of the demographic impact of the epidemic. In the model this highly variable incubation interval is described with a gamma distribution. The mean of this distribution is 9.3 years, and 90 percent of infected individuals are assumed to be at risk of contracting AIDS. These parameters were obtained by fitting a cumulative gamma distribution to observed proportions progressing to AIDS in a cohort of homosexuals in a San Francisco city clinic (Hessol *et al.*, 1987).
- *Death from AIDS.* The interval between the onset of AIDS and death is assumed to be exponentially distributed, and all AIDS cases are assumed to die eventually. The average survival time for an AIDS patient is assumed to be 1.5 years.

In the discussion of HIV infection routes, only sexual and perinatal transmissions have been mentioned thus far. Other modes of HIV transmission do exist in Africa, but they are believed to contribute only a minority of infections. Piot and Carael (1988) estimate that perhaps 5 to 10 percent of HIV infections among adults are due to transfusions with infected blood. This percentage is probably higher among infected infants and children. In addition, injections with contaminated needles (e.g., for vaccinations) may cause some infections although this is difficult to document conclusively. These factors are also included in the model, but their effect is assumed to decline over time, because inexpensive screening tests will make it possible to reduce infection from blood transfusions in the future.

9.4   The Relationship Between HIV Seroprevalence and AIDS Mortality

A set of model simulations was carried out to determine the mortality effects of epidemics of different sizes. Before presenting the main results of this exercise, selected findings of an earlier application of the model are examined briefly. The objective of this previous application was to project the future course of epidemiological and demographic variables in a hypothetical Central African country with a severe HIV epidemic (Bongaarts, 1988). *Table 9.2* presents the principal input parameters for this simulation. *Figure 9.2* plots the projected trajectory of HIV seroprevalence for the period 1975–2000. The epidemic is assumed to have started in 1975, and by 1987 seroprevalence had reached 11 percent among adults, a level roughly comparable with that of Uganda. The projection to the year 2000 indicates substantial further growth of the epidemic, approaching a plateau with HIV seroprevalence at 21 percent by the end of the century. *Figure 9.2* also plots the corresponding trend in AIDS mortality (measured in AIDS deaths per 1,000 total population). The rise in AIDS mortality occurs several years after the increase in seroprevalence. In the model AIDS mortality is estimated at 3.5 per 1,000 population in 1987, and by the end of the century it triples to 10.5. About three-quarters of this mortality occurs among adults,

Table 9.2. Input parameters for the illustrative projection of an HIV/AIDS epidemic in Africa.

Disease progression	
Average duration of incubation period (years)	9.3
Average interval between AIDS onset and death (years)	1.5
Proportion infected at risk of developing AIDS	0.9
Sexual behavior	
Monthly frequency of sexual contact before marriage	
highly mobile males/females	10/25
Monthly frequency of sexual contact after marriage	
highly mobile males/females	4/100
Monthly frequency of sexual contact between spouses	8
Proportion highly mobile before marriage (males/females)	0.4/0.2
Proportion highly mobile after marriage (males/females)	0.2/0.02
Age at marriage	20
Annual risk of marital disruption	0.02
Proportion remarrying	1.0
Average number of wives per married male	1.25
Determinants of infectiousness	
Standard transmission risk per contact	
male to female/female to male	0.001/0.0005
Cofactor multiplier (highly mobile/other)	3.0/1.5
Infectiousness multiplier for ARC and AIDS cases	10.0
Frequency of contact multiplier for AIDS cases	0.0
Proportion using condoms	0.1
Nonsexual transmission	
Probability of perinatal transmission	0.35
Proportion of infections among infants/adult females	
due to blood transfusion	0.2/0.1
Demographic structure	
Initial population size (millions)	100.0
Initial population growth rate (percent)	3.0
Initial life expectancy at birth in years (male/female)	44/47
Annual increment in life expectancy (male/female)	0.3/0.3
Annual decrement in fertility rate (births per woman)	0.02

Source: Bongaarts, 1988.

with the remainder occurring among children. Three key conclusions are drawn from this particular simulation of a severe epidemic (Bongaarts, 1988):

1. HIV seroprevalence will roughly double between 1987 and 2000.

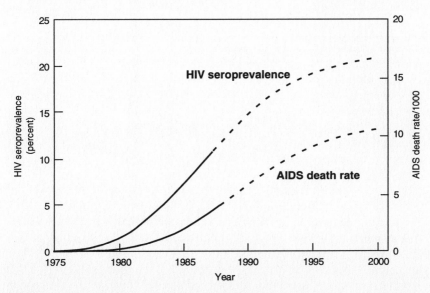

Figure 9.2. Model projection of HIV seroprevalence and AIDS death rate for a severe African epidemic.

2. Rapid changes in HIV seroprevalence and AIDS mortality occur in the first 25 years of the epidemic, but thereafter relatively stable levels are achieved for these variables.

3. AIDS mortality causes a substantial decline in the population growth rate, but, given the high birth rates that exist in much of Africa, the rise in the crude death rate is insufficient to produce negative population growth.

Most countries in Africa are experiencing epidemics that are less severe than the one just described. To obtain simulations of epidemics of different sizes, model input parameters related to sexual behavior and cofactors were varied. Two findings from these simulations are noteworthy. First, the AIDS death rate was directly related to the size of the epidemic. *Figure 9.3* plots the relationship between these two variables in the year 2000. Interestingly, the effect of epidemic size on AIDS mortality is close to linear. As a simple rule of thumb, the number of AIDS deaths per 1,000 population in the year 2000 is about half of the HIV seroprevalence among adults in that year. For smaller epidemics mortality is slightly lower than this rule implies, but the resulting modest overestimate of AIDS

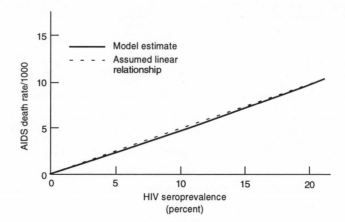

Figure 9.3. Estimated relationship between AIDS death rate and adult HIV seroprevalence in 2000.

mortality was considered acceptable. Second, the patterns of change over time in seroprevalence and AIDS mortality are similar to those for the severe epidemic depicted in *Figure 9.2*; nevertheless, the smaller an epidemic is, the later equilibrium tends to be reached.

The results of these simulations are used in Section 9.5 to make alternative projections for the African continent as a whole.

9.5 Projection of AIDS Mortality for the African Continent

One approach to estimating the future death rate attributable to AIDS would be to simulate epidemics in the urban and rural parts of each African country, and then to aggregate these country-specific results into a continentwide estimate of mortality. Such an exercise would be very time consuming and difficult because accurate statistics for many epidemiological and demographic variables are lacking for most African countries. Fortunately, a much simpler approach is available. This alternative is made possible by the essentially linear relationship between the seroprevalence level and the corresponding AIDS death rate in the year 2000 (see *Figure 9.3*). As a consequence of this linear relationship one can estimate AIDS mortality for the African continent from the average seroprevalence in Africa in 2000, rather than from country-specific projections. This shortcut gives quite accurate results, because (assuming linearity) the AIDS death rate is not sensitive to variation in epidemic size around the average. In other words, it is the average African seroprevalence that matters, and for our purpose it is not important that epidemics in many countries will in fact be much larger or smaller than average.

To estimate the AIDS death rate for all of Africa in the year 2000, answers to two questions have to be provided: (1) how large will the HIV epidemic be by the end of the century; and (2) given this epidemic size, what is the related AIDS death rate? To answer the second question we use the simple rule derived from *Figure 9.3*: the AIDS death rate per 1,000 population is estimated at half the HIV seroprevalence (in percent of adults). This leaves the much more difficult first question. Needless to say, it is impossible to estimate the future course of the African HIV epidemic with any accuracy. However, it is possible to set plausible upper and lower limits for the epidemic. The upper limit for the African continent is set here at 21 percent seroprevalence, based on the simulation of a Uganda-like epidemic as summarized in *Figure 9.2*. The implied assumptions for this scenario are that no important behavioral or epidemiological differences exist among African countries and that it is only a matter of time before all of Africa will experience the explosive epidemic observed in parts of Central Africa. The lower limit for seroprevalence in 2000 is derived by assuming that the relative increase in seroprevalence over time found in the simulation of the less severe epidemics (roughly a doubling between 1990 and 2000) will apply to all of Africa. Since HIV seroprevalence currently is estimated at about 1.7 percent this gives a lower limit of 3.4 percent for the epidemic in 2000. The implied assumption in this best case scenario is that current differences in seroprevalence among African countries are largely attributable to specific epidemiological and behavioral factors and that those differences will be maintained in the future. To sum up, the estimates for the year 2000 are:

Worst case: HIV seroprevalence, 21 percent of adults; AIDS death rate, 10.5 per 1,000 population.

Best case: HIV seroprevalence, 3.4 percent of adults; AIDS death rate, 1.7 per 1,000 population.

Since the evidence reviewed earlier suggests that sexual behavior and cofactors are the principal determinants of the existing variation in epidemic sizes in African populations, it appears likely that actual future trends in HIV seroprevalence and AIDS mortality will be closer to the low end than to the high end of the spectrum of projections presented here.

9.6   Conclusion

The available country-specific evidence on the spread of HIV indicates very large differences in the size of epidemics between and within African countries. Seroprevalence is low or negligible in large parts of Africa, particularly in rural areas, while a few urban areas are very heavily infected. Since the majority of Africans live in rural areas, HIV seroprevalence for Africa as a whole is currently "only" about 1.7 percent among adults. But there is little doubt that the epidemic will grow substantially in the future.

Given the uncertainty about the past course of the epidemic and about the roles of different behavioral and biological determinants, precise projections are not possible. However, results from computer simulations can be used to project ranges of future epidemic sizes and the corresponding mortality impacts. A key finding from a set of simulations was that the death rate (per 1,000 population) in the year 2000 will be approximately equal to half the HIV seroprevalence (percent of adults) in that year. Based on this simple relationship, two alternative projections for the African continent have been made. In the worst case scenario all of Africa is assumed to follow the route of the most severely affected countries in Central Africa, resulting in an AIDS death rate of over 10 per 1,000 population in the year 2000. In this extreme case, the AIDS death rate will approach the rate from all other causes of death, but the population growth rate, while substantially reduced, will remain positive. An African epidemic of this magnitude would of course have disastrous effects on the health care system, the economy, and the society in general. At the other end of the plausible spectrum for the evolution of the epidemic, a doubling of seroprevalence throughout Africa is projected between 1990 and 2000. In that case the death rate attributable to AIDS will grow to about 1.7 per

1,000, implying a minimal impact on population growth in Africa as a whole. But even in this most optimistic scenario AIDS will become a major cause of mortality in many countries.

Finally, the projections presented here do not take into account two factors that may affect the course of the epidemic and its mortality impact. The first is a change in sexual behavior that may occur (or may have already occurred) in response to the epidemic. It seems likely that at least some adults with high sexual mobility will change their behavior once they learn of the potentially fatal consequences of this behavior. Any reduction in the frequency of sexual intercourse and/or the number of sexual partners would tend to dampen the epidemic. At present no solid evidence indicates a change in sexual behavior, although such a change may be responsible for the reported recent leveling off of the HIV epidemic in Kinshasa (N'Galy *et al.*, 1988). A second factor that is not taken into account in our projections is the potential impact of the AIDS epidemic on mortality from other causes of death. The AIDS epidemic will put strains on an already overburdened health care system, and resources devoted to AIDS will tend to reduce the effectiveness of programs aimed at fighting other diseases. Since these two factors tend to offset one another and are of unknown magnitude, it is not clear whether their net impact will be positive, negative, or negligible, and for that reason they have been excluded from this analysis.

References

Anderson, R.M., and Maym, R.M., 1992, Understanding the AIDS pandemic, *Scientific American* May:58–66.

Anderson, R.M., May, R.M., Boily, M.C., Garnett, G.P., and Rowley, J.T., 1991, The spread of HIV-1 in Africa: Sexual contact patterns and the predicted demographic impact of AIDS, *Nature* **352**:581–589.

Bongaarts, J., 1988, Modeling the demographic impact of AIDS in Africa, in R. Kulstad, ed., *AIDS 1988: AAAS Symposium Papers*, AAAS Press, Washington, DC, USA.

Bongaarts, J., 1989, A model of the spread of HIV infection and the demographic impact of AIDS, *Statistics in Medicine* **8**:103–120.

Bongaarts, J., Reining, P., Way, P., and Conant, F., 1989, The relationship between male circumcision and HIV infection in African populations, *AIDS* **3**:373–377.

Bos, E., and Bulatao, R.A., forthcoming, The Demographic Impact of AIDS in Sub-Saharan Africa: Short- and Long-term Projections,

Mimeo, Population, Health, and Nutrition Division, World Bank, Washington, DC, USA.

Brookmeyer, R., 1991, Reconstruction and future trends of the AIDS epidemic in the United States, *Science* **253**:37–41.

Centers for Disease Control (USA), 1987, Human immunodeficiency virus infection in the United States: A review of current knowledge, *Morbidity and Mortality Weekly Report* **36**(5–6):1–48.

Fink, A.J., 1986, A possible explanation for heterosexual male infection with AIDS, *The New England Journal of Medicine* **315**(18):1167.

Frank, O., 1983, Infertility in sub-Saharan Africa: Estimates and implications, *Population and Development Review* **9**:137–144.

Godefroid, B., Augustin, N., and Didacem, N., 1988, Etude sur la séropositivé liée à l'infection au Virus de l'Immunodéficience Humaine au Rwanda, *Revue Medicale Rwandaise* **20**(54):37.

Hessol, N., Lifson, A.R., Rutherford, G.W., O'Malley, P.M., Franks, D.R., Darrow, W.W., and Jaffe, H.W., 1987, The natural history of human immunodeficiency virus infection in a cohort of homosexual and bisexual men: A 7-year prospective study, in *Abstract Volume, III International Conference on AIDS*, Washington, DC, USA.

N'Galy, B., Ryder, B., and Francis, H., 1988, HIV Prevalence in Zaire, 1984 to 1988, 4th International Conference on AIDS, June, abstract 5632, Stockholm, Sweden.

Piot, P., and Carael, M., 1988, Epidemiological and sociological aspects of HIV infection in developing countries, *British Medical Bulletin* **44**(1):68–88.

Piot, P., Plummer, F., Mhalu, F., Lamboray, J., Chin, J., and Mann, J., 1988, AIDS: An international perspective, *Science* **239**:573.

Plummer, F.A., Simonson, J.N., Ngugi, E., Cameron, D.W., Piot, P., and Ndinya-Achola, J.O., 1987, Incidence of human immunodeficiency virus (HIV) infection and related disease in a cohort of Nairobi prostitutes, in *Abstract Volume, III International Conference on AIDS*, Washington, DC, USA.

Plummer, F.A., Simonson, J.N., Cameron, D.W., Ndinya-Achola, J.O., Kreiss, J.K., Galeinya, M.N., Waiyaki, P., Cheang, M., Piot, P., Ronald, A.R., and Ngugi, E.N., 1991, Cofactors in male-female sexual transmission of human immunodeficiency virus type 1, *The Journal of Infectious Diseases* **163**:233–239.

Quinn, T.C., Mann, J.M., Curran, J.W., and Piot, P., 1986, AIDS in Africa: An epidemiological paradigm, *Science* **234**:955–963.

Quinn, T.C., Piot, P., McCormick, J.B., Feinsod, F.M., Taelman, H., Kapita, B., Stevens, W., and Fauci, A.S., 1987, Serologic and immunologic studies in patients with AIDS in North America and Africa, *Journal of the American Medical Association* **257**:2617–2621.

Simonson, J.N., Cameron, D.W., Gakinya, M.N., Ndinya-Achola, J.O., D'Costa, L.K., Karasira, P., Cheang, M., Ronald, A.R., Piot, P., and Plummer, F.A., 1988, Human immunodeficiency virus infection among men with sexually transmitted diseases, *The New England Journal of Medicine* **319**(5):274–278.

UN, 1991a, *The AIDS Epidemic and its Demographic Consequences*, Department of International Economic and Social Affairs, United Nations, New York, NY, USA.

UN, 1991b, *World Population Prospects: 1990*, Population Studies, No. 120, Publication No. ST/ESA/SER.A/120, Department of International Economic and Social Affairs, United Nations, New York, NY, USA.

US Bureau of the Census, 1991, *Recent HIV Seroprevalence Levels by Country: November 1991*, Research Note No. 4, Health Studies Research, Center for International Research, Washington, DC, USA.

WHO, 1991, *Current and Future Dimensions of the HIV/AIDS Pandemic*, Global Program on AIDS, World Health Organization, Geneva, Switzerland.

Chapter 10

How Many People Can Be Fed on Earth?

Gerhard K. Heilig

Many distinguished writers have studied the question whether food is a limiting factor for population growth. Since the time when Malthus started the debate some 200 years ago (see Malthus, 1967; Ricardo, 1964) thousands of books, research papers, and study reports have been published on the subject (Boserup, 1965, 1981; Clark, 1967; Clark and Haswell, 1964; Livi Bacci, 1991).[1] Despite these intense efforts, we are still far from consensus. A screening of available literature on estimating the earth's population carrying capacity reveals surprising diversity of results (see *Table 10.1*).

In 1945 Pearson and Harper calculated that between 902 million and 2.8 billion people could be supported by the earth's agriculture. Some 20 years later Clark (1967) estimated the sustainable population maximum of the earth to range between 40 and 157 billion! However, in the 1970s Buringh *et al.* (1975) considered the world food production potential equivalent to just 5.3 billion people. In the late 1970s and early 1980s a large FAO study (Higgins *et al.*, 1983) concluded that – only on Third World soils – between 3.9 and 32.4 billion people could be fed, depending on the level of agricultural inputs. Only a decade ago, Simon's (1981) *Ultimate Resource*

207

Table 10.1. Estimates of the earth's population carrying capacity during the past 100 years.

Source	Earth's maximum population carrying capacity	Date
Ravenstein (1891)	6 billion	1891
Penck (1925)	7.7–9.5 billion	1925
Pearson and Harper (1945)	0.9–2.8 billion	1945
Baade (1960)[a]	30 billion	1960
Clark (1967)[b]	47–157 billion	1967
Revelle (1967)[a]	41 billion	1967
Mückenhausen (1973)[c]	35–40 billion	1973
Buringh et al. (1977, 1975)	2.7–6.7 billion	1975
Westing (1981), Mann (1981)	about 2 billion	1981
Simon (1981), Kahn (1982)	no meaningful limitation	1982
FAO/UNFPA/IIASA[d] (Higgins et al., 1982)	for 1975: 1.957–32.407 billion for 2000: 3.590–33.195 billion	1982
Gilland (1983)[a]	7.5 million	1983
Resources for the Future (1984)	6.1 billion	1984
Marchetti (1978)	1 trillion	1978
World Hunger Program[e] (Cohen, 1992)	2.8–5.5 billion	1992
Ehrlich et al. (1993)	< 5.5 billion	1993

[a] Estimates are based on very low estimates of average food caloric consumption. According to Norse (1992) the three estimates of the global population carrying capacity would be much lower, if an average grain consumption of 800 kilograms per year were applied. Baade's estimate would be more than 18 billion; Revelle's would be 14 billion; and Gilland's would be 8.8 billion.

[b] "If we take world resources of agricultural land at 10.7 billion hectares of standard land equivalent, this could feed, at maximum standards, 47 billion people. ... For people living at Japanese standards of food consumption and Asian standards of timber requirements only 680 sq.m./person is required, and the world's potential agricultural and forest land could supply the needs of 157 billion people." See Clark (1967).

[c] Mückenhausen's estimate was based on a report of the US President's Science Advisory Commitee in 1967 which analyzed the world's production capacity of soils (US, 1967).

[d] The FAO/UNFPA/IIASA study estimated the global population carrying capacity for 1975 and 2000 at three agricultural input levels (low, medium high). For details see Appendix Tables 1 and 2 in Higgins et al. (1982).

[e] "The World Hunger Program at Brown University estimated that, with present levels of food production and an equal distribution of food, the world could sustain either 5.5 billion vegetarians, 3.7 billion people who get 15 percent of their calories from animal products, ... or 2.8 billion people who derive 25 percent of their calories from animal products" (Cohen, 1992).

Among other sources the author uses a compilation on "Estimates of Arable Land: Past Studies" in Shah et al. (1985).

became a popular book. It resolutely denied any limits to (population) growth; people were considered the "ultimate resource." Today *Beyond the Limits* by Meadows *et al.* (1992) is a bestseller. They argue that we have already passed the limits of sustainability and are on the way to ecological disaster. In 1992 the World Resources Institute published a wealth of data and analyses which imply that we are already approaching ecological limits in many sectors of our economies, including agriculture.

Most recently Ehrlich *et al.* (1993) analyzed the subject. According to their estimate it is "doubtful ... whether food security could be achieved indefinitely for a global population of 10 or 12 billion people." They thought it "rather likely that a sustainable population, one comfortable below Earth's nutritional capacity, will number far fewer than today's 5.5 billion people." There are many other studies, but probably the highest estimate of the globe's population carrying capacity was published by Marchetti (1978), who argued that a world population of 1 trillion people would not be impossible.

Obviously, these numbers are not much help to the student of future population trends. One reason for the large discrepancies is methodological divergences of the various approaches. Some authors deal with global averages of carrying capacity; others study small agro-ecological areas and only later aggregate the results. Some authors base their estimates on the most advanced agricultural technology or assume future innovation; others define the carrying capacity in terms of current, and in some regions rather low, levels of agricultural output. Biologists usually explain carrying capacity as the balance between natural resources and the number of people; social scientists consider human resources the critical factor and accentuate social limits to growth. More systematically, we can identify four reasons for the conceptual confusion: dissent about the reference area, disagreement about the means of sustenance, controversy on the mode of reaction to limitations, and confusion about the time frame. We discuss some of these problems in detail in later sections of this chapter. For now we can only conclude that there are more dimensions to the problem than one would expect at first sight. It seems to be necessary to combine the various aspects of the earth's carrying capacity into a consistent theoretical framework.

10.1   Dimensions of the Earth's Carrying Capacity

To visualize the major dimensions of the problem, imagine a pipe
through which the earth's food resources have to pass before they
can be used for feeding people (see *Figure 10.1*). The diameter of
the pipe, however, is not constant. While it is quite large on the
"input" side, it is significantly smaller on the "output" end. The
pipe's stepwise decreasing diameter symbolizes different kinds of restrictions to the earth's carrying capacity – technological, economic,
ecological, and sociocultural.

10.1.1   The hypothetical maximum carrying capacity

On the input side of our conceptual pipe we have the theoretical
maximum of the earth's food production capacity. This purely hypothetical measure is roughly equivalent to what biologists have
termed the net primary production (NPP) of the earth. The measure is based on the assumption that the ultimate limitation of food
production is given by the energy conversion ratio of photosynthesis. This is the basic biochemical process by which green plants
transform solar radiation into biomass. Since we (roughly) know
the total solar radiation input of the earth, we can calculate the
globe's maximum biomass production, which quantifies the initial
product of all animal and human food chains.

The NPP is only restricted by physical constants, such as the
total solar radiation energy input of earth, and by natural laws that
govern the biochemical processes of plant growth.[2] In its most
extreme version the measure ignores not only economic, social, cultural, and political restrictions of food production, but also technical
constraints and ecological feedback mechanisms. It assumes homogeneous implementation of most advanced agricultural technologies
throughout the world. Authors who have adopted this rather narrow definition of carrying capacity estimate the maximum world
population that can be sustained indefinitely into the future in the
range of 16 to 147 billion people, depending on the specific method
applied.[3] Marchetti's (1978) monstrous estimate of several trillion
carrying capacity of the earth is based on a similar approach.

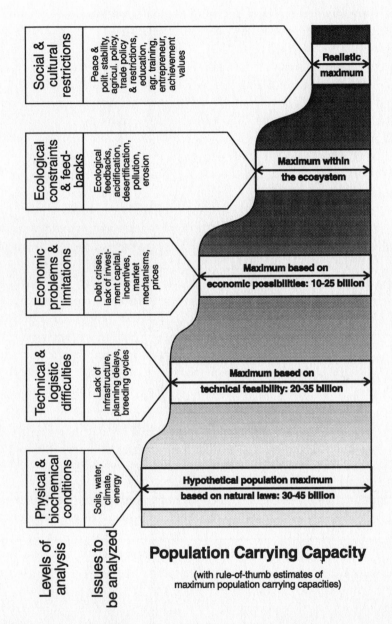

Figure 10.1. Conceptual model for analyzing the earth's population carrying capacity.

10.1.2   Technical and logistic restrictions and chances

The previous definition of carrying capacity assumes homogeneous distribution and instantaneous implementation of (advanced) food production technology. But this is impossible in reality. Even with existing agricultural technologies we would need years before we could use them throughout the world. They have to be adapted to local conditions; they must be integrated with existing food distribution channels; and they often require previous implementation of service and support schemes. The production and distribution of regionally adapted high-yield seeds, for instance, can take years or decades. Also the breeding cycles in husbandry have to be considered.

In addition to the usual delays in technology transfer, we have to realize that advanced agricultural methods are primarily available for good-quality soils in temperate climates and for subtropical and tropical irrigation cultures (such as Asian paddy rice crops). In the arid and semiarid zones of Africa, however, we still have traditional pastoral systems which survived quite well as long as animal and human population density was low. But since the population has doubled or tripled, the socioecological system is out of balance. The situation obviously requires new technology to increase productivity of food production. However, we cannot be sure that high-tech alternatives of animal husbandry, which could potentially boost productivity by orders of magnitude, are adaptable to the hot and dry climate. Current experiments are not too promising. It is not impossible that there simply is no high-tech alternative to traditional cattle ranging and primitive agriculture in certain parts of the world. We are just beginning to apply scientific methods to the management of arid and tropical soils, and it will probably take years or decades before we have drought-resistant, high-yield crops and livestock.

This indicates that the global carrying capacity is certainly diminished by agro-technical and logistic restrictions and delays. Some studies have tried to take this into account by defining different input levels for various agro-climatic regions. The FAO/UNDP/IIASA (1982) study, for instance, assumed three levels of agricultural input which largely correspond to levels of technology.

10.1.3   Economic barriers

Nothing in the world is free. Also the implementation of advanced agricultural technology and the expansion of agricultural areas into previously unused land is costly. One needs investment capital, functioning price mechanisms, adequate incentives for farmers, and a whole set of other economic conditions and mechanisms to boost food production for a world population of several billion. Current estimates of a global carrying capacity usually ignore these economic dimensions. However, in reality we find numerous economic difficulties and limitations which could further restrict global carrying capacity. On the other hand, few spheres in human life are capable of generating more powerful incentives and driving forces than the economy. Recent history has shown (for instance, in China) that agriculture can modernize within a few years and double or triple its productivity when the economic framework is right. Only few studies have developed agricultural models that take into account economic mechanisms, such as prices and (international) trade. Unfortunately these models are extremely complex and their methodology and assumptions are highly debatable (Parikh *et al.*, 1988).

It is an illusion to believe that economic development is predictable for more than a few years. The fundamental changes in global economic patterns, from the rise of the Asian Tigers (Taiwan, South Korea, Singapore, Thailand, Malaysia) and the economic boom in China to the total breakdown of Soviet and East European economies, should have taught us a lesson. The economic framework of agriculture is man-made and can be changed for the better or the worse.

The earth's carrying capacity in the 21st century will be a matter of economic decisions at least to the same extent as it will be a matter of sufficient natural resources. Three aspects are most important: the conditions of international agricultural trade, the dissemination of agricultural technology, and the implementation of functioning incentive structures. We can strengthen or weaken worldwide agricultural productivity, depending on what we do with trade restrictions and food subsidies. We can speed up or slow down agricultural modernization, depending on what we do with the results of agricultural research and development. We can block farmers' initiative or encourage their entrepreneurial spirit, depending on

how we arrange property rights, taxation, price mechanisms, access
to modern agricultural inputs, and education. The earth's carrying
capacity not only depends on natural conditions and technology, it
is also a function of specific economic arrangements.

10.1.4   Ecological constraints and feedback mechanisms

Since agriculture and livestock production – as everything else –
is embedded into a natural environment, we also have to take into
account ecological constraints and feedback mechanisms, such as
acidification, soil loss, groundwater pollution, or desertification.
These consequences of intense agriculture and animal production
can gradually diminish returns. Some ecologists have argued that
the overutilization of arable land and forest areas in Europe and
North America has already degraded the soils to such an extent
that artificial fertilization and soil management techniques cannot
repair the damage.

However, there is more to the ecological perspective than the
necessary modification of production systems in order to minimize
harmful impact on the environment. For instance, we need to reserve space for the (still remaining) fauna and flora, if we want to
avoid additional termination of whole strains of evolution. Keeping biodiversity at a high level is not (only) a matter of aesthetics
and respect – a large pool of plant and animal genes could be a
primary resource for future bio-sciences. We must also reserve natural space for human recreation. The 10 billion world population
of the 21st century, cramped into multi-million urban agglomerates,
will certainly need some of the potential crop area for leisure activities, such as playing golf or riding a horse. Finally, a significant
proportion of our environment cannot be utilized for agriculture or
cattle ranging because it has vital functions in stabilizing the climate. Cutting down tropical rain forests for agricultural expansion
would probably backfire. It would trigger or speed up climate change
which could worsen agricultural conditions elsewhere and diminish
overall food production. These examples show that the ecologically
sustainable population maximum is certainly below a level that is
determined by physical laws, technological possibilities, or optimal
economic structures.

10.1.5   Social, cultural, and political conditions

Some people believe that we just have to provide land, tractors, high-yield seeds, fertilizers and pesticides, agricultural training, and free markets to make a farmer highly efficient. This technocratic approach, however, ignores the social nature of man. We must realize that probably the most serious restrictions for maximal utilization of the earth's population carrying capacity arise from social, political, and cultural conditions.

Social and cultural constraints which prevent optimal land utilization can be found not only among traditional food collectors, hunters, and cattle rangers of Africa and Asia. In many societies we have political and social conditions which hinder farmers from fully exploiting the carrying capacity of their land. In some cases these restrictions are voluntary and based on ecological considerations. For instance, a growing number of European farmers and agricultural politicians have realized that maximizing food production by means of agrochemistry and mechanization cannot be the ultimate goal of agriculture. They begin to exclude land from cultivation to make it available for natural reservations or recreational purposes. In Germany, for instance, 911,576 hectares (or 7.8 percent) of arable land was taken out of production between 1988–1989 and 1990–1991. In the new states of eastern Germany even 12.8 percent of the arable land was excluded from cultivation in 1990–1991. There are similar trends in all European countries, especially in Italy and France, where 357,922 and 113,922 hectares of land were taken out of agricultural production (Bundesministerium für Raumordnung, Bauwesen und Städtebau, 1991:62–64).

However, this noble self-restriction of agriculture (which is facilitated by substantial government subsidies) is rather untypical. Usually, there are other, more unpleasant sociocultural and political constraints. Many farmers throughout the world are working their fields amid (civil) wars, suffer from lack of technology and modern inputs, or are restricted by ridiculously low producer prices or market regulations. They are forced into collectivization by fanatical bureaucrats, and their children are deprived of adequate education and training. These kinds of sociocultural and political constraints probably restrict the carrying capacity of the earth much more than anything else.

To my knowledge there is no estimate of carrying capacity which takes into account all five kinds of restrictions. Scientists particularly shy away from addressing sociocultural and political constraints. Usually, the concept is defined in terms of natural resources available for food production at a given level of agricultural technology. This reflects widespread ignorance of key factors – economic, social, cultural, and political – that limit food production. In Section 10.2 we examine the multiple dimensions of the earth's carrying capacity in greater detail.

10.2 Natural Resources

According to our pipe concept of carrying capacity, natural conditions (such as the globe's solar radiation input) and basic biochemical processes (such as photosynthesis) ultimately determine the earth's food production potential. If we could transform the total solar energy input of the earth into biomass – and if we could eat this biomass – we could probably feed 1 trillion people. But this is just a theoretical exercise (which we discuss later). For all practical purposes we have to consider real agro-climatic conditions. Four natural resources and conditions directly limit the globe's carrying capacity: land, water, climate, and fossil energy.

10.2.1 Land

Since the beginning of the debate on the globe's carrying capacity, the land factor has usually been considered a limitation for increasing food production. The world's land area is, undoubtedly, limited, and only a small proportion is suitable for agriculture (*Table 10.2*). Many physical and chemical constraints restrict the arable area – some land is too steep or too shallow, other areas have drainage or tillage problems. There are serious constraints of soil fertility, such as low nutrient retention capacity, aluminum toxicity, phosphorus fixations hazards, low potassium reserves, or excess of salts or sodium.

Both in its 1990–1991 and 1992–1993 reports on world resources, the World Resources Institute (WRI) published detailed estimates of these physical and chemical soil constraints by climatic class for major regions and on a country-by-country basis. The estimates in

Table 10.2. Cropland in percent of land without soil constraints, 25 highest and lowest, in 1989.

Country	Population (1000)	Land area (1000 ha)	Cropland (1000 ha)	Land without soil Constraints (1000 ha)	Cropland in % of land without soil constraints
Lesotho	1724	3035	320	1	32000.0
Malaysia	8451	32855	4880	196	2489.8
Lao PDR	4024	23080	901	37	2435.1
Thailand	54857	51089	22126	983	2250.9
Burundi	5315	2565	1336	66	2024.2
Mauritius	1069	185	106	7	1514.3
Rwanda	6994	2467	1153	91	1267.0
Sierra Leone	4049	7162	1801	187	963.1
Syrian Arab Rep.	12085	18406	5503	643	855.8
Vietnam	65276	32549	6600	989	667.3
Uganda	18118	19955	6705	1210	554.1
Bangladesh	112548	13017	9292	1719	540.5
Benin	4493	11062	1860	360	516.7
Lebanon	2694	1023	301	59	510.2
India	835610	297319	168990	33232	508.5
Côte d'Ivoire	11552	31800	3660	730	501.4
Brazil	147283	845651	78650	17081	460.5
Togo	3424	5439	1444	319	452.7
Cambodia	8044	17652	3056	695	439.7
Nigeria	105015	91077	31335	7797	401.9
Pakistan	118476	77088	20730	5250	394.9
Cuba	10500	10982	3329	888	374.9
Cameroon	11453	46540	7008	1949	359.6
Ethiopia	47942	110100	13930	30079	46.3
Mexico	86672	190869	24710	55930	44.2
Kenya	23187	56969	2428	7342	33.1
Argentina	31914	273669	35750	111781	32.0
Botswana	1256	56673	1380	4792	28.8
Sudan	24487	237600	12510	50390	24.8
Peru	21105	128000	3730	15264	24.4
Somalia	7257	62734	1039	4519	23.0
Bolivia	7115	108439	3460	15415	22.4
Uruguay	3077	17481	1304	6100	21.4
Kuwait	1971	1782	4	31	12.9
Egypt	51186	99545	2585	24633	10.5
Chad	5539	125920	3205	34160	9.4
Niger	7492	126670	3605	41388	8.7
Namibia	1725	82329	662	9308	7.1
Mali	8938	122019	2093	40865	5.1
Libya	4382	175954	2150	54004	4.0
Saudi Arabia	13585	214969	1185	30579	3.9
Yemen, PDR	2416	33297	119	3870	3.1
Oman	1446	21246	48	3897	1.2
United Arab Emirates	1538	8360	39	3707	1.1
Albania	3186	2740	707	96958	0.7
Mauritania	1970	102522	199	58867	0.3

this discussion are from the 1992–1993 WRI report and are based on a complex methodology, which combines the Fertility Capability Classification (FCC) system developed at North Carolina State University (Sanches *et al.*, 1982), agro-climatic data from FAO's Agro-Ecological Zones project (FAO 1978a, 1978b, 1981a, 1981b), and the FAO/UNESCO soil map of the world.

The estimates are shocking. The most seriously handicapped region is Southeast Asia: more than 93 percent of the soils have physical or chemical constraints. The situation is not much better in Southwest Asia: only 12 percent of the soils are free of inherent fertility constraints. In South America 80 percent and in Africa 82 percent of the soils have constraints. Central America is a little better: "only" 73 percent of the soils are hampered by physical or chemical restrictions (World Resources Institute/United Nations Environment Programme/United Nations Development Programme, 1990:286–287).[4] On a country-by-country basis the estimates are even more dramatic. For India, the WRI reports just 33.2 million hectares of unconstrained soils; this would be equivalent to just 0.04 hectares (or 400 square meters) per person. Bangladesh's unconstrained soil resources would be even less: only 0.02 hectares per person. Pakistan, the Philippines, and Indonesia would have from 0.4 to 0.6 hectares per person of soil without inherent physical or chemical constraints.

What do these statistics indicate? The WRI reports that "the extent of land with soil constraints is an important indicator of agricultural costs, the *potential and success of future expansion* [emphasis added], and the comparative advantage of a nation's agricultural production" (World Resources Institute/United Nations Environment Programme/United Nations Development Programme, 1990:289).

The WRI further explains that "in the past 10 years, the FCC system has proven a meaningful tool for describing fertility limitations on crop yields" (*ibid*:289). Do the estimates – in other words – indicate that we are already short of fertile soils for future expansion of food production?

Not at all! First, one has to read the footnotes attached to the WRI tables. Here we find a few hints that explain what is meant by the various soil constraints. It turns out that most of the so-called constraints are just specific natural conditions that can be somewhat easily overcome with modern agricultural technology. Consider the case of soils with "low potassium reserves" which constrain crops because of potassium deficiency. There is a simple solution: throw potassium fertilizer on them! Other examples of soil constraints are "steep slopes" or "drainage problems": would one think that many of these soils can be found in the extremely productive paddy rice and wheat areas of Asia, where agriculture in some places has been practiced for more than 8000 years (as in China)? "Aluminum toxicity" is also a so-called constraints that turn out to be less dramatic than its name: it limits the growth of common crops, "unless lime is applied" (World Resources Institute/United Nations Environment Programme/United Nations Development Programme, 1992:284) – a practice that should not be completely impossible.

There are, of course, serious soil constraints that cannot be overcome by technology, but the WRI data do not distinguish between these and simple problems of soil management. For thousands of years farmers had to cope with soils that were less than perfect. They had to build terraces, add (natural) fertilizers, irrigate or drain the soil. But this did not hinder them from supplying some of the most prominent empires of history, such as the dynasties of China or the kingdoms of ancient Egypt.

There is a second reason why the WRI data on soil constraints are worthless as indicators of the earth's carrying capacity: they do not match with current trends in food production – to be more precise, in some cases the indicators are just absurd when compared with agricultural performance. For instance, according to the WRI the continent-size nation of India has only 33.2 million hectares of internally unconstrained soils, but FAO reports that India's farmers are cultivating some 169 million hectares of cropland – which is five times the area of "unconstrained soils" (cropland equals arable land plus land under permanent crops). In other words, according to the WRI most of India's farmers are producing on marginal land, which should limit crop yields. But just the opposite has happened during the past 30 years. Between 1961 and 1989 India's farmers increased cereal production by a spectacular 129 percent (from 87,376,000 to 199,816,000 tons). They also increased the cereal yields from 947 to 1,921 kg per hectare area harvested. In Thailand just 983,000

hectares are free of soil constraints, according to WRI data. Is
it not strange that the country's farmers actually cultivated 22.1
million hectares of cropland – nearly 23 times the area of the unconstrained soils? Only the rice area harvested was 10 times the size
of the unconstrained soils area. Thailand's farmers also managed to
increase cereal production by 131 percent between 1961 and 1989.
Most absurd are the estimates of soil constraints for Malaysia. According to WRI data only 0.6 percent (or 196,000 hectares) of the
country's land area is covered by unconstrained soils. Obviously
this did not have a great effect on the country's farmers, who cultivated 4.9 million hectares of cropland in 1989 – 25 times the area of
unconstrained soils. It also did not affect their productivity, since
they managed to increase cereal production by 62 percent between
1961 and 1989. These are only a few examples. We can find a
large number of countries where the farmers expanded cultivation
far into the area of so-called constrained soils, while at the same
time substantially increasing crop yields.

There is a third reason why WRI's soil data have limited relevance: a high percentage of unconstrained soils in a country does
not correlate with good agricultural performance. For example, according to the WRI, Chad has one of the largest areas of excellent
soils – 34.2 million hectares have no inherent physical or chemical
constraints, an opulent 6.2 hectares per person. Is it not strange
that the farmers use less than 10 percent of this area for cultivation
and that famines are notorious in a place with one of the largest per
capita resources of first-rate soils? This is not just an isolated case.
According to WRI data, nearly all typical famine countries of Africa
(Ethiopia, Sudan, Somalia, Mali) have huge areas of top-rated soils
which are many times the size of their actual cropland.

Given these examples it is obvious that factors other than soil
quality by itself are responsible for agricultural performance. There
is simply no correlation between food production and soil constraints
as reported by the WRI.

On the other hand, we have a large number of agricultural techniques available that could help to either expand the arable land and
increase yields on marginal soils or improve the overall efficiency of
crop production.

First, we could expand the area of multiple harvests. In many places farmers could use their land several times during a growing season instead of only once or twice. Modern seeds, advanced agricultural technology, artificial fertilizers, and other agricultural inputs have made these techniques of multi-cropping possible. It is a myth that we are already overutilizing the world's arable land. This is only true in some European and Asian regions. Large parts of Latin America and Africa have excellent soils which are still cultivated with most primitive agricultural technology. Crop yields are often 60 to 90 percent below the average European level. Better inputs and modern agricultural methods could substantially expand the area of multiple harvests.

Second, we could expand cultivation to marginal land. There is still plenty of dry land that could be irrigated, swamps that could be drained, steep hills which could be terraced. We could cover land with greenhouses in cold regions or use forests for multilayered cultivation. It is also possible to convert shallow seas into agricultural land. The Netherlands have demonstrated that even in an adverse climate one can produce more than enough (tropical) fruits and vegetables on artificially climatized and drained land. In most countries it was not necessary to increase arable land during the past decades, but some agricultures have demonstrated that a spectacular expansion of cultivation is still possible. Libya, for instance, has converted desert into circles of irrigated cropland; between 1961 and 1989 its area of irrigated agriculture nearly doubled from 121,000 to 242,000 hectares (Allan, 1976). Burundi, which is already densely populated, managed to increase its arable land from 765,000 to 1,120,000 hectares and the area of irrigated agriculture from 3,000 to 72,000 hectares. Tanzania nearly doubled its arable land and increased the irrigated agriculture more than seven times. There are still spectacular land reserves in parts of Africa and Latin America. Of course, some of these expansions are rather absurd in terms of energy efficiency or economic costs; one might even consider the idea of growing wheat in the desert a form of hypocrisy. But these cases show what could be done in agriculture if money and technology were accessible and environmental concerns could be ignored.

Third, we can expand food production areas to the water bodies of our globe – lakes, rivers, and seas (Sindermann, 1982). While there is certainly a danger of exploiting the natural fish population of the sea, efforts are being made to begin exploring the potential of fish farming. There is already some fish farming on the northern coast of England, in Norwegian fjords, along the coast of Sweden, and in Chinese paddy rice fields. A significant proportion of Europe's salmon supply is produced in fish farms near the Shetland Islands. But these are still small production sites compared with the huge coastal zones of our continents. It has been argued that large-scale fish-farming schemes might disturb the natural balance of the maritime ecosystem, which, in turn, could limit its production potential (Uthoff, 1978; UNO/FAO, 1976). However, recent research has found only a minimal risk of local sea pollution caused by a discharge of nutrients in intense fish farming (Ackefors and Enell, 1990).

Fourth, we can switch from nonfood to food crops. Currently, a significant proportion of fertile land is used not for food production in a narrow sense, but to grow lifestyle-related cash crops, such as tobacco, tea, cocoa, or coffee. It is hard to estimate the areas wasted for the illegal cultivation of drugs (marijuana, coca, etc.), but it must be substantial. Farmers also spend arable land for producing natural fibers, such as jute, flax, or sisal – nonfood products for which synthetic substitutes are available. In some countries, such as Brazil, there is substantial energy-cropping (sugar cane), and some European governments encourage farmers to grow rape seed and produce bio-fuel. In some countries (Italy, Spain) large areas are used to grow wine. And – last but not least – we spend considerable amounts of land to produce hops, which is mainly used for brewing beer. According to FAO statistics, it is quite likely that some 20 percent of all arable land worldwide is used to produce nonfood or lifestyle-related products, including drugs (see *Table 10.3*).

Previously it was thought that a given plot of land can only feed a fixed number of people. Later, scientists realized that it is not only the size and natural quality of the land, but mainly the level of agricultural technology which determines the land's food production capacity. This basic understanding is still rare among today's environmental doomsdayers, such as the World Resources

Table 10.3. Lifestyle-related and nonfood agricultural production.

	Area harvested (1000 ha)		Growth (%)	In % of total arable land	
	1961	1990	1961–1990	1961	1990
Drugs (marijuana, coca)	?	?	?	?	?
Wine	?	?	?	?	?
Tobacco leaves	3,397	4,629	36.6	0.3	0.3
Hops[a]	55	79	43.6	0.0	0.0
Tea	1,318	2,442	85.3	0.1	0.2
Coffee	9,706	11,241	15.8	0.8	0.8
Cocoa beans	4,100	5,312	29.6	0.3	0.4
Sugar beets	6,917	8,656	25.1	0.6	0.6
Sugar cane	8,914	17,120	92.1	0.7	1.3
Flax fiber	2,041	1,113	−45.5	0.2	0.1
Hemp fiber	685	233	−66.0	0.1	0.0
Jute, jutelike fibers	2,629	2,218	−15.6	0.2	0.2
Linseed	7,615	4,078	−46.4	0.6	0.3
Rape seed[a]	6,277	17,588	180.2	0.5	1.3
Sunflower seed	6,667	16,913	153.7	0.5	1.3
Seed cotton[a]	31,897	32,984	3.4	2.5	2.4
Sesame seed[a]	5,051	6,336	25.4	0.4	0.5
Soybeans	23,806	56,351	136.7	1.9	4.2
Castor beans	1,233	1,657	34.4	0.1	0.1
Groundnuts	16,641	20,135	21.0	1.3	1.5
Total	138,949	209,085	50.5	11.1	15.5

[a]1961–1991.

Source: Food and Agricultural Organization, 1994: PC-AGROSTAT, Rome.

Institute. They continue to focus their attention on the physical conditions of soils, collecting ever-more detailed inventories of soil characteristics. But they are obviously blind to the fact that these characteristics are becoming relevant. The size and quality of soils are just two variables in a multiterm equation of agricultural productivity, which is mainly determined by technological, economic, sociocultural, and political factors.

10.2.2 Water

Some experts have argued that it is not land, but water which is the critical resource for the global carrying capacity (Rivière, 1989). The most prominent Cassandra of a world water crisis is Malin Falkenmark. She has argued that "water scarcity [is] now threatening two-thirds of the African population" (Falkenmark, 1989:118). Her pessimism, however, is not shared by prominent hydrologists who have collected detailed water resource inventories for Africa. Almost three dozen water experts, assisted by five major hydrological institutes, contributed to a UN publication which concluded:

> There is almost nowhere in Africa where groundwater is not found at one depth or another.... Mineral-water and thermo-mineral springs abound in the African continent in the fracture zones. They constitute a major potential resource which has been explored and exploited in only a few places. [UN, 1988:13–14]

Other water experts have raised the argument that we should not confuse man-induced regional or local water shortages with climate-related resource scarcity (Bandyopadhyay, 1989).

Globally around 70 percent of all water withdrawal is used in agriculture (*Table 10.4*). This explains why the water situation is, in fact, important to the food production capacity of the earth. There are also some reasons for concern. Available statistics confirm that in some river basins, freshwater is being extracted for human use (including agriculture) at rates approaching those at which the supply is renewed. In particular, Egypt is probably on the brink of a water crisis. The country's renewable freshwater resources include some 58.3 km^3, of which 56.5 km^3 are from the Nile's annual flow and 1.8 km^3 from other internal renewable resources. Some 97 percent of these resources (or 56.4 km^3) are already being withdrawn. Egypt's agriculture needs 49.6 km^3 of water. Only 2.8 km^3 are used in industry, and the withdrawal for domestic purposes is about 3.9 km^3.

Libya's agriculture might also be limited by extreme water shortages. According to recent estimates the country has a renewable freshwater resource of some 0.7 km^3 per year – mostly from underground aquifers. Libya's annual withdrawal, however, is estimated at 2.83 km^3 – which is four times the rate of natural replacement. Some 75 percent of this unsustainable withdrawal is used in agriculture. The country's spectacular increase of grain production is obviously borrowed from future generations.

Table 10.4. Freshwater resources and withdrawals for selected countries: sorted by withdrawal in percent of total resources.

	Annual river inflow (km³)	Annual internal renewable water resources				Annual withdrawal per capita (m³)	Annual withdrawal in % of total water resources[a]	Agricultural withdrawal in % of total withdrawal
		Total (km³)	Per capita (m³)	Per 10000 ha of cropland[b]	Per 10000 ha of land			
Congo	621	181	90.77	10.77	0.05	20	0	11
Zaire	x	1019	28.31	1.30	0.04	22	0	17
Gambia	19	3	3.50	0.17	0.03	33	0	91
Cambodia	410	88.1	10.68	0.29	0.05	69	0	94
Paraguay	220	94	21.98	0.42	0.02	111	0	78
Cameroon	x	208	18.50	0.30	0.04	30	0	35
Uganda	x	66	3.58	0.10	0.03	20	0	60
Angola	x	158	15.77	197.50	0.01	43	0	76
Haiti	x	11	1.69	0.12	0.04	46	0	68
Zambia	x	96	11.35	0.18	0.01	86	0	26
Benin	x	26	5.48	0.14	0.02	26	0	58
Chad	x	38.4	6.76	0.12	0.00	35	0	82
Brazil	1760	5190	34.52	0.66	0.06	212	1	40
Uruguay	65	59	18.86	0.45	0.03	241	1	91
Ghana	x	53	3.53	0.19	0.02	35	1	52
Guatemala	x	116	12.61	0.62	0.11	139	1	74
Tanzania	x	76	2.78	0.14	0.01	36	1	74
Indonesia	x	2530	14.02	1.19	0.13	96	1	76
Niger	30	14	1.97	0.04	0.00	44	1	74
Bangladesh	1000	1357	11.74	1.46	0.94	211	1	96
Côte d'Ivoire	x	74	5.87	0.20	0.02	68	1	67
Nigeria	47	261	2.31	0.08	0.03	44	1	54
Lesotho	x	4	2.25	0.13	0.01	34	1	56
Mozambique	x	58	3.70	0.19	0.01	53	1	66
Vietnam	x	376	5.60	0.57	0.11	81	1	78
Canada	x	2901	109.37	0.63	0.03	1752	1	8
Nepal	x	170	8.88	0.64	0.12	155	2	95
Malawi	x	9	1.07	0.04	0.01	22	2	49
Ethiopia	x	110	2.35	0.08	0.01	48	2	86
Malaysia	x	456	26.30	0.93	0.14	765	2	47
Mali	x	62	6.62	0.30	0.00	159	2	97

Table 10.4. Continued.

| | Annual river inflow (km³) | Annual internal renewable water resources | | | | Annual withdrawal per capita (m³) | Annual withdrawal in % of total water resources | Agricultural withdrawal in % of total withdrawal[a] |
		Total (km³)	Per capita (m³)	Per 10000 ha of cropland[b]	Per 10000 ha of land			
Rwanda	x	6.3	0.87	0.05	0.02	23	2	68
Argentina	300	694	21.47	0.19	0.03	1059	3	73
Burundi	x	3.6	0.66	0.03	0.01	20	3	64
AFRICA	x	4184	6.46	0.22	0.01	244	3	88
Yugoslavia	115	150	6.29	0.19	0.06	393	3	12
Senegal	12	23.2	3.15	0.04	0.01	201	4	92
Swaziland	x	6.96	8.82	0.42	0.04	414	4	93
Hungary	109	6	0.57	0.01	0.01	502	5	36
Australia	0	343	20.48	0.07	0.00	1306	5	33
Zimbabwe	x	23	2.37	0.08	0.01	129	5	79
Somalia	0	11.5	1.52	0.11	0.00	167	7	97
Kenya	x	14.8	0.59	0.06	0.00	48	7	62
USSR	300	4384	15.22	0.19	0.02	1330	8	65
Turkey	7	196	3.52	0.07	0.03	317	8	57
WORLD	x	40673	7.69	0.28	0.03	660	8	69
Philippines	0	323	5.18	0.41	0.11	693	9	61
Syria	27.9	7.6	0.61	0.01	0.00	449	9	83
Greece	13.5	45.15	4.49	0.12	0.03	721	12	63
Romania	171	37	1.59	0.04	0.02	1144	12	59
Sudan	100	30	1.19	0.02	0.00	1089	14	99
Sri Lanka	0	43.2	2.51	0.23	0.07	503	15	96
Dominican Rep.	x	20	2.79	0.14	0.04	453	15	89
ASIA	x	10485	3.37	0.23	0.04	526	15	86
EUROPE	x	2321	4.66	0.17	0.05	726	15	86
Mexico	x	357.4	4.03	0.14	0.02	901	15	33
Peru	x	40	1.79	0.11	0.00	294	15	72
Algeria	0.2	18.9	0.75	0.02	0.00	161	16	74
Portugal	31.6	34	3.31	0.09	0.04	1062	16	48
Netherlands	80	10	0.68	0.11	0.03	1023	16	34
China	0	2800	2.47	0.29	0.03	462	16	87
Korea, Rep.	x	63	1.45	0.30	0.06	298	17	75
Thailand	69	110	1.97	0.05	0.02	599	18	90

Table 10.4. Continued.

	Annual river inflow (km³)	Annual internal renewable water resources				Annual withdrawal per capita (m³)	Annual withdrawal in % of total water resources[a]	Agricultural withdrawal in % of total withdrawal
		Total (km³)	Per capita (m³)	Per 10000 ha of cropland[b]	Per 10000 ha of land			
India	235	1850	2.17	0.11	0.06	612	18	93
South Africa	x	50	1.42	0.04	0.00	404	18	67
USA	x	2478	9.94	0.13	0.03	2162	19	42
Japan		547	4.43	1.18	0.14	923	20	50
Korea, DPR	x	67	2.92	0.34	0.06	1649	21	73
France	15	170	3.03	0.09	0.03	728	22	15
Oman	0	2	1.36	0.42	0.00	325	24	94
Germany, Fed. Rep.	82	79	1.30	0.11	0.03	668	26	20
Poland	6.8	49.4	1.29	0.03	0.02	472	30	24
Italy	7.6	179.4	3.13	0.15	0.06	983	30	59
Pakistan	170	298	2.43	0.14	0.04	2053	33	98
Morocco	0	30	1.19	0.03	0.01	501	37	91
Iran	x	117.5	2.08	0.08	0.01	1362	39	87
Spain	1	110.3	2.80	0.05	0.02	1174	41	62
Jordan	0.4	0.7	0.16	0.02	0.00	173	41	65
Iraq	66	34	1.80	0.06	0.01	4575	43	92
Afghanistan	x	50	3.02	0.06	0.01	1436	52	99
Tunisia	0.6	3.75	0.46	0.01	0.00	325	53	80
Belgium	4.1	8.4	0.85	0.10	0.03	917	72	4
Israel	0.45	1.7	0.37	0.04	0.01	447	88	79
Malta	0	0.025	0.07	0.02	0.01	68	92	16
Egypt	56.5	1.8	0.03	x	0.00	1202	97	88
Yemen, PDR	0	1.5	0.60	0.13	0.00	1167	129	93
Saudi Arabia	0	2.2	0.16	0.02	0.00	255	164	47
United Arab Emirates	0	0.3	0.19	0.08	0.00	565	299	80
Libya	0	0.7	0.15	0.00	0.00	623	404	75

[a]Total water resources include both internal renewable resources and river flows from other countries.
[b]Cropland includes arable land and land under permanent crops.
x = unknown/no data available.
Source: WRI/UNEP/UNDP (1992): World Resources, 1992–1993. New York, Oxford (Oxford University Press), pp. 328–329, 274–275.

Another interesting case is Saudi Arabia. Since 1961 the desert country has increased its wheat production by a spectacular 4706 percent, from merely 85,000 to 4,000,000 metric tons. Today, the country's farmers are not only able to provide more than 35 percent of the domestic food supply – which is a spectacular achievement in itself – but they actually produce more grain than the country needs. In 1991 Saudi Arabia's net export of wheat was 1,805,000 metric tons, as compared with a net import of 67,600 metric tons in 1974. Ecologists have argued that the bumper harvests were mainly achieved by exploiting fossil – that is nonrenewable – water resources below the desert. They estimate that in 1988 the country withdrew some 20.5 km^3 of water, 90 percent from nonrenewable fossil groundwater aquifers. They also estimate that Saudi Arabia's agriculture needs 90 percent of the water available, with 35 percent of the agricultural water consumption being used in wheat production. According to the *Middle East Economic Digest* (Hopes dry up..., 1989:15), which cites a confidential US Government agency report, at the current rate of depletion Saudi Arabia's fossil groundwater would be exhausted by 2007.

Many authors have argued that Africa is a parched continent (Pearce, 1991). The most pessimistic position maintains that by the year 2000, Tunisia, Kenya, Malawi, Burundi, and Rwanda will suffer a permanent water crisis (Falkenmark, 1989:116).

There is also much concern about the arid regions of the north China plain. According to recent calculations by the World Resources Institute, the 200 million population is already exploiting the freshwater resources to a large extent. The WRI concludes that "if present trends continue, the region will have 6 percent less water than needed by the end of the century" (World Resources Institute/United Nations Environment Programme/United Nations Development Programme, 1992:163). These examples certainly seem to confirm the conclusion that water is a critical factor for limiting global carrying capacity, but there is also empirical evidence that does not fit into the pessimistic outlook.

According to the most recent estimate the earth's total annual freshwater resource is some 40,673 km^3. The annual agricultural withdrawal is about 2,236 km^3, which is less than 6 percent of the globe's renewable water. Worldwide industrial and domestic water consumption together account for another 995 km^3, or just 2.5 percent of the total water resource (World Resources Institute/United Nations Environment Programme/United Nations Development Programme, 1992:328). It is hard to imagine that we are approaching global limits of freshwater withdrawal when more than 92 percent of the known reserves are still untouched.

If there is no scarcity at the global level, the uneven regional distribution of resources might be the problem. Africa is frequently considered an example of continentwide agricultural stagnation – triggered, or at least intensified, by water scarcity (Falkenmark, 1991). Available statistics, however, do not confirm this theory. Africa has 4,184 km^3 of annual internal renewable water resources, which was nearly 6,500 m^3 per person per year in 1990. This is almost five times the per capita freshwater availability of West Germany, which was only 1,300 m^3. Moreover, Africa's freshwater is not only located in the tropical areas, as one might suspect. There are large reserves all over the continent: famine ridden Somalia has more than twice the per capita internal freshwater resource of the Netherlands (1,520 versus 680 m^3).[5] The "arid" Chad has internal freshwater sources of 6,760 m^3 per person – more than three times the per capita water resource of the rainy United Kingdom (which is only 2,110 m^3). In Angola there are 15,770 m^3 of freshwater for each person – nearly 28 times more than, for instance, in Hungary, which has just 570 m^3 available.

There is also more than enough freshwater in South America. The total resource is estimated at 10,377 km^3 which is equivalent to the combined renewable water resources of Europe, the whole (former) Soviet Union, and Africa. On average, each inhabitant of South America has potential access to 34,960 m^3 of freshwater, which is 7.5 times more than in Europe. All large South American nations have abundant per capita freshwater resources, ranging from 18,860 m^3 in Uruguay to 43,370 m^3 in Venezuela (which is many times the typical ratio for Europe, Asia, or the USA). Only Peru is somewhat "shorter" in freshwater: 1,790 m^3 per person are available – a still abundant amount, however, if compared with the 850 m^3 of Belgium's internal renewable water resource.

The situation in North America and Central America is mixed: very large resources in Canada, more limited resources on the

Caribbean Islands. However, there is no indication that freshwater resources are running out in the region. Mexico, for instance, has larger internal freshwater resources than Italy: 4,030 versus 3,130 m^3 per person per year.

The freshwater resources of Asian countries are very different. At the national level, China has enough water – 2,470 m^3 per person per year.[6] India, Pakistan, and Thailand have a little less (2,170, 2,430, and 1,970 m^3 per person per year, respectively), but are far from critical. There is abundant freshwater in Indonesia (14,020 m^3), Bangladesh (11,740 m^3), and Malaysia (2,630 m^3).

An interesting indicator of water stress is the proportion of annual withdrawals from available resources. In 51 countries the annual withdrawals are equal to or less than 1 percent of the renewable freshwater resources – including populous nations such as Indonesia, Brazil, and Nigeria. China uses 16 percent of its annual freshwater resource; India, 18 percent; Kenya, just 7 percent. In all of Africa, including the drought-affected Sahel, only three countries extract more than 50 percent of their annual freshwater resource, namely, Egypt (90 percent), Libya (404 percent), and Tunisia (53 percent). Most African countries are extracting less than 3 percent of their resources. In South America the highest extraction is reported from Peru: a mere 15 percent. All other South American nations have not even touched their renewable water reserves – they use typically less than 2 percent. Even in Asia, where the situation is a little tighter, extraction rates typically range between 1 and 30 percent. Only Afghanistan, Israel, and Cyprus have extraction rates of more than 50 percent. For these countries the situation is certainly serious. Jordan, Algeria, and Tunisia are also critical. The real "dramatic" cases, however, are only a small number of states of the Arabian Peninsula: Qatar, Saudi Arabia, United Arab Emirates, and Yemen. They are all withdrawing water at much higher rates than those at which their resource is renewed.

These statistics indicate that at the national level only a very small number of countries are facing water resources shortages. On the other hand, local or regional water shortages are well known, as well as strong seasonal variation of availability. It is also obvious that groundwater pollution is a major problem in some places, such as in very intensely used agricultural or industrial areas. Can we solve these water problems, or will they impose serious restrictions on the world's agricultural production? To answer these questions three aspects have to be taken into account.

First, with a 10 to 15 billion world population there is no alternative to the implementation of (advanced) water management and exploitation technologies. It will also be necessary to find political solutions for water conflicts. But this is nothing new. Water – as well as air – has always been a natural resource that must be managed. No one knew this better than the ancient civilizations along the Nile or in the desert. They developed highly sophisticated methods of water exploitation, storage, distribution, and conservation. We tend to forget that large irrigation systems were built in the Middle East some 4,000 to 5,000 years ago and that during the Roman Empire the capital city could flourish only because it was supplied with water through aqueducts across hundreds of miles. We have to advance these methods (Meybeck *et al.*, 1990). Most likely it will be necessary to pump freshwater to agricultural areas over long distances (such as from northern United States to southern California); we certainly will have to settle conflicts over limited water resources between neighboring countries (such as between Israel and Lebanon); some islands (such as Malta) and some densely populated agricultural regions (such as northern China) will require the implementation of advanced water conservation and recycling schemes. These methods are not impossible, and they have proved to be successful in the past.

Second, we have to understand that water use is essentially a recycling process: frequently water is just moved through biological and technical systems for cleaning or as some kind of biological catalyst. Much of the freshwater withdrawal (especially in agriculture) is not consumed, but directly returned to a river or underground aquifer. From there it can be used several times before it finally reaches the sea. We usually do not consume water in the same way we exploit fossil fuels or scarce minerals. These natural resources have a much lower recycling rate than water – they are actually destroyed or at least removed from natural cycles for a very long time through human consumption. Consumptive uses of water, such as the evaporation from industrial cooling towers and irrigation systems, make up only a small proportion of water withdrawal. The real water problem is not its natural scarcity, but the pollution we add to the returning flows and the carelessness with which we use freshwater in households, industries, and agriculture.

Finally, both industries and private households have already caused serious local or regional water contamination. Unfortunately, high-tech agriculture itself is a major polluter of groundwater and river flows (Biswas, 1993). In some intensively cultivated agricultural areas of Europe the excessive use of fertilizers has raised the nitrate concentration in groundwater to dangerously high levels. We can also observe pesticide contamination of freshwater resources in some areas of North America and Europe (Hallberg, 1989; Leistra and Boesten, 1989). An increase in food production could easily lead to further deterioration of water resources. On the other hand, this trend is not inevitable. All experts agree that there is still a huge potential for improving the efficiency of fertilizer use, irrigation, water treatment, and recycling (Biswas and Arar, 1988). Much has already been done to clean lakes and rivers in Europe. Twenty-five years ago the lakes in southern Germany frequently had to be closed to swimmers because of pollution with coli bacteria; today one could drink the water. European farmers have also realized the danger of overfertilization. Contrary to popular belief they have not increased nitrogen fertilizer application per hectare of arable land during the past 10 years.

On the basis of these considerations we cannot see water as a serious limitation for the globe's carrying capacity. No doubt, there are nations with rather limited resources. As well, local or regional shortages will require expensive water infrastructures. However, the only dramatic shortages can be found in a small number of desert states of North Africa and West Asia. Most of these countries are enormously wealthy oil exporters that could artificially "produce" water for their unconventional high-tech agriculture – in fact, this is what they are doing with the highest density of desalination plants in the world. But is the natural water scarcity of some oil billionaires really worth the concern?

10.2.3 Climate

The globe's food production potential certainly depends on the climate. The annual fluxes of precipitation and evapotranspiration which determine the potential water supply available for human exploitation (runoff) vary greatly by region. They are much higher at the equator than in the arid or semiarid regions around the latitudes of 40° north or 30° south (Baumgartner and Reichel, 1975). The vast deserts and arid lands of Asia and Africa that have emerged from these climatic conditions are certainly among the most hostile environments for agriculture on earth. The lowest precipitation and evapotranspiration, and consequently the lowest potential water supply for human exploitation, can be found at the poles.

The spatial pattern of the global water cycle not only influences the water supply for rainfed agriculture, but also determines variations in the flux of solar radiation energy, which is the fuel of photosynthesis – the basic process of plant growth. In the arid or semiarid mid-latitudes of low precipitation, cloud cover is rare or absent so that less solar radiation is absorbed or reflected. Consequently, insolation in these regions is some 20 percent higher than at the equator, where one would expect the highest solar energy flux (Stanhill, 1983). Since there is also a low level of actual evaporation in these arid zones, the solar energy input mainly heats up the ground and the air, which further increases the region's water deficit and worsens environmental conditions for agriculture.

It is not only the (absolute) shortage of water and the high temperatures in arid and semiarid regions that make agriculture difficult or impossible. There is also the interannual variation in precipitation, which is typically three or four times greater in these regions than in temperate regions. This high climatic variability explains why the desert can widen and narrow in an unpredictable temporal pattern. During the early 1970s we experienced a global redistribution of rainfall which led to the 1970–1972 Sahel drought and contributed to widespread famines in the Sahel and Ethiopia. The bioclimatic zones of the Sahel moved to the south and expanded the area of high desertification risk.

During the 1970s and 1980s many authors considered desertification – triggered by climate variation – a major cause of declining food production potential in large parts of Africa and Asia. But there is no general consensus. Other scientists reported evidence for a major anthropogenic component in the desertification process (Garcia, 1981; Rubenson, 1991; Kiros, 1991). We also have to take

into account that the transformation from arid and semiarid lands
to desert during the Sahel drought was (at least partially) compen-
sated by higher precipitation north of the Sahara (Stanhill, 1989).
There is still a debate over whether the total desert area really expanded or just shifted southward into densely populated and more
intensely cultivated areas, causing serious famines.

There is also evidence that the climatic risk of desertification in
the arid and semiarid regions of Africa is amplified by unsustainable
practices of agriculture, deforestation, and cattle ranging in this region. According to some authors, human mismanagement of land
resources are major factors of desertification in the African Sahel
(Stanhill, 1989). Finally, climate data show that the drought was
not restricted to the famine areas of the Sahel. Much higher precipitation anomalies were observed during the same period in Asia
and south of the equator. The absence of serious famines in these
regions indicates that factors other than climatic conditions must
have caused the great African famines (Lamb, 1982).

Climate conditions are certainly important factors restricting
the area of profitable agriculture, but this does not mean that we
are totally dependent on them. We can grow tropical fruits in cold
climates or wheat in the desert. We can heat or cool, irrigate or
drain cultures. This is a matter of technology, food prices, and
investment capital. Of course, farmers are still restricted by natural
conditions, such as soils or climates, but they have also made great
steps toward reducing their dependence. Between 1961 and 1990
Finland, which certainly does not have the most favorable climate
for agriculture, increased its total production of cereals from 1.94
to 4.30 million tons (by almost doubling average yields from 1.88 to
3.54 tons per hectare).

Farmers in Sweden and Norway could also achieve spectacular
increases of cereal production. By comparison, climatically privileged Argentina only increased its cereal yields from 1.41 to 2.22
tons per hectare, and Brazil's farmers could only improve yields from
1.35 to 1.76 tons per hectare. Obviously, there must be important
conditions other than climate (and soils) which determine agricultural output. As we discuss in Section 10.3, agricultural technology
plays a major role in agricultural output.

10.2.4 Fossil energy input

Most experts agree that we could boost food production in many developing regions if we modernize agriculture. Crop yields in Africa and Latin America are frequently 70 to 80 percent below the European average. Modern agricultural inputs, such as nitrogenous fertilizers, irrigation, pesticides, and agricultural machinery, could easily double or triple the output. There is no doubt that nitrogen fertilizer production has to increase substantially to meet the food demand of the rapidly growing Third World population. Recently it was estimated that, until the year 2000, world nitrogen production must increase by 15 million tons, which is equivalent to the output of 10 large new plants each year (Constant and Sheldrick, 1992:115). With modern technology after-harvest losses could also be reduced. These losses are substantial in many developing countries. This modernization, however, is linked to one basic factor: commercial energy. Therefore, some authors have argued that (fossil) energy is the limiting factor for the global carrying capacity.[7]

However, available statistics and research on energy consumption in agriculture give no indication that fossil energy will be a limiting factor for agricultural modernization. Modern agriculture does not consume large amounts of commercial energy. On average, just 3 percent of worldwide fossil energy consumption is used in agriculture, and less than 1 percent is needed for the production of (nitrogenous) fertilizers (Smil, 1987). Most likely it takes more fossil energy to fly the doomsday advocates of the global food problem to their many international conferences than it would cost to produce adequate amounts of crop nutrients, pesticides, and fungicides for the stagnating agricultures in Africa and Latin America.

Some critics have rejected agricultural modernization as an option for increasing global food production on the basis of its supposedly high consumption of fossil energy. They obviously misunderstand energy statistics which indicate that some 70 to 80 percent of all commercial energy is used in the food sector. While these numbers might certainly be correct, they only indicate the overall fossil energy consumption in human food chains. Most of this energy, however, is not spent in agriculture, but used for packaging, cleaning, transport, conservation, bottling, canning, refrigeration, and preparation of food. We spend enormous amounts of fossil

energy for post-harvest processing of food and for running a most
energy-consuming international food distribution network (Heilig,
1993). We have accepted the preposterous situation that, for instance, French or Austrian mineral water is bottled and shipped to
the USA or Australia – completely unaware of the fact that a huge
amount of fossil energy is needed to produce the bottles and ship
the water halfway around the globe. Most of the energy consumption in the food sector has nothing to do with agriculture, but with
lifestyles, trade regulations, state subsidies, or marketing strategies.
If we would discontinue only the most absurd practices in the food
processing and distribution sector, we could save much more fossil
energy than is needed for modernization of agricultures in developing countries.

10.2.5   Conclusion: Are the natural resources limited?

If we take into account the creative potential of man, there is no
foreseeable limitation to the basic natural resources of food production, which are space, water, climate conditions, solar energy, and
man-made inputs. All these resources are either unlimited or can be
expanded, better utilized, or redesigned to a very large extent. This
might be the reason why several experts have denied any upper limit
to population growth. The notion of "physical limits to growth" is
a faulty concept. It makes it easy for agricultural technocrats to
deny any basic problems in boosting the world food supply. Better arguments must be found to convince people that global food
production may be limited.

10.3   Technical Limitations and Chances

Technology is certainly one of the most important determinants of
the earth's carrying capacity. If the human race would have failed to
invent agriculture some 10,000 years ago, only a few million people
could have survived on this planet as hunters and gatherers. Cut
and burn agriculture, which was the next step in the evolution of
human sustenance, lifted the carrying capacity to at least twice or
three times the level of primitive food collectors (Pimentel, 1984:4).
The invention of soil cultivation and animal husbandry in stable
settlements, which was the first agricultural revolution, prepared

the way for the empires at the Nile, Euphrates, and Tigris and along the great Asian rivers.

Since World War II, the second – chemo-technological – revolution of agriculture has established a new level of sustenance. We are certainly capable of producing enough food for a world population of 5 to 6 billion; in fact we are facing severe problems of overproduction. Now, the important question is whether technologies will be available that could further increase the earth's carrying capacity? And what are the restrictions and risks for their implementation?

10.3.1 Chances

Despite nearly hysterical criticism by some scholars, only the application of modern technology to agriculture will provide the necessary tools for increasing the earth's carrying capacity. Of course, we are not talking about simple-minded high-input agriculture which – for the sake of short-term increase of yields – would degrade soils, pollute groundwater, or harm the environment in some other way. We are talking about the numerous technical options that could improve yields, while at the same time reduce the environmental impact of agriculture. In general these technical options would be targeted to improve energy and water efficiency, refertilize exhausted soils, or minimize pesticide application. They would optimize crop rotation, adapt cultivation methods to local soil conditions, or prevent adverse effects of large-scale irrigation.

10.3.2 Fertilizer application

Many people are not aware that in some developing countries there is a threat to the environment, not because of too much use of modern technology, but because of too little. A case in point is fertilizer application. Especially in less developed Africa there is the problem of excessive nutrient removal or "nutrient mining" from soils. While farmers try to respond to the growing food demand by using better crop seeds, reducing fallow periods, and so on, they have frequently failed to prevent the constant nutrient removal which is typical for modern crops. These require an essential supply of plant nutrients (such as nitrogen, phosphorus, and potassium), because with each harvest the farmer permanently removes some 100 to 150 kg/ha of

these major plant nutrients from his field. Therefore it is imperative
that (artificial) fertilizers are applied to ensure sustained productivity of the soil. However, according to recent estimates, African
farmers replace only some 50 percent of the harvest-related crop
nutrient loss in their soil by applying (artificial) fertilizers. They
permanently degrade their soils because of a less than optimal input of fertilizers (Constant and Sheldrick, 1992:114).

10.3.3 Irrigation

One possibility for increasing the earth's food production capacity
is the expansion of irrigation. However, since two-thirds of global
freshwater withdrawal is already used in agriculture it would be essential to implement only those technologies that improve irrigation
efficiency, reduce water loss, and prevent environmental damage in
irrigation schemes. Fortunately, techniques are available that could
achieve these objectives. In a study on agricultural water efficiency
Xie *et al.* (1983) conclude:

> Technologically, there is great potential to improve water use effi-
> ciency in both the agriculture and urban sectors. Despite demon-
> strated success in water saving and favorable experience in many
> developing countries, advanced technologies, such as sprinkler and
> drip systems, are applied to less than 3 percent of the world's ir-
> rigated lands.

We cannot go into detail, but list a few options that are considered rather promising by agricultural experts (most examples are
from Stanhill, 1989).

An obvious technical option is the conservation of existing water resources (rather than the exploitation of new ones). In most
irrigation schemes efficiency is incredibly low – usually less than 25
percent of the applied water is consumed by plants. In the USA it
was possible to double water use efficiency by simple means, such
as laser land leveling and automatic pulsed water application.

Runoff control, cleaning, and recycling of agricultural wastewater could also contribute to the conservation of existing water
resources.

A modification of cropping practices could save water or increase
yields with available resources. For instance, farmers could switch
to crops that can be grown during seasons of lower climatic water

demand – which are the cooler and more humid seasons of the year. This simple measure could increase yields per unit of water by up to 50 percent. Only by carefully timing planting dates are substantial yield increases possible.

Insufficient leaching is one of the most serious dangers in irrigation agriculture.[8] To avoid problems farmers tend to apply more water to their irrigated fields than would be necessary. This frequently results in serious soil damage and has already destroyed large irrigation areas. Agricultural science and technology could prevent this irrigation mismanagement. There are methods for calculating and applying the amount of water needed for leaching requirements, which take into account soil salinity and evaporation.

Desertification and soil loss is frequently triggered by removal of significant areas of the vegetation cover – through overgrazing, cattle trampling, or deforestation. Intelligent land-use practices which avoid phases of total vegetation removal could substantially increase the local water availability. Afforestation on water catchment areas would also help to conserve water resources.

Modern technology could reduce water evaporation losses. The three major sources of water evaporation in agriculture are water storage and conveyances, irrigation systems, and plant evapotranspiration. All three can be reduced by technical means. There are several methods for reducing plant transpiration (Stanhill, 1986), but the gains are probably not too big and negative side effects are likely. Much, however, could be done to reduce evaporation in irrigation, such as better timing of water application and trickle irrigation. The evaporation from lakes and conveyances could be reduced by removing water plants and by building deep, instead of shallow, reservoirs. It was estimated that lake Nasser, dammed by the Aswan Dam, is losing more water by evaporation than it makes available for irrigation (Stanhill, 1989:268).

Water harvesting is also a very attractive technical option for increasing local water resources for agriculture (Reij *et al.*, 1988). For example, special kinds of fences can be used at high altitude to "milk" water out of clouds, as is being done in some places in the Andes Mountains. A very cost-efficient method is cloud seeding. Certain chemicals are used to increase the number of condensation nuclei in the atmosphere which can trigger precipitation. Recently detailed studies were undertaken to assess the possibility of water harvesting in Burkina Faso, Kenya, Niger, Somalia, Sudan, and Zimbabwe (Critchley *et al.*, 1992). Rapid development of desalination technologies has also been observed. Prices for the desalination of water are declining rapidly as larger plants with better technology are set up (Wangnick, 1990).

Finally we can exploit previously neglected sources of water, such as the large bodies of brackish water. Also several great rivers are practically unused for irrigation, such as the Shari and Logone rivers in Chad (Melamed, 1989). Their combined water flow is comparable to Egypt's withdrawal from the Nile. Well-designed irrigation schemes could make the desert bloom.

Many arid and semiarid countries in Africa have vast resources of fertile soils. If these countries were able to apply proper irrigation technology to their lands (such as Israel did under similar climatic conditions), they could significantly increase food production.

10.3.4   Breeding, bioengineering

Apart from irrigation there are many technological options to boost rainfed agriculture. We have just started to explore the potential of bioengineering for increasing crop yields (Gasser and Fraley, 1989) and livestock efficiency (Pursel *et al.*, 1989). In a few years or decades the *creation* of new plants by techniques of bioengineering could replace traditional breeding methods. This would speed up the process of adapting animal and plant species to marginal environments, such as arid regions or wetlands. The new techniques could also lead to high-yield food and feed crops which bind nitrogen from the air and thus require less fertilizer inputs. There is also speculation about bioengineering plants and animals that have a natural resistance against many kinds of diseases, which would reduce the consumption of pesticides and animal medicines. Most experts agree that these techniques could possibly boost food production by orders of magnitude (Holló, 1986).

Photosynthesis is the complex and still poorly understood biochemical process by which plants build up biomass. It is fueled by solar radiation energy, and needs – among other things – atmospheric carbon, plant nutrients, and water as inputs. Until today not much could be done to increase the overall efficiency of the process – other than creating artificially CO_2-enriched atmospheres in greenhouses. However, there is a chance that recent advances in biochemistry and plant genetics can somewhat improve the net efficiency of photosynthesis by reducing the respiratory losses of CO_2 (Smil, 1987:165–166). The gains will probably not be spectacular in food grain, but it is possible that animal food with very high photosynthetic efficiency can be bioengineered.

10.3.5   Food processing

Much can be done to optimize post-harvest crop processing, drying, transport, and storage. In some parts of the Third World (such as India) enormous amounts of food and feed crops are lost to mice, rats, and fungi. Improper storage and transport frequently causes after-harvest losses of up to between 40 and 50 percent.

Much can also be done to improve the processing, transport, and preparation of food. Most people are not aware that some 90 percent of fossil energy use in the food chain is linked to nonagricultural activities – only 5 to 10 percent is consumed on the farm.

Also, if we were to reduce meat consumption in Europe and North America by a few percent we could save enormous amounts of grain. Finally, we could boost the productivity of agriculture by optimizing system integration of farms, such as linking energy generation (biogas) and livestock production.

10.3.6   "Frankenfood"

Finally, there is the option of synthetic food production. Those who shiver from abhorrence about this possibility have coined the term "frankenfood"; but they should think twice about this option. We are already using considerable amounts of artificial ingredients in our food. The yeast in our beer and bread is industrially produced in bioconverters, and citric acid and hundreds of food preservatives are manufactured by the biochemical industry.[9] The taste of fruit yoghurt is usually a synthetically redesigned and enforced "natural" flavor. The colors of meat sausages or fruit juices often come straight from the chemical laboratory. In the not-too-distant future it is very possible that we will produce "synthetic" meat or vegetable

protein in cell cultures. If this perspective affects your appetite, it
is just because you are not familiar with what is currently done in
slaughterhouses or chicken farms all over the world. Actually, it
might be more humane to feed a 10 or 12 billion world population
on bioengineered protein than to breed and kill billions of animals
or convert the last natural ecosystems into paddy rice fields.

A big step toward synthetic food production was recently made
in Japan, where 12 *lettuce factories* began production. They look
like high-tech electronic laboratories; the *lettuce farmers* wear white
gloves and breathing masks. The production sites are so-called clean
rooms – hermetically isolated and sterilized chambers which prevent introduction of fungi, insects, and crop diseases. There is no
soil, rainfall, or sun. The lettuce is grown on a synthetic fiber, the
roots are automatically sprayed with fertilizer-enriched water, and
radiation energy (for photosynthesis) is applied by special electric
lights. Lettuce output is 10 times that of natural cultivation and
highly profitable. The taste of this high-tech lettuce cannot be distinguished from the naturally grown plant. Rash critics might jump
to the conclusion that this high-tech production is rather energy-
inefficient as compared with conventional cultivation, but this is
most likely not the case. More fossil energy is used to control the
production environment (heating, lighting, irrigation), but much less
is needed for production of pesticides, fungicides, weed killers, and
insecticides because of the sterile growing conditions.

Moreover, high-tech cultivation needs much less space and can
be located close to the consumers, such as in the middle of a city.
Thus, enormous amounts of fossil energy for transportation, conservation, and storage can be saved. (Usually, the fossil energy consumption needed for the production of lettuce and other vegetables
is a small fraction of the energy that is spent in packaging, transportation, and storage of the product.) In some Japanese supermar-
kets lettuce is already produced directly on the spot and *harvested*
by the sales personnel according to demand. It is very likely that
the urban agglomerates of the 21st century will be supplied locally
with vegetables and fruits. This is not science fiction. Large proportions of the tomatoes, cucumbers, zucchini, and eggplants we eat
in Europe are already produced in a similar way in the high-tech
greenhouses of the Netherlands.

10.3.7 Limitations

After reading the previous section one might have the impression that technology is the "golden key" to open the earth's unlimited resources of food, but this is not the case. Agro-science and agrotechnology have limitations and dangers.

First, there are unintended side effects of agricultural technology. Especially the input-oriented large-scale technology of the 1970s and early 1980s has caused many problems, such as soil degradation, over-fertilization, salination or water logging in irrigated soils, groundwater pollution, and toxification of agricultural workers by pesticides. These problems are usually caused by lack of know-how, poor management techniques, faulty maintenance of irrigation systems and agricultural machinery, or simply corruption and ignorance.

Second, we have consequences of agricultural modernization and expansion that were well predicted but seem to be inevitable. When farmers transform natural ecosystems into cropland or meadows, they inevitably disturb their biological balance. A new, artificial balance has to be re-established. This requires careful planning and proper long-term management of soils, water sources, and infrastructure. One of the greatest threats to natural ecosystems – such as the tropical rain forests – is the "unconfined cut-down, plant, and move" exploitation by poorly trained, inexperienced farmers (or ignorant and cynical agribusinesses).

Third, there is the problem of education and sociocultural adaptation. It is obvious that not every culture and ethnic group is flexible enough to learn new ways of food production. Chinese farmers, for instance, quickly adapted to using modern technology when the government abandoned many restrictions of the communist economy during the 1970s. Within a few years China experienced one of the most spectacular increases in nitrogenous fertilizer consumption and tractor use – and a tripling of cereal production. Compare this to Nigeria, the oil-wealthy African nation. The country has all the resources (including capital, land, water, and fossil energy for fertilizers) to make it the breadbasket of Africa, but agriculture has stagnated for the last three decades.

Finally, there are enormous costs for implementing a more efficient agricultural technology. We are not only referring to farmers who need investment capital. There is also the need for upgrading the general infrastructure. Agricultural modernization requires a steady supply of inputs (fertilizers, water for irrigation, crop sanitation products) for which working transportation and distribution systems have to be implemented. There are also significant social costs. Agricultural modernization inevitably increases the pressures on the rural labor force. Both farmers and landless agricultural workers have to adapt to new methods and conditions. They must accept retraining and technical education, and there are always groups of the population that lack the necessary flexibility for change. It is also very likely that agricultural modernization will produce rural unemployment, even if labor-intensive production methods are applied.

10.4   Ecological Limits

Ecological constraints and feedback mechanisms are frequently considered limiting factors of growing food production (Chen, 1990). Currently scientists are discussing four types of problems. First, the expansion of agricultural areas and increases in the catch of fish could destroy large ecological systems. This would lead to a reduction of biodiversity in the fauna and flora and diminish the global gene pool. Second, the increase of agricultural inputs, such as fertilizers, pesticides, fungicides, weed killers, and other chemicals, could pollute groundwater bodies, lakes, and the sea. It could change the chemistry of the soils and speed up soil erosion. Third, genetically modified plants (and animals) could be a danger to the natural environment. Finally, a significant increase in food production could even change the global climate; emissions of greenhouse gases, such as methane, could dramatically increase due to the expansion of livestock and paddy rice production. What evidence do we have that these ecological consequences are in fact unavoidable?

10.4.1   Shrinking of natural ecological systems

There is little doubt that feeding an ever-growing number of people will further diminish the living space of other species. For many kinds of wild animals we leave only small niches of natural ecosystems. This competitive race between man and other living creatures (including plants) is probably unavoidable. It seems to be an evolutionary constant. The best we can hope for is that we will be able to preserve key natural habitats in order to stop further extinction of species. The only realistic protection of the planet's natural "gene pools" and "green lungs," such as the Amazonas, is a combination of strictly managed natural parks and careful economic utilization with a minimum of environmental damage. If we want to reserve the tropical rain forests exclusively for butterfly catchers, anthropologists, and botanists in the face of millions of landless hungry farmers, we have to answer some tough questions on our moral standards.

Food production, however, is not the only activity that tends to diminish the natural ecosystem. The spread of human settlements, infrastructures, and industries must be added to a possible expansion of agricultural land. Undoubtedly, the human race is changing the surface of the earth with unprecedented speed.

10.4.2 Soil degradation (acidification, soil loss) and water pollution

Many agricultural practices can have a destructive impact on the environment. Excessive use of fertilizers can contaminate the groundwater; crop monocultures and unsuitable tillage practices can aggravate soil erosion; the use of pesticides poses health risks on farm workers; and the runoff of pesticides can pollute groundwater. There are concerns that "artificial" pest and weed control can trigger the emergence of resistant animal and plant species, which in turn would require the further increase of pesticides. In some parts of Europe we have industrial-size livestock production systems which produce enormous amounts of manure. If the manure is not properly processed and is only spread in large quantities on crop fields and meadows, it can run off into rivers and lakes, seep into the groundwater, or increase the already existing nitrogen overload of the soil. In Africa's pastoral societies overgrazing and trampling by cattle is an enormous problem.

These environmental risks of agriculture are well known and certainly diminish the actual carrying capacity of many regions. A recent study conducted by the International Soil Reference and Information Centre in Wageningen has estimated that agricultural activities have caused moderate to extreme soil degradation of 1.2

billion hectares worldwide – which is about the combined size of China and India (Oldemann *et al.*, 1990). This does not mean that the soils are completely unproductive, but that their natural fertility is more or less diminished. The impact of agriculture on the water is also well documented: some 25 percent of the population in the European Union is already drinking water with a nitrate level greater than the recommended maximum of 25 milligrams per liter (Gardner, 1990:5). Pesticides can be found in the groundwater of 34 states in the USA.

These problems of intensive crop and livestock production are serious, but there is no reason why we should not be able to solve them. With modern technology, agricultural know-how, and better agricultural policy it would be possible to expand food production, while reducing its environmental impact. A good example is Europe's agriculture. Contrary to widespread belief, the farmers did not just proceed with their practices of overfertilization and mindless use of pesticides (which they in fact had adopted during most of the 1970s and 1980s).

If the FAO statistics are correct the consumption of nitrogenous fertilizers significantly declined during the past six or seven years in most European countries, while production increased. In all of Europe the consumption of nitrogenous fertilizers fell from some 15.1 in 1983–1984 to about 13.6 million tons in 1990–1991 – a decline of more than 10 percent (FAO, 1992:56). In West Germany farmers consumed 1.52 million tons in 1985; four years later consumption was down to 1.48 million tons (FAO, AGROSTAT). The fertilizer input in kilograms per hectare of cropland fell from 464 to 404 between 1977–1979 and 1987–1989 (World Resources Institute/United Nations Environment Programme/United Nations Development Programme, 1992:275).

Modern methods of crop management have tried to optimize, rather than maximize, the input of crop nutrients and pesticides. We also have to take into account that in large parts of the Third World, especially in Africa, fertilizer consumption is a small fraction of what is typical in Europe or some Asian countries. Even if these farmers doubled or tripled fertilizer consumption they would be far from the levels that are typical for high-input agriculture.

10.4.3 Risks of genetic engineering and advanced breeding practices

Previously we mentioned that genetic engineering could be a great opportunity for increasing food production, especially if we could breed drought- and pest-resistant crops, but it could also be a danger. There was much concern that genetically manipulated plants and animals could *escape* and drive out other natural species from their habitat. Also several other unintended side effects have been under discussion. However, governments in Europe and North America have recently loosened restrictions for field experiments with genetically modified plants. They obviously consider the risks rather low as compared with possible benefits.

10.4.4 Climate change

In theory, there are two links between climate change and global food production. First, the expansion and intensification of agriculture, which is necessary for sustenance of the growing world population, could be a driving force for global warming. Emissions of methane (CH_4), which is the third most important greenhouse gas, could increase when livestock and paddy rice areas are expanded. Livestock and paddy rice areas are important sources of anthropogenic methane emission to the atmosphere (Heilig, in press). Agricultural mechanization could boost CO_2 emissions. The second link between climate change and agriculture works the other way: global warming could reduce (or increase) agricultural output. One of the most detailed approaches to the problem was IIASA's integrated climate impact assessment which – for the first time – analyzed not only first-order consequences of global warming to agriculture, but also second-order impacts (Parry *et al.*, 1988). This is not the place to analyze this major scientific study, but it should be pointed out that Parry and Carter (1988) are very cautious about the predictive validity of their research. In a summary of results they write:

> The estimates reported in this volume are *not predictions* [italics in Parry and Carter] of future effects. Present-day uncertainties and inaccuracies in simulating the behavior of the world's climate and in evaluating the agricultural implications of climatic change do not permit realistic predictions to be made. Furthermore, we cannot forecast what technological, economic and social

developments in agriculture will occur over the next half century. The estimates should therefore be considered as measures of the *present-day sensitivity* [italics in Parry and Carter] of agriculture to climate change. [Parry and Carter, 1988:69]

No doubt, there are links between climate and agriculture, but it is also obvious that these links are not just simple one-way causations. They work through a complex system of intermediate variables, which not only can modify their strengths, but also can turn them around from positive to negative (and vice versa). The most important intermediate variables are the availability of advanced technology, the existing economic arrangements, the political situation, and the level of education and training among the farmers. If farmers have no access to advanced technology, are hampered by poor education and training, or are restricted by stupid economic arrangements, a worsening of climate conditions (such as the increase of drought or unstable precipitation) can seriously diminish agricultural output. However, the climate change could also have the opposite effect: it could trigger the development of advanced agricultural methods, which in the end are even more productive. Israel's and Finland's farmers have demonstrated that high productive agriculture is possible under harsh, and diverse, agro-climatic conditions.

Our knowledge is too limited to decide whether the projected climate change would reduce global carrying capacity. However, we believe that a possible (but by no means certain) global warming would be a gradual process, which would give us enough time to adapt the socioeconomic framework of agriculture and implement new technologies in order to counterbalance its negative effects.

10.5   Social, Economic, and Political Dimensions of Carrying Capacity

For decades the scientific discussion on the food–population nexus has avoided a key issue. While the scientists spent their time elaborating hypotheses with rather weak empirical evidence (such as the law of diminishing returns) or engaged in intellectual self-gratification by building all kinds of complex models of global carrying capacity, they mostly ignored the political, social, and economic dimension of food production. The news media, however, reported the facts on a day-by-day basis: in most cases it was colossal policy failure which caused widespread undernutrition and famine during the past four decades. Agricultural stagnation and food deficits were usually unrelated to a shortage of soil, water, rainfall, fossil energy, or investment capital. They were also unrelated to high population growth. Typically, food crises could be found where social, cultural, and economic conditions have prevented agricultural modernization, as in large parts of Africa.

There are so many sociocultural constraints to agricultural modernization that we could dedicate an entire chapter to this problem. Due to space limitation we mention only a few of the most important factors.

Policy failure. The most serious famines in recent times had nothing to do with population pressure, crop failure, or natural disasters. They were directly and intentionally triggered by unscrupulous regimes as a means for executing their political strategies as the Khmer Rouge did in Cambodia (Becker, 1986; Barnett *et al.*, 1980), accepted as necessary side effects of coercive development measures as in China's Great Leap Forward during the Mao Tse-Tung era (Bernstein, 1984), or simply emerged from cynical ignorance because the regimes were more interested in other political and military issues as in most civil wars of Africa from Ethiopia to Somalia (Griffith, 1988).

False economic policy and corruption. The stagnation of agricultural production in some parts of the Third World – especially in sub-Saharan Africa and in parts of Latin America – was closely related to the notorious inefficiency, massive corruption, unbelievable incompetence, and ideological blindness of political leaders and their administration. Many of these incompetent regimes in Africa simply transplanted the Soviet model of a centrally planned command economy to their preindustrial society. They eliminated traditional market mechanisms by fixing food prices at ridiculously low levels to appease urban masses (Bale, 1981). They collectivized most of the fertile land (as in Ethiopia) and forced the farmers to sell their production to state-owned trade agencies for prices that were

close to production costs (as in Tanzania). The ideologically le-
gitimized lack of incentives discouraged the farmers and prevented
agricultural modernization (Bates, 1981). In Latin America military
regimes stabilized feudalistic rural societies and prevented agricultural modernization. Very often these disasters of agricultural policy
were joined by a general failure of development policy. The political
and administrative elites in many developing countries of Africa and
Latin America did not do much to modernize infrastructure; they
neglected technical education and training and blocked industrial
modernization. Huge amounts of development aid were wasted on
expensive but useless prestige projects or simply vanished into bank
accounts of the small ruling class. Even rich countries, such as exporters of oil and other natural resources (Nigeria), neglected the
agricultural sector.

Social inequality. There is still chronic undernutrition and hunger
among certain groups of the population in food surplus countries, as
in India or Indonesia. However, this kind of food problem can also
be found in highly developed, affluent countries, such as the USA.
It is a problem of income distribution and has nothing to do with
the availability of food. Lack of entitlements to acquire adequate
food in the lowest classes of society is the cause of the problem. The
class and cast structure of some societies also prevents adequate
distribution of agricultural land.

Development of human resources (health, education). Much land
in the Third World cannot be cultivated in the most efficient way
because farmers are suffering from chronic diseases (malaria, river
blindness) or are hampered by a lack of education and agricultural
know-how. Several studies, for instance, have shown the impact
of malaria among rural populations on food production (Bradley,
1991). A dramatic situation is evolving in parts of Africa and Asia
(Thailand) because of AIDS. The spread of this disease among rural
populations in East Africa has already made a measurable impact
on food production (Norse, 1991). Is it not rather absurd that we
spend considerable efforts on the collection of soil inventories to

determine Africa's carrying capacity, while whole villages in Africa are wiped out by a virus infection?

Traditions.   Many traditions help people improve their sustenance. Agricultural societies have developed numerous rules, habits, taboos, and traditions to prevent food crises, maintain soil fertility, or improve the environment for the next generation. Consider the traditional rules of crop rotation or the tradition to plant a tree on certain occasions. Unfortunately some cultural values also prevent agricultural modernization and a full utilization of resources. For instance, in most of Africa agriculture is considered low-prestige women's work. It is part of their household duties – in addition to cooking and caring for children. Whenever a man can afford to avoid working on a field, he will do so. This traditional disregard of food production, deeply embedded in African men, can be also found in development plans and investment decisions of African governments.

Culture and food are closely related. A society can only develop sciences, technology, and arts when it has a highly productive system of food supply. As long as everyone is busy collecting or hunting food, no real modern development is possible. We can study this link between cultural development and food in early agricultural societies that originated in the alluvial lowlands and river floodplains of Africa and Asia. These ancient people developed complex social and economic systems, which included bureaucratic hierarchies and specialized professions. The social differentiation was necessary to solve typical problems of agriculture, such as water management or storage administration. The societies also institutionalized mechanisms of conflict resolution – for instance, to settle conflicts of water distribution and land ownership. They developed cognitive systems which helped them to understand and predict the natural cycles of floods and rainfalls. They also managed to establish a stable (if not always peaceful) relationship with their neighbors. This social and cultural framework was essential for making their agriculture prosper – and in turn, the highly productive agriculture also propelled social and cultural development. In his many books on Indonesia, Clifford Geertz (1963) has studied these dialectics of food and sociocultural development.

10.6   Discussion

From a system-analytic point of view, most studies on carrying capacity are surprisingly unrealistic in their economic and social assumptions. They usually define carrying capacity in terms of direct agricultural self-supply – as a population supporting capacity of land, given a certain level of agricultural technology. This concept might be sufficient to describe traditional rural societies, which lack a clear division of labor, international trade, political organization, science, and industry. But this concept is inadequate for today's functionally differentiated societies and economies. Here the division of labor expands from the household to the national economy and the international market. During the last decades, Arab nomads in the deserts of Saudi Arabia could feed their families quite well from the scarce land by selling their oil resources on the world market – for instance, to French farmers, who in turn produced a significant proportion of their meat supply.

Today, the supply of food, which once was a simple process of collecting, hunting, or self-sufficient local agriculture, has evolved into a complex international network of production activities, industrial processes, market and price mechanisms, trade arrangements, food policies, and distribution channels. At each stage of this widely expanding food chain we might find conditions that could limit the food supply of a population. It might be a shortage of fertile soils or water; it might be adverse climate conditions; or it could be a lack of fossil energy for fertilizer production. But the limitation might also arise from widespread analphabetism and a lack of agricultural know-how in a population; it could be caused by the persistence of inefficient market structures and production regulations; or it might be the consequence of international trade restrictions.

The carrying capacity of the earth not only depends on its natural resources or the level of technology, but essentially on the quality of our worldwide economic, social, and political arrangements. Land, water, climate, and energy are just four parameters in a much more complex set of equations for calculating a realistic measure of carrying capacity. These equations must describe the world as a system of interdependencies – a system of exchange mechanisms (food trade) and complementary production activities, which can counterbalance regional variations in the density of natural and human resources. Today, carrying capacity cannot be defined at a purely local or regional level. It cannot be calculated from the availability of natural resources. We know that the natural supporting potential of land can only be realized if there are educated and trained people who can live in peace, who have access to (world) markets, who can use modern agricultural and industrial techniques and inputs, who are not punished and unmotivated by a centrally planned command economy.

10.7   Conclusion

How many people can be fed on earth if we take into account technical, ecological, political, and social constraints? Most experts would probably agree that we could sustainably supply the current 5.5 billion world population. At the moment European governments are pressing their farmers to reduce food production; grain is cheap on international markets; and Asian countries are harvesting bumper crops year after year. The scandal of famines in Africa is not a result of agriculture approaching carrying capacity; it is mostly a consequence of massive policy failures, corruption, ethnic conflicts, ignorance, and incompetence of ruling elites. There are different and more complex reasons for widespread undernutrition in some parts of Asia, but they have nothing to do with natural limitations. Certain groups of the population lack the means to acquire food, which would be available in principle. Here we obviously have the socioeconomic and cultural problems of uneven distribution of entitlements. Latin America has vast resources of land, freshwater, and – at least in some cases – oil money. The real problem is the feudalistic distribution of land which prevents a more efficient agriculture.

But could we also feed 10 or 15 billion people? Most likely, if we can prevent (civil) wars with soldiers plundering harvests or devastating crop fields with land mines; if we can stop the stupidity of collectivization and central planning in agriculture; if we can agree on free (international) trade for agricultural products; if we redistribute agricultural land to those that actually use it for production; if we provide credits, training, and high-yield seeds to poor farmers; if we can adapt the modern high-yield agriculture to the agro-climatic and sociocultural conditions of arid regions and use it

carefully to avoid environmental destruction; if we implement optimal water management and conservation practices. If we do all this
during the next few decades, we would certainly be able to feed a
doubled or tripled world population.

There are many "ifs" in our conclusion. Almost certainly, business as usual will not provide the conditions which are necessary for
feeding the world population of the 21st century. We need fundamental political, social, and economic changes, especially in Africa,
Latin America, and parts of Asia. Only a democratization in these
regions will open the gates for the development of human resources,
for better education and training, for private economic initiatives,
and for functioning markets.

There are positive and negative signs that this change will be
possible: the governments of China, India, and some other Asian
countries have removed economic controls which prevented agricultural productivity; they have provided a relatively stable political
environment and they have actively supported agricultural modernization (the green revolution). Consequently, they doubled or
tripled domestic food production within two or three decades. Many
African governments, on the other hand, neglected the agricultural
sector. They introduced rigid methods of central planning; sup-
pressed free markets; and collectivized or coercively resettled the
farmers. They did not stop the devastation of agricultural areas
due to civil wars, and they mostly failed in introducing modern
techniques of crop production and livestock management. It is no
wonder that per capita food production stagnated or declined in
most parts of Africa during the past three decades.

Let us do a simple exercise: How many people can be fed in
Sudan? The FAO estimated that at a low input level the country's arable land could sustain nearly 60 million people – 3.7 times
the actual population of 1975 (which was 16 million); a high-input
agriculture could feed 1.036 billion Sudanese, which would be twice
the actual population of Africa. All we hear from Sudan, however, are reports of persistent famines and slow degeneration of the
agricultural system. Theoretically, Sudan could be the breadbasket of Africa; in practical terms it is one of the continent's famine
areas. On the other hand, the FAO has estimated that Algeria's
agro-climatic conditions could support only 7 million people at low

inputs and 24.6 million at medium inputs. Currently Algeria has a population of 25 million and not much can be heard about food shortages in this country. Given the substantial restraints and difficulties that can slow down or even prevent the theoretically almost unlimited increase of global food production, we have to lower our expectations. It is unlikely that the world food problem will be solved within the next decades, despite the fact that it would be possible in theory. There are serious social, economic, and political limits to growth.

We should come back to the initial concept that visualizes the problem of carrying capacity in a pipe with a declining diameter. Using this image, we can conclude that the key for balancing people and food is the speed with which the social, economic, cultural, and political constraints are pushed back that hinder people to utilize the full potential of the earth's food resources in a sustainable way. If we can open the pipe quickly enough, if we can stop some of our collective stupidities, we could produce more than enough food for the people of the 21st century. The carrying capacity of the earth is not a natural constant – it is a dynamic equilibrium, essentially determined by human action.

Notes

[1] Malthus was not the first scholar dealing with the problem, but probably the most influential.

[2] Usually the total solar radiation input of earth is seen as a (near) constant. However, at the soil level, it can certainly vary considerably with specific atmospheric conditions, such as water vapor and dust concentration in the higher atmosphere, as well as cloud cover conditions in the lower atmosphere.

[3] Clark (1967) estimated that the earth could support between 47 billion people on an American-type diet and 147 billion on a cereal-subsistence diet.

[4] These data are from the 1992–1993 WRI report. The estimates of soil constraints in the 1990–1991 report were even higher for most countries.

[5] River flows from other countries are an unreliable source of water supply, since they can be influenced by neighboring countries. Therefore we compare only "annual internal renewable water resources," such as underground aquifers.

[6] The situation within this continentlike country is, however, different. There is water scarcity in the northeastern agricultural areas.

[7] In 1974 *The Futurist* wrote that Lester Brown "refuses to own an automobile and uses public transportation, so that more energy can go into food production" (cited in Smil, 1987:100).

[8] In irrigation systems a certain proportion of the water applied is not intended for plants, but for washing out (leaching) soluble salts which are concentrated in the topsoil by evapotranspiration. Especially in arid and semiarid areas this practice is absolutely essential. Otherwise soil salinity would build up to toxic levels. Frequently farmers apply too much water for leaching, which not only is a waste of the resource, but also results in serious soil damage.

[9] This is a highly profitable industry; Austria's richest man made his fortune by producing citric acid for the European food industry.

References

Ackefors, H., and Enell, M., 1990, Discharge of nutrients from Swedish fish farming to adjacent sea areas, *Ambio* **19**(1):28–35.

Allan, J.A., 1976, The Kufrah agricultural schemes, *The Geographical Journal* **142**(1):48–56.

Baade, F., 1960, *Der Wettlauf zum Jahre 2000*, Oldenburg, Munich, Germany (in German).

Bandyopadhyay, J., 1989, Riskful confusion of drought and man-induced water scarcity, *Ambio* **18**(5):284–292.

Bale, M.D., 1981, Price distortions in agriculture and their effects: An international comparison, *American Journal of Agricultural Economics* **63**(1):8–22.

Barnett, A., Kiernan, B., and Boua, C., 1980, The bureaucracy of death: Documents from inside Pol Pot's torture machine, *New Statesman*, May 2.

Bates, R.H., 1981, *Markets and States in Tropical Africa: The Political Basis of Agricultural Politics*, University of California Press, Berkeley, CA, USA.

Baumgartner, A., and Reichel, E., 1975, *The World Water Balance*, Elsevier Scientific Publishers, Amsterdam, Netherlands.

Becker, E., 1986, *When the War was Over: The Voices of Cambodia's Revolution and its People*, Simon & Schuster, New York, NY, USA.

Bernstein, T.P., 1984, Stalinism, famine, and the Chinese peasants: Grain procurements during the Great Leap Forward, *Theory and Society* **13**:339–377.

Biswas, A.K., 1993, Water for agricultural development: Opportunities and constraints, *Water Resources Development* **9**(1):3–12.

Biswas, A.K., and Arar, A., 1988, *Treatment and Reuse of Wastewater*, Butterworths, London, UK.

Boserup, E., 1965, *The Conditions of Agricultural Growth*, Aldine, Chicago, IL, USA.

Boserup, E., 1981, *Population and Technological Change*, University of Chicago Press, Chicago, IL, USA.

Bradley, D.J., 1991, Malaria, in R. Feachem and D. Jamison, eds., *Disease and Mortality in Sub-Saharan Africa*, World Bank/Oxford University Press, New York, NY, USA.

Bundesministerium für Raumordnung, Bauwesen und Städtebau, eds., 1991, *Raumordnungsbericht 1991*, Bonn, Germany.

Buringh, P., and Van Heemst, H.D.J., 1977, *An Estimation of World Food Production Based on Labour-oriented Agriculture*, Centre for World Food Market Research, Agricultural Press, Wageningen, Netherlands.

Buringh, P., Van Heemst, H.D.J., and Staring, G.J., 1975, *Computation of the Absolute Maximum Food Production of the World*, Centre for World Food Market Research, Wageningen, Netherlands.

Chen, R.S., 1990, Global agriculture, environment, and hunger: Past, present, and the future, *Environmental Impact Assessment Review* **10**:335–358.

Clark, C., 1967, Population and food, in *Population Growth and Land Use*, Macmillan, London, UK.

Clark, C., and Haswell, M., 1964, *The Economics of Subsistence Agriculture*, Macmillan, London, UK.

Cohen, J.E., 1992, How many people can earth hold? *Discover*, November:114–119.

Constant, K.M., and Sheldrick, W.F., 1992, *World Nitrogen Survey*, Technical Paper No. 174, World Bank, Washington, DC, USA.

Critchley, W., Reij, C., and Seznec, A., 1992, *Water Harvesting for Plant Production, Volume 2: Case Studies and Conclusions for Sub-Saharan Africa*, World Bank, Washington, DC, USA.

Ehrlich, P., Ehrlich, A., and Daily, G.C., 1993, Food security, population, and environment, *Population and Development Review* **19**(1):1–32.

Falkenmark, M., 1989, The massive water scarcity now threatening Africa: Why isn't it being addressed? *Ambio* **18**(2):112–118.

Falkenmark, M., 1991, Water, energy, and development, Rapid population growth and water scarcity: The predicament of tomorrow's Africa, in K. Davis and M.S. Bernstam, eds., *Resources, Environment, and Population: Present Knowledge, Future Options, (Population and Development Review*, A Supplement to Volume 16, 1990, Oxford University Press, New York, NY, USA.

FAO, 1978a, *Report on the Agro-Ecological Zones Project, Volume 1: Methodology and Results for Africa*, World Soil Resources Report 48/1, Food and Agriculture Organization, Rome, Italy.

FAO, 1978b, *Report on the Agro-Ecological Zones Project, Volume 2: Results for Southwest Asia,* World Soil Resources Report 48/2, Food and Agriculture Organization, Rome, Italy.

FAO, 1981a, *Report on the Agro-Ecological Zones Project, Volume 3: Methodology and Results for South and Central America,* World Soil Resources Report 48/3, Food and Agriculture Organization, Rome, Italy.

FAO, 1981b, *Report on the Agro-Ecological Zones Project, Volume 4: Results for Southeast Asia,* World Soil Resources Report 48/4, Food and Agriculture Organization, Rome, Italy.

FAO, 1992, *Fertilizer Yearbook,* Food and Agriculture Organization, Rome, Italy.

FAO/UNDP/IIASA, 1982, *Potential Population Supporting Capacities of Lands in the Developing World,* Technical Report of the Project, FPA/INT/513, Food and Agriculture Organization, Rome, Italy.

Garcia, R., 1981, *Drought and Man: The 1972 Case History,* Volume 1: Nature Pleads Not Guilty, Pergamon Press, New York, NY, USA.

Gardner, B., 1990, European Agriculture's Environmental Problems, Paper presented at the First Annual Conference of the Hudson Institute, Indianapolis, IN, USA.

Gasser, C.S., and Fraley, R.T., 1989, Genetically engineering plants for crop improvement, *Science* **244**(16 June):1293–1299.

Geertz, C., 1963, *Agricultural Involution: The Process of Ecological Change in Indonesia,* University of California Press, Berkeley, CA, USA.

Gilland, B., 1983, Considerations on world population and food supply, *Population and Development Review* **9**(2):203–211.

Griffith, I., 1988, Famine and war in Africa, *Geography* **73**(1):59–61.

Hallberg, G.R., 1989, Pesticides pollution of groundwater in the humid United States, *Agriculture, Ecosystems and Environment* **26**:299–367.

Heilig, G.K., 1993, Food, lifestyles, and energy, in D.G. van der Heij, ed., *Food and Nutrition Policy,* Proceedings of the Second European Conference on Food and Nutrition Policy, The Hague, Netherlands, 21–24 April 1992, Pydoc, Wageningen, Netherlands.

Heilig, G.K., 1994, Neglected dimensions of global land-use change: Reflections and data, *Population and Development Review,* September.

Heilig, G.K., in press, The greenhouse gas methane: Sources, sinks and possible interventions, *Population and Environment.*

Higgins, G.M., Kassam, A.H., Naiken, L., Fischer, G., and Shah, M.M., 1982, *Potential Population Supporting Capacities of Lands in the Developing World,* Technical Report FPA/INT/513 of Project Land Resources for Population of the Future, Food and Agriculture Organization, Rome, Italy.

Holló, J., 1986, Foreseeable developments in food production and processing, United Nations, Economic Commission for Europe: Biotechnology and Economic Development, Papers from the Economic Commission for Europe Symposium on the Importance of Biotechnology for Future Economic Development, Szeged, Hungary, June 1985, Pergamon Press, Oxford, UK [Published as *Economic Bulletin for Europe* **38**(1)].

Hopes dry up for food security, 1989, *Middle East Economic Digest* **33**(40).

Kahn, H., 1982, *The Coming Boom*, Simon and Schuster, New York, NY, USA.

Kiros, F.G., 1991, Economic consequences of drought, crop failure and famine in Ethiopia, 1973–1986, *Ambio* **20**(5):183–188.

Lamb, H.H., 1982, *Climate, History and the Modern World*, Methuen, London, UK.

Leistra, M., and Boesten, J., 1989, Pesticides contamination of groundwater in Western Europe, *Agriculture, Ecosystems and Environment* **26**:369–389.

Livi Bacci, M., 1991, *Population and Nutrition: Essay on the Demographic History of Europe*, Cambridge University Press, Cambridge, UK.

Malthus, R., 1967 [1798], *Essay on the Principle of Population*, 7th Edition, Dent, London, UK.

Mann, D.W., 1981, Fewer people for a better world: A plea for negative population growth, *Environmental Conservation* **8**(40):260–261.

Marchetti, C., 1978, On 10^{12} : A Check on Earth Carrying Capacity for Man, RR-78-7, International Institute for Applied Systems Analysis, Laxenburg, Austria.

Meadows, D.H., Meadows, D.L., and Randers, J., 1992, *Beyond the Limits: Global Collapse or a Sustainable Future*, Earthscan, London, UK.

Melamed, A., 1989, Commentary on Gerald Stanhill's Paper, in S.F. Singer, ed., *Global Climate Change. Human and Natural Influences*, Paragon House, New York, NY, USA.

Meybeck, M., Chapman, D., and Helmer, R., 1990, *Global Environment Monitoring System: Global Freshwater Quality: A First Assessment*, Blackwell Reference for WHO/UNEP, Cambridge, MA, USA.

Mückenhausen, E., 1973, Die Produktionskapazität der Böden der Erde, Vorträge N234, Rheinisch-Westfälische Akademie der Wissenschaften, Germany (in German).

Norse, D., 1991, Socioeconomic Impact of AIDS on Food Production in East Africa, Paper prepared for the Seventh International Conference on AIDS, 16–21 June, Florence, Italy.

Norse, D., 1992, A new strategy for feeding a crowded planet, *Environment* **34**(5):6–39.

Oldemann, L.R., Hakkeling, R.T.A., and Sombroek, W.G., 1990, *World Map of the Status of Human Induced Soil Degradation: An*

Exploratory Note, International Soil Reference and Information Centre, Wageningen, Netherlands.

Parikh, K.S., Fischer, G., Frohberg, K., and Gulbrandsen, O., 1988, *Towards Free Trade in Agriculture*, Nijhoff, Dordrecht, Netherlands.

Parry, M.L., and Carter, T.R., 1988, The assessment of effects of climatic variations on agriculture: Aims, methods and summary of results, in M.L. Parry, T.R. Carter, and N.T. Konijn, eds., *The Impact of Climate Variations on Agriculture*, Volume 1, Kluwer, Dordrecht, Netherlands.

Parry, M.L., Carter, T.R., and Konijn, N.T., eds., 1988, *The Impact of Climate Variations on Agriculture*, Volumes 1 and 2, Kluwer, Dordrecht, Netherlands.

Pearce, F., 1991, Africa at a watershed, *New Scientist*, March 23:34–40.

Pearson, F.A., and Harper, F.A., 1945, *The World's Hunger*, Cornell University Press, New York, NY, USA.

Penck, A., 1925, Das Hauptproblem der physischen Anthropogeographie, *Zeitschrift für Geopolitik* 2 (in German).

Pimentel, D., 1984, Energy flow in the food system, in D. Pimentel and C.W. Hall, eds., *Food and Energy Resources*, Academic Press, Orlando, FL, USA.

Pursel, V.G., Pinkert, C.A., Miller, K.F., Bolt, D.J., Campbell, R.G., Palmiter, R.D., Brinster, R.L., and Jammer, R.E., 1989, Genetic engineering of livestock, *Science* 244(16 June):1281–1288.

Ravenstein, G., 1891, Lands of the globe still available for European settlement, *Proceedings of the Royal Geographic Society* 13(27).

Reij, C., Mulder, P., and Begemann, L., 1988, *Water Harvesting for Plant Production*, Technical Paper No. 91, World Bank, Washington, DC, USA.

Resources for the Future, 1984, Feeding a hungry world, *Resources* 76:1–20.

Revelle, R., 1967, The resources available for agriculture, *Scientific American* 235(3):165–178.

Ricardo, D., 1964, *The Principles of Political Economy and Taxation*, Dent, London, UK.

Rivière, J.W.M., 1989, Threats to the world's water, *Scientific American*, Special Issue: Managing Planet Earth, 261(3):48–55.

Rubenson, S., 1991, Environmental stress and conflict in Ethiopian history: Looking for correlations, *Ambio* 20(5):179–182.

Sanches, P.A., Couto, W., and Buol, S.W., 1982, The fertility capability soil classification system: Interpretation, applicability and modification, *Geoderma* 27:283–309.

Shah, M.M., Fischer, G., Higgins, G.M., Kassam, A.H., and Naiken, L., 1985, Estimates of arable land: Past studies, in *People, Land, and*

Food Production, CP-85-11, International Institute for Applied Systems Analysis, Laxenburg, Austria.

Simon, J., 1981, *The Ultimate Resource*, Princeton University Press, Princeton, NJ, USA.

Sindermann, C.J., 1982, Aquatic animal protein food resources: Actual and potential, in R.G. Woods, ed., *Future Dimensions of World Food and Population*, 2nd Printing, A Winrock International Study, Westview Press, Boulder, CO, USA.

Smil, V., 1987, *Energy, Food, Environment: Realities, Myths, Options*, Clarendon Press, Oxford, UK.

Stanhill, G., 1983, The distribution of global solar radiation over the land surfaces on earth, *Solar Energy* **31**:95–104

Stanhill, G., 1986, Water use efficiency, *Advances with Agromanagement* **39**:53–85.

Stanhill, G., 1989, World water problems: Desertification, in S.F. Singer, ed., *Global Climate Change: Human and Natural Influences*, Paragon House, New York, NY, USA.

UN, 1988, *Ground Water in North and West Africa*, Natural Resources/Water Series No. 18, Department of Technical Co-operation for Development and Economic Commission for Africa, United Nations, New York, NY, USA.

UNO/FAO, 1976, *Report of the FAO Technical Conference on Aquaculture*, Kyoto 1976, FAO Fishery Report No. 188, Food and Agriculture Organization, Rome, Italy.

US, 1967, *The World Food Problem*, A Report of the President's Science of Advisory Committee, Volume 11, Washington, DC, USA.

Uthoff, D., 1978, Endogene und exogene Hemmnisse in der Nutzung des Ernährungspotentials der Meere, 41, Deutscher Geographentag Mainz 1977, Tagungsberichte und Wissenschaftliche Abhandlungen, pp. 347–361, Wiesbaden, Germany.

Wangnick, K., 1990, *IDA Worldwide Desalting Plants Inventory*, Report No. 11, Prepared for the International Desalination Association (Wangnick Consulting), Gnarrenburg, Germany.

Westing, A.H., 1981, A world in balance, *Environmental Conservation* **8**(3):177–183.

World Resources Institute/United Nations Environment Programme/United Nations Development Programme, 1990, *World Resources, 1990–1991*, Oxford University Press, New York, NY, USA.

World Resources Institute/United Nations Environment Programme/United Nations Development Programme, 1992, *World Resources, 1992–1993*, Oxford University Press, New York, NY, USA.

Xie, Mei, Küffner, U., and LeMoigne, G., 1983, *Using Water Efficiently: Technological Options*, World Bank Technical Paper No. 205, World Bank, Washington, DC, USA.

Editor's Note for Part III

The papers in this part indicate that mortality in developing countries has experienced very impressive declines over the past decades, which were mostly due to the decline in infectious diseases. Until recently there was widespread optimism that these declines would continue in the future and eventually approach the level of industrialized countries as some individual developing countries have already done. The AIDS pandemic, the return of other infectious diseases such as malaria, and increasing uncertainty about future food supply and environmental problems have significantly weakened this optimism. Although at the global level there should be enough food for a possible future world population of 15 billion, local political and environmental problems as well as distributional problems may cause at least temporary famine-related excess mortality. AIDS will definitely have an effect on mortality in the most affected regions of Africa and South Asia, but it is still unclear by how much it will increase mortality.

Given this significant uncertainty in Africa, a decline in life expectancy of three years per decade is assumed as the worst case and an increase of three years as the best case. This roughly corresponds to the estimates of possible future AIDS mortality given in Chapter 9. Because under favorable conditions there are still great potentials for increases in life expectancies, in most other regions average increases of two years have been assumed with a significant range of uncertainty. These issues are discussed more extensively in Chapter 15.

Part IV

Future Fertility and Mortality
in Industrialized Countries

Chapter 11

Future Reproductive Behavior in Industrialized Countries

Wolfgang Lutz

For countries that have fully passed through fertility transition from high fertility to modern family limitation, there is no convincing theory on what should happen to fertility trends in the future. This is not for lack of trying. Approaching the issue from several different disciplines, scientists have made innumerable efforts to analyze and understand past trends and derive from these hypotheses about the future.

Economists tended to look at the fertility fluctuations, trying to discover regularities in the sequence of ups and downs and associations with economic cycles. Demographers have given much attention to the comparison of period and cohort fertility rates. Sociologists and psychologists have studied myriads of survey data and developed theories of increasing individualization and changing gender roles. Family historians have pointed at the changing structure and function of the family. And the medical profession has contributed to the issue by looking at sub-fecundity and effectiveness of contraceptives. In sum, there is a large array of interesting ideas and somewhat explicit hypotheses that tend to refer to specific aspects of reproductive behavior, but they are of limited value for predicting the final outcome, namely, age-specific fertility rates in the years to come.

The ideas in this chapter are based on the huge literature on the determinants of fertility in modern industrialized countries which cannot be exhaustively summarized here (this chapter has been influenced by Kiernan, 1993). The chapter is guided by the goal of determining reasonable and defendable assumptions about alternative high and low paths of future fertility trends in modern industrialized countries. In doing this, we first look at unambiguous empirical evidence from the past years, and then list possible arguments that could be used to support the alternative assumptions of either further declining fertility or increasing fertility levels. The final section focuses on how these alternative assumed forces could work in a heterogeneous society and result in specific assumed fertility levels.

11.1   Recent Trends in Partnership Formation and Dissolution

Human procreation is intimately linked to the institution of marriage in virtually all historical and contemporary societies. In some populations this link has been stronger than in others, and recently, in highly industrialized countries, new forms of partnership have been spreading that are in direct competition with traditional marriage. With respect to fertility, this bears the obvious question whether such changes in living arrangements and partnership have affected and will affect the average number of children born to women and men. For this reason we first must look at changes in the marital status composition of industrialized populations.

Over recent decades the proportion of the adult population that is married has declined markedly in many industrialized countries. *Table 11.1* gives these proportions for 1960 and 1985 in selected European countries. This decline was most significant in Sweden, where the proportion of married women declined from more than 60 percent in 1960 to only 48 percent in 1985. The decline for men was of similar magnitude. It is mostly attributable to increases in the proportions never married and divorced. This pattern is similar in the other Scandinavian countries and in the UK. In the FRG the

Table 11.1. Distribution of the population above age 15 by marital status in selected European countries: 1960 and 1985.

Country	Women				Men			
	Never married	Mar-ried	Di-vorced	Wid-owed	Never married	Mar-ried	Di-vorced	Wid-owed
France								
1960	20.7	60.3	2.5	16.6	27.3	66.4	1.9	4.3
1985	24.5	56.6	4.6	14.3	31.5	61.9	3.6	3.1
FRG								
1960	22.7	57.7	2.6	17.0	26.8	67.9	1.5	3.9
1985	24.4	54.3	4.4	16.9	33.5	59.8	3.5	3.2
Hungary								
1960	17.3	64.4	2.6	15.7	23.7	71.5	1.4	3.4
1985	14.2	61.5	6.9	17.4	23.1	68.0	5.0	3.8
Italy								
1960	29.1	58.0	0.0	12.9	34.4	62.1	0.0	3.5
1985	24.5	61.1	0.4	14.0	30.8	65.8	0.3	3.1
Netherlands								
1960	26.9	63.0	1.3	8.8	30.7	64.9	0.8	3.6
1985	26.4	57.6	4.8	11.2	33.5	60.0	3.9	2.6
Sweden								
1960	26.2	60.7	3.0	10.1	31.6	61.9	2.3	4.3
1985	30.0	48.4	8.7	12.9	38.7	50.4	7.3	3.5
UK								
1960	21.9	63.6	0.9	13.6	25.6	70.0	0.6	3.9
1985	24.0	56.4	5.7	13.9	31.4	60.2	4.8	3.5

Source: Prinz, 1994.

decline in the proportion married was much stronger for men than for women, which is largely explained by a significant increase in the never-married male population. Of the countries listed, Italy shows a slight increase between 1960 and 1985 which is due to the fact that in Italy, the decline in marriage rates started later than in other countries and had not yet had much effect by 1985. This table clearly shows that the proportion married is a cumulative indicator which is largely determined by past trends; therefore it is hardly appropriate to study recent behavioral changes.

Trends in contemporary marriage behavior are well described by age-specific marriage rates. An analysis of such rates in the industrialized countries since the 1960s makes it apparent that men

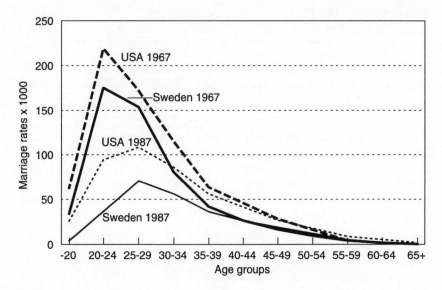

Figure 11.1. Age-specific marriage rates in Sweden and the USA: 1967 and 1987. Source: National Statistical Yearbooks, various years.

and women have changed their behavior toward later marriage and lower probabilities of marriage. To illustrate this pattern, *Figure 11.1* plots age-specific marriage rates of women for the USA and Sweden in 1967 and 1987. In both countries in 1967, marriage rates peaked in the 20–24 age group with around 20 percent of all women in this group marrying. Twenty years later the peak moved to the 25–29 age group with marriage intensities at about half their 1967 levels in the USA and less than that in Sweden. The figures include remarriages which explains why rates especially in the USA are still rather high in the late 30s and 40s. In the USA marriage rates even among women aged 40–44 are higher than in Sweden for women in the traditional prime age group for marriage 20–24. While marriage and especially remarriage after divorce still seem to be popular in the USA, the new Swedish pattern can only be explained by a significant societal change in the role of marriage as opposed to other living arrangements.

Table 11.2 gives data on the evolution of nonmarital unions in Europe between 1960 and 1985. It shows for Sweden that despite a

Table 11.2. Evolution of nonmarital unions in Europe.

Country	Changes 1960 to 1985 in percentage points of women living in		Proportion of consensual unions among all unions by age of woman (in %) ca. 1985		
	Marriage	All unions	20–24	25–29	30–34
Austria	−3.0	1.6	25.8	8.2	3.5
Finland	−7.0	5.0	49.7	23.9	11.6
France	−4.6	4.6	35.8	14.0	10.1
Germany	−6.1	−1.5	30.0[a]	6.2[a]	6.2[a]
Hungary	−2.8	0.1	3.3	2.4	2.7
Italy	4.4	5.9	2.1	1.8	1.6
Netherlands	−9.1	−1.7	36.3	15.9	6.7
Norway	−9.8	1.1	47.0	23.0	12.0
Sweden	−20.3	−0.4	77.1	48.1	29.6
UK	−11.3	−5.4	29.0	12.8	6.8

[a]Data only given for 15–24 and 25–34 age groups.
Source: Prinz, 1994.

20 percent decline in proportions married, the proportion of women living in unions (marriages and consensual unions) remained virtually unchanged. Not surprisingly this trend toward nonmarital unions is strongest for younger couples. In Sweden of all women aged 20–24 and living together with a man, only 23 percent were married. This trend toward nonmarital unions was less extreme in other European countries but still went in the same direction. In all countries a decline in proportions married was associated with an increase in nonmarital unions. Of the countries listed, only Hungary and Italy stand out with very low proportions of women living in nonmarital unions in 1985.

The other significant trend over recent decades was the increase in divorce rates that could be observed in all industrialized countries. *Figure 11.2* plots the crude divorce rates (the number of divorces per 1,000 inhabitants) for eight selected countries. At every point in time between 1950 and 1990, divorce rates were by far the highest in the USA. Between 1965 and 1980 the rate more than doubled. In one year approximately 5 out of 1,000 inhabitants in the USA (including children) experience a divorce. Currently about every second marriage ends in divorce in the USA. In Europe this proportion ranges from about 1 out of 10 marriages in Southern Europe to

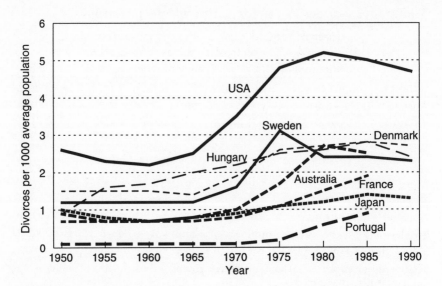

Figure 11.2. Crude divorce rates from 1950 to 1990 in selected industrialized countries.

3 out of 10 in Central Europe, and about 4 out of 10 in Scandinavia and the UK.

In the present context the crucial question with regard to future fertility levels is to what extent changes in the patterns of union formation and dissolution affect the number of children. The empirical evidence so far is very mixed. In Sweden the fertility of nonmarital unions is not much different from that of married couples, although dissolution rates of such unions are still much higher. In Southern and Eastern Europe fertility is still closely tied to marriage. In western Germany, a very advanced country in many respects, with rapidly declining proportions married, only 10 percent of all children are born out of wedlock. In the USA, this proportion has recently increased to about 25 percent (Pagnini and Rindfuss, 1993). For most industrialized countries it seems likely that a possible future decline in the prevalence of marriage and marital stability will tend to decrease fertility, but the extent of this decline will largely depend on whether other countries follow the Swedish or the German pattern. This issue is discussed in Sections 11.4 and 11.5.

11.2   Recent Trends in Period and Cohort Fertility

Fertility can be measured and described with respect to different demographic dimensions, such as age, duration of marriage, time between births, and calendar year. One principal conceptual distinction is whether to consider the reproductive experience of birth cohorts of women over their life span (cohort approach) or to study the fertility of different age groups in a specific calendar year (period approach). For population projections the number of children born in a particular year is needed as an input parameter, which is derived from the application of age-specific period fertility rates to the age structure of the female population. Hence assumptions need to be defined in terms of period fertility. If one believes, however, that cohort fertility – because it has greater stability or because it better captures the life course of women – is the more appropriate indicator for making assumptions, assumed cohort fertility can be translated into period rates if additional assumptions about the timing of births over the course of a life are made.

Table 11.3 gives the period total fertility rates, i.e., the mean number of children per woman implied by age-specific fertility rates of a year, for 30 industrialized countries for the period 1950–1990. In all countries except for Eastern Europe, Malta, and Japan, fertility increased during the late 1950s. This is the famous postwar baby boom which peaked around 1960 in the most affected countries. Of the 30 countries listed, in 1960–1965 only Estonia and Hungary had fertility rates below two children per woman, and several countries had rates above 3.0. The 1970s were a period of fertility decline in practically every industrialized country. By 1980–1985 only Iceland, Ireland, and Poland had a fertility level above 2.1. For all industrialized countries together – which comprised 0.8 billion people in 1950 and 1.2 in 1990 (UN, 1993) – fertility declined from 2.82 in 1955–1960 to 2.44 in 1965–1970, 2.00 in 1975–1980, and 1.92 in 1985–1990.

As to regional differences in fertility trends, there seems to be a West European pattern with a moderate baby boom and a steep decline during the 1970s. Southern Europe follows the pattern with some delay. Eastern Europe shows rather stable moderate levels

Table 11.3. Total fertility rates 1950 to 1990 in 30 industrialized countries.

TFR	1950–1955	1955–1960	1960–1965	1965–1970	1970–1975	1975–1980	1980–1985	1985–1990
Australia	3.18	3.41	3.28	2.87	2.54	2.09	1.93	1.86
Austria	2.09	2.52	2.78	2.53	2.01	1.64	1.62	1.45
Belarus[a]	–	–	2.55	2.26	2.29	2.11	2.06	1.91
Belgium	2.34	2.51	2.66	2.34	1.94	1.71	1.59	1.56
Bulgaria	2.48	2.27	2.18	2.15	2.17	2.18	2.01	1.92
Czechoslovakia	2.89	2.57	2.40	2.08	2.34	2.35	2.09	2.00
Denmark	2.53	2.54	2.59	2.24	1.96	1.70	1.43	1.54
Estonia[a]	–	–	1.96	1.97	2.15	2.07	2.06	2.06
Finland	2.97	2.78	2.58	2.06	1.62	1.64	1.69	1.66
France	2.73	2.71	2.85	2.61	2.31	1.86	1.87	1.82
Germany, West	2.16	2.30	2.49	2.32	1.64	1.52	1.46	1.44
Greece	2.29	2.27	2.20	2.38	2.32	2.32	1.96	1.53
Hungary	2.73	2.21	1.82	1.97	2.09	2.11	1.81	1.82
Iceland	3.70	4.02	3.94	3.15	2.84	2.29	2.25	2.12
Ireland	3.37	3.67	3.96	3.86	3.80	3.46	2.87	2.28
Italy	2.32	2.35	2.55	2.49	2.27	1.92	1.55	1.33
Japan	2.75	2.08	2.01	2.00	2.07	1.81	1.76	1.68
Luxembourg	1.97	2.22	2.36	2.22	1.96	1.50	1.45	1.47
Malta	4.14	3.73	3.10	2.17	2.07	2.02	1.96	2.02
Netherlands	3.05	3.09	3.12	2.73	1.97	1.58	1.51	1.56
Norway	2.60	2.84	2.90	2.72	2.25	1.81	1.69	1.80
Poland	3.62	3.29	2.65	2.27	2.25	2.26	2.33	2.15
Portugal	3.05	3.04	3.09	2.86	2.76	2.42	1.99	1.60
Russia[a]	–	–	2.40	2.06	2.01	1.95	1.97	1.89
Spain	2.57	2.75	2.89	2.93	2.89	2.63	1.86	1.46
Sweden	2.21	2.23	2.33	2.12	1.89	1.65	1.65	1.91
Switzerland	2.28	2.33	2.50	2.27	1.81	1.53	1.53	1.55
Ukraine[a]	–	–	2.17	1.99	2.07	1.99	2.00	1.85
UK	2.18	2.50	2.82	2.52	2.04	1.72	1.80	1.81
USA	3.45	3.71	3.31	2.55	2.02	1.78	1.82	1.92

[a]From Lutz and Scherbov, 1989. Data in last column refer to 1990 only (Lutz *et al.*, 1994).
Source: UN, 1993.

before the 1991 transition, which is mostly associated with steep fertility declines (eastern Germany currently has a TFR of 0.8). *Figure 11.3* depicts these trends in more detail for seven selected countries. The United States clearly falls out of the general pattern:

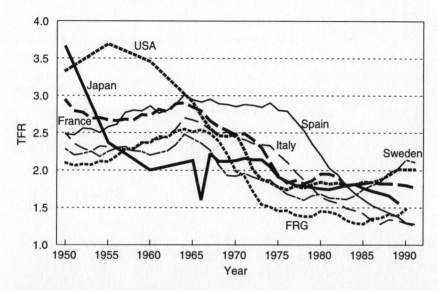

Figure 11.3. Total fertility rates from 1950 to 1991 (annual data) in selected industrialized countries.

because of the baby boom, it reached fertility levels of 3.7 in 1955, which is above any level registered in Europe since early in this century. Japan shows a completely different pattern with a steep fertility decline during the 1950s which brought down total period fertility from 3.6 in 1950 to 2.0 in 1960. An East Asian peculiarity is the low fertility in 1966 which is attributable to the *Hinoeuma* ("fire horse") year during which it was considered unpropitious to have a daughter (Atoh, 1989).

As can be expected the completed fertility of generations (cohorts) shows a much smoother trend as plotted in *Figure 11.4*. The figure gives the average number of children born between 1940 and 1960 to women by age 45. For cohorts born after 1945, the data are partly based on estimations because the women have not yet reached age 45. There seem to be two types of countries, those that show a steadily declining trend, such as the FRG, Switzerland, Italy, and the UK, and those that do not show much of a decline, such as Sweden and Czechoslovakia. France also shows only little decline. Under this cohort perspective, fertility declines over recent decades look less dramatic than under the period perspective. The baby

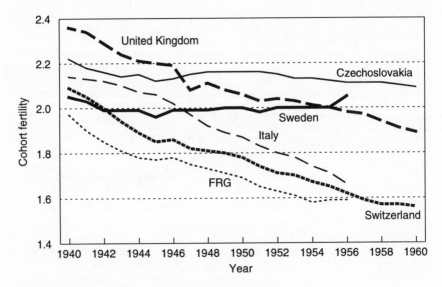

Figure 11.4. Completed fertility for birth cohorts born between 1940 and 1960. Source: Council of Europe, 1991.

boom and the following bust are not clearly visible because these events were largely phenomena of timing of births.

11.3 Desired Family Size and Childlessness

Since the information derived from the analysis of past fertility trends in industrialized countries that have already completed the demographic transition does not suggest any obvious future trend, one may look for other sources of information, such as reproductive intentions as stated in interview surveys. For the short-term future, such expressed intentions are clearly a relevant piece of information although they cannot be readily translated into fertility rates because of various biases.

The most recent survey with comparable data for a large number of industrialized countries was given in an annex to the Eurobarometer 1991 which asked identical questions in the 12 countries of the European Community. *Table 11.4* lists the answers to the question regarding the ideal number of children in a family. Despite some variation across countries, the general pattern is similar: very few

Table 11.4. Answer to question: "[In your country] today what do you think is the ideal number of children for a family like yours or the one you might have?" Poll taken in 1989.

Country	Number of children (in %)					Mean
	0	1	2	3	4 or more	
Belgium	5	18	52	21	3	2.01
Denmark	3	9	65	20	4	2.13
Germany, West	7	14	58	18	3	1.97
Greece	2	13	42	33	11	2.42
France	3	19	47	28	4	2.13
Ireland	2	9	33	30	27	2.79
Italy	2	9	61	24	4	2.20
Luxembourg	3	21	56	19	3	1.99
Netherlands	3	5	65	22	5	2.23
Portugal	3	21	55	16	4	2.01
Spain	4	22	55	15	3	1.94
UK	2	10	67	15	6	2.14
EC12	4	14	57	21	4	2.10

Source: Eurobarometer, 1991.

European men and women find a childless family ideal; the proportion is highest in West Germany with 7 percent and Belgium with 5 percent. In all countries there is a clear majority for the two-child family. In the UK, the Netherlands, and Denmark, up to two-thirds of the population thinks that two children are desirable. About one-fifth thinks that three children are ideal. The proportion wanting three children is 30 percent or higher only in Ireland and Greece. In the UK and Spain it is as low as 15 percent. Again with the exception of Ireland and Greece, the proportion mentioning four or more children is extremely small. The mean family size resulting from these answers is lowest in Spain, West Germany, Luxembourg, Portugal, and Belgium. While the results for Germany are not surprising, the results for Spain and Portugal are because they still had rather high fertility recently (in the World Fertility Survey, Portugal was considered part of the high fertility/developing country group). The low levels of stated ideal family size in these countries also support the view that the present low period fertility rates are not just a temporary phenomenon.

Table 11.5. Answers to questions on family size in Austria, 1981–1982, for women married five to eight years.

Number of children	Societal ideal	Personal ideal	Desired number of children	Expected number of children	Children already born (incl. pregnancies)
Zero	0.1	2.4	2.2	2.2	10.1
One	1.4	7.3	13.8	14.1	30.7
Two	72.3	53.4	51.6	50.0	46.0
Three	24.5	28.1	24.6	25.3	10.8
Four	1.4	6.6	5.9	6.5	1.8
Five or more	0.3	2.2	1.9	1.9	0.6
Mean	2.27	2.37	2.25	2.26	1.65

However, a stated ideal family size is not an actual family size, especially if the ideal refers to an abstract average family rather than one's personal life. Like several other surveys, an Austrian fertility survey conducted during the early 1980s asked five different questions related to family size to better understand the personal biases involved. *Table 11.5* gives the answers to questions on the societal ideal, the personal ideal, the actual desired number of children, the realistically expected number of children, and the children already born after five to eight years of marriage. A comparison shows the interesting pattern that the further away the question is from one's personal life, the greater the concentration on the two-child family. It is especially dominant for the societal ideal.

Only 2 percent of the married women want to remain childless, but the data on actual fertility show that the proportion childless will be much higher. Because the Austrian data come from a panel study, it was possible to analyze how many women have met their stated plans over a three- to four-year period (see Lutz, 1985). Of all children planned for that period, more than half were not born (pregnancies were also counted as births). On the other hand, 13 percent of the women had more children than they planned. This resulted in a significant net deficit. It also implies that if unplanned pregnancies could be avoided by better contraception, the deficit may become even larger.

The most significant case of a personal deficit, i.e., having fewer children than originally intended, seems to be with respect to the first birth. The actual number of childless women tends to be much

Table 11.6. Evolution of childlessness in German-speaking countries by cohorts.

		Childless among all women		Childless among women married 11 to 15 years	
Age	Year of birth	Austria (%)	East Germany (%)	Year of marriage	West Germany (%)
80	1901	33.8	27.1	1956–1960	11.2
75	1906	29.9	21.9	1961–1965	13.7
70	1911	26.2	17.8	1966–1970	15.8
65	1916	23.2	16.7	1971–1975	19.3
60	1921	20.9	17.9		
55	1926	20.5	16.9		
50	1931	16.4	12.4		
45	1936	14.4	10.5		
40	1941	14.7	9.2		
35	1946	15.8	7.7		
30	1951	23.2	9.9		

Source: Büttner and Lutz, 1990b.

higher than the number of women who say in their early adulthood that they want to be childless. It is quite difficult to calculate the proportion of women remaining without children (and complete family-size distributions) as implied by period fertility rates because birth-order specific information is required. A recent survey article by Feeney and Lutz (1991) describes alternative methods and shows estimates of childlessness among all women above age 45 in the early 1980s of 27 percent in the USA, 31 percent in the Netherlands, and 28 percent in Austria.

More accurate but less contemporary information on childlessness can be given for cohorts of women. *Table 11.6* compares the evolution of cohort childlessness in three German-speaking countries (Austria, East Germany, and West Germany) over the course of this century (see Büttner and Lutz, 1990b). For West Germany the data are only available for married women. In both Austria and East Germany the proportion of childless women declined significantly from around 30 percent for cohorts born at the beginning of the century to just above 10 percent. This decline is evidence of the disappearance of the "European marriage pattern" under which high proportions of women remained unmarried. Childlessness has always been somewhat lower in East Germany, but after the cohort of 1940 the trend completely diverges from that in Austria, with further decreases in East Germany and increases in Austria. As is discussed later the very low levels of childlessness in East Germany are partly attributable to government policies. The increasing proportion in Austria is probably a mixture of actually increasing childlessness and the fact that not all children were born to these young cohorts.

In West Germany the existing data for marriage cohorts show a clear increase over time of childlessness after 11 to 15 years of marriage. Since one can assume that the overwhelming proportion of first children is already born after 11 to 15 years of marriage, these figures should come close to final childlessness. Taken together with the fact that the proportion of women that marry has been declining and that fertility outside marriage is very low, this implies very high levels of cohort childlessness in West Germany.

These family-size distributions, including childlessness, also have direct implications on distributional and equity issues, such as the concentration of childbearing and the division of labor for society's reproduction among women of one generation. The rather even distribution and low childlessness in East Germany in the late 1980s implies that 33 percent of all women have half the children born, whereas in Austria 23 percent of all women have half the children. In West Germany 29 percent of all married women have half the children, but for all women together the proportion should be lower than in Austria, i.e., the concentration higher. The concentration of childbearing has many implications which are discussed in Lutz (1989).

One issue which is also relevant for future fertility levels is whether there will be a trend toward some women specializing in childrearing while the rest are career-oriented with few or no children. Such a pattern, if accepted, could result in higher total fertility, but this is very unlikely. All empirical information shows that very few women want to have a large number of children and that the overwhelming majority wants to have at least one child or two children. The normative trend toward the two-child family at least as a goal seems to be very strong. This would imply lower concentration in the future rather than an increase.

11.4 Arguments Assuming Higher Fertility

In several countries period fertility has been below the so-called replacement-level fertility for more than two decades. Is this a stable and sustainable pattern of reproduction in modern industrialized societies, or is it only a transitory state that will be followed by higher fertility? One can think of several arguments and mechanisms that can potentially lead to higher average fertility in these countries.

11.4.1 The homeostasis argument

The usual interpretation of the demographic transition theory is that an initial equilibrium between high birth rates and high death rates is disturbed by declining mortality which in course triggers a fertility decline that will bring birth and death rates back to an equilibrium at low levels. However, history has shown that fertility declines with all their irregularities and national particularities generally do not stop at replacement level, but continue to decline further. The homeostasis argument would stress that this is simply an overshooting that will be reversed after some inevitable societal adjustments. Most explicitly this has recently been expressed by Vishnevsky (1991) who does not see fertility levels as the sum of individual behavior, but rather as one aspect in the evolution of a system that determines behavior. He believes that the development of the demographic system is directed by a proper, inherent goal. In the process of self-organization the system aims at self-maintenance and survival. For human beings at a certain stage of the evolution, a new and higher goal is assumed to appear that goes beyond pure population survival – namely, that of maintaining homeostasis in the population's reproduction, even in the face of considerable fluctuations in external conditions (see Vishnevsky, 1991:265).

It is not yet possible to empirically test this hypothesis. Trends such as the recent fertility increase in Sweden, which has been a forerunner in many other social issues, may be taken as evidence by its supporters. But the hypothesis is not specific enough to be tested (e.g., it does not state by how much fertility should increase over a period). Since studies have not addressed the mechanisms and motivations that induce couples to have more children, it remains largely a philosophical argument. Nevertheless, it seems worthwhile considering at this individual level, although it is highly controversial, and authors such as Westoff (1991) criticize the assumption of a "magnetic force" toward replacement.

11.4.2   Assumption of fertility cycles

Several views summarized under this heading contend that the present low level of period fertility is just the bottom of a cycle and that the future will bring an upward trend. These shall be grouped into arguments with respect to the timing of fertility within cohorts and to intergenerational fertility fluctuations. The first argument is based on the observation that in many countries the recent declines in total fertility were accompanied by declines in the fertility rates of younger women. Hence, one could assume that observed trends only reflect a delay in childbearing (the timing of fertility) and do not indicate a decline in the number of children a woman has over her life span (the quantum of fertility). Especially in France there has been a heated debate on this issue even beyond scientific circles; it has been pointed out that the fertility of cohorts born until the late 1950s was still above 2.0 children per woman (Le Bras, 1991). As described above it is evident in all countries that declines in cohort fertility have been slower than in period fertility. But in most European countries, meanwhile, cohort fertility is also below 2.0, and in several countries even below 1.7.

It is difficult to evaluate the argument that women will soon catch up and have their delayed births, hence increasing period fertility. The slight recovery in total fertility over the last years in several European countries may be partly attributable to this phenomenon. Studies for Sweden have also shown that the presently high period fertility is largely due to such a timing phenomenon and is likely to decline soon (Hoem, 1990). This timing phenomenon could only have a sizable impact on future period fertility levels if one assumes that cohort fertility tends to be substantially higher than present period rates. This may be the case in Southern Europe, where period fertility recently declined extremely fast, but generally there is no clear substantive reason to assume that a significant catch-up phenomenon will occur. For longer-term fertility trends (more than 10 years) such timing aspects are irrelevant in any case.

The second argument focuses on longer-term cycles. It assumes that the fertility level of the parent generation is a determinant of their children's reproductive behavior. Best known in this context is Easterlin's relative income hypothesis (Easterlin, 1980). In short, it assumes that fertility is determined by income relative to aspirations with cohort size determining income: generation one has low relative income and low fertility; generation two grows up with low aspirations for wealth but finds advantages in labor market conditions because of few competitors, hence having high relative income and high fertility; generation three is numerous and has high aspirations resulting in low relative income and low fertility. Empirically, this model fits nicely to the US baby boom in the 1960s and the subsequent fertility decline. But this is only half a cycle. So far a new baby boom has failed to materialize. For other countries even the historical application fits less well. There are also a number of conceptual problems such as the fact that within a generation fertility is unevenly distributed among families – some have many children, others only one (see discussion in Lutz, 1989) – and that women have children at different ages which soon smoothes out any cycles. But even if this assumed mechanism is not a dominating factor for fertility trends, it may well play some role as one among several factors.

11.4.3   Pronatalistic policies

Governments in countries with very low fertility have reason to worry about the long-term implications of subreplacement together with increasing life expectancy at higher ages on the pension system and other social-security issues such as health care. Because the baby boom generation is presently in their main productive ages, the economic dependency burden is still quite favorable. But projections indicate that in Western Europe, the proportion of the population that is above age 60 will increase significantly over the next few decades. This is an extremely serious threat to present forms of pay-as-you-go pension schemes, where the active people pay for the pensioners. For this and other reasons, several European countries have tried to stimulate fertility through policies that make it more profitable to the individual to have another child. It needs to be stressed, however, that most countries that provide extensive childcare benefits do this for social policy rather than population policy (Höhn, 1991). But still such policies might be relevant for individual reproductive decisions.

If the reproductive behavior of couples reacts to incentives in the way other human behavior does, then changes in the incentive structure will have an impact on fertility. Monetary incentives for having children are only one possible mechanism of government policies directed toward higher fertility. There is very little evidence that such monetary policies actually work. Compare, for instance, the high direct and indirect child benefits in Germany and Austria to the almost nonexisting benefits in the USA; and yet fertility is much lower in Germany and Austria. Also over time it is hard to detect responses of fertility rates to changes in government benefits (Chesnais, 1985; Klinger, 1985). One exception is the marked fertility increase in the GDR between 1976 and 1977, which can clearly be attributed to the introduction of a package of social-policy measures (Büttner and Lutz, 1990a; Vining, 1984). But conditions in the GDR were very specific: there was a severe housing shortage, and the birth of a child was an easy way to get access to an apartment and other benefits. Since these benefits provided for basic needs that otherwise could hardly be met, the motivation for childbearing became very strong. But this already goes beyond the usual understanding of incentives, because it is associated with deprivations that are hardly acceptable in democratic free market societies.

Beyond material incentives, social pressure and changing attitudes as well as infrastructural arrangements for childrearing may be very important. Because no monetary transfer can realistically compensate the cost of children, including the opportunity costs, nonmaterial motivation for parenthood remains the key issue. These can also be influenced by government policies which try to remove institutional and other obstacles for women to combine motherhood with a professional career. In Sweden, the universal and low-cost provision of public child-care starting at very young ages and easy opportunities for part-time work may be important factors in explaining the high level of fertility.

11.4.4   National identity and ethnic rivalry

While it cannot be expected that macroeconomic concerns, such as the pension gap, influence individual reproductive behavior without intervening public policies, this may well be the case with respect to the issue of national identity. Fears related to the ethnic composition of the population and ingroup-outgroup feelings can be powerful emotional forces that may directly influence individual reproductive behavior. Examples of this may be found in Israel, Northern Ireland, and the Baltic states, where there is clear rivalry between two groups of the population that seems to be associated with higher fertility levels than could be expected from their socioeconomic standing and comparison to other populations. One possible hypothesis is that through international migration such rivalry may also affect other industrialized countries. But there are strong counterexamples, such as francophone Canadians, non-Hispanic Californians, or Germans living in cities with many Turks, where ethnic-linguistic rivalry is carried out by means other than fertility levels.

11.5   Arguments Assuming Lower Fertility

11.5.1   Trend toward individualism

According to the sociological theories of Durkheim (1902) and Tönnies (1887) the process of "modernization" is characterized by a transition from "community" (*Gemeinschaft*) to "society" (*Gesellschaft*). While "community" refers to a lasting and complete living together under a relatively stable structure, "society" means a mere proximity of persons who are independent of one another and is characterized by relatively open structures. In this process of transition, an increasing number of functions that used to be met by the family are now taken over by anonymous institutions. This means an increase in equality and personal freedom, but also an increase of individualism and a weakening of interpersonal bonds.

With respect to the future of the family, Hoffmann-Nowotny (1987) assumes that the trend of increasing differentiation as well as multiple and partial integration will continue, especially for women. From a sociological point of view, he concludes that there is little reason to believe that the family as we know it can and will survive as the mainstream model for future living patterns. This view is not too different from the notion of a "second demographic transition" put forward by Lestaeghe (1983) and van de Kaa (1987) to characterize a new phase of demographic behavior that expresses itself through lower marriage propensities, higher instability of unions, increase in extramarital fertility, and lower total fertility.

Another psychological aspect of this supposed trend toward individualism is that men and women are increasingly reluctant to make decisions which have long-term consequences and clearly limit the future freedom of choice. The decision to have a child predetermines many choices for the next two decades, and makes second thoughts impossible once the child is born. If the trend toward greater mobility in all aspects of life continues, this might well mean fewer responsible men and women daring to become parents.

There is little empirical basis to evaluate the validity of these presumptions for the future, but they seem to be powerful arguments and plausible explanations of recent trends. In the future it might well happen that, if this trend goes to an extreme, counterforces will be mobilized to compensate some of the negative aspects of this trend. But a return to traditional patterns of "community" with their restrictions on individual freedom is very unlikely. Most of the following arguments are related to this general "continued modernization" argument, but they are mentioned individually because they carry some specific weight in themselves.

11.5.2   Economic independence of women

One recent trend that has often been singled out as a dominating feature of societal change is the increasing economic independence of women. Female labor force participation has steeply been increasing in virtually all industrialized countries over the past decades. The increase has been strongest in Scandinavia, where labor force participation is almost universal among adult women below age 50. But female activity rates in North America are not much lower. In Italy over the last decade, female labor force participation increased by more than one-third. It seems obvious that this fundamental change in the role and orientation of women with respect to economic activity is connected to changing reproductive patterns. Increasing economic independence of women also tends to result in a postponement of marriage which typically is associated with lower fertility.

One must be cautious, however, in pointing out female economic activity as a major determinant of declining fertility. It may also be that the lower desired number of children motivates women not to stay at home but rather to enter the labor force, or there may be a joint driving force behind both trends. This statement is supported by the evidence that in several countries fertility rates have recently improved, despite very high and still increasing female labor force participation. The key question in this multifaceted issue seems to be how women can combine parenthood with participation in the labor market (see, e.g., Kiernan, 1991). This may be a decisive question for future European birth rates. Nevertheless, even with flexible legal regulations and good child-care systems, working women on average will not have very large families.

11.5.3 Instability of partnership

As described above, marital stability has been declining in all industrialized countries. Part of the reason for this phenomenon clearly lies in the increasing economic independence of women. Women are no longer economically forced to stay in an unsatisfactory union if they earn an independent income. Other reasons may lie in the general increase in mobility in modern industrialized societies and in a decreasing threshold in the level of dissatisfaction necessary to attempt to change conditions. Whatever the social and psychological reasons may be, a young couple today can count less on actually staying together for 20 years, the minimum time required from the children's perspective.

Increasing evidence from empirical studies (Kiernan, 1992) shows that the separation of parents actually does more harm to children than had been assumed in the past. Such effects range from indicators of social behavior and intellectual performance to happiness and feelings of security. Thus responsible prospective parents who are sensitive about their children's likely psychological well-being and would not like them to experience a trauma of separation from one parent may decide not to have children, if they have doubts about the stability of their partnership. This may be true for marriages, but even more so for the increasing number of nonmarital unions which seem to have much lower stability, as indicated by statistical data, e.g., in Sweden.

One possible counterargument would be that remarriage (or formation of new nonmarital unions) may actually be an incentive to have an additional child to strengthen the relationship with the new partner. Although this may happen in individual cases, empirical analysis on data cross-classified by marital status and number of children for Finland (see Lutz, 1993) show that a slight effect of this kind exists, but is clearly not significant for total fertility.

11.5.4 Consumerism and use of time

Commentators of the recent fertility decline often mention the increase in consumerism as a basic underlying cause. Under this form of materialism, people would supposedly rather invest in pleasure for themselves than in children; they would rather buy a new car than have another child; they would rather spend their time watching TV than changing diapers. Underlying this view is the notion that having children is work and not fun. As pointed out by Keyfitz (1991), in earlier times couples had to work harder and more hours to earn a living and still found the time to have many children. The extra leisure time they have now is not being spent on having children. Having children is defined as work and therefore one talks about its opportunity cost. In the words of Keyfitz (1991:239): "No one complains about the opportunity cost of having sex. Thus to talk about opportunity cost of children indeed highlights the problem of non-childbearing." He suggests thinking of a work–fun continuum and trying to move childbearing toward the fun end of that continuum.

Whether or not childbearing, and especially childrearing, will become a more favored leisure-time activity of men and women will depend on the trade-offs between fun and burden. Some European cities already have more dogs than children. Obviously the work–fun balance is more favorable for pets, who mean less of a commitment and in the worst case can always be given away. This argument clearly suggests that unless the burden of having children is diminished or the rewards from children is enhanced, the balance will continue to be negative for childbearing.

11.5.5   Improving contraceptives

The final argument in this series is less concerned with changing values but is at a more mechanical level. It is an empirical fact that in all industrialized societies, a significant number of children are born without being planned either for that specific time or at all. Demographers often distinguish between timing failure (pregnancy too early) and quantum failure (unwanted pregnancy). Both could be reduced by more efficient contraceptive use: for the latter this would clearly imply lower fertility; for the former it is theoretically neutral. In practice one can assume that a certain fraction of the births categorized as timing failures may not have been realized at a later point in time because of changing living conditions, such as disruption of a union, a more demanding job. With respect to unwanted pregnancies, Westoff *et al.* (1987) estimate that for a number of low fertility countries, completely efficient contraception would bring down fertility rates by somewhat less than 10 percent, but would also have a significant effect in bringing down the number of abortions.

Currently, we are still far from a perfect contraceptive that requires no effort to use and has no negative side effects. An increasing number of women report being tired of using the pill, yet sterilization is not appealing to all (especially in continental Europe) because of its irreversibility. This may have recently resulted (there is little new empirical data yet) in an increase in the number of risk-takers or couples practicing less reliable natural methods. A hypothetical new perfect contraceptive without any side effects, which is only taken once and then requires some reverse action to become pregnant, certainly would change the situation because in the numerous cases of ambivalence and risk-taking this would clearly inhibit pregnancies which presently are still quite numerous. It will make quite a difference for future fertility levels whether one must go to the doctor to have a child or not to have a child, as is the case now.

11.6   Fertility Assumptions and Population Heterogeneity

The above-stated arguments – and there are many more that are not listed – suggesting the assumption of a tendency toward lower or higher future fertility levels have some degree of justification. All these aspects will impact on future reproductive behavior in industrialized countries, but it is unclear what the possible balance, the synergism of these partly contradictory developments will be. For this reason we cannot provide one estimate but can rather suggest alternative scenario assumptions.

A probable situation is that the synergism of these various trends will not result in a uniform pattern of childbearing in all population groups. Heterogeneity of reproductive behavior has been increasing since the baby boom of the 1960s, and there is no indication that this heterogeneity is likely to diminish. Quite the contrary, the above-mentioned trend toward a societal structure labeled "society" rather than "community" implies lower normative pressure toward uniform behavioral patterns. There may be many subgroups and subcultures in society that have quite different reproductive behavior. On the other hand, it is often argued that mass media exert a powerful force toward standardization. But with respect to fertility it is not clear in which direction the standardization goes. Among TV "protagonists" you find singles, childless couples, and traditional families. It seems to be the case that the plurality of lifestyles is in itself one of the key messages from the media.

Heterogeneity of the population has important impacts on demographic dynamics. In mortality, heterogeneity affects the overall dynamics of the system through selection processes resulting in changing weights of the subgroups. As to differential fertility – aside from individual biological differences – subgroups with higher fertility grow more rapidly and hence gain more weight in the population. Empirically this can be observed for certain high fertility religious groups but also with respect to foreigners who have not fully adapted to the host country's average fertility level. In Germany, for instance, the recent slightly positive balance of births and deaths was attributable to the large birth surplus of foreigners living in Germany. While only 1 in 12 inhabitants of Germany is a foreigner, 1 in 8 children born has foreign citizenship. In other words, without the foreigners the German fertility rate would still be lower.

Such considerations of heterogeneity also entered the final numerical choice of fertility assumptions for the four industrialized regions considered in this study. At least in the long run, fertility levels should not be seen independently from migration levels. For this reason the population scenarios to the end of the next century consider such interdependencies while the systematic permutation scenarios until 2030 are based on the assumption of independence. But in the assumed independent fertility level, heterogeneity resulting from past immigration levels is indirectly reflected.

Figure 11.5 shows the fertility assumptions for Western Europe and North America together with the recent trend in total fertility rates. The high, central, and low assumptions reflect different mixes of the trends described above. The often-assumed replacement-fertility level was not used as a benchmark because there is little substantive reason for such a "magic" level. The low values of the TFR to be reached by 2010, and then assumed to stay constant, are 1.3 in Eastern Europe, Western Europe, Japan/Australia, and 1.4 in North America. The assumed high values are 2.1 in Western Europe and Japan/Australia, and 2.3 in Eastern Europe and North America. The range of uncertainty is assumed to be highest in Eastern Europe, which is currently experiencing a profound transition, the result of which is hardly predictable. The assumed central values are always the arithmetic means of the low and high values. They may be seen as the values with the greatest probability. In all cases fertility levels for the period between 1990 and 2010 were derived from linear interpolation starting from the 1990 values.

For the scenario calculations up to 2100, i.e., more than a century from today, a very different approach was chosen because fertility in more than 100 years will hardly depend on today's fertility level in a specific region. To propose an alternative to the ubiquitous replacement fertility assumption, which is most prominent in the World Bank's long-range projections, the long-term calculations in the Appendices of this volume assume fertility to be dependent on the population density in the region. Within a predefined range, it will be assumed that the lower the population density is, the higher the fertility. This rationale, which has been inspired by ecological considerations, needs to be discussed and evaluated in a much broader context. Some empirical evidence, such as the higher fertility in sparsely populated Scandinavia compared with the fertility level in densely populated Central Europe, suggests that the idea may at least be considered on an equal basis with the

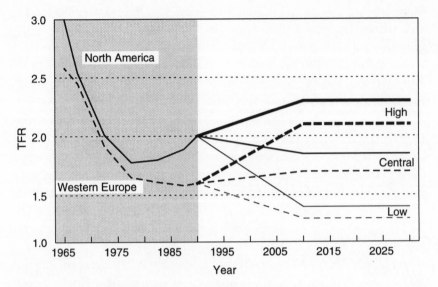

Figure 11.5. Total fertility rates since 1965 and assumptions until 2030 in North America and Western Europe.

replacement-level assumption that also has no behavioral theory behind it. If this assumption of density dependence of the ultimate fertility level helps initiate a discussion, it will have served part of its purpose. In the long-range projections the assumptions will not only be applied to the four regions of today's industrialized countries but also to the other world regions that are assumed to have completed their demographic transition over the course of the next century. More details on this are given in the projection chapters.

References

Atoh, M., 1989, Trends and differentials in fertility, Reprinted from *Country Monograph Series No. 11, Population of Japan,* UN ESCAP, 1984, Reprint Series No. 9, Institute of Population Problems, Ministry of Health and Welfare, Tokyo, Japan.

Büttner, T., and Lutz, W., 1990a, Estimating fertility responses to policy measures in the German Democratic Republic, *Population and Development Review* **16**(3):539–555.

Büttner, T., and Lutz, W., 1990b, Vergleichende Analyse der Fertilitätsentwicklungen in der BRD, DDR und Österreich, *Acta Demographica* 1:27–45, Physica-Verlag, Heidelberg, Germany.

Chesnais, J.-C., 1985, Les conditions d'efficacité d'une politique nataliste: examen theoretique et exemples historiques (The conditions of efficiency of a pronatalist policy: Theoretical considerations and some historical examples), *International Population Conference, Florence 1985* 3:413–425, International Union for the Scientific Study of Population, Liège, Belgium.

Council of Europe, 1991, *Recent Demographic Developments in Europe,* Council of Europe Press, Strasbourg, France.

Durkheim, E., 1902, *De la Division du Travail social,* Felix Alcan, Paris, France.

Easterlin, R.A., 1980, *Birth and Fortune: The Impact of Numbers on Personal Welfare,* Basic Books, New York, NY, USA.

Eurobarometer, 1991, Desire for children, *Eurobarometer* **32**.

Feeney, G., and Lutz, W., 1991, Distributional analysis of period fertility, in W. Lutz, ed., *Future Demographic Trends in Europe and North America: What Can We Assume Today?* Academic Press, London, UK.

Hoem, J.M., 1990, Social policy and recent fertility change in Sweden, *Population and Development Review* **16**(4):735–748.

Hoffmann-Nowotny, H.-J., 1987, The future of the family, in *Plenaries. European Population Conference 1987: Issues and Prospects,* Central Statistical Office of Finland, Helsinki, Finnland.

Höhn, Ch., 1991, Policies relevant to fertility, in W. Lutz, ed., *Future Demographic Trends in Europe and North America: What Can We Assume Today?* Academic Press, London, UK.

Keyfitz, N., 1991, Subreplacement fertility: The third level of explanation, in W. Lutz, ed., *Future Demographic Trends in Europe and North America: What Can We Assume Today?* Academic Press, London, UK.

Kiernan, K., 1991, *The Respective Roles of Men and Women in Tomorrow's Europe,* Human Resources in Europe at the Dawn of the 21st Century, Eurostat, International Conference, 27–29 November, Luxembourg.

Kiernan, K., 1992, The impact of family disruption in childhood on transitions made in young adult life, *Population Studies* **46**.

Kiernan, K., 1993, The future of partnership and fertility, in R. Cliquet, ed., *The Future of Europe's Population,* Population Studies 26, Council of Europe Press, Strasbourg, France.

Klinger, A., 1985, Population policy measures: Effects on reproductive behavior in Hungary, *Population Bulletin of the United Nations* **17**:64–79.

Le Bras, H., 1991, *Marianne et les lapins: l'obsession démographique,* Olivier Orban, Paris, France.

Lestaeghe, R., 1983, A century of demographic and cultural change in Western Europe: An exploration of underlying dimensions, *Population and Development Review* **9**(3):411–435.

Lutz, W., 1985, Realisation und Veränderung von Kinderwünschen: der dynamische Aspect, in R. Münz, ed., *Leben mit Kindern: Wunsch und Wirklichkeit*, Vienna, Austria.

Lutz, W., 1989, *Distributional Aspects of Human Fertility: A Global Comparative Study,* Academic Press, London, UK.

Lutz, W., 1993, Effects of children on divorce probabilities and of divorce on fertility: The case of Finland 1984, *Yearbook of Population Research in Finland* **31**:72–80.

Lutz, W., and Scherbov, S., 1989, Modellrechnungen zum Einfluß regional unterschiedlicher Fertilitätsniveaus auf die zukünftige Bevölkerungsverteilung in der Sowjetunion, *Zeitschrift für Bevölkerungswissenschaft* **15**(3):271–292.

Lutz, W., Scherbov, S., and Volkov, A., eds., 1994, *Demographic Trends and Patterns in the Soviet Union Before 1991,* Routledge, London, UK.

Pagnini, D.L., and Rindfuss, R.R., 1993, The divorce of marriage and childbearing: Changing attitudes and behavior in the United States, *Population and Development Review* **19**(2):331–348.

Prinz, Ch., 1994, Patterns of marriage and cohabitation in Europe, with emphasis on Sweden, *POPNET* 24 (Spring), International Institute for Applied Systems Analysis, Laxenburg, Austria.

Tönnies, F., 1887, *Gemeinschaft und Gesellschaft: Grundbegriffe der reinen Soziologie,* Wissenschaftliche Buchgesellschaft, Darmstadt, Germany.

UN, 1993, *World Population Prospects: The 1992 Revision,* United Nations, New York, NY, USA.

van de Kaa, D., 1987, Europe's second demographic transition, *Population Bulletin* **42**(1), Population Reference Bureau.

Vining, D.R., Jr., 1984, Family salaries and the East German birth rate: A comment, *Population and Development Review* **10**(4):693–696.

Vishnevsky, A., 1991, Demographic revolution and the future of fertility: A systems approach, in W. Lutz, ed., *Future Demographic Trends in Europe and North America: What Can We Assume Today?* Academic Press, London, UK.

Westoff, Ch.F., 1991, The return to replacement fertility: A magnetic force? in W. Lutz, ed., *Future Demographic Trends in Europe and North America: What Can We Assume Today?* Academic Press, London, UK.

Westoff, C.F., Hammerslough, R., and Paul, L., 1987, The potential impact of improvements in contraception on fertility and abortion in western countries, *European Journal of Population* **3**:7–32.

Chapter 12

The Future of Mortality at Older Ages in Developed Countries

James W. Vaupel and Hans Lundström

Death in developed countries usually strikes at older ages. In most developed countries the life table probability of survival to age 65 is over 75 percent for men and over 85 percent for women. Median life table life spans typically exceed 75 years for men and 80 years for women. Populations are aging, but even given current age distributions, about one-third of male deaths and half of female deaths in developed countries occur after age 80.

Not only is mortality concentrated at advanced ages in developed countries, but uncertainty about the future of mortality in these countries largely stems from uncertainty about the future of death rates among the elderly. There may be some surprises in trends at younger ages, analogous perhaps to the unanticipated epidemic of AIDS, but it seems plausible that the death rates at most ages under 65 will continue to fall at rates of perhaps 1 or 2 percent per year. In some countries for some subpopulations and in some age categories – e.g., males in their 20s – death rates may rise somewhat, at least in the short term. In the longer term, however, any such rise in mortality will produce public health responses that will probably lead to mortality improvements.

Whether or not it will be possible to continue to reduce death rates at older ages is, in contrast, an open and highly controversial question. Many gerontologists and demographers believe that death rates at advanced ages cannot be substantially reduced and that life expectancy will not increase beyond 85 years (Fries, 1980; Fries *et al.*, 1989; Olshansky *et al.*, 1990; Lohman *et al.*, 1992; Harman, 1991; Hayflick, 1977; Bourgeois-Pichat, 1978; Keyfitz, 1978; Demeny, 1984). Most deaths after age 80 are taken to be natural, senescent deaths due to intrinsic, intractable aging process. Little, then, can be done about saving lives (i.e., substantially postponing deaths) among the oldest-old. Opinions differ about whether this barrier to progress is due primarily to biological causes or to practical impediments, but the canonical view is that death rates at advanced ages in developed countries are close to limits that can only be relaxed by fundamental and currently unforeseeable breakthroughs in slowing the process of aging itself. This assumption underlies the long-term mortality forecasts published by the World Bank, the United Nations, and many national statistical offices.

Other researchers are skeptical about the existence of an upper limit to life expectancy, at least at an age as early as 85. They foresee continuing and perhaps even accelerating progress in reducing mortality rates at all ages, including the most advanced ages (Manton *et al.*, 1991). Some projections suggest that the life expectancy of the current generation of children in the United States might be 100 years or more if progress in reducing mortality rates continues over the next century (Vaupel and Gowan, 1986; Guralnik *et al.*, 1988).

If progress can be made, growth of the oldest-old population will quicken, with major economic and social consequences, including escalation of the cost of public health care and retirement programs. Progress is most important at the ages when most deaths occur; it is the weighted average of age-specific rates of mortality improvement, with weights corresponding to the product of death counts and remaining life expectancy, that determines change in life expectancy. As a rule of thumb, an average rate of improvement of 1 percent would yield an increase of one year in life expectancy per decade;

an average progress rate of 2 percent would yield a two-year increase per decade (Vaupel, 1986). At current mortality levels a newborn girl in most developed countries has a life expectancy of about 80 years. If progress in reducing mortality rates could be maintained at an average of 1 percent per year, then her life expectancy would be about 90 years. Sustained 2 percent progress would imply that the typical newborn girl in developed countries will live to celebrate her 100th birthday (Vaupel and Owen, 1986; Vaupel and Gowan, 1986).

Such an increase in female life expectancy and a corresponding increase in male life expectancy would result in a radical increase in the number of persons at advanced ages. For instance, according to one projection for the United States that assumes 2 percent annual progress (Ahlburg and Vaupel, 1990), the population above age 85 could increase from 3 million in 1990 to 72 million in 2080. This figure may be contrasted with the estimate of 17 million persons in the "middle projection" of the US Bureau of the Census (Spencer, 1989), which assumes much lower rates of mortality improvement, especially after 2005.

The conjunction of these three considerations – most deaths in developed countries occur at older ages, future trends in death rates at older ages are particularly uncertain, and alternative trends have very different demographic implications – suggests that studies of the future of mortality in developed countries should pay particular attention to the future of death rates at older ages. In this chapter we therefore review the reasons for the uncertainty surrounding the future of death rates at older ages and then present some new evidence based on Swedish data.

12.1   85 or 100+?

A major biomedical uncertainty lies at the core of the disagreement between those who foresee life expectancy leveling off at about 80 or 85 years and those who predict more radical increases to a century or more. Does the force of mortality (i.e., the age-specific hazard of death) sharply and inexorably rise for the typical individual to extremely high levels around age 85 or increase after age 85 at about the same rate or even at a slower rate than before age 85, with the

likelihood that the rate of progress being made in reducing the force
of mortality among the very old will be of the same magnitude as
the rate of progress being made among the younger old?

The first perspective implies that life spans are limited. Individuals may differ somewhat in their maximum potential life spans,
with some individuals having a potential of 100 years and others a
potential of 75 years. On average, however, the typical individual's
longevity is unlikely to exceed the natural limit of 85 years or so that
has prevailed. Most of those who adhere to this perspective believe
that continued progress in reducing mortality rates up to age 75 or
so is likely to be made, so that death before age 75 will become
rare. Consequently, life expectancy will approach the length of the
typical maximum life span, i.e., about 85 years. Eventually, some
extraordinary breakthroughs may be made that permit humans to
live beyond their natural life spans, but when such breakthroughs
will occur, if ever, is uncertain.

This general point of view is often illustrated with diagrams
showing an increasing rectangularization of survivorship curves or
showing bell-shaped distributions, centered at age 85, of what Fries
(1983) describes as "natural death (due to senescent frailty)." Such
survivorship curves and distributions of deaths imply that little or
no progress can be made in reducing death rates after age 80.

The second perspective implies that the force of mortality rises
fairly smoothly to very advanced ages exceeding 100 years or more;
there is no sharp increase for the typical individual around age 85,
and there may even be some gradual lessening of the rate of increase
after age 90 (as implied by the power function or the logistic function
used instead of an exponential function in some models of mortality).
Furthermore, there is no discontinuity around age 85 in the rate of
progress that is likely to be made in reducing the force of mortality,
so that substantial reductions in mortality rates will probably be
achieved at all ages. Consequently, life expectancy will continue
to gradually but steadily increase and may rise to 90, 95, or even
longer by the year 2050. Major biomedical breakthroughs are likely
over the course of the next century, although the exact nature and
significance of these breakthroughs cannot now be foreseen: these
breakthroughs may result in some acceleration in the rate of progress
made in reducing the force of mortality, so that a life expectancy of

well over 100 years less than 100 years from now cannot be ruled out. In contrast to the limited life-span paradigm, this might be called the mortality-reduction paradigm.

Given current knowledge, no judicious researcher can claim to know for sure which of these two paradigms is more correct – or whether some combination of them or some entirely different perspective will eventually prove to be true. Furthermore, each paradigm has numerous variants that have not yet been conclusively shown to be inconsistent with reliable empirical evidence.

Broadly speaking and with many caveats, the limited life-span paradigm can be associated with the stream of research done by Pearson (1897), Pearl (1923), Clarke (1950), Bourgeois-Pichat (1952, 1978), Comfort (1964), Ryder (1975), Hayflick (1977, 1980), Sacher (1977), Keyfitz (1978), Kohn (1982), and their colleagues. The most prominent advocate and popularizer of this general perspective is Fries (1980, 1983, 1984; Fries and Crapo, 1981; Fries *et al.*, 1989); useful reviews are also provided by Rosenfeld (1976) and Gavrilov and Gavrilova (1991). These researchers generally assume that there are biological barriers to longer life expectancy; in contrast, Olshansky *et al.* (1990) stress practical barriers that may effectively limit life expectancy to values less than 85. Whether the barriers are practical or genetic is, however, rarely explicitly addressed: in much of the gerontological literature it is simply accepted as a stylized fact that natural or senescent death implies that mortality rates cannot be substantially reduced at advanced ages. Harman (1991) and Lohman *et al.* (1992) provide two recent examples of the strength and persistence of this point of view.

The possibility that the mortality-reduction paradigm may be more correct is implied by most of the process models of mortality developed from Gompertz (1825) onward. This viewpoint has been cogently argued by Manton (1982; Manton and Soldo, 1985; Manton and Woodbury, 1987; Myers and Manton, 1984; Manton *et al.*, 1991), and is supported either explicitly or implicitly by Schatzkin (1980), Schneider and Brody (1983), Peto *et al.* (1986), Vaupel and Owen (1986), Vaupel and Gowan (1986), Schneider and Guralnik (1987), Poterba and Summers (1987), and Rowe and Kahn (1987).

The key reason that the controversy between the limited life-span and mortality-reduction paradigms has not been resolved is that there is relatively little reliable data on mortality rates over age, time, and sex among the oldest-old (i.e., after age 85). Indeed, it is remarkable how little is known considering the rapidly increasing population at advanced ages and the high life table probability, approaching 50 percent for females in some countries, of survival past age 85.

Very few published human life tables extend past age 85, and the population and death counts that are available for the oldest-old tend to be suspect. As reviewed by numerous demographers (including Shryock and Siegel, 1976; Mazess and Forman, 1979; Rosenwaike, 1981; Horiuchi and Coale, 1983; Spencer, 1986; Coale and Kisker, 1986, 1990; Kannisto, 1988), various kinds of gross errors are common in reported age-specific deaths and population sizes above age 85. These errors – such as age-heaping caused by rounding off ages to the nearest age divisible by five or ten, the tendency of some older people to falsify their age, the fact that relatively few errors in misclassifying younger people as very old people can swamp actual counts of very old people, or failures to remove the deceased from population registers so that the dead appear to survive eternally – may represent systematic biases across populations. Hence it may be impossible to reduce these errors by the usual statistical expedient of examining many data sets and either formally or informally averaging them. It is consequently essential that large, reliable data bases on oldest-old human mortality be assembled and analyzed.

The most reliable data on mortality rates up to the most advanced ages over a long period of time pertain to Sweden. Excellent data exist for Sweden since 1750; superlative data have been archived since 1895. The published Swedish data that are readily available are highly accurate, but even these data have some deficiencies at advanced ages. In particular, a large part of the published data has been smoothed by actuarial methods after age 90 or so, and the most widely available mortality rates are based on aggregated data on several years of age and time rather than by single years of age and time. Furthermore, the data, once published, have not been revised as new information (from censuses or cohort death counts) has become available.

Using unpublished information in the archives of Statistics Sweden, one of the authors (Hans Lundström) is in the process of meticulously verifying, correcting, and computerizing the death counts and population counts needed to estimate mortality rates at advanced ages in Sweden from 1750 to 1992. For this presentation, we made use of a nearly completed version of the data base for 1895 to 1990. Minor changes may be made to a few of the death and population counts in this data base, but the version used is undoubtedly extremely close to the final version.

12.2　Force of Mortality at 85, 90, and 95

Figure 12.1 plots the force of mortality for Swedish females at ages 85, 90, and 95 from 1900 through 1990. Other ages between 80 and 100 show similar patterns.

The force of mortality, also known as the hazard or intensity of death, is a measure favored by demographers to capture the level of mortality. It is defined, at age x and time y, by

$$\mu(x) = -\frac{ds(x,y)/dx}{s(x,y)} \ , \quad y = y_o + x \ ,$$

where $s(x,y)$ is the proportion of the cohort born x years ago that is surviving at time y and y_0 is the time the cohort was born. The Swedish data are available by single years of age and time, so a discrete approximation must be used to estimate μ. We used the standard approximation

$$\mu(x,y) = -\ln[1 - D(x,y)/N(x,y)] \ ,$$

where $D(x,y)$ represents the number of deaths among the cohort of people who were between exact ages $x - 1$ and x on January 1 of year y and $N(x,y)$ represents the number of people in this cohort on January 1. It should be noted that the members of this cohort attain exact age x (i.e., celebrate their x-th birthday) over the course of year y. Also in- and out-migration is ignored: net migration is negligible in Sweden after age 80.

Population sizes are small, especially at age 95, so the trajectories in *Figure 12.1* show considerable random fluctuation. The overall trends, however, are clear. There was little progress in reducing the force of mortality at advanced ages before 1940 or 1950.

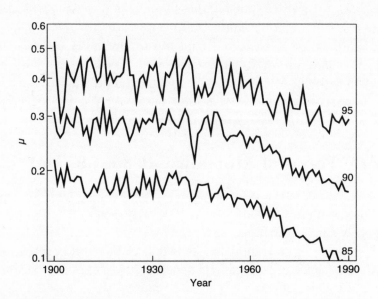

Figure 12.1. Force of mortality for females, ages 85, 90, and 95, Sweden: 1900–1990.

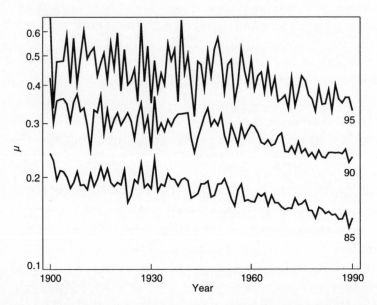

Figure 12.2. Force of mortality for males, ages 85, 90, and 95, Sweden: 1900–1990.

Table 12.1. Average annual rates of progress in reducing mortality rates in various age categories and over various time periods.

Sex	Age category	1900–09 to 1920–29	1920–29 to 1940–49	1940–49 to 1960–69	1960–69 to 1980–89
Males	60–69	0.50	0.44	0.28	0.62
	70–79	0.37	0.20	0.19	0.62
	80–89	0.36	0.13	0.36	0.53
	90–99	0.27	0.11	0.36	0.56
	100+	1.76	−1.07	0.97	0.18
Females	60–69	0.24	0.61	1.88	1.63
	70–79	0.18	0.22	1.25	2.08
	80–89	0.19	0.10	0.78	1.64
	90–99	0.13	0.03	0.60	0.94
	100+	0.23	0.41	0.80	0.49

Afterward, the force of mortality declined considerably, even at age 95. At age 85 the force of mortality declined from about 0.2 to about 0.1. At age 90 the decline was from a level of about 0.3 to about 0.2. An absolute decline on the order of magnitude of 0.1, from about 0.4 to about 0.3, is also apparent at age 95.

As shown in *Figure 12.2*, the trends for Swedish males are roughly similar although less dramatic. It is clear that the force of mortality for very old males in Sweden was substantially lower in 1990 than it was in 1900, although the reduction was less for males than for females and the levels of mortality were higher for males than for females. At each age, the absolute decline for males was on the order of magnitude of 0.05 in contrast to the decline of roughly 0.1 for females.

12.3 Average Annual Rates of Progress in Reducing Mortality Rates

To summarize the overall pattern of reduction, *Table 12.1* presents average annual rates of progress in reducing the force of mortality for Swedish females and males over successive 20-year time periods and for people in their 60s and 70s as well as octogenarians, nonagenarians, and centenarians.

For males and for females, the average level of the force of mortality over a decade of time and age was calculated as follows:

$$\bar{\mu}(x_o, y_o) = \frac{\sum\limits_{y=y_o}^{y_o+9} \sum\limits_{x=x_o}^{x_o+9} \tilde{N}(x)\mu(x,y)}{\sum\limits_{y=y_o}^{y_o+9} \sum\limits_{x=x_o}^{x_o+9} \tilde{N}(x)} \ .$$

In this equation $\tilde{N}$ is used to standardize the age composition of the population. We calculated $\tilde{N}$ from the population of Sweden in the 1980s:

$$\tilde{N}(x) = \sum_{y=1980}^{1989} N(x,y) \ .$$

The values of $\mu(x, y)$ were calculated as described above. If the death count equaled the population count, then the standard approximation μ equals 2 was used. Occasionally, at ages greater than 100, it was impossible to estimate μ for some specific years because no one was alive at that age and year. In such cases, the μ term was dropped from the numerator and a corresponding correction was made in the denominator. The average annual rate of progress in reducing the force of mortality was then calculated using

$$\rho(x_o, y_o) = -\left\{ \left[\frac{\bar{\mu}(x_o, y_o + 20)}{\bar{\mu}(x_o, y_o)} \right]^{0.05} - 1 \right\} \ .$$

Table 12.1 indicates that progress has been made in Sweden in reducing the force of mortality at all ages after 60 for both males and females. Estimated rates of progress fluctuate erratically for centenarian males, probably because there are so few observations in this category, but even so the general trend is toward a reduction in mortality rates. For females and for younger age categories, the picture is clear: mortality rates among the elderly are declining in Sweden and at a faster pace in recent decades than in the first decades of the century.

For males in the most recent time period, the rate of progress is roughly the same – about half a percent per year – for men in their

60s, 70s, 80s, and 90s. For females in the most recent time period, the rate of progress is about 2 percent for women in their 70s and half as much for women in their 90s. However, the rate of progress for women in their 80s is the same, 1.6 percent, as that for women in their 60s.

If rates of progress in the first 20 years of the century are compared with the most recent 20-year period, it is apparent that there has been a considerable acceleration of rates of progress. The acceleration is greater for females than for males. The acceleration is also greater in older age categories than in younger ones, at least in the age categories below age 100, where there are substantial numbers of observations.

The overall acceleration in rates of progress and the greater acceleration at older ages may reflect actual changes at the individual level: the elderly today may be healthier than in the past, and they may be receiving better health care. A supplemental explanation was suggested by Vaupel *et al.* (1979). Progress in reducing mortality rates at younger ages makes it more difficult to make progress at subsequent ages if the persons whose lives are saved are frail and vulnerable. In effect, progress in reducing cohort mortality rates at younger ages masks the true rate of progress (controlling for compositional changes) at older ages. As, however, mortality rates in an age category decline, this effect diminishes in importance, resulting in an apparent acceleration in rates of progress.

12.4   Lexis Maps of Force of Mortality

Another way to summarize data concerning a surface of demographic rates over age and time is to present a Lexis map, i.e., a shaded contour map of the surface (Vaupel *et al.*, 1987). *Figure 12.3* displays a Lexis map of the force of mortality for Swedish females at ages 80 to 111 and from 1900 through 1990. *Figure 12.4* displays a corresponding map for Swedish males.

The data available include death counts by year of birth as well as by current age and year. Furthermore, the data include population counts of those attaining a specific age in some year (e.g., the number of those who celebrated their 85th birthday in 1970) as well as counts of the number of people at a given age on January 1 of a

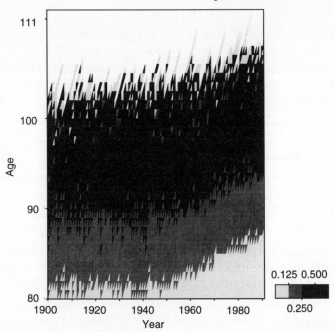

Figure 12.3. Force of mortality for females, ages 80–111, Sweden: 1900–1990.

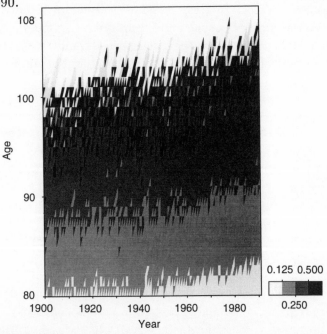

Figure 12.4. Force of mortality for males, ages 80–111, Sweden: 1900–1990.

given year. Hence it is possible to estimate the force of mortality for triangular categories of age and time. Let $q = D/N$ be the ratio of the death count to the population at risk in one of these triangles. To convert this to an annual probability of death, let

$$q^* = 1 - (1 - q)^2 \ .$$

Then, analogous to the formula used earlier, the force of mortality can be estimated by

$$\mu = -\ln(1 - q^*) \ .$$

The four shades of gray in *Figures 12.3* and *12.4* represent four levels of this estimated force of mortality. The light gray tones along diagonals above age 100, terminated by a black triangle, generally represent cohorts with one remaining member: the force of mortality is zero until this person dies.

Consider the age at which the force of mortality for females crosses the level of 0.125, as shown in *Figure 12.3*. Until 1945 or so, this age is around 81; by 1990 the age is up around 87. One interpretation of this is that an 87-year-old Swedish female in 1990 was as healthy (at least in terms of probability of death) as an 81-year-old Swedish female in the first four decades of the 20th century. The age at which the force of mortality for females crosses the level of 0.250 increases by about five years from a level fluctuating around 89 to a level of 94. Despite substantial statistical noise, a shift upward is also apparent at the level of 0.5, and there is also a clear increase in the maximum age attained. The record longevity is 111 years, attained by the grandmother of an employee of Statistics Sweden.

For males, as shown in *Figure 12.4*, the surface of mortality rates is higher than for females. Furthermore, the upward shift is less substantial at the 0.125, 0.25, and 0.5 levels and in the maximum age attained. Nonetheless, it is clear that there has been a definite shift on the order of three years. As noted above, this can be interpreted as the result of a downward shift in mortality curves or, alternatively, as a delay in the aging process: elderly Swedish males in 1990 can be considered to be three years *younger* (in terms of their risk of death) than Swedish males of the same age in the first part of this century.

Table 12.2. Age when remaining life expectancy is two years or five years.

Period	Two years left		Five years left	
	Males	Females	Males	Females
1900–1909	93.9	95.3	80.5	81.7
1910–1919	94.1	95.7	80.7	81.8
1920–1929	95.3	96.1	81.2	82.0
1930–1939	94.4	95.4	80.9	81.5
1940–1949	95.0	96.9	81.6	82.3
1950–1959	95.9	97.3	81.8	82.9
1960–1969	96.3	99.0	82.5	84.0
1970–1979	97.6	99.7	83.2	85.8
1980–1989	98.1	100.1	83.7	86.7

12.5   Remaining Life Expectancy

A final perspective on the decline in oldest-old mortality rates in Sweden is presented in *Table 12.2.* For the various decades from 1900 until 1990, the table gives, for males and females, the age when remaining life expectancy is two years and the age when remaining life expectancy is five years.

The numbers given are based on decennial life tables. The age-specific mortality rates, for single years of age, that form the basis of these life tables were calculated using the following formula:

$$q(x, y_o) = \frac{\sum_{y=y_o}^{y_o+9} D(x,y)}{\sum_{y=y_o}^{y_o+9} N(x,y)} \quad ,$$

where, unlike above, $D(x,y)$ now represents the number of deaths of people who attain exact age x in year y and $N(x,y)$ represents the number of people who attain age x in year y.

It should be noted that in *Table 12.2*, for both males and females and when remaining life expectancy is either two years or five years, there was little net change between the decade from 1900 to 1909 and the decade from 1930 to 1939. From the 1930s to the 1980s, however, the shifts were substantial. For males, the age when two years of life expectancy are left increased by almost four years, from 94.4 to 98.1. For females, the corresponding shift was close to five years, from 95.4 to 100.1. The age at which remaining life expectancy is five years increased for males by almost three years, from 80.9 to 83.7. For females, the increase was five years, from 81.5 to 86.7.

As suggested earlier, one interpretation of these shifts is that the process of aging has been slowed or delayed in Sweden such that elderly Swedish men are effectively three or four years *younger* than they used to be, and elderly Swedish females are five years younger. Caution is required because these figures are based entirely on mortality statistics, with no information about morbidity or disability. Nonetheless, treated judiciously, this perspective suggests that certainly mortality, and perhaps health more generally, is plastic even at the most advanced ages. It has been possible, at least in Sweden, to lower the force of mortality and to significantly postpone death even among the oldest-old.

12.6 Discussion

Swedish life expectancy has been among the very longest in the world for many decades. If progress can be made in Sweden in lowering mortality rates at advanced ages, then the contention that oldest-old mortality rates cannot be significantly reduced seems questionable. Using highly reliable data, we presented four perspectives on mortality changes in Sweden since 1900 among the elderly. As shown in *Figures 12.1* and *12.2*, the force of mortality at ages 85, 90, and 95 has substantially declined, especially since 1945, and more for females than for males. As shown in *Table 12.1*, rates of progress in reducing mortality rates among the elderly have accelerated over the course of the century, and from the 1960s to the 1980s ran at an average annual rate of 1 to 2 percent for females and half a percent for males. As shown in *Figures 12.3* and *12.4*, the age at which the force of mortality attains the levels of 0.125, 0.25, and 0.5 has shifted upward substantially since 1945, by about five years for females and three years for males. Finally, as shown in *Table 12.2*, the age when remaining life expectancy reaches two years or five years has also shifted upward, by about five years for females and three or four years for males. These four perspectives are consistent with each other. They indicate that the theory that oldest-old mortality rates cannot be significantly reduced is incorrect.

A variety of other strands of evidence, reviewed by Manton *et al.* (1991), point in the same direction. Most of this evidence pertains to small special populations followed for short periods of time or is based on the results of sophisticated mathematical modeling. The evidence from Sweden is highly reliable, pertains to a sizable national population followed since 1900, and is so straightforward that it does not have to be filtered through a statistical model.

The available evidence, taken together, suggests that if historical rates of progress in reducing mortality rates continue to prevail in the future, today's newborns can expect to live about 90 years on average. If, as health and biomedical knowledge develops, progress accelerates so that age-specific mortality rates come down at an average rate of about 2 percent per year, then the typical newborn in developed countries will live to celebrate his or her 100th birthday.

If our children survive to become centenarians, what will their health be like during their extra life span? Will the added years be active, healthy years or years of decrepitude, disability, and misery? The answer to this question is central to forecasting the impact of population aging on health and social needs and costs, on retirement decisions and policies, and on other questions in the economics of aging, but very little is currently known about what the answer might be.

12.7   Conclusion

Let us return now to the original question: What is the future of mortality in developed countries? It has been argued that the answer to this question hinges on a narrower question: What is the future of mortality at older ages? This question in turn hinges on the question: Is it possible to substantially reduce death rates after age 80? The Swedish data, together with other data reviewed by Manton *et al.* (1991), indicate that it is possible. However, whether progress in reducing mortality rates will continue at historical levels or even accelerate is, of course, an open question.

Biomedical research may fail to continue to produce the advances needed to reduce mortality rates. Social and economic conditions may become unfavorable to further improvements. Environmental conditions may substantially deteriorate. Nuclear war may kill millions or even billions. New diseases, like AIDS, may decimate populations.

On the other hand, the acceleration of mortality improvement at older ages may continue, so that mortality rates may fall not at 1 or 2 percent per year but at 3 or 4 percent per year over the course of the 21st century. Biological, medical, and gerontological breakthroughs could lead to considerable extensions of the human life span. The life sciences may be poised at roughly the point the physical sciences were at a century ago, and biological innovations comparable to electricity, automobiles, television, rockets, and computers may be forthcoming. Fundamental advances could occur over the next few decades in genetic engineering, in the prevention and treatment of such diseases as arteriosclerosis, cancer, or diabetes, and perhaps even in understanding and controlling human aging itself.

The future is not just uncertain: it is surprisingly uncertain. As Ascher (1978), Keyfitz (1981), Stoto (1983), and others reviewed by Ahlburg and Land (1992) have demonstrated, the actual course of demographic events often leads to outcomes beyond the most extreme projections. Consequently, forecasts ought to include wide bands of uncertainty that spread outward at an accelerating pace into the more and more distant future.

Recent research by Lee (1992), Lee and Carter (1992), and Tuljapurkar (1992) provides a good starting point. Using time-series methods, Lee and Carter project life expectancy in the United States, with confidence bands. Their forecast is that life expectancy at birth in the United States in 2065 will be around 86 years with a 95 percent confidence interval of plus or minus 4 or 5 years. This projection, however, is based entirely on analysis of historical trends of US data. The future of developed countries may not be like the past of the United States: that is an important source of additional uncertainty. The results presented above for Sweden plus the research summarized by Manton *et al.* (1991) suggest that future improvements in death rates at older ages may be more rapid than in the past.

Taking those two considerations into account and using methods of subjective probability assessment (as explained, e.g., in Behn and Vaupel, 1982), a more judicious guesstimate might be that life expectancy in the typical developed country in 2065 is not 86 plus or minus 4 or 5 but perhaps the following. There is a 50/50 chance that life expectancy will be above or below 92. There is a 50 percent chance that life expectancy will be between 85 and 100 and a 50 percent chance it will be outside this range. There is a 5 percent chance that life expectancy will be below its current level of about 75 and a 5 percent chance that it will exceed the current record longevity of 120. This is speculation, as are all predictions, but it is informed speculation that takes into account our vast ignorance of what breakthroughs or catastrophes the future might bring.

References

Ahlburg, D.A., and Land, K.C., 1992, Population forecasting: Guest editors' introduction, *International Journal of Forecasting* **8**(3):289–299.

Ahlburg, D.A., and Vaupel, J.W., 1990, Alternative projections of the US population, *Demography* **27**:639–652.

Ascher, W., 1978, *Forecasting: An Appraisal for Policy Makers and Planners,* Johns Hopkins University Press, Baltimore, MD, USA.

Behn, R.D., and Vaupel, J.W., 1982, *Quick Analysis for Busy Decision Makers,* Basic Books, New York, NY, USA.

Bourgeois-Pichat, J., 1952, Essai sur la mortalité "biologique" de l'homme, *Population* **7**:381–394.

Bourgeois-Pichat, J., 1978, Future outlook for mortality declines in the World, *Population Bulletin of the United Nations,* No. 11, United Nations, New York, NY, USA.

Clarke, R.D., 1950, A bio-actuarial approach to forecasting rates of mortality, *Proceedings of the Centenary Assembly of the Institute of Actuaries,* University Press, Cambridge, UK.

Coale, J.A., and Kisker, E.E., 1986, Morality crossovers: Reality or bad data? *Population Studies* **40**:389–401.

Coale, J.A., and Kisker, E.E., 1990, *Asian and Pacific Population Forum* **4**(1):1–36.

Comfort, A., 1964 [1979], *The Biology of Senescence,* 3rd Edition, Elsevier, New York, NY, USA.

Demeny, P., 1984, A perspective on long-term population growth, *Population and Development Review* **10**:103–126.

Fries, J.F., 1980, Aging, natural death, and the compression of morbidity, *New England Journal of Medicine* **303**:130–135.

Fries, J.F., 1983, The compression of morbidity, *Milbank Memorial Fund Quarterly/Health and Society* **61**:397–419.

Fries, J.F., 1984, The compression of morbidity: Miscellaneous comments about a theme, *The Gerontologist* **24**:354–359.

Fries, J.F., and Crapo, I.M., 1981, *Vitality and Aging*, W.H. Freeman, San Francisco, CA, USA.

Fries, J.F., Green, L.W., and Levine, S., 1989, Health promotion and the compression of morbidity, *The Lancet* **I**:481–483.

Gavrilov, L.A., and Gavrilova, N.S., 1991, *The Biology of Life Span*, Harwood Academic Publishers, Chur, Switzerland.

Gompertz, B., 1825, On the nature of the function expressive of the law of human mortality, and on a new mode of determining the value of life contingencies, *Philosophical Transactions of the Royal Society of London*, Series A 115:513–585, Abstract in *Abstracts of Philosophical Transactions of the Royal Society of London*: 252–253.

Guralnik, J.M., Yanagishita, M., and Schneider, E.L., 1988, Projecting the older population of the United States: Lessons from the past and prospects for the future, *Milbank Memorial Fund Quarterly* **66**:283–308.

Harman, D., 1991, The aging process: Major risk factor for disease and death, *Proceedings of National Academy of Sciences USA* **88**:5360–5363.

Hayflick, L., 1977, The cellular basis for biological aging, in C.E. Finch and L. Hayflick, eds., *Handbook of the Biology of Aging*, Van Nostrand Reinhold, New York, NY, USA.

Hayflick, L., 1980, The cell biology of human aging, *Scientific American* **242**:58–65.

Horiuchi, S., and Coale, A.J., 1983, Age Patterns of Mortality for Older Women: Analysis Using the Age-Specific Rate of Mortality Change with Age, Paper presented at the 1983 Annual Meeting of the Population Society of America.

Kannisto, V., 1988, On the survival of centenarians and the span of life, *Population Studies* **42**:389–406.

Keyfitz, N., 1978, Improving life expectancy: An uphill road ahead, *American Journal of Public Health* **68**:954–956.

Keyfitz, N., 1981, The limits of population forecasting, *Population and Development Review* **7**(4):579–593.

Kohn, R.R., 1982, Cause of death in very old people, *Journal of American Medical Association* **247**:2793–2797.

Lee, R.D., 1992, Stochastic demographic forecasting, *International Journal of Forecasting* **8**:315–328.

Lee, R.D., and Carter, L., 1992, Modeling and forecasting the time series of US mortality, *Journal of the American Statistical Association* **87**:659–671.

Lohman, P.H.M., Sankaranarayanan, K., and Ashby, J., 1992, Choosing the limits to life, *Nature* **357**:185–186.

Manton, K.G., 1982, Changing concepts of mortality and morbidity in the elderly population, *Milbank Memorial Fund Quarterly* **60**:183–244.

Manton, K.G., and Soldo, B.J., 1985, Dynamics of health changes in the oldest old: New perspectives and evidence, *Milbank Memorial Fund Quarterly* **63**:177–451.

Manton, K.G., and Woodbury, M.A., 1987, Biological Models of Human Mortality and the Limits to Life Expectancy, Paper presented at the Annual Meeting of the Population Association of America, 29 April–2 May, Chicago, IL, USA.

Manton, K.G., Stallard, E., and Tolley, H.D., 1991, Limits to human life expectancy: Evidence, prospects, and implications, *Population and Development Review* **17**(4):603–637.

Mazess, R.B., and Forman, S.H., 1979, Longevity and age exaggeration in Vilcabamba, Ecuador, *Journal of Gerontology* **34**:94–98.

Myers, G.C., and Manton, K.G., 1984, Compression of mortality: Myth or reality? *The Gerontologist* **24**:346–353.

Olshansky, S.J., Carnes, B.A., and Cassel, C., 1990, In search of Methuselah: Estimating the upper limits of human longevity, *Science* **250**: 634–640.

Pearl, R., 1923, *The Rate of Living*, Alfred Knopf, New York, NY, USA.

Pearson, K., 1897 [1923], *The Chances of Death, and Other Studies in Evolution*, Arnold, London, UK.

Peto, R., Parish, S.E., and Gray, R.G., 1986, There is no such thing as aging, and cancer is not related to it, in A. Likhachev *et al.*, eds., *Age-Related Factors in Carcinogenesis*, International Agency for Research on Cancer, Lyon, France.

Poterba, J.M., and Summers, L.H., 1987, Public policy implications of declining old-age mortality, in G. Burtless, ed., *Work, Health, and Income among the Elderly*, Brookings, Washington, DC, USA.

Rosenfeld, A., 1976 [1985], *Prolongevity*, 2nd Edition, Knopf, New York, NY, USA.

Rosenwaike, I., 1981, A note on new estimates of the mortality of the extremely aged, *Demography* **18**:257–266.

Rowe, J.W., and Kahn, R.L., 1987, Human aging: Usual and successful, *Science* **237**:143–149.

Ryder, N.B., 1975, Notes on stationary populations, *Population Index* **41**(1):3–28.

Sacher, G.A., 1977, Life table modification and life prolongation, in C.E. Finch and L. Hayflick, eds., *Handbook of the Biology of Aging*, Van Nostrand Reinhold, New York, NY, USA.

Schatzkin, A., 1980, How long can we live? A more optimistic view of potential gains in life expectancy, *American Journal of Public Health* **70**:1199–1200.

Schneider, E.L., and Brody, J.A., 1983, Aging, natural death, and the compression of morbidity: Another view, *New England Journal of Medicine* **309**:854–856.

Schneider, E.L., and Guralnik, J., 1987, The compression of morbidity: A dream which comes true someday! *Gerontologica Perspecta* **1**:8–13.

Shryock, H.S., and Siegel, J.S., 1976, *The Methods and Materials of Demography*, Academic Press, New York, NY, USA.

Spencer, G., 1986, The First-Ever Examination of the Characteristics of Centenarians in the 1980 Census, Paper presented at the 1986 Annual Meeting of the Population Association of America.

Spencer, G., 1989, *Current Population Reports, Series P-25, No. 1018, Projections of the Population of the United States, by Age, Sex, and Race*, US Bureau of the Census, US Government Printing Office, Washington, DC, USA.

Stoto, M., 1983, The accuracy of population projections, *Journal of the American Statistical Association* **78**:13–20.

Tuljapurkar, S., 1992, Stochastic population forecasts and their uses, *International Journal of Forecasting* **8**:385–392.

Vaupel, J.W., 1986, How change in age-specific mortality affects life expectancy, *Population Studies* **40**:147–157.

Vaupel, J.W., and Gowan, A.E., 1986, Passage to Methuselah: Some demographic consequences of continued progress against mortality, *American Journal of Public Health* **76**:430–422.

Vaupel, J.W., and Owen, J.M., 1986, Anna's life expectancy, *Journal of Policy Analysis and Management* **5**:383–389.

Vaupel, J.W., Manton, K.G., and Stallard, E., 1979, The impact of heterogeneity in individual frailty on the dynamics of mortality, *Demography* **16**:439–454.

Vaupel, J.W., Gambill, B.A., and Yashin, A.I., 1987, *Thousands of Data at a Glance: Shaded Contour Maps of Demographic Surfaces*, RR-87-16, International Institute for Applied Systems Analysis, Laxenburg, Austria.

Editor's Note for Part IV

The nature of uncertainties in fertility and mortality in today's industrialized countries is very different from that in developing regions. For future trends in life expectancy the relevant questions are what will happen to old age mortality and is life expectancy already approaching an upper limit. This is a highly controversial issue in the present scientific discussion. The Swedish evidence presented in Chapter 12 suggests that mortality at very high ages also shows a declining trend, and that there is no good reason to assume that a limit will soon be reached. In our scenarios this optimistic view is translated into an assumed increase of three years of life expectancy per decade. The alternative view of stagnating improvements is reflected in the low assumption of only one year of improvement per decade. The central assumption is two years. Among industrialized regions, the uncertainty seems to be greatest in Eastern Europe, where life expectancy has recently stagnated or even declined. This stagnation either could continue or, under better socioeconomic conditions, could even close some of the gap to Western mortality conditions.

As to fertility, even in industrialized countries the direction of future change is unclear. Fertility could further decline if certain social trends such as increasing individualism and consumerism continue. On the other hand, fertility may increase to replacement level or above if certain counterforces such as community orientation become stronger and social services that make it easier for women to combine motherhood and work are improved. Nevertheless more factors seem to point toward lower fertility, but the issue remains open. This can be translated into possible low values of 1.3–1.4 children and high values of 2.1–2.3 children per woman depending on the specific region.

317

Part V

The Future of Intercontinental Migration

Chapter 13

Migration to and from Developing Regions: A Review of Past Trends

Hania Zlotnik

At least since the "discovery" of the Americas in 1492, intercontinental migration has been a key factor influencing the demographic evolution of the developing world. During the first decades of this century, the major international flows originated in Europe and were directed mostly to the "New World," that is, to the overseas countries of permanent resettlement and certain Latin American countries. Despite the dampening effects of the two world wars and the Depression, major intercontinental flows continued to be dominated by Europeans until the early 1960s. Since then, migration from developing to developed countries has been growing and important interregional flows within the developing world have also gained prominence. This chapter provides a comprehensive view of the main migration flows either originating in or directed toward seven developing regions, namely, sub-Saharan Africa, North Africa and West Asia, South Asia, China, the rest of developing Asia (called

---

The views and opinions expressed in this paper are those of the author and do not necessarily reflect those of the United Nations.

East and Southeast Asia), Central America and the Caribbean, and
South America.[1]

The task of quantifying migration to and from the regions is
far from straightforward. A variety of data sources must be used to
piece together the facets of the phenomenon. The lack of comparability between data sources severely constrains the types of estimates
that can be derived, so that in most cases only rough indications of
the magnitude of flows can be presented. On the other hand, the
use of major regions as units of analysis precludes the need to consider every flow between developing countries. Most flows occurring
between neighboring countries, which are often the main sources of
migrants in specific countries, are excluded from the analysis.

Given the state of international migration statistics, more information is available on migration to and from developed regions than
on that between developing regions. Therefore, most of the quantitative analysis presented in this chapter focuses on statistics derived
from developed countries. Problems arising from lack of quantitative
information on a given flow are pointed out as appropriate. Before
proceeding with the presentation of migration estimates from a comparative perspective, an overview of the main data sources used and
their limitations is provided.

13.1   The Statistics Used

13.1.1   The universe covered

There are basically two different sources of information on international migration: those producing data on the stock of migrants
at a given time and those producing statistics on the flow of immigrants or emigrants over a given period. Clearly, the latter are
the most useful in tracking the evolution of migration through time
and thus providing the basis to project it. However, whereas adequate estimates of migrant stocks can be obtained from censuses
that may be carried out at relatively lengthy intervals, the availability of flow statistics depends on the existence of relatively sophisticated data-collection systems that must function continuously. Only
a few countries have those systems in place, and both their existence
and adequacy are highly correlated with whether a country considers

itself to be a recipient of immigrants or a sender of emigrants. Indeed, most countries that gather information on migration on a continuous basis do so for administrative purposes and, consequently, tend to identify migrants on the basis of administrative or regulatory principles rather than on demographic ones (Zlotnik, 1987). The USA, for instance, gathers information on immigrants defined as aliens granted the right of permanent residence. Since that right may be granted to aliens who are already present in the country under a temporary permit, the number of immigrants admitted annually by the USA is not equivalent to the number of new arrivals of aliens. In contrast, the statistics gathered on aliens granted only temporary permission to stay in the USA refer to their entries into the country. Consequently, to the extent that some such persons enter the USA several times during a year, the statistics available overestimate the number of persons involved.

Aside from data on permanent immigration to the United States, this chapter makes use of those available for the other countries of permanent resettlement, namely, Australia, Canada, and New Zealand. Information on immigration to Israel is also used, together with those available for European countries having flow statistics, namely, Belgium, Germany (the data refer only to the former West Germany), the Netherlands, Sweden, and the United Kingdom. Selected data on immigration to France are also used.

The data for Canada resemble those available for the United States, because they reflect only the number of foreigners who are granted the right of permanent residence. Australian and New Zealand statistics are gathered at the time of entry and conform better to demographic concepts. The Australian data in this chapter refer to the arrivals of persons admitted as permanent settlers and to their permanent departures. For New Zealand, the data also reflect the number of arrivals of permanent immigrants and their departures when they intend to stay away permanently. In all cases, the data are classified by place of birth. No emigration data are available for either Canada or the USA.

In the case of Israel, the data used represent the number of immigrants and the so-called potential immigrants entering the country and classified by place of birth. Although some statistics on departures are gathered by the Israeli government, they are not tabulated by place of birth, thus precluding the estimation of net migration by region of origin.

In France, l'Office National d'Immigration (ONI), which became in 1988 l'Office des Migrations Internationales (OMI), has been in charge of gathering statistics on the number of migrant workers and their families being "introduced" into the country. However, since the data are gathered through control procedures from which many migrants are exempt by law, they have generally been incomplete. In particular, after Algeria became independent in 1962, Algerians have been subject to a special immigration regime that has precluded a statistical accounting of their inflow (Tribalat and Muñoz-Pérez, 1989). Given that France is a major receiving country of citizens from the Maghreb countries (Algeria, Morocco, and Tunisia) and Turkey, statistics on both workers and family members from those countries are used as indicative of migration from North Africa and West Asia to France. The data regarding Algerians have been derived from estimates presented by Benamrane (1983) and Tapinos (1975). It must be noted that OMI statistics include both new arrivals and persons regularizing their status after being present in France for a time.

Several European countries gathering information on migration flows do so as part of the normal operation of their population registers (Belgium, Germany, the Netherlands, and Sweden). Therefore, the definition of immigrant and emigrant is derived in each case from the rules establishing who can be added to or deleted from the register. In the Netherlands a person is removed from the register when he or she intends to stay abroad for at least a year. However, Dutch citizens who have been abroad are inscribed in the register when they intend to stay in the Netherlands for at least one month and aliens are inscribed if they intend to stay for at least six months (Verhoef, 1986). Statistics on immigrants and emigrants are apparently adjusted to take into account only persons who intend to stay in the country or out of it for a year or more (Schoorl and Voets, 1990).

In Belgium, an emigrant is someone coming from abroad and intending to establish permanent residence in the country, whereas an emigrant is someone giving up permanent residence (UN, 1978). Similarly, in Germany, an immigrant is a person coming into the country to establish residence and an emigrant is a person departing and intending to give up residence in the country (UN, 1978). In both cases, "residence" is a legal concept that remains ill-defined since it is not clear under what circumstances foreigners are allowed to establish residence.

In Sweden, incoming persons must register if they intend to stay in the country for at least a year and those leaving must de-register if they intend to stay abroad for a year or more. Different definitions, however, are applied to immigrants and emigrants from Nordic countries in order to harmonize registration practices among them (Nilsson, 1990).

In the United Kingdom, information on immigration and emigration is gathered via the International Passenger Survey (IPS), a survey of travelers entering or leaving the United Kingdom by the principal air and sea routes. The IPS has been operational since 1964 and, although it gathers information on both British and foreign travelers, persons moving between the United Kingdom and Ireland are beyond its scope (Haskey *et al.*, 1989). The IPS is based on definitions of immigrant and emigrant consistent with United Nations standards, using an intended stay of over a year and an intended absence of over a year to identify each group, respectively.

It must be noted that both the systems based on population registers and the British IPS gather information on both immigration and emigration. Furthermore, similar coverage is extended to citizens and aliens. Consequently, there are major differences between the data produced by such systems and those yielded by the administrative records used by Canada, France, or the USA. Aside from the fact that the latter records lack information on emigration, both of nationals and foreigners, their statistics are only rough indicators of true population flows. Indeed, in the USA, a major problem of interpretation has arisen lately because normal immigration statistics have been artificially swollen by the regularization of undocumented aliens carried out under the provisions of the Immigration Reform and Control Act (IRCA) of 1986.

According to the IRCA, two groups of undocumented aliens could legalize their status (US Immigration and Naturalization Service, 1991). The first and larger group consisted of persons who could prove that they had been present in the USA since before

1 January 1982 and who began regularizing their status in 1989.
The second group consisted of "special agricultural workers" who
had to prove that they had worked in agriculture at least 90 days
during each of the three years preceding 1 May 1986 and who became eligible to start adjusting their status to permanent resident
on 1 December 1989. Therefore, although these two groups began
appearing in the immigration statistics only in 1989, the first entry
of the former group must have taken place before 1982 and that of
the latter group before 1984. Since other evidence suggests that illegal immigration to the United States grew significantly during the
1970s, the data presented here have been estimated assuming that
those persons regularizing their status during 1989–1992 as part of
the first group entered during 1972–1991. Their entries over that period were distributed according to a linearly increasing trend. That
assumption is validated, to a certain extent, by the terms of the regularization drive itself. With regard to special agricultural workers,
however, assumptions about their entry and stay in the USA are
less straightforward, particularly because many fraudulent applications were reportedly filed. Thus the group of migrants regularized
under the special agricultural worker program is likely to include
an important number of undocumented migrants who arrived in the
USA after the 1 January 1982 cutoff date and even up to the time at
which the IRCA was passed. It was decided, therefore, to distribute
their numbers uniformly over the 1982–1986 period.

13.1.2   Problems of data classification

Regarding the criteria used to identify region of origin, data classified by country of last or next residence would appear to be the
most useful for projection purposes, since they allow straightforward demographic accounting. However, aside from the misreport-
ing problems arising from the different possible interpretations of
the term "residence," data thus classified are often not available.
Consequently, consideration of data classified by place of birth or
citizenship becomes mandatory, though their use involves the tacit
assumption that persons born in a given country who leave another
are intending to return to their country of birth or that citizens of a
country who leave another are intending to return to their country
of citizenship (and the equivalent in terms of arrivals).

The data used in this paper as indicative of migration flows are classified by place of birth for Australia, Canada, Israel, New Zealand, and the USA; by citizenship for Belgium, France, and the Netherlands; and by country of last and next residence for Germany, Sweden, and the United Kingdom. However, citizenship being a criterion so intrinsically linked to the international migration process, it often colors the manner in which other criteria are used. Thus, the data for Australia, Canada, Israel, and the USA include only foreigners. In addition, German data distinguish between foreigners and German citizens, thus permitting the consideration of only foreigners as originating in or leaving for developing regions. Similarly, the United Kingdom publishes data that are classified first by citizenship (Commonwealth citizens vs. other) and then by place of residence. Only the data thus classified distinguish between Commonwealth citizens originating in Central American and Caribbean countries and non-Commonwealth citizens originating mostly in South America. British data classified only by place of last or next residence make no distinction between the two regions of the Americas. Hence, the two series have been used, as appropriate, in presenting the data by regions (see *Table 13.1*).

Although the use of data classified by citizenship has been kept to a minimum, the series for the Netherlands is based on that criterion; consequently Dutch citizens from overseas Dutch territories migrating to the Netherlands cannot be identified separately. In particular, the relatively large flow of Dutch Surinamese who migrated to the Netherlands just before and after Suriname's independence in 1975 shows up as an increased inflow of Dutch citizens during the 1970s. To take this group into account in interregional migration, an annual net gain of 4,000 persons during 1970–1974 and 6,000 during 1975–1979 has been added to the estimated number of migrants to the Netherlands originating in South America (the net migration gain of Dutch citizens during the 1970s was roughly of that magnitude, whereas during earlier or later periods net gains of Dutch citizens were negative or virtually nil).

A further caveat relates to the actual classification by country of origin used by the various receiving countries in publishing flow statistics. The practice of listing separately only the countries of origin of sizable numbers of migrants and grouping the rest into a

Table 13.1. Average annual number of immigrants originating in the different developing regions and average annual net migration by country of destination and period: 1960–1991; panel 1.

Origin Sub-Saharan Africa	1960–64	1965–69	1970–74	1975–79	1980–84	1985–89	1990–91
Emigrants to							
Canada	794	2,217	5,819	5,707	3,585	6,174	–
USA	1,106	1,888	4,276	10,110	13,921	14,768	16,191
Israel	318	465	670	807	2,803	1,330	4,329
Subtotal	2,218	4,570	10,765	16,624	20,309	22,272	20,520
Australia	1,604	2,551	3,401	2,719	4,308	5,708	3,960
New Zealand	468	172	431	404	146	–	–
Belgium	7,932	7,919	7,660	5,774	3,176	4,403	–
Germany	5,355	3,829	8,695	7,644	11,672	16,106	–
Netherlands	–	–	444	1,196	1,602	5,008	–
Sweden	–	–	–	–	698	2,367	–
UK	–	25,940	34,200	27,640	20,220	23,760	–
Subtotal	15,359	40,411	54,831	45,377	41,822	57,352	3,960
Net emigration to							
Australia	1,529	2,286	3,033	2,531	4,079	5,548	3,865
New Zealand	377	52	367	322	67	–	–
Belgium	6,565	5,174	4,736	2,929	541	824	–
Germany	3,145	1,262	3,872	1,589	2,056	5,297	–
Netherlands	–	–	139	761	1,032	4,282	–
Sweden	–	–	–	–	445	2,096	–
UK	–	–6,960	–1,320	2,060	–5,520	13,160	–
Subtotal	11,616	1,814	10,827	10,192	2,700	31,207	3,865
Total emigrants	17,577	44,981	65,596	62,001	62,131	79,624	24,480
Maximum net loss	13,834	6,384	21,592	26,816	23,009	53,479	24,385

single figure often precludes an adequate calculation of regional indicators. Problems encountered fairly frequently include the practice of reporting together all persons originating in the People's Republic of China and in Taiwan; the separate listing of only a few countries in a continent thus precluding the proper identification of persons originating in the different subregions; the practice of using idiosyncratic regions (e.g., the British Commonwealth); and the use of different classifications through time which lead to spurious variations in the regional estimates. Though there is no ideal solution for any of these problems, the data on China were accepted as given (if given) and the "other Asia" category was assigned to the East and Southeast Asia region, "other Africa" was generally assigned to sub-Saharan

Table 13.1. Continued, panel 2.

Origin North Africa & West Asia	1960-64	1965-69	1970-74	1975-79	1980-84	1985-89	1990-91
Emigrants to							
Canada	3,146	6,534	4,698	6,858	4,878	9,829	–
USA	5,348	9,652	14,620	19,180	22,105	21,653	26,521
Subtotal	8,494	16,185	19,319	26,038	26,983	31,482	26,521
Australia	2,133	4,777	9,027	7,461	2,625	6,217	5,701
New Zealand	38	14	60	–	–	–	–
Belgium	5,402	3,084	3,455	7,043	6,089	4,231	–
France	40,869	48,245	79,159	32,474	43,841	22,623	–
Germany	38,721	85,143	201,123	133,466	88,874	77,084	–
Netherlands	843	9,595	16,522	18,882	15,066	16,666	–
Sweden	113	569	686	1,393	1,135	1,411	–
UK	–	–	–	7,420	13,140	15,360	–
Subtotal	88,119	151,428	310,034	208,139	170,769	143,591	5,701
Net emigration to							
Australia	2,090	4,673	8,841	7,281	2,455	6,039	5,621
New Zealand	29	4	45	–	–	–	–
Belgium	4,732	1,210	2,647	4,236	1,925	965	–
Germany	29,144	44,813	121,251	17,017	-26,939	25,304	–
Netherlands	746	6,599	13,132	14,563	8,244	10,770	–
Sweden	94	488	486	1,228	994	1,315	–
UK	–	–	–	-8,160	-9,700	260	–
Subtotal	36,835	57,787	146,403	36,164	-23,021	44,652	5,621
Total emigrants	96,613	167,613	329,349	234,177	197,752	175,073	32,222
Maximum net loss	86,198	122,218	244,881	94,675	47,802	98,757	32,142
Israel Immigrants from North Africa & West Asia	30,779	8,562	4,840	2,359	1,627	716	612
Immigrants from elsewhere	26,233	19,698	26,532	31,089	15,101	13,323	198,904
Total immigrants	57,012	28,260	31,373	33,448	16,727	14,039	199,516
Net loss for North Africa & West Asia	-59,965	-102,520	-218,348	-63,586	-32,701	-85,434	166,762

Subtotals and totals may not add up due to rounding.

Africa, and no general rule was followed for "other America." Because of the ensuing ambiguities in the last case, a region comprising the whole of Central America, the Caribbean, and South America (denominated Americas–developing) was also considered.

Table 13.1. Continued, panel 3.

Origin South Asia	1960–64	1965–69	1970–74	1975–79	1980–84	1985–89	1990–91
Emigrants to							
Canada	1,365	5,815	11,713	10,450	11,361	16,990	–
USA	1,387	5,393	17,335	25,739	45,271	54,540	64,553
Israel	3,007	3,014	2,194	1,647	858	1,158	162
Subtotal	5,759	14,222	31,242	37,836	57,490	72,689	64,715
Australia	1,042	2,521	4,547	1,909	2,166	5,687	8,280
New Zealand	330	276	342	–	43	–	–
Germany	4,234	3,318	4,395	7,170	10,636	21,824	–
UK	–	32,440	21,600	28,260	26,280	23,520	–
Subtotal	5,606	38,555	30,884	37,339	39,125	51,031	8,280
Net emigration to							
Australia	980	2,408	4,388	1,793	2,075	5,607	8,235
New Zealand	226	150	285	0	31	–	–
Germany	2,528	586	1,536	2,999	3,165	12,486	–
UK	–	23,880	12,560	22,520	20,800	17,020	–
Subtotal	3,734	27,024	18,769	27,312	26,071	35,113	8,235
Total emigrants	11,365	52,777	62,126	75,175	96,615	123,720	72,995
Maximum net loss	9,493	41,246	50,011	65,148	83,561	107,802	72,950

Problems of classification by country of origin prevented the use of the flow statistics available for Switzerland, a fairly important migrant-receiving country in Europe. Since most of the migrants in Switzerland originate in other European countries, exclusion of Swiss data is not likely to lead to important biases. Indeed, the data available did not identify separately a single category of migrants originating in the developing world, though a fair number of Turkish citizens and at least some Vietnamese refugees are known to have been admitted by Switzerland.

The data discussed so far have been used to derive the estimates presented in *Table 13.1*, which shows for each major region of origin the number of emigrants that have originated in that region and that have been recorded as immigrants by each receiving country discussed. In addition, whenever possible net emigration from the region of origin being considered has been presented. In general, the table makes a distinction between the receiving countries that have immigration and emigration statistics and those that have only immigration statistics by region of origin. The sum of all emigrants

Table 13.1. Continued, panel 4.

Origin East & Southeast Africa	1960–64	1965–69	1970–74	1975–79	1980–84	1985–89	1990–91
Emigrants to							
Canada	692	7,237	15,602	21,064	27,850	34,871	–
USA	9,156	21,783	66,070	114,762	186,948	168,707	183,552
Israel	26	23	20	19	79	21	677
Subtotal	9,874	29,043	81,692	135,845	214,877	203,599	184,229
Australia	1,010	2,071	3,910	10,661	23,059	31,759	43,069
New Zealand	391	472	496	1,080	925	–	–
Belgium	752	1,298	2,219	2,932	3,206	3,675	–
Germany	3,449	3,988	10,097	19,140	26,439	41,502	–
Netherlands	2,213	2,258	3,214	5,981	6,329	8,679	–
Sweden	–	–	–	–	3,144	12,559	–
UK	–	25,420	27,100	29,800	30,100	32,680	–
Subtotal	7,815	35,507	47,036	69,594	93,202	130,854	43,069
Net emigration to							
Australia	888	1,880	3,689	10,450	22,710	31,285	42,739
New Zealand	287	222	357	798	679	–	–
Belgium	464	849	1,250	1,552	1,655	1,778	–
Germany	2,257	1,836	6,243	10,932	9,378	22,776	–
Netherlands	1,886	1,830	1,971	4,298	4,186	6,475	–
Sweden	–796	–1,409	–2,634	–2,059	1,365	11,808	–
UK	–	6,860	5,000	4,140	6,200	6,960	–
Subtotal	4,986	12,068	15,876	30,111	46,173	81,082	42,739
Total emigrants	17,689	64,550	128,728	205,439	308,079	334,453	227,298
Maximum net loss	14,860	41,111	97,568	165,956	261,050	284,681	226,968

originating in a certain region and recorded as immigrants by the receiving countries listed in the table is presented under the label "total emigrants." That number can be interpreted as representing the gross emigration from the region of origin considered.

Since net emigration figures are available for certain receiving countries, a second indicator of overall emigration is calculated by adding the data for receiving countries without emigration statistics to the net gains or losses recorded by the rest. This second indicator, denominated "maximum net loss," represents an upper limit for the number of emigrants originating in a given region or, equivalently, the maximum net gain by the developed countries listed as receiving countries of immigrants from the developing region considered.

Table 13.1. Continued, panel 5.

Origin China	1960–64	1965–69	1970–74	1975–79	1980–84	1985–89	1990–91
Emigrants to							
Canada	1,123	4,288	4,865	5,055	7,230	6,572	–
USA	4,116	13,142	16,434	21,390	26,642	26,492	30,223
Israel	10	8	6	5	9	7	29
Subtotal	5,249	17,438	21,305	26,450	33,881	33,071	30,252
Australia	694	393	376	883	1,452	4,150	4,690
New Zealand	110	103	70	–	–	–	–
Germany	108	27	53	308	1,245	2,733	–
Subtotal	912	523	499	1,191	2,697	6,883	4,690
Net emigration to							
Australia	655	342	320	832	1,406	4,062	4,615
New Zealand	81	69	50	–	–	–	–
Germany	72	5	25	123	461	1,245	–
Subtotal	808	416	396	955	1,867	5,306	4,615
Total emigrants	6,160	17,961	21,804	27,641	36,578	39,954	34,942
Maximum net loss	6,057	17,854	21,701	27,405	35,748	38,377	34,867

All data are presented in terms of average annual number of emigrants or average annual net emigration for the periods indicated. Average annual numbers were used not only to make comparisons easier and thus facilitate the derivation of projection assumptions on the basis of such a measure, but also to obviate the problem of missing information for selected years: 1961, 1962, and 1989 in the case of Belgium; 1960 in the case of Germany; 1988 and 1989 in the case of British data for the Caribbean and South America only; and 1991 for Australia and Israel. Indeed, the set of data available for the 1990s is so incomplete that it is only presented for illustrative purposes.

13.1.3   Asylum seekers

A major development in the 1980s was the sharp increase in the number of persons seeking asylum in developed countries, particularly those of the European Community. Since a large proportion of asylum seekers originates in developing countries, their numbers must be considered in this overview. However, it is difficult to decide

Table 13.1. Continued, panel 6.

Origin Central America & Caribbean	1960–64	1965–69	1970–74	1975–79	1980–84	1985–89	1990–91
Emigrants to							
Canada	2,381	8,947	16,490	13,244	9,822	15,176	–
USA	76,977	123,664	165,308	304,958	372,592	276,725	178,201
Israel	121	122	130	136	127	92	93
Subtotal	79,479	132,733	181,928	318,338	382,541	291,993	178,294
Australia	179	638	3,645	507	533	1,798	2,341
New Zealand	28	42	84	36	9	–	–
Belgium	–	–	–	147	283	169	–
Germany	1,245	1,591	2,120	2,217	2,912	4,730	–
Netherlands	–	–	442	6,451	6,570	5,323	–
Sweden	371	389	794	2,728	1,671	674	–
UK[a]	–	–	5,280	4,460	3,000	3,667	–
Subtotal	1,823	2,660	12,365	16,546	14,978	16,361	2,341
Net emigration to							
Australia	165	588	3,494	443	485	1,754	2,311
New Zealand	21	29	78	21	3	–	–
Belgium	–	–	–	4	9	30	–
Germany	707	375	820	526	705	1,323	–
Netherlands	–	–	187	5,599	5,201	4,454	–
Sweden	91	85	406	2,271	1,173	366	–
UK[a]	–	–	–2,000	1,280	–400	1,000	–
Subtotal	984	1,077	2,985	10,144	7,176	8,927	2,311
Total emigrants	81,302	135,393	194,293	334,884	397,519	308,354	180,635
Maximum net loss	80,463	133,810	184,913	328,482	389,717	300,920	180,605

[a]The data for the UK are classified by both citizenship and place of previous residence.

how to use such numbers as indicators of migration since they have several shortcomings.

First, statistics on asylum seekers represent applications filed rather than persons and, at least during the 1980s, a person could lodge asylum applications in several countries simultaneously. Second, asylum seekers are not necessarily new arrivals: some were already legal, albeit temporary, residents of the country where they filed an application. Third, it is not clear what is the overlap between asylum statistics and normal migration statistics. In countries having population registers, for instance, at what point are asylum seekers who are allowed to stay and work pending consideration of their application inscribed in the register? Clearly, if such

Table 13.1. Continued, panel 7.

Origin South America	1960–64	1965–69	1970–74	1975–79	1980–84	1985–89	1990–91
Emigrants to							
Canada	1,031	2,555	7,139	8,773	5,452	7,492	–
USA	20,026	23,844	22,495	37,870	44,498	44,316	46,732
Israel	1,894	1,667	2,132	2,442	1,633	1,675	2,522
Subtotal	22,951	28,066	31,766	49,085	51,583	53,483	49,254
Australia	–	–	809	3,300	1,164	2,399	1,604
New Zealand	9	7	39	102	15	–	–
Belgium	496	844	1,076	956	815	725	–
Germany	2,322	2,297	3,393	3,052	3,701	3,140	–
Netherlands	–	–	4,000	6,000	–	–	–
Sweden	–	–	–	–	1,212	3,966	–
UK[a]	–	–	1,140	1,160	1,400	1,333	–
Subtotal	2,827	3,148	10,457	14,570	8,307	11,563	1,604
Net emigration to							
Australia	–	–	797	3,167	1,002	2,265	1,529
New Zealand	5	–	36	90	3	–	–
Belgium	281	499	286	290	277	272	–
Germany	1,249	882	1,459	813	704	1,027	–
Netherlands	–	–	4,000	6,000	–	–	–
Sweden	–	–	–	–	896	3,416	–
UK[a]	–	–	–240	–560	–200	–	–
Subtotal	1,535	1,381	6,338	9,800	2,682	6,979	1,529
Total emigrants	25,778	31,214	42,223	63,655	59,890	65,046	50,858
Maximum net loss	24,486	29,447	38,104	58,885	54,265	60,462	50,783

[a]The data for the UK are classified by both citizenship and place of previous residence.

inscription takes place at any time (which it must, at least in the case of persons granted refugee status or who are otherwise allowed to stay), asylum seekers will be counted twice. *Table 13.2* presents the data on asylum applications lodged in European countries during 1983–1990 classified by region of citizenship of the persons involved.

13.2 Overview of the Main Interregional Migration Flows

13.2.1 Sub-Saharan Africa

Information on migration flows affecting sub-Saharan Africa since 1960 is highly asymmetric: there is more information on migration

Table 13.1. Continued, panel 8.

Origin Americas (developing)	1960–64	1965–69	1970–74	1975–79	1980–84	1985–89	1990–91
Emigrants to							
Canada	3,413	11,502	23,629	22,017	15,274	22,668	–
USA	97,003	147,508	187,804	342,828	417,090	321,041	224,933
Israel	2,014	1,789	2,262	2,578	1,759	1,767	2,615
Subtotal	102,430	160,799	213,695	367,423	434,123	345,476	227,548
Australia	179	638	4,454	3,807	1,698	4,197	3,945
New Zealand	37	49	123	139	23	–	–
Belgium	496	844	1,076	1,102	1,098	894	–
Germany	3,567	3,888	5,513	5,269	6,613	7,870	–
Netherlands	–	–	4,442	12,451	6,570	5,323	–
Sweden	371	389	794	2,728	2,883	4,640	–
UK	–	16,080	8,980	8,520	6,780	6,760	–
Subtotal	4,650	21,888	25,382	34,016	25,666	29,684	3,945
Net emigration to							
Australia	165	588	4,291	3,610	1,487	4,019	3,840
New Zealand	26	29	114	111	6	–	–
Belgium	281	499	286	294	286	302	–
Germany	1,956	1,257	2,278	1,340	1,409	2,349	–
Netherlands	–	–	4,187	11,599	5,201	4,454	–
Sweden	91	85	406	2,271	2,069	3,783	–
UK	–	5,080	–1,200	1,360	–180	420	–
Subtotal	2,519	7,538	10,363	20,585	10,278	15,327	3,840
Total emigrants	107,080	182,687	239,077	401,439	459,788	375,160	231,493
Maximum net loss	104,949	168,337	224,058	388,008	444,401	360,803	231,388

originating in the region than on that directed toward the region. Although sub-Saharan Africa attracted considerable numbers of European and Asian migrants before 1960, the decolonization process led to a reversal of the flow. Not only did the independence of certain countries trigger important repatriation flows directed mostly to European countries, but there were also cases of outright expulsion (e.g., that of British Asians from Uganda ordered by President Idi Amin in 1972).

As the first panel of *Table 13.1* indicates, the total number of immigrants originating in sub-Saharan Africa and recorded by the selected set of receiving countries considered rose significantly between 1960–1964 and 1970–1974 and remained fairly stable until the late 1980s when another increase was recorded. Although the

Table 13.1. Continued, panel 9.

Origin All regions	1960–64	1965–69	1970–74	1975–79	1980–84	1985–89	1990–91
Emigrants to							
Canada	88,008	181,976	158,857	130,127	114,056	137,910	–
USA	283,803	358,947	422,206	628,397	801,189	692,250	680,058
Israel	57,012	28,260	31,373	33,448	16,727	14,039	199,516
Subtotal	428,822	569,184	612,436	791,971	931,972	844,199	879,574
Australia	115,021	147,213	141,588	70,635	94,258	114,485	121,458
New Zealand	31,292	31,002	31,713	13,673	11,434	–	–
Belgium	69,056	65,583	64,688	58,271	47,862	48,559	–
France	174,285	203,735	192,585	70,398	78,889	36,660	–
Germany	576,211	706,144	873,051	527,483	502,179	817,754	–
Netherlands	57,746	71,009	115,425	103,571	79,419	90,567	–
Sweden	26,140	42,221	38,938	36,114	27,069	40,488	–
UK	–	215,540	205,340	186,580	186,340	232,120	–
Subtotal	1,049,752	1,482,447	1,663,329	1,066,724	1,027,449	1,380,634	121,458
Net emigration to							
Australia	106,824	128,387	112,532	54,525	81,351	103,865	115,408
New Zealand	16,281	5,439	16,921	-2,777	-4,340	–	–
Belgium	33,785	24,080	17,073	5,281	-10,801	-4,783	–
Germany	212,104	197,449	306,211	6,352	3,040	377,695	–
Netherlands	6,528	10,679	38,952	43,833	17,457	35,079	–
Sweden	15,321	27,821	11,874	18,929	8,126	27,291	–
UK	–	77,520	-50,400	-21,100	-27,580	24,160	–
Subtotal	390,844	316,335	453,163	105,042	67,254	563,307	115,408
Total emigrants	1,478,574	2,051,631	2,275,765	1,858,695	1,959,421	2,224,833	1,001,032
Maximum net loss	993,951	1,089,254	1,258,183	967,411	1,078,115	1,444,166	994,982

Totals and subtotals may not add up due to rounding.

Table 13.2. Average annual number of asylum seekers in Europe by region of citizenship: 1983–1990.

Region of citizenship	1983–1984	1985–1989	1990[a]
Sub-Saharan Africa	15,890	38,991	76,660
North Africa and West Asia	12,896	60,266	97,671
South Asia	26,375	58,029	65,867
East and Southeast Asia	6,071	3,971	13,671
China	0	869	1,946
Central America and Caribbean	1,097	1,318	867
South America	2,682	5,629	3,544
Total	88,024	240,876	412,889

[a]Data for 1990 are preliminary and do not necessarily refer to the whole year.

evolution of net migration (i.e., net emigration from sub-Saharan Africa) paralleled that of gross emigration as of 1970 (it changed relatively little between 1970 and 1985, to rise sharply thereafter), during the 1960s the trend in net emigration was the opposite of that in gross emigration. The United Kingdom was mainly responsible for such contrasting trends during the 1960s since, although it received nearly 26,000 immigrants annually from sub-Saharan Africa during 1965–1969, it sent out an annual average of 33,000 during the period. However, British data include both British citizens and foreigners, so that it is likely that a significant proportion of those leaving for or coming from sub-Saharan Africa were British citizens.

The first panel of *Table 13.1* also indicates that, since 1960, there has been a steady rise in the number of persons from sub-Saharan Africa admitted as immigrants by the main countries of permanent resettlement. For Israel, in particular, the admission of Ethiopian Jews led to the rise registered during the 1980s. Although gross immigration from sub-Saharan Africa to European countries has also, by and large, been growing, the changes registered during the 1980s are the most significant: net emigration from the region to Europe rose from 2,700 annually during 1980–1984 to over 31,000 annually during 1985–1989, with Germany, the Netherlands, and, especially, the United Kingdom registering very substantial gains. Not surprisingly, the number of citizens from sub-Saharan African countries seeking asylum in Europe also rose dramatically: from 16,000 annually during 1983–1984 (an average that would be considerably lower if the data for the full five-year period were available) to 39,000 in 1985–1989 (see *Table 13.2*). Furthermore, preliminary data for 1990 already indicate that the number of Africans from south of the Sahara filing asylum applications in Europe rose to nearly 77,000.

In addition to the flows documented in *Tables 13.1* and *13.2*, between 500,000 and 800,000 inhabitants of the Portuguese colonies of Angola, Cape Verde, Guinea-Bissau, and Mozambique returned to Portugal during the 1970s when those countries gained independence (Ferreira de Paiva, 1983). The majority of these returnees were Portuguese citizens. However, African nationals have also emigrated to Portugal. By 1990, over 45,000 citizens of African countries, mainly from Cape Verde (over 28,000), Angola (5,000), and Guinea-Bissau (3,500), were legal residents of that country (OECD, 1991, 1992).

Italy has also experienced important inflows of migrants from sub-Saharan Africa, especially during the 1980s. By the end of 1990, 75,000 citizens of countries in the region were registered as legal residents in Italy: 25,000 from Senegal, 12,000 from Ethiopia, 11,000 from Ghana, and 9,000 from Somalia. At least 17,000 of the total had been regularized in 1986 and 36,000 in 1990. However, the increase in these figures cannot be interpreted as necessarily indicating an increase in inflows, since much depends on the stringency of the regularization drive.

In Spain, where regularization drives were carried out in 1985 and 1991, the number of citizens from sub-Saharan African countries who were officially registered as residents increased from about 1,000 by the end of 1980 to nearly 9,000 by the end of 1990 (Spain, 1991). Among the 43,800 persons filing for regularization in 1985, 3,600 were Senegalese and 2,700 were Gambian (OECD, 1990). Preliminary data regarding the 1991 regularization drive are only available for selected nationalities of applicants (OECD, 1992).

Information on inflows of migrants from other regions to sub-Saharan Africa is mostly lacking. Indirect indications can be obtained from stock data derived from censuses, though very few countries have two censuses with comparable information. In Liberia, for instance, the population born outside of Africa increased from 8,600 to 11,800 between 1962 and 1974, in Réunion it rose from 16,300 to 30,200 during 1974–1982, and in Swaziland it increased from 4,200 to 6,700 during 1976–1986. The population of non-African citizenship also rose from 5,500 in 1974 to 8,300 in 1984 in the Congo and from 7,600 to 8,800 between 1963 and 1974 in Sierra Leone. A very rough estimation of net migration based on the figures spanning the 1975–1980 period would suggest that at least 2,500 persons immigrated annually to sub-Saharan Africa from other regions.

More recent data for the Republic of South Africa suggest that this country alone may have recorded even higher net migration gains. Thus, its foreign-born population rose from 426,000 to 450,000 between 1980 and 1985. Making allowance for mortality at the level of 8 per 1,000 (lower than the 11 per 1,000 estimated by the United Nations for the total population of South Africa to make some allowance for the selectivity of migration), the estimated net inflow of migrants to South Africa during 1980–1985 would have been of the order of 41,000 – that is, about 8,200 per year. However, it is likely that at least some of those migrants have already been accounted for by the emigration data of the United Kingdom.

Given the paucity of the information available, only guesses are possible regarding the possible net inflow to sub-Saharan Africa of persons originating in countries other than those presented in *Table 13.1*.

To conclude, it is worth noting that sub-Saharan Africa hosts the second largest number of refugees in the world, amounting to about 5.2 million in early 1991 (UN, 1994). Most of the refugees, however, have found asylum in neighboring countries and have therefore remained within the region as defined here. Their movements, therefore, need not be taken into account in projecting the total sub-Saharan population.

13.2.2 North Africa and West Asia

The region comprising the northern part of Africa and the western part of Asia has been one of the most dynamic in terms of its participation in interregional migration flows, both as a region of origin and as one of destination. There have also been important intraregional flows that need not be documented here. The main sources of interregional emigration have been the Maghreb countries (Algeria, Morocco, and Tunisia) and Turkey.

Because the region encompasses many of the oil-rich countries of the developing world, particularly those having a limited work force both in general terms and, more importantly, in terms of needed skills, it has been a major destination of migrant workers, particularly those originating in countries of South, East, and Southeast Asia. The region also includes Israel, one of the few countries pursuing an active policy of permanent resettlement. Lastly, as a result of both internal and international conflict, the region has been the source of important outflows of population both to neighboring regions (South Asia) and, to a lesser extent, to the rest of the world (via, for instance, the emigration of Lebanese).

13.2.3   North Africa and West Asia

The second panel of *Table 13.1* shows that the region has been the source of very sizable migrant outflows directed mainly to European countries, especially France and Germany. However, at least in the case of Germany, gross inflows have been considerably larger than net migration. The same may apply to France, although lack of information on emigration from that country prevents an adequate assessment of net gains. Indirect evidence suggests that net migration from the Maghreb countries to France was positive during the late 1970s but very low or possibly negative during at least part of the 1980s. Thus, the number of citizens of Algeria, Morocco, Tunisia, and Turkey enumerated by the censuses of France increased from 1,161,000 in 1975 to 1,560,000 in 1982 and only to 1,614,000 in 1990 (OECD, 1992). Whereas the number of Moroccans, Tunisians, and Turks in France grew between 1982 and 1990, that of Algerians declined sharply, passing from 805,000 in 1982 to 620,000 in 1990. Although some of that change may have been due to naturalization or better reporting of citizenship by persons of Algerian descent (many of whom have the right to French citizenship), return migration is also likely to have contributed to the change observed.

In 1990, Belgium, France, Germany, the Netherlands, and Sweden were hosting a total of 2,196,000 Turks, 951,000 Moroccans, 631,000 Algerians, and 242,000 Tunisians (OECD, 1992). Sizable Turkish populations were also present in other European countries. Thus, between 1980 and 1990, the number of Turks in Norway and Switzerland increased from 40,600 to 69,700, and the number of

Turkish workers in Austria rose from 28,300 to 50,500. At least part of the increase in the Turkish population in Europe was associated with the very sizable inflows of Turkish asylum seekers. As *Table 13.1* shows, the number of asylum seekers from North Africa and West Asia rose very markedly between the early and late 1980s, and Turks accounted for much of that increase (figures not shown).

Among the other nationalities, about 2,200 Moroccans were reported to be present in Norway in 1990 and they figured prominently in the regularization drives carried out by Italy and Spain since 1985. In Italy, for instance, 146,000 persons from North Africa and 12,000 from West Asia were present in 1990, of which 78,000 were Moroccan, 41,000 Tunisian, 20,000 Egyptian, and 6,000 each Lebanese and Jordanian. Of the total 158,000 North Africans and West Asians present in 1990, 39,000 had regularized their status as a result of the 1990 drive and 18,400 during that held in 1986 (OECD, 1991).

In Spain, the register of foreigners indicates that the North African and West Asian population declined slightly from 1975 to 1980 (from 7,500 to 6,800), rose to 9,200 in 1985, and then increased sharply to reach 21,100 by the end of 1990 (Spain, 1991). This rise was partly due to the 1985 regularization drive where at least 8,000 Moroccans lodged applications for regularization (OECD, 1990). Preliminary results from the 1991 drive indicate that a further 40,000 Moroccans may be regularized (OECD, 1992).

Lastly, it must be noted that the changes taking place in the former East Bloc countries have made Turkey a migrant-receiving country. Indeed, in 1989, 314,000 Bulgarians of Turkish ethnic origin moved into the country. By September of 1991 there were 358,000 Bulgarians in Turkey. Nearly two-thirds had settled permanently and virtually all had acquired Turkish citizenship (OECD, 1992).

13.2.4 Israel

Panel 2 of *Table 13.1* indicates that gross immigration to Israel, most of which has originated outside the region in recent years, has contributed significantly to reduce the net emigration balance of the region (see the last line of the second panel). The high levels of immigration recorded by Israel during the 1970s and again during the 1990s are associated with the arrival of Soviet Jews whose emigration during the 1970s was permitted as part of "détente" and during the 1990s as a result of the liberalization of the Soviet and now the Russian regime. In 1990 alone, 185,200 Soviet Jews immigrated to Israel, and the figure for 1991 is 147,800 (Sabatello, 1992). The 1989 census of the USSR enumerated 1.45 million ethnic Jews. Taking into account Jews registered under other "nationalities" and their non-Jewish relatives, an estimated 1.8 to 2 million persons might still be eligible for eventual admission to Israel (Sabatello, 1992).

Unfortunately, information on emigration from Israel by region of origin or region of destination could not be obtained. Available information on net migration indicates that during 1975–1979, it amounted to only 12,200 persons annually (UN, 1985), a level far lower than the gross immigration figure of 33,400 shown in *Table 13.1*. In addition, data on the number of Israeli residents who left in a given year and had not yet returned by May 1990, indicate that, on average, 9,700 emigrated annually during 1976–1979, 12,100 did so during 1980–1984, and 22,700 during 1984–1988 (Israel, 1990). Of course, the last figure is likely to underestimate permanent emigration somewhat because the time elapsed since departure is shorter. However, such figures indicate the approximate levels of emigration that Israel has been experiencing, levels that would reduce considerably the gross gains presented in *Table 13.1*.

13.2.5 Oil-rich countries

It is well known that the oil-rich countries of North Africa and West Asia have been major importers of foreign labor. Even before the dramatic rises in the price of oil during the early 1970s, several countries in the region had been resorting to foreign workers. The most complete estimates on worker migration to the region indicate that, between 1975 and 1980, the total number of foreign workers employed in Bahrain, Iraq, Jordan, Kuwait, Libya, Oman, Qatar, Saudi Arabia, the United Arab Emirates, and Yemen increased from 1.8 to 2.8 million (Birks and Sinclair, cited in UN, 1985). The largest proportions (43 percent in 1975 and 36 percent in 1980) were employed in Saudi Arabia. Libya with 19 percent in 1980, the United Arab Emirates with 15, and Kuwait with 13 followed.

Until 1980, most foreign workers in the region also originated in countries of North Africa and West Asia: 71 percent in 1975 and

63 percent in 1980. The rest were mostly citizens of India, Iran, and Pakistan (25 percent in 1975 and 27 in 1980). Whereas Indians and Pakistanis worked in almost every possible receiving country, Iranians were mostly concentrated in Iraq and Kuwait.

During the late 1970s a new trend took hold. The main labor-importing countries in the region turned to migrant workers from East and Southeast Asia. *Table 13.3* shows the average annual number of persons granted permission to work abroad under temporary contractual agreements by various sending countries in both South Asia and East and Southeast Asia. The data, though probably fairly incomplete for earlier periods, indicate that by 1975–1979 an annual average of 330,000 persons were being granted permission to work abroad. During the 1980s, the equivalent figure remained above 1 million. The distribution by region of origin changed substantially since 1975. Whereas during 1975–1979, 52 percent of all workers securing permits to go abroad originated in South Asia, by 1980–1984 their share had dropped to 43 percent, and during 1985–1989 it decreased further to 30 percent.

Care must be taken in interpreting the figures presented in *Table 13.3*. They represent generally the number of exit permits granted by government authorities to persons wishing to work abroad. Since temporary engagements are possible, multiple work permits may be issued to a single person during a given year. Furthermore, even from year to year, figures cannot be interpreted as representing new workers joining the expatriate labor force. The policy of worker rotation adopted by many receiving countries implies that foreign workers usually remain abroad for relatively short periods (one or two years) and need to return home before having their contracts renewed. Unfortunately, figures on net flows are not available. On the other hand, since workers have been known to emigrate "illegally" without obtaining the necessary permits, the figures presented may be subject to a counterbalancing negative bias. Lastly, although the oil-rich countries of West Asia have been a major destination of migrants originating in most of the countries listed in *Table 13.3*, it is by no means certain that they are the only destination. Data classified crudely by region of destination indicate that, at least for Indonesia, the Philippines, the Republic of Korea, and Thailand,

Table 13.3. Average annual number of migrant workers leaving from selected countries of South Asia, East and Southeast Asia, and China: 1970–1991.

Region and country of origin	Average annual number of work permits issued (thousands)				
	1970–74	1975–79	1980–84	1985–89	1990–91
South Asia					
Bangladesh	–	13.8	53.0	78.0	125.5
India	–	53.6	236.5	139.7	–
Nepal	–	–	–	0.2	0.3
Pakistan	7.3	92.3	133.9	80.3	128.3
Sri Lanka	–	11.5	28.5	$(12.7)^a$	–
Sri Lanka (final approvals)	–	–	–	15.3	53.8
Subtotal	7.3	171.2	451.9	313.5	307.9
East and Southeast Asia					
Indonesia	–	4.7	24.4	66.3	105.5
Korea, Republic of	2.9	72.3	171.1	77.0	–
Myanmar	–	–	–	1.6	9.8
Philippines	15.5	75.9	330.9	$(460.3)^a$	$(650.3)^a$
Philippines (deployed)	–	–	$(70.2)^a$	426.0	530.6
Thailand	0.1	6.3	60.0	97.0	63.5
Vietnam	–	–	13.3	38.9	2.1
Subtotal	18.5	159.2	599.7	706.8	711.5
China	–	–	–	27.6	73.9
Total	25.8	330.4	1,051.6	1,047.9	1,093.3

^{a}Entry has not been used in calculation.

the proportion of workers intending to go to the Middle East has varied substantially since 1975 (see *Table 13.4*).

Unfortunately, data relative to the countries of destination are generally lacking. In particular, no reliable information is available regarding the size and composition of the foreign population present in the main labor-importing country of the region, Saudi Arabia. Although it has been estimated that the number of foreign workers in the member states of the Gulf Cooperation Council – Bahrain, Kuwait, Oman, Qatar, Saudi Arabia, and the United Arab Emirates – increased from 2.1 to 5.1 million between 1980 and 1985 (Russell, 1990), the bases for such estimates remain obscure. Data on entries to and departures from Saudi Arabia indicate that the country has

Table 13.4. Distribution of average annual number of migrant workers originating in countries of East and Southeast Asia by destination: 1975–1988.

Country of origin and intended destination	Average annual number of work permits issued		
	1975–1979	1980–1984	1985–1988
Korea, Republic of[a]			
Total workers	97,500	171,800	96,200
Workers to Middle East	77,800	128,400	42,600
Percentage to Middle East	79.8%	74.7%	44.2%
Indonesia			
Total workers	–	24,400	61,400
Workers to Middle East	–	15,800	48,100
Percentage to Middle East	–	64.8%	78.4%
Philippines			
Total workers	75,900	330,900	433,500
Workers to Middle East	28,500	232,300	278,700
Percentage to Middle East	37.6%	70.2%	64.3%
Thailand			
Total workers	6,300	60,000	89,900
Workers to Middle East	5,100	56,400	75,600
Percentage to Middle East	81.2%	93.9%	84.1%
Total			
Total workers	179,800	587,100	681,000
Workers to Middle East	111,500	432,900	445,000
Percentage to Middle East	62.0%	73.7%	65.3%

[a]Data on Middle East destinations are available only since 1977.

been gaining population from regions other than North Africa and West Asia, particularly from South Asia and East and Southeast Asia (see *Table 13.5*). However, the usual drawbacks of entry and departure statistics make them less than ideal indicators of long-term migration to the country.

Lastly, a word must be said about the effects of the Gulf War on migration to and from West Asia. The invasion of Kuwait by Iraq led to the outflow of large numbers of expatriate workers. At least 700,000 were reported to have fled to Jordan from where they were eventually repatriated to their countries of origin. Estimates by the ILO indicate that of the 2.6 million foreigners present in Iraq and Kuwait before the invasion, only 1.4 million remained two months

Table 13.5. Average annual migration to Saudi Arabia by region of citizenship: 1977–1984.

Region of citizenship	1977–1979	1980–1984
Southern Africa	8,998	−5,281
North Africa and West Asia	22,938	4,208
South Asia	59,144	102,894
East and Southeast Asia	51,937	37,663
China	1,865	−1,131
Rest of the world	9,076	−84,530
Total	153,958	53,823
Total from outside North Africa and West Asia	131,020	49,615

later. Among those departing, there were some 229,000 persons from South Asia and 49,000 from the Philippines and Thailand, as well as 68,000 from other Asian countries (ILO, 1990). There is as yet no information about the resumption of labor migration after the war, but the task of reconstruction is likely to have attracted not only those who fled but other workers as well. Indeed, reports about the decision of Kuwaiti authorities to dispense with Palestinian workers suggest that workers from other countries may have to be imported to take their place.

The war also caused major dislocations in Iraq. In particular, 1.4 million Kurdish and Shiite refugees from Iraq fled to Iran between February and May 1991. Their repatriation, however, was swift. By early July, only 252,000 remained in Iran (De Almeida e Silva, 1991). Yet, continued instability in Iraq may lead to further outflows to neighboring countries.

13.2.6   South Asia

The major countries of South Asia, by virtue of having been under British colonial rule, have traditionally had close migration ties with the United Kingdom and other developed members of the British Commonwealth. As panel 3 of *Table 13.1* shows, since 1970 the region has been an important source of immigrants for the USA and Canada, and over the period considered net migration between South Asia and the United Kingdom has been positive. Important contingents of South Asians have also been recorded recently in Germany, a development that is likely to be associated with the movement of asylum seekers from the region to Europe. As *Table 13.2* shows, the number of asylum seekers from South Asia increased from an annual average of 26,000 during 1983–1984 to 58,000 during 1985–1989. The main sources of asylum seekers in the region have been Iran and Sri Lanka.

As discussed in Section 13.2.5, South Asia has also been an important source of labor migration for the oil-rich countries of West Asia. Data on the outflow of workers from the main sending countries in South Asia are presented in *Table 13.3*. It is worth noting that, particularly for India and Sri Lanka, the number of work permits issued to those intending to work abroad is thought to underestimate true outflows. Sri Lanka's worker migration has attracted attention because of the high proportion of women it involves. Most of them work as maids in West Asian countries. Although there is no information on the country of destination of the South Asian workers who have been granted exit permits, it is safe to assume that most of them intend to work in West Asia. Only lately have there been reports of an increasing number of South Asian workers finding employment in other Asian countries, such as Japan or Taiwan. However, most of them work illegally. Japanese statistics show that during 1985–1990, 11,600 citizens of Bangladesh, 10,700 of Pakistan, 1,000 of Sri Lanka, 700 of each Iran and India, and 400 of Nepal were deported. For each nationality, the number of deportations rose rapidly over the period considered.

South Asian workers are also finding their way to Europe. Toward the end of 1990, Italy recorded 34,100 citizens of Bangladesh, India, Pakistan, and Sri Lanka as legally residing in the country, 13,400 of whom had legalized their status during the 1990 regularization drive and 12,100 during that held in 1986 (OECD, 1990). In Spain, the number of South Asian nationals legally present by the end of 1990 amounted to nearly 8,000, a substantial increase from the 2,600 registered in 1980 (Spain, 1991).

Some of the largest population outflows have occurred within the South Asian region itself. According to statistics on the foreign-born, India was the second largest migrant-receiving country in the world in 1980. Most of the migrants thus identified had moved to

India from Bangladesh or Pakistan, probably as a result of partition. In addition, the region hosts the largest refugee population originating in a single country, Afghanistan. As of early 1991 an estimated 6.2 million Afghani refugees were present in Iran and Pakistan (UN, 1994). Furthermore, by mid-1991 Iran was still hosting 252,000 Iraqi refugees.

13.2.7   East and Southeast Asia

The East and Southeast Asia region has been a major source of migrants for both the developed countries and the labor-importing countries of West Asia. As *Table 13.1* indicates, immigrants from the region have constituted the second largest contingent admitted by the USA since 1970–1974. The close strategic, military, or even colonial ties that link several countries in the region with the USA have fostered such migration. Thus, the Philippines, the Republic of Korea, and Vietnam have been among the main sources of immigrants to the USA for over a decade. Migration from Vietnam, Cambodia, and Laos has occurred mostly within the framework of refugee resettlement. It is estimated that between 1975 and 1988 nearly 1.5 million Indo-Chinese refugees were resettled abroad, the vast majority (1.15 million) in developed countries, including 108,000 in France, 8,000 in Switzerland, and 6,000 each in Norway and Japan (UN, 1992). The Vietnamese resettled in other developed countries are already reflected in the statistics presented in *Table 13.1*. In addition, during the 1980s China admitted 284,000 ethnic Chinese from Vietnam for resettlement.

Emigration from Vietnam has also occurred in the context of labor migration. Newly available statistics from the former German Democratic Republic indicate that by the end of 1989 there were over 60,000 Vietnamese in that country, a number that had declined to 35,000 by the end of 1990 (OECD, 1992). In the former Czech and Slovak Federal Republic 34,000 Vietnamese workers were present in 1990, but their number had declined to barely 10,000 by 1991 (OECD, 1992). Vietnamese workers are also known to have migrated to the former Soviet Union, but no information on their numbers is available. *Table 13.3*, however, indicates that during the 1980s a growing number of Vietnamese received clearance to work abroad.

At least part of the growth of the number of East and Southeast Asian immigrants recorded by the countries listed in panel 4 of *Table 13.1* is attributable to the intake of Indo-Chinese refugees after the fall of Saigon in 1975. However, especially during the 1980s, the numbers of migrants originating in countries like the Philippines, Hong Kong, or Malaysia have also been growing. Indeed, the planned devolution of Hong Kong to the People's Republic of China has fueled emigration from the Crown Colony. Countries like Australia, Canada, and the United States have established special immigration categories aimed, at least in part, at attracting affluent Hong Kong residents. Although emigration from Hong Kong has been increasing, net migration to the Colony may still be positive. Estimates of net migration for earlier periods indicate that Hong Kong gained an annual average of 11,500 persons during 1961–1971, 20,400 during 1971–1976, and 80,000 during 1976–1981 (Skeldon, 1986). The sharp rise registered in the late 1970s was due to the increased inflow of illegal migrants from China lured by the possibility of regularizing their status in Hong Kong if they managed to reach the urban areas of the Colony. The rise in illegal migration prompted British authorities to remove that possibility in 1980. The effects of such a change are noticeable in the evolution of the Hong Kong population born in China. Whereas the 1976 census of Hong Kong showed that 1.66 million Hong Kong residents were born in China and the 1981 census put that figure at 1.97 million, the 1986 census showed that the population born in China increased only to 2 million (Hong Kong, 1988). The figures imply that net Chinese migration would have amounted to an annual average of 79,000 during 1976–1981 (assuming a mortality of 10 per 1,000) and of some 25,000 during 1981–1986 under unchanging mortality conditions.

The growing variety of sources of emigration from East and Southeast Asia has been paralleled by an increasing diversification of possible destinations. During the 1980s, not only did increasing numbers of East and Southeast Asian workers secure permits to work in West Asian countries, but the proportion obtaining permits to work elsewhere rose in the Philippines, the Republic of Korea, and Thailand (see *Table 13.4*). Although many of those workers found employment in other countries of the region, such as Brunei, Hong Kong, Malaysia, Singapore, or Taiwan, others went further afield.

Rising numbers of Filipinos, in particular, have been recorded in Japan (49,000 were registered aliens in 1990 compared with only 5,500 in 1980), Italy (34,000 in 1990), and Spain (where 2,500 applied for regularization in 1991). In addition, during 1985–1990, 31,400 Filipinos were deported from Japan, 72 percent of whom were women. The same proportion of women was found among the 7,100 Thai migrants deported from Japan during 1985–1990. In contrast, among the 6,600 Malaysians deported during the same period, women amounted to only 12 percent (Japan, 1990).

To conclude, the number of citizens from East and Southeast Asia seeking asylum in Europe has remained relatively small (see *Table 13.2*). The generous resettlement opportunities granted to Indo-Chinese refugees during most of the 1980s are probably responsible for these trends. However, as conflict in Indochina subsides and a growing number of would-be refugees are denied asylum in the region, they may start seeking it elsewhere.

13.2.8   China

The fact that in 1980 over 26 million Chinese or descendants of Chinese were estimated to be living in countries other than mainland China or Taiwan (Poston and Yu, 1990) proves that Chinese emigration has been significant in modern times. However, during the first three decades of the People's Republic of China (from the late 1940s to the late 1970s), Chinese emigration from the mainland was severely restricted and only a small number of people left legally during the period. More recently, as Chinese authorities have increasingly opened the country to foreigners, emigration levels have risen somewhat (see panel 5 of *Table 13.1*) but, in general, Chinese emigration remains highly restricted.

As panel 5 of *Table 13.1* indicates, the main receivers of Chinese emigrants have been the USA and Canada. Only during the 1980s did Chinese immigration to Australia or Germany surpass the 1,000 mark. However, as already noted, Chinese emigration to neighboring countries, particularly Hong Kong, has been considerably larger. In addition, the number of Chinese registered as resident aliens in Japan has been rising in recent years, passing from 49,000 in 1975 to 75,000 in 1985 and reaching 150,000 in 1990 (Japan, 1990). It is not clear, however, whether the data refer only to mainland Chinese or also to those of Hong Kong or Taiwanese origin.

As *Table 13.2* indicates, the number of Chinese asylum seekers in Europe, though small, has been increasing. Chinese became more likely to obtain asylum after the events of Tienamin Square in 1989. The USA passed at the time a Deferred Enforced Departure Act that allowed virtually every Chinese student in the country and his or her dependents to stay. By August 1992, a bill that would grant permanent residence to an estimated 80,000 Chinese students and dependents in the USA had been passed (FAIR, 1992).

Chinese are securing entry to developed countries not only via asylum procedures but also as needed workers. In Italy 18,700 Chinese were resident aliens by the end of 1990, 4,500 of whom had regularized their status in 1986 and a further 9,700 in 1990. A high proportion of them were registered as own-account workers. In addition, Chinese authorities themselves are promoting the export of labor. As *Table 13.3* indicates, the number of Chinese workers obtaining permits to work abroad increased markedly from an annual average of 27,600 during 1985–1989 to nearly 74,000 during 1990–1991. Given the increasing misgivings that West Asian countries are having about hiring Muslim workers from other Asian countries (Economist Intelligence Unit, 1990), resorting to Chinese labor may be a desirable option during the 1990s.

13.2.9 Central America and the Caribbean

According to the data presented in *Table 13.1*, the region identified here as Central America and the Caribbean, which includes Mexico, has been the main source of emigrants during 1960–1984. Only for the period 1985–1989 did the gross number of emigrants originating in East and Southeast Asia surpass those coming from Central America and the Caribbean. However, the data in panel 6 of *Table 13.1* include the over 2 million legalizations from Central America and the Caribbean that were registered during 1989–1992 and that have been redistributed over the period 1972–1986. As a result of such redistribution, the average annual number of admissions of permanent immigrants from Central America and the Caribbean by the USA increased from 133,000 to 165,000 in 1970–1974, from 158,000 to 305,000 in 1975–1979, from 162,000 to 373,000 in 1980–1984, and from 198,000 to 277,000 in 1985–1989. Since most of the legalizations correspond to Mexican citizens, Mexico became the main source of migrants to the USA during the late 1970s.

In fact, any attempt at incorporating undocumented migration into overall migration estimates would make Mexico a major country of emigration. Indeed, because the regularization established by the Immigration Reform and Control Act of 1986 imposed time limits on those who could have their status legalized, it did not eliminate entirely the undocumented population present in the USA. It has been estimated that, even taking into account the regularization results, by June 1988 nearly 1.9 million undocumented migrants were still in the country, 1.1 million of whom were Mexican and another half a million originated in the rest of North America (Woodrow and Passel, 1990). Furthermore, some 70,000 were estimated to have entered the country during 1987–1988. However, that number of entries was not statistically significant (Woodrow and Passel, 1990).

Not only do the figures on immigration to the USA presented in panel 6 of *Table 13.1* exclude estimates of undocumented migration, they also exclude the inflow of persons from Caribbean Islands whose inhabitants are US citizens. Puerto Rico is probably the main source of such migrants. According to census figures, the number of net migrants from Puerto Rico amounted to an average annual intake by the United States of 17,700 during 1955–1960, 19,200 during 1965–1970, and 20,000 during 1975–1980 (Ortiz, 1986).

It is noteworthy that relatively few migrants from the region have found their way to overseas countries. Although migration from the English-speaking Caribbean to the United Kingdom was significant during the late 1950s and early 1960s, as the data in *Table 13.1* show, the net migration of Commonwealth citizens from the Caribbean and Belize to the United Kingdom has been relatively small or even negative since 1970. However, several Caribbean countries have been the source of emigrants to other regions. Cuba, for instance, sent both troops and workers to Angola, and it was also a source of workers for certain East Bloc countries. There were, for instance, 8,000 Cubans in the former German Democratic Republic in 1989, only 3,000 of whom remained by 1990 (OECD, 1992). In the Czech and Slovak Federal Republic, 1,100 Cuban workers were present in 1990, but by 1991 only 100 remained.

Citizens from the Dominican Republic have also migrated in search of work to both regional and overseas destinations. Thus, the 1980–1981 regularization drive of Venezuela recorded 4,300 Dominicans and 1,900 persons from other countries of Central America and the Caribbean (Torrealba, 1985). In addition, by the end of 1990, 4,400 citizens from the Dominican Republic were registered as legal resident aliens in Italy, and 5,000 more applied for regularization in Spain in 1991 (OECD, 1992). Interestingly, the foreign population of Central American and Caribbean origin residing legally in Spain changed relatively little, declining from 13,700 to 10,800 between 1975 and 1985 and then rising to 14,000 by 1990 (Spain, 1991).

Although during the 1980s several countries of Central America were important sources of refugees, relatively few persons from the region have applied for asylum in Europe (see *Table 13.2*). Again in this instance, the USA and Canada have been the preferred destinations of asylum seekers from Central America and the Caribbean. During 1984–1990, US authorities adjudicated 102,000 applications for asylum filed by citizens of just three Central American countries, namely, El Salvador, Guatemala, and Nicaragua. Those applications constituted 64 percent of all the asylum cases adjudicated in the USA during the period, and the vast majority (88,000) were denied. Since most applicants remained in the USA even after their asylum request was turned down, they became undocumented aliens and were probably adequately reflected by the statistics on undocumented alien stocks reported above. However, as a result of a lawsuit by human rights advocates, US authorities granted all Salvadorans present in the country as of 19 September 1990 and all Guatemalans present on 1 October 1990 the right to new hearings on their asylum claims and the possibility of staying in the country and working until 30 June 1992 (UN, 1994). Approximately 185,000 Salvadorans have benefited from the temporary protected status thus granted (Weintraub and Díaz-Briquets, 1992).

13.2.10   South America

Until the late 1950s, South America was a region of immigration, since countries like Argentina, Brazil, Chile, and Uruguay attracted an important number of immigrants from European countries after the end of World War II. The main sources of European migration to the Americas were Italy, Spain, Portugal, and several East European countries. By the 1960s, however, the inflow of Europeans had largely run its course. Only Venezuela was successful in attracting overseas migrants well into the 1970s. Entry and departure statistics for Venezuela indicate that during 1974–1979 the country registered, on an annual basis, a net inflow of some 10,000 European immigrants and another 1,000 from other regions (Torrealba, 1982). During 1980–1981, however, the net flow became negative and is likely to have remained so during the rest of the decade.

Census data from two of the main receiving countries in the region, Argentina and Brazil, suggest that during the 1970s net migration became negative. In Argentina the population born in Europe declined from 1.47 million in 1970 to 1.08 million in 1980, a reduction that cannot be accounted for by mortality alone. In Brazil the population of European nationality declined from 803,000 in 1970 to 638,000 in 1980. Although such a change could be the result of naturalization, return migration is likely to have also contributed to it.

As panel 7 of *Table 13.1* shows, South America has been a relatively important source of immigrants to the USA. A fair number of them remained in that country illegally because, although the numbers legalizing under IRCA were small in comparison to those of undocumented aliens from Central America and the Caribbean, the trend since 1970 has been affected by the redistribution of those legalizing during 1989–1992. In particular, without the IRCA legalizations, the average annual number of admissions of South Americans by the USA would have amounted to only 31,000 instead of 38,000 in 1975–1979, to 37,000 instead of 45,000 in 1980–1984, and to 42,000 instead of 44,000 in 1985–1989.

Emigration from South America is likely to have grown significantly during the 1980s. Part of it, however, is difficult to measure, since it involves the emigration of second- and third-generation migrants (i.e., the children and grandchildren of the original immigrants) who have been granted citizenship rights by the countries of origin of their forebears. Thus, Italy and Spain have been receiving the inflow of Italian or Spanish citizens born overseas who do not appear on statistics relative to foreigners. According to statistics on the foreign stock, there were 47,000 South American citizens in

Italy at the end of 1990 (14,000 of whom were Brazilian and 13,000 Argentine citizens), and the number of South American citizens in Spain nearly doubled, passing from 24,000 in 1975 to 30,000 in 1985 and then to 49,000 in 1990 (Spain, 1991). In addition, about 7,000 nationals of Argentina and 5,000 of Peru lodged applications for regularization during the 1991 drive carried out in Spain.

Perhaps one of the most interesting cases of return migration among the descendants of former immigrants is the migration of Brazilians and Peruvians of Japanese descent to Japan. Between 1985 and 1990, the population of South American origin in Japan increased dramatically, rising from 3,600 to 71,500. Underlying such a change was the decision of Japanese authorities to permit the establishment in Japan of persons of Japanese descent. Both Brazil and Peru host relatively sizable subpopulations of Japanese ethnic origin that may decide to go back to their roots.

The number of South American asylum seekers in Europe has remained modest. Until the 1990 change of government in Chile, citizens of that country were likely to obtain asylum in Europe, particularly in the Nordic countries. The new Chilean government is planning to facilitate the repatriation of those wishing to return.

13.3 Conclusion

This overview of migration trends to and from the main developing regions, though fairly comprehensive, is still a weak basis on which to estimate current interregional migration or derive assumptions regarding future trends. Although data on migration flows are not entirely lacking, those available are often incomplete (they do not refer to all possible long-term movements), and they are not easily comparable from one country to another. In addition, when the main countries of destination are located in the developing world, data on migration flows are often entirely lacking or cannot be readily obtained. The political sensitivity of the migration phenomenon is such that existing information is often treated as highly classified material that must be protected. Countries are often guilty of benign neglect, preferring to ignore the magnitude of flows than measure them adequately. Despite efforts to improve the quality and availability of international migration statistics, little progress has been made. In the meantime, migration continues to increase and its complexity rises. Part of that complexity stems from the barriers that potential countries of destination are using to control or stop migration. When legal migration is highly restricted or not desired under any circumstances, different varieties of illegal or undesirable flows will arise. Such a situation makes the job of the forecaster even more difficult, since policy aims are at odds with likely outcomes.

On the other hand, consideration of any time series on migration is a sobering experience. As *Table 13.1* indicates, relatively drastic changes in trends can and have occurred over the course of the past 30 years in many developing regions. Events like the Gulf War can trigger large interregional flows over relatively short periods. Given the difficulties in forecasting such events and their likely effects on migration, population projections are often based on relatively simplistic assumptions regarding future migration trends. Perhaps the most common assumption is that migration will, in the long run, have little effect on population dynamics, so that it can be assumed to be zero. Otherwise, migration assumptions are generally made in terms of net numbers of migrants gained or lost during each of the projection quinquennia (see, for instance, Arnold, 1989). When the latter approach is taken, nonzero assumptions are typically made for a few projection periods (usually one to four, thus covering at most a span of 20 years) and from then on migration is assumed to taper off to zero or to remain constant at the last assumed level. Although undoubtedly simplistic, such practices have much to recommend them, particularly when one is dealing with large and complex regions such as the ones considered in this paper. Given the relatively large population bases of most regions, estimated net migration levels of the magnitude presented in *Table 13.1* are likely to have relatively small effects on the overall evolution of the population.

At the level of individual countries or smaller regions, however, the situation may be different. Migration is also likely to be an important component of population change when fertility has reached very low levels, especially if it remains below replacement for a certain period (see, for instance, OECD, 1991). Yet, even in countries facing such fertility prospects, projections continue to be made using the type of migration assumptions described above: total net numbers of migrants that vary minimally over time. Although the construction of more complex assumptions is technically possible, policy considerations usually dissuade technicians, who are mostly at the service of governments, from using more realistic scenarios, especially if these scenarios are likely to run counter major policy stances. Whether such scenarios, if available, would help or hinder the debate on migration, its desirability, or the degree to which it must be tolerated is a matter that needs to be considered carefully.

Note

[1] Definitions of developing regions used.

Sub-Saharan Africa: East Africa – British Indian Ocean Territory, Burundi, Comoros, Djibouti, Ethiopia, Kenya, Madagascar, Malawi, Mauritius, Mozambique, Réunion, Rwanda, Seychelles, Somalia, Uganda, Tanzania, Zambia, and Zimbabwe; Central Africa – Angola, Cameroon, Central African Republic, Chad, Congo, Equatorial Guinea, Gabon, Sao Tome & Principe, and Zaire; Southern Africa – Botswana, Lesotho, Namibia, South Africa, and Swaziland; West Africa – Benin, Burkina Faso, Cape Verde, Côte d'Ivoire, Gambia, Ghana, Guinea, Guinea-Bissau, Liberia, Mali, Mauritania, Niger, Nigeria, St. Helena, Senegal, Sierra Leone, and Togo.

North Africa and West Asia: North Africa – Algeria, Egypt, Libya, Morocco, Sudan, Tunisia, and West Sahara; West Asia – Bahrain, Cyprus, Gaza Strip (Palestine), Iraq, Israel, Jordan, Kuwait, Lebanon, Oman, Qatar, Saudi Arabia, Syria, Turkey, United Arab Emirates, and Yemen.

South Asia: Afghanistan, Bangladesh, Bhutan, India, Iran, Maldives, Nepal, Pakistan, and Sri Lanka.

East and Southeast Asia: East Asia – Hong Kong, Korea (Democratic People's Republic), Korea (Republic), Macau, and Mongolia; Southeast Asia – Brunei Darussalam, Cambodia, East Timor, Indonesia, Lao People's Democratic Republic, Malaysia, Myanmar, Philippines, Singapore, Thailand, and Vietnam.

China.

Central America and the Caribbean: Central America – Belize, Costa Rica, El Salvador, Guatemala, Honduras, Mexico, Nicaragua, and Panama; Caribbean – Anguilla, Antigua & Barbuda, Aruba, Bahamas, Barbados, British Virgin Islands, Cayman Islands, Cuba, Dominica, Dominican Republic, Grenada, Guadeloupe, Haiti, Jamaica, Martinique, Montserrat, Netherlands Antilles, Puerto Rico, St. Kitts & Nevis, St. Lucia, St. Vincent & the Grenadines, Trinidad & Tobago, Turks & Caicos Islands, and US Virgin Islands.

South America: Argentina, Bolivia, Brazil, Chile, Colombia, Ecuador,

358 Hania Zlotnik

Falkland Islands (Malvinas), French Guiana, Guyana, Paraguay, Peru, Suriname, Uruguay, and Venezuela.

References

Arnold, F., 1989, Revised estimates and projections of international migration 1980–2000, Policy, Planning, and Research Working Papers, Population and Human Resources Department, World Bank, Washington, DC, USA.

Benamrane, D., 1983, *L'Emigration Algerienne en France*, Société Nationale d'Edition et de Diffusion, Algiers, Algeria.

De Almeida e Silva, M., 1991, Persian Gulf exodus stretched resources, *Refugees* 87(October):12–15 (Geneva).

Economist Intelligence Unit, 1990, *Saudi Arabia: Country Report*, No. 2.

FAIR (Federation for American Immigration Reform), 1992, Chinese student amnesty legislation passes, *FAIR Immigration Report* 12(8):3.

Ferreira de Paiva, A., 1983, Portuguese migration: A critical survey of Portuguese studies on the economic aspects of the phenomenon since 1973, *International Migration Review* 17(1):138–147.

Haskey, J., Shaw, C., Grebenik, E., Coleman, D., Balajaran, R., and Bulusu, L., 1989, Country Report: Great Britain, Paper prepared for the Working Group on Immigrant Populations.

Hong Kong, 1988, *Hong Kong 1986 By-Census: Main Report*, Volume 1, Census and Statistics Department, Government Printer, Hong Kong.

ILO, 1990, Informal Report on Migrant Workers Affected by the Gulf Crisis, International Labour Office, Geneva, Switzerland.

Israel, 1990, *Monthly Bulletin of Statistics*, Central Bureau of Statistics, Jerusalem, Israel.

Japan, 1990, *Statistics on Immigration Control*, Tokyo, Japan.

Nilsson, A., 1990, A Comparison of the Statistics on the Migration Flows between Sweden and the Other Nordic Countries: 1945–1988, Paper presented at the Conference of European Statisticians, 9–11 April, Geneva, Switzerland,

OECD, 1990, *SOPEMI: Continuous Reporting System on Migration 1989*, Organisation for Economic Co-operation and Development, Paris, France.

OECD, 1991, *SOPEMI: Continuous Reporting System on Migration 1990*, Organisation for Economic Co-operation and Development, Paris, France.

OECD, 1992, *SOPEMI: Trends in International Migration*, Organisation for Economic Co-operation and Development, Paris, France.

Ortiz, V., 1986, Changes in the characteristics of Puerto Rican migrants from 1955 to 1980, *International Migration Review* 20(3):612–628.

Poston, D.L., and Yu, M.Y., 1990, The distribution of the overseas Chinese in the contemporary world, *International Migration Review* **24**(3):480–508.

Russell, S.S., 1990, Policy Dimensions of Female Migration to the Arab Countries of Western Asia, Paper presented at the Meeting on International Migration Policies and the Status of Female Migrants, 26–31 March, San Miniato, Italy.

Sabatello, E., 1992, Migrants from the USSR to Israel in the 1990s: Socio-Demographic Background and First-year Occupational Trends, Paper presented at the Conference on Mass Migration in Europe – Implications in East and West, 5–7 March, Laxenburg, Austria.

Schoorl, J.J., and Voets, S.Y., 1990, Country Report: The Netherlands, Paper prepared for the Working Group on Immigrant Populations.

Skeldon, R., 1986, Hong Kong and its hinterland: A case of international rural-to-urban migration? *Asian Geographer* **5**(1):1–24.

Spain, 1991, *Anuario Estadístico*, Instituto Nacional de Estadística, Madrid, Spain.

Tapinos, G., 1975, *L'Immigration Etrangère en France: 1946–1973*, Presses Universitaires de France, Paris, France.

Torrealba, R., 1982, La migración internacional hacia Venezuela en la década de 1970: Características socio-demográficas, Consejo Nacional de Recursos Humanos, Caracas, Venezuela.

Torrealba, R., 1985, El trabajador migrante en situación irregular y su legalización en Venezuela, International Migration for Employment Programme, International Labour Office, Geneva, Switzerland.

Tribalat, M., and Muñoz-Pérez, F., 1989, Rapport Français, Groupe de Travail sur les Migrations Internationales de l'Association Européenne pour l'Etude de la Population.

UN, 1978, *Demographic Yearbook 1977*, Statistical Office, United Nations, New York, NY, USA.

UN, 1985, *World Population Trends, Population and Development Inter-relations and Population Policies: 1983 Monitoring Report*, Volume 1, United Nations, New York, NY, USA.

UN, 1992, *World Population Monitoring, 1991*, Population Studies, No. 126, United Nations, New York, NY, USA.

UN, 1994, *World Population Monitoring, 1993*, ESA/P/WP.121, United Nations, New York, NY, USA.

US Immigration and Naturalization Service, 1991, *1990 Statistical Yearbook of the Immigration and Naturalization Service*, Government Printing Office, Washington, DC, USA.

Verhoef, R., 1986, The Netherlands population registers as a source of international migration statistics, in *National Data Sources and Programmes for Implementing the United Nations Recommendations on*

Statistics of International Migration, Department of International Economic and Social Affairs, United Nations, New York, NY, USA.

Weintraub, S., and Díaz-Briquets, S., 1992, The Use of Foreign Aid to Reduce Incentives to Emigrate from Central America, Working Paper, Work Employment Programme Research, International Labour Office, Geneva, Switzerland.

Woodrow, K.A., and Passel, J.S., 1990, Post-IRCA undocumented immigration to the United States: An assessment based on the June 1988 CPS, in F.D. Bean, B. Edmonston, and J.S. Passel, eds., *Undocumented Migration to the United States: IRCA and the Experience of the 1980s,* Urban Institute Press, Washington, DC, USA.

Zlotnik, H., 1987, The concept of international migration as reflected in data collection systems, *International Migration Review* **21**(4):925–946.

Chapter 14

Spatial and Economic Factors in Future South–North Migration

Sture Öberg

The objective of this chapter is to estimate future migration flows between less developed countries and more developed countries. This could be an easy task, where earlier flows are used as a basis for trend projections, or an aim far too complex for the scope of this chapter.

The solution here is close to the first idea. The estimated figures are based on three factors that determine the probabilities of future migration. The first is present trends as they are measured by the UN (see Chapter 13). The second is an estimate of public attitudes toward immigrants. The assumption is that these attitudes do not change easily over time. Attitudes are also reflected in contemporary flows, so these two factors are interrelated. The third factor examines the proximity of push and pull regions, present contacts between people living in rich and poor regions, and the welfare gap between regions. This factor is of course also interrelated with the other two.

There is no official prognosis on future international migration, a fact which has to do with political politeness. For a sending country it is not easy to accept in hard figures that it will not be able to organize its labor market or food production in the near future via emigration. For a receiving country, it is not easy to reveal, for example, that it will deny citizenship to refugees in the future or that it will continue to accept mostly well-educated immigrants from poor countries. Prognoses of this kind therefore have to be personal guesses made by individuals not working for UN agencies or any other official authority.

Another reason for the lack of migration prognoses is the fairly low interest in migration figures among demographers and others working with forecasts. Migration figures are small compared with other demographic changes. Every day there are 250,000 more inhabitants on the globe (UN, 1992). Every day 25,000 children and adults die of starvation and diseases related to lack of nutrition (Durning, 1989). Compared with this, the number of net migrants from the South to the North during one day is a small number, about 5,000 each day. Per year, it is fewer than 1 inhabitant out of 2,000 in developing countries that migrate North. This could partly explain the lack of prognoses on international migration.

The numbers are small, but the resulting political tension in both sending and receiving countries is a fact. Even small streams are visible and create positive and negative changes in the industrialized world. In the long run, say after one generation, small numbers add up to large numbers and to more impressive demographic-ethnic changes. But of course, at a very aggregated level, the size of the numbers is still smaller than the numbers influenced by future changes in fertility and mortality patterns.

Before the prognosis in this chapter is presented let us define some concepts and then determine how theories from different scientific disciplines could be used to contribute to an understanding of historical and current flows which in turn would make it easier to speculate about future flows. This discussion is based on Öberg and Wils (1992).

14.1   Definitions

The *North* is synonymous with the industrialized countries where the income, on average, is roughly six times higher than in the

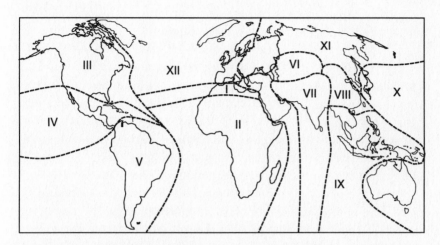

Figure 14.1. The world regions used in this book.

developing countries, the *South*. The North consists of Europe, North America, Japan, and Oceania.

Europe is sometimes divided into Western Europe, which is part of the North, with around 400 million inhabitants and a high per capita income, and the rest of Europe, the former communist countries, with more than 300 million inhabitants and a much lower per capita income, thus statistically part of the South. North America consists of the USA and Canada. Oceania is dominated by Australia and New Zealand.

The *regions* used in this chapter are consistent with the regions defined in other chapters in this book. Thus, there are 12 groups of nations forming the regions: Europe, the USA and Canada, Japan, Oceania, sub-Saharan Africa, North Africa and West Asia (including Iran), South Asia, China (including Hong Kong), East and Southeast Asia, Central America and the Caribbean, South America, and finally the Asian part of the former USSR. The regions are presented in *Figure 14.1*.

Migration usually means "relatively permanent" changes of residence. Since we define regions as continents or groups of nations, interregional migration refers to movements across the boundaries of these regions. Permanence stands for several years, preferably a lifetime.

Of the large number of persons who enter or leave a country, only a small portion are defined as migrants. Tourists, business executives, temporary workers, and asylum seekers trying to find a new home (Rogge, 1992) are usually not defined as migrants. This definition makes it easier to make a prognosis because the accepted flows are statistically better known than the illegal and temporal ones. Most of the discussion in this chapter uses a wider definition of migrants, but the prognosis at the end of the chapter is only concerned with migrants receiving permission to stay permanently, including those who later become citizens of the new country.

Citizenship is an individual person's formal membership of a state. This is a purely legal definition that serves as the basis for a number of rights and duties. The most important here is the legal right for a person to stay in the country where he or she is a citizen. There are also other aspects, like political and psychological ones, but they are not considered here (see Reinans and Hammar, 1993).

14.2   Theories on International Migration

Today, migration is understood as a process of complexity and heterogeneity. It can be analyzed from several perspectives and within different conceptual frameworks or paradigms. It can concentrate on individuals or structures, on micro or macro factors. It occurs in response to a wide range of historical processes and contemporary situations.

Migration concerns individuals, and thus it is a result of unique responses to an actual, potential, or perceived understanding of many processes. It is partly a voluntary and partly a forced action controlled not only by the migrant but also by others, including regulating governments. With this complexity in mind, researchers still try to find regularities which could be used for theories or prognoses. Different scientific disciplines have specialized in different aspects on regularities or prevailing ideas behind migration processes.

The basic idea in the scientific literature on migration between less developed and more developed countries, South–North migration, is that people should migrate North. This will equalize the capital per worker ratio and thus increase efficiency and hence incomes and welfare. A majority of the population in the North will gain from migration (Simon, 1993). Industrialists are happy to employ less-expensive labor. An increased supply of labor would decrease the wage level. Rich and well-educated people would also be better off if they could afford to employ housemaids and gardeners for low wages. People in possession of real estate will earn money on increased demand for housing.

Many people in the South would also gain. Migrants would be better off in their new countries. They could help new migrants settle in the North. They would probably send money home to their relatives in the less developed countries. At present the remittances are about $75 billion annually, substantially more than development aid.

The first ideas on international migration that were developed into a theoretical framework are more than two centuries old. In a study by Kryger (1764), a Swedish social scientist, causes of international migration were discussed as well as how authorities could influence the size of the flows. His idea was that migration cannot be explained in simple words. Individual households could have several reasons for migrating, and the gross migration flows could have several causes. At that time the academic disciplines were broader and fewer than today, but Kryger's study could be labeled "applied economics." As Sweden at that time was a poor country, he concentrated his analysis on push factors, like low wages in some sectors, unfair taxation, badly organized social-security systems, and lack of a well-functioning food distribution system. Several of these factors are still push factors in today's poor countries.

A little more than a century later, several researchers like Ravenstein (1885) in England and Rauchberg (1893) in Austria formulated theories on interregional migration that could be extended to international migration. A French researcher (Lavasseur, 1885) discussed, as we often do today, "the increased facilities for communication, and the multiplicity of the relations existing between the countries of emigration and immigration" as two of the main factors behind migration.

An example of a summary of present knowledge on regularities can be found in Lee (1966). He deals with a prevailing set of factors both in the sending and in the potential receiving regions. These factors could be positive, neutral, or negative. Added to them are potential barriers to migration, "intervening obstacles," such as spatial and cultural distances between regions, costs of migration, or government restrictions. Böhning (1981) provides a more general overview. A recent survey of macro determinants of international migration is given by Greenwood and McDowell (1992).

Today, economic theory is less applied than during Kryger's time and thus further from actual socioeconomic processes. It is a scientific discipline with a hard and coherent theory, based on a number of simplified assumptions about people and society. However, several economists are struggling to develop theories that can be applied to real world situations, like international migration (e.g., Lucas, 1981; MacPhee and Hassan, 1990; Blanchard et al., 1991). According to economic theory we could expect not only labor to move North but also capital to move South. This would increase the total production of goods and services. In a hypothetical future with only economic considerations, no restrictions on international migration, and no ethnic tension or social problems, the greatest economic efficiency would be attained by a very large redistribution of the population.

In reality, economic theory cannot be used in this simplified way. Rather than calculating the flows necessary to achieve a theoretically efficient equilibrium, economic theory should be used to indicate the direction of the flows – not only migrants but also capital and trade commodities – and the marginal returns of these flows.

In geography, a more applied discipline, researchers on migration have been concerned mainly with intranational migration, including urbanization. Strong theories, like the gravitation approach from the 1940s, could then be applied to make probable prognoses on migration flows. However, South–North migration is not only dependent on factors such as distances, information flows, the size of populations, or the number of employment opportunities in different regions. Legal restrictions in the rich countries prevent many foreigners from entering. With present trends, less than 1 percent of the population in the South will probably migrate to the North before 2010.

The well-known mobility transition theory (Zelinsky, 1971), which sometimes is treated as a deterministic theory, tells us that there are historical phases, for example, the demographic transition, when movement is related to general processes of urbanization, industrialization, and modernization. It is, however, not self-evident how these ideas could be applied to South–North migration.

Political science can teach us about public institutions and public decision systems, concerning, for example, the formation of immigration policies (Kelley and Schmidt, 1979). Law can explain the background and practice of immigration rules. However, neither discipline has a theory on international migration flows.

The geopolitical future of the world, studied by geographers and political scientists, is important, but there are no good theories which could help us make forecasts. We know that the lack of congruence between ethnic settlements and political borders will continue to be a problem – it is a problem in several regions. The present situation in Africa is shown in *Figure 14.2*. In Europe, a strong ethnic chauvinism not only created more than a dozen new nations over the last years, but also caused "ethnic cleansing." Unwanted minorities have been either expelled from their settlements or killed in a systematic way. This type of geopolitics is currently taking place in the former Yugoslavia.

Sociology can explain some of the flows. According to one theory (Hoffman-Nowotny, 1981), some flows have to do with the distribution of power and prestige in a social system. A typical migrant would first live in a poor country with a specific status among friends and neighbors, then migrate to a rich country where he or she would work hard, accumulate savings, and finally move back to the poor country with the savings and with a higher status than before. The attractive aspect of this theory is that it fits many movements between South and North.

Demographers speculate less than other researchers. They want clear assumptions and established methods. A typical study would, for instance, assume that 20,000 migrants with a specific ethnic belonging and age and sex distribution settle permanently in Australia every year. The study would then make calculations on how this flow would change the demographic structure of the Australian population over time. Lutz and Prinz (1992), in their study on hypothetical migration flows from Eastern Europe to Western Europe, show that assimilation processes would soon reduce the number of "foreigners" in the West to very small numbers.

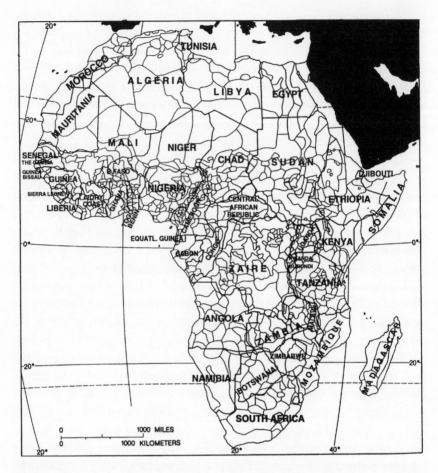

Figure 14.2. Ethnic territories and national boundaries in Africa. Present boundaries were drawn with very little consideration of ethnicity and long-lasting peaceful coexistence within and between nations. Source: Peoples and Bailey, 1991.

The dependency burden is one of the central concepts in demography, and an international gap in this burden would lead to migration flows. The discrepancy of an elderly (and wealthy) population in the more developed countries and a young (and poor) population in the less developed is repeatedly pointed out by demographers. This creates a "demographic potential" for migration.

Demographers are also concerned with feedback and return flows, as are scientists in other fields, such as geography and sociology. It is a well-known fact that small, pioneer flows of a new group of migrants into a region later generate larger flows. First a small group of new migrants is established in a new region. If the members in this group are doing better there than others are doing at home, they can receive friends or relatives and give them a base to start from; these friends can in turn receive others, and so on. A further example of feedback effects is that a migration flow grows as agencies (formal and informal) are set up in the sending country to help potential migrants by providing them with information and practical assistance.

Another well-known fact is that migration flows in one direction will later cause counterflows. An early reference with both ideas and empirical evidence on this statement regarding international migration flows is Ravenstein (1885). For example, a large proportion of the immigrants, legal and illegal, to the USA from Mexico returns home after a work season or a few years.

History is, of course, not only an academic discipline; it is also the empirical source of all applied social science. We understand the world by observing it. By knowing more about past and present migration flows it is hoped that we will be better prepared for expected future flows. There have been many mass migration flows over long distances. In the last century, Europeans migrated to North America, South America, and Australia; Russians colonized parts of Asia; Chinese went South. The British, Ottoman, and, more recently, the Russian empires fell, resulting in large numbers of British, Turkish, and Russian settlers belonging to the ruling class migrating from conquered territories. In recent decades, the Rio Grande and the Mediterranean have become symbols of borders that are crossed by large numbers of migrants. Today, the need for foreign labor in the USA, Europe, and the oil-producing countries is resulting in large flows of labor migrants, staying for shorter or longer periods, some of them becoming citizens in their new countries.

Can these and other earlier movements tell us anything about the future? Yes, they can teach us that a few thousand net migrants per year add up to many millions over several decades. During the 1970s and 1980s about 4 percent (net) of the Mexican population migrated to the USA. History also tell us that economic booms in the North result in large labor flows in the future. Less comforting is that history also tells us that several flows were not regarded as probable before they became a fact. For sure, like other disciplines, history cannot tell us about future details, only probable patterns.

The main factors influencing historic and contemporary international migration are well known, and will continue to be important. There are many ways to label them. Economic factors include wage differences, different access to economic wealth, and material standard of living. Social factors comprise proximity to relatives and friends. Cultural factors, like lifestyles and ethnicity, include social organizations, religion, and values. Geopolitical factors concern tension or conflict, political instability, and threats to life. Environmental factors, such as the carrying capacity of land for inhabitants with limited resources, cause large migration flows, especially when they are combined with geopolitical instability.

The causal links between these factors and the flows are generally clear. For example, if everything else is equal, most people prefer higher wages, nearness to family, and religious freedom.

Migrants from the South usually go directly to the North, but sometimes they first migrate to another developing country before continuing to an industrialized country. For example, ethnic Turks from the Balkan states often migrate to Turkey in a first move and then to Western Europe. A study of such indirect international migration to the United States was carried out by Greenwood and Trabka (1991).

14.3 Push Factors

The welfare gap between countries in the South and North, factors such as a structural income gap or physical proximity, do not change easily over time. The income gap between Eastern Europe and Western Europe or between North America and South America will not disappear before the year 2020 (Öberg and Boubnova, 1993). Also even with unrealistically large investments in the South (for example, 50 percent), it may still take a long time to reduce this gap. If present policies continue, the gap could even be larger in the

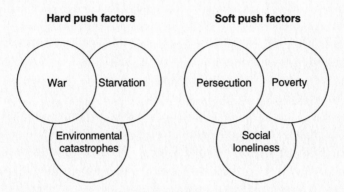

Figure 14.3. Hard and soft push factors of migration.

future than it is today. There are more dollars invested per person in the North today than the total income per person in the South.

As indicated earlier, causes of migration are sometimes divided into two groups – push factors and pull factors. The ways these factors influence South–North migration are discussed by several authors (e.g., Golini *et al.*, 1991; Heyden, 1991). Push factors can be structural, like the rapid global population growth with its effects on competition for food and other resources. Population growth is most severe in poor countries, where it is already a major problem for individuals to afford food. Another structural cause is the welfare gap between the North and the South. There are several other structural forces, but they are all somewhat internally interrelated in a causal structure.

Push factors can also be related to individual motives as shown in *Figure 14.3*. There are no indications that these factors will become less important in the future. Without being pessimistic, it is easy to believe the opposite for several reasons.

Wars between or within nation-states are usually caused by a combination of long-lasting ethnic tensions and economic inequalities. They can create large migration flows. For example, in the past migration flows occurred in many former African colonies such as Algeria, Angola, Guinea-Bissau, Mozambique, Namibia, and Zimbabwe (Rogge, 1992). Today these migration flows are taking place in former Yugoslavia, Sudan, and Sri Lanka. Usually people try to move to neighboring countries. In some cases, they may move to distant places if relatives and friends are already located there. Indonesians migrated to the Netherlands, Armenians to the USA, and Croats to Sweden. War between nations usually occurs where it has occurred before, where ethnic hate exists, and where the social systems are under too loose control (anarchy) or too strict control (dictatorship).

In some parts of Africa, the Balkan area, or Southeast Asia, the risk of war in the coming decades is higher than in North America or Western Europe. Countries like South Africa and Israel have more tension in relations to their neighbors than Switzerland or Canada, and thus the risk for future war is higher in the former countries. However, higher risks do not forecast future outcome. Peace can come unexpectedly in some areas; tension can rise fast in peaceful regions.

Persecution exists in many parts of the world, such as in Sudan, Burma, former Yugoslavia, and El Salvador. Ethnic tension leads to murder in war times and persecution in peace times. It will continue to be a problem in most parts of the world in the coming decade. Africa may see more of this problem than other parts of the world in the near future.

Starvation with high mortality is already prevalent in many countries (Dréze and Sen, 1989). In most African countries the consumption of calories has decreased in the last decade: 35 out of 47 countries were worse off in 1989 than in 1980, according to FAO statistics. The worst decline was in sub-Saharan countries like Angola, Botswana, Gabon, Mozambique, and Rwanda. Starvation in the future is more probable in poor countries with a small domestic food production or in nondemocratic nations, since "no democratic country with a relatively free press has ever experienced a major famine" (Sen, 1993). Starvation is also more probable in countries with ethnic/political tension since it is a weapon that can be used to hurt enemies, for example, in the Ukraine in the 1930s, Biafra in the 1960s, and southern Sudan in the 1990s. Areas with current low income, high debts, and low food consumption are shown in *Figure 14.4*.

Poverty is probably the largest single factor behind current and future migration flows. According to one estimation from the UN (1993), 100 million migrants have left their home countries because

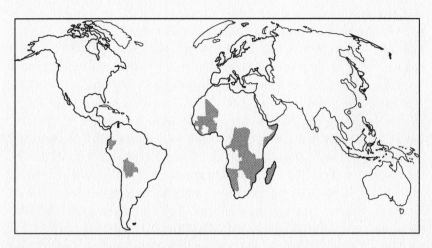

Figure 14.4. Potential emigration areas. The map shows countries with low income per capita, large debts in relation to income, and low food consumption. A quarter of a billion people live in these countries. Low income is defined as less than $1,500 per person in 1990; high debts mean more than one year's GNP; and at present low food consumption implies that the supply of food is lower than 2,300 calories per person per day. Source: UNEP and UNDP, 1992.

of poverty. It is of course hard to define poverty gaps, but they certainly constitute a contemporary and a future main force behind international migration. The search for a good living standard can be combined with all the push factors mentioned earlier, such as parenthood or ethnicity. Poverty has indirect effects on migration flows in the sense that we do not find the poorest part of the population among the migrants. Large numbers of very poor in a country will increase competition for resources, add to crime and violence, and thus decrease the living standard for others, including the lower and upper middle class. It is in these latter groups that we find most migrants.

Environmental catastrophes are often discussed as a common future cause behind large migration flows. Nuclear power stations or factories producing atomic, biological, or chemical (ABC) weapons could pollute large areas, like Chernobyl did in the Ukraine in 1986. A rise in sea level or more hurricanes, which are phenomena discussed as a possible scenario if global warming becomes a reality, will create floods in lowlands in many countries. With less ozone protection in the atmosphere, large areas will be uninhabitable. For the moment there are no good prognoses of where future environmental catastrophes are likely to occur. Most environmental catastrophes have occurred in developing countries. Drought, floods, soil erosion, and desertification are widespread, recurrent problems. According to a 1992 report by the International Organization for Migration, environmental migration will be caused by the following disruptions: elemental, biological, slow-onset accidents; disruptions caused by development; and finally, environmental warfare. Each category covers a spectrum of disruptions ranging from mild to catastrophic. For an excellent overview of the literature on links between environmental degradation and migration see Suhrke (1993).

Social loneliness is a problem of much less general importance than others mentioned here. Furthermore, it will be a problem only for a very small minority in the South, such as some parents with their children in the North. However, this small group can be a substantial proportion of the migrants going North, since they are usually allowed to move to their close relatives (Jasso and Rosenzweig, 1986).

Summarizing the short discussion of push factors is easy. They are overwhelming and will probably change the world in many ways. We may be facing an unrecognizable world in the year 2020 with migration flows of the same magnitude as during the last century when Europeans flooded other parts of the world.

The North will be affected in an unforeseeable way, especially if the future flows are determined by the supply of emigrants in the South instead of, as today, by the demand for immigrants in the North. However, a large part of these international flows will continue to be between neighboring countries in the South. A large part will also be refugees who will not be allowed to stay permanently or temporary workers; neither group is defined as migrants in this chapter.

The basic assumption in this chapter is that changes are not very spectacular. Restrictions put up by countries in the North will regulate future immigration. Future changes in restrictions are assumed to be mainly influenced by present attitudes toward strangers, attitudes that will not change during one generation.

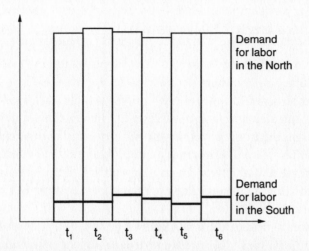

Figure 14.5. The gap between demand for cheap labor in the North and the South is so large that minor changes in the demand only influence migration flows indirectly through policy formation.

14.4 Pull Factors

The distinction between push and pull factors is usually unclear from a scientific point of view. Wealth can be a pull factor in the North, attracting migrants from less wealthy countries, but this phenomenon could also be described as a push factor, lack of wealth, in the South. With this in mind, caution must be taken when push and pull concepts are under study.

From a technical point of view, it is difficult to distinguish between the importance of push and pull factors in relation to South–North migration. The gap between indicators such as salary, security, and demand for cheap labor is usually so large between the South and the North that changes in either the push or pull factor only marginally affect it.

Also, theoretically a distinction is combined with severe problems. A larger flow of migrants during a period of low demand in poor countries could be dependent either on the low demand during the period, in which case it is a push factor, or on a delayed response to an earlier situation with a high demand in the rich countries, in which case it is a pull factor (see *Figure 14.5*). Thus, not only could data be selected in different ways, but the same information can also be interpreted in many ways. Concerning, for example, the early migration flows between Sweden and the United States, Wilkinson (1967) states that they were mainly determined by labor demand in the USA, while Thomas (1941) reports that the economic conditions in Sweden were more important. Quigley (1972) shows that conditions in both the sending country and the receiving country were important. An overview of these and other empirically based studies on patterns and dynamics of push and pull factors can be found in Greenwood and McDowell (1992). The most successful studies of international migration are theoretically weak but empirically strong.

Models of migration are specific to the relative importance of push or pull factors. Depending on which theory a researcher uses, he or she is restricted to specific mathematical tools. Each modeling technique emphasizes either push or pull factors. For example, a Markov model "pushes" migrants between time steps in the future depending on earlier trends. An overview on how different methods rely on push or pull ideas can be found in the geographic literature (Alonso, 1974).

In the literature, pull factors are expressed in terms of gaps. A high demand for labor with a corresponding high salary level is related to the wage gap between countries. Pull factors of this kind are difficult to trace in empirical figures because the gap is so enormous that it is not theoretically sound to relate marginal changes directly to migration flows.

It would be better to relate pull factors indirectly to migration flows through the formation and implementation of immigration policies in the North. According to this idea, there is always a long-lasting, large structural welfare gap between the North and the South. The average income on one side of a geographical border can be more than 2000 percent higher than on the other side – for example, along the northern Mexican border or along the eastern Finnish border. An increase in the wage level of a few percentages on either side of the border does not change the gap as such. However, in some situations, pull factors in the North, like a shortage of labor, could make it easier for the people in the North to accept immigrants. Policies could change and migration flows could increase. This view makes the distinction between push and pull factors instrumental in studies of South–North migration.

Related to this idea is the concept of migration pressure. This commonly used expression roughly means unrealized migration desires. The migration pressure from the South thus increases either if fewer people are allowed to migrate through a more restrictive policy or if a larger proportion of the population in the South would like to move North.

Pull factors that could change migration policies are related to economic and humanitarian ideas. Economic considerations are stronger than humanitarian factors. If influential actors in the North could earn money on immigration, this would probably be the most important pull factor. A few can always gain – farmers in California or fishermen in Sicily – but they must be supported by other groups, usually more than half of the population in democracies.

Looking ahead, there are different opinions on the future demand of labor in the North. One extreme argument is that there will not be a future need for more immigrants. The demand for labor has changed structurally in recent decades. In the future few laborers will be employed in modern agriculture in the North, yet this sector will produce more food than ever. Furthermore, there will not be a future need for industrial workers in the North. This is not only because of the increasing competition from the newly industrializing countries but also because of new technologies in the production system. More investments in industry and its productivity will only decrease demand for employees. Robots and computers will run the machines in some rich countries. For example, in the Netherlands, only three workers out of ten in the labor market are in farming or in industry.

A further argument for why there is no need for immigration is that even with a future demand for labor in a booming economy, many millions of homemakers in the North can enter the labor market. Today, the low labor market participation in southern Europe, for example, functions as a reserve supply of labor.

The opposite argument is that the demand for labor in the North will increase as a function of income, not as a function of demand for labor in agriculture and industry. Service employment must also be included in the analysis. For example, many of rich old people in the

North will need help in the future, but a shortage of people willing
to care for them has been projected. The shortage is due partly to a
new demographic situation, with a decrease in working-age groups,
and partly to the fact that it is difficult to recruit people living in
the North for jobs with a low status.

The humanitarian rationale for accepting refugees as immigrants has been quite strong, and will probably maintain its strength
in the future. A tendency to decrease its influence on migration is
the argument that more refugees could get help for the same amount
of money if they did not have to migrate to the North. Temporary
refugee camps in the South will probably be more common in the
future. Another tendency is that attitudes toward immigration are
slowly changing. Right-wing political parties tend to try to promote
policies that result in fewer accepted migrants (Vandermotten and
Vanlaer, 1993; Fielding, 1993). It is hard to see how the humanitarian pull factor can change policies so that more migrants will be
accepted in the future. Yet, if a change in attitudes occurs, it could
influence immigration much more than changes in the labor market.

14.5   Policies

In this chapter, the most important factor for future permanent immigration flows to the developed countries is assumed to be attitudes
toward foreigners within the receiving countries. These attitudes
determine regulation policies in the North. Ethnicity in a broad
sense plays an important part in this context. Feelings of superior-
ity among rich majority groups in the North or of hate or fear of
potential immigrant groups belonging to other ethnic groups cause
decreases in future flows. Native ethnic Estonians are afraid of large
flows from Russia. Ethnicity also plays an important role when internal flows in the South are determined. Muslims in Pakistan are
not interested in large flows of Hindus from India.

Since there is no comparative study of this sensitive issue on
feelings on ethnicity and attitudes toward other ethnic groups, the
current international discussion among researchers is based on a
combination of nonsystematic interviews with colleagues from different countries, official policies, and statistics on actual permissions
for foreigners to obtain citizenship. According to this soft approach,

Japan, the oil-rich Muslim countries, and Australia will be hesitant to accept immigrants from other cultures; North America will welcome large streams; and Western Europe will hold a position in between these two.

Within Western Europe, current practice varies: Sweden accepted one non-European asylum seeker for every 80 inhabitants during the 1980s; Finland accepted almost no non-European immigrants. On average, there are large migration flows within Europe but very limited immigration from other parts of the world.

However, small labor flows from neighboring regions continue. For example, in Germany, Belgium, and the Netherlands, the Turkish population increased from 1.6 million to 1.8 million between 1985 and 1988. During the same period, the number of Algerians, Moroccans, and Tunisians living in those countries rose from 330,000 to 370,000 (UN, 1992:179). The majority of the labor migrants are legal. Most of the illegal migrants are now in Italy. There are several estimates on the number of illegal migrants, but most of them are estimates of about 1 million (Montanari and Cortese, 1993).

In the past the immigration policy in Western Europe varied from country to country, but a more coherent policy is now emerging (Widgren, 1992). Five countries (Germany, France, the Netherlands, Belgium, and Luxembourg) have signed an agreement to harmonize immigration. This group of countries, the Schengen group, will directly or indirectly influence other countries to adjust their policies in the same direction. Europeans are very restrictive to non-European immigrants. On average, around 1 percent of the population are non-Europeans. France, the UK, Germany, Sweden, and Belgium have higher figures.

Within the former USSR, which consists of a European part (the Baltic states, Russia, Ukraine, Belarus, and Moldova) and an Asian part (including Georgia, Armenia, Azerbaijan, and Kazakhstan), there are now flows from Asia to Europe. Ethnic Russians migrate to Europe from territories where they used to belong to a ruling minority, or where they were working for high salaries as compensation for poor working conditions. The same is true for ethnic Ukrainians and Belarussians (Öberg and Boubnova, 1993).

The two countries in the North American region are of special interest in this chapter since they have traditionally accept immigrants

Table 14.1. Principal countries[a] of resettlement of refugees and asylum seekers.

Resettlement country	1975–1990	Ratio refugees/population
Sweden	121,000	1/71
Canada	325,000	1/82
Australia	183,000	1/96
USA	1,478,000	1/171
France	200,000	1/238
Germany[b]	91,000	1/869

[a]Some countries with very small populations – Denmark, Norway, and New Zealand – have high ratios, as high as those in the USA or France.
[b]Excludes ethnic Germans from Eastern Europe. If this group is included, Germany has the same ratio as France.
Source: USCR, *World Refugee Survey*, 1992, cited in Rogge, 1992.

with different ethnic backgrounds. The United States accepts more immigrants than any other country in the world. The USA and Canada belong to the principal countries of resettlement of refugees and asylum seekers (see *Table 14.1*). Canada accepts fewer immigrants in absolute numbers but more than the USA in relative terms. The USA granted permanent resident status to nearly 6 million people and Canada to 1 million during the 1980s.

The US immigration policy legalized the stay of another 0.5 million people in 1989. For more than a decade, immigration has been increasing. About one-third of the immigrants today are admitted because they are adult children or siblings of US citizens, another third are spouses, children, and parents, and the last third are humanitarian or economic immigrants without close relatives living in the USA.

The Canadian immigration policy has always been based on humanitarian ideas and economic considerations (Green, 1976). Family reunions and protection of refugees belong to the former category; labor market needs, to the latter. Approximately one-third of the immigrants belong to the latter group. They have desired skills or occupations or business intentions, or they are members of a family having this labor market advantage. In recent years, labor market needs have become more important, and there are discussions on increasing this group of immigrants still further.

The majority of the population in Oceania lives in Australia and New Zealand. Australia admitted about 0.8 million immigrants from countries outside Oceania during the 1980s. New Zealand, a country with net emigration, admitted less than half in relative terms, which is approximately one-tenth in absolute numbers. Roughly every fifth person moving to Australia was skilled and defined as a "business migrant." Every tenth (between 1986 and 1989) was a refugee or a person admitted under the Special Humanitarian Program.

Japan is a rich country with a demand for foreign labor. It is by tradition a closed society. However, its strong and successful economy has increased the demand for labor within the country to a degree where legal and illegal imports become a factor. The legal workers are mainly women entertaining Japanese men, 71,000 in 1988 (UN, 1992). The unregistered, illegal workers are increasing in numbers but are still less than 1 percent of the labor force (Shah, 1992). Thus there are some foreigners working in Japan, but they seldom get permission to settle in the country. A reasonable guess is that present attitudes toward non-Japanese will not change within one generation. The result could then be a large number of temporary guests or guest workers employed in Japan but not allowed to be citizens.

The rich oil-producing countries, especially in West Asia, will probably use the same strategy; they will continue their policy to allow workers to stay in the country on temporary jobs but will not allow foreigners to become citizens. Today, they accept large numbers (perhaps 2 or 3 million) of foreign workers: people of Arab origin (e.g., Egyptians, Palestinians, and Jordanians), people from countries in South Asia (e.g., India, Pakistan, and Bangladesh), and people from Southeast Asia (e.g., the Philippines, Republic of Korea, and Thailand). By 1985, it was estimated that 63 percent of all workers in the six Gulf States (Bahrain, Kuwait, Oman, Qatar, Saudi Arabia, and the United Arab Emirates) were from South or Southeast Asia (Shah, 1992). Since these workers are not allowed to be citizens in West Asian countries, they are all temporary visitors and are not treated as (permanent) immigrants in this chapter. The assumption is that even in the coming decades, very few people will be allowed to become permanent immigrants to this rich part of the world.

Hong Kong, which is a part of China in this book (and will formally be a part of China as of July 1997), has an unpredictable future. Many inhabitants have already moved to other countries, like Canada. The UK says that it will no longer accept the inhabitants as privileged members of the Commonwealth, except for 50,000 people with their families.

China will, according to a probable scenario, become more integrated with the economy of the rest of the world in the coming decades. This event could result in larger migration flows to North America where there is a positive attitude toward immigrants from Asia. Also, Australia could be affected demographically by more intense economic cooperation with China.

The attitudes toward immigration in the rich countries are generally in favor of strong regulations and limitations on the numbers allowed to enter. The attitudes vary from a more generous North America to a restrictive Japan. Australia is similar to North America, but has clear ethnic priorities. Europe is, on average, closer to Japan, but some individual countries are exceptions.

The discussion of attitudes is mainly based on knowledge from historic and current situations. Attitudes toward future immigrants are based on attitudes toward immigrants today. These attitudes are already known indirectly through the size of contemporary migration flows. Previous migration flows between South and North, to a large extent, determine future flows. There are at least three reasons for this. First, an existing flow tells us that the receiving rich country accepts immigrants. Second, earlier immigrants, now living in the North, with social contacts to people in the South, make it easier for potential migrants to realize their wishes and thus become new immigrants. Large proportions of present immigrants are related to earlier immigrants. For example, more than one-third of the immigrant flow to the USA consists of close relatives of US citizens (spouses, children, and parents). Third, if many immigrants of one ethnic background move to a country with a democratic society, they become a political force because they have many votes, have economic power, and can organize lobbies. The Hispanic part of the US population is a good example of an immigrant group reaching the point of being able to exercise political power.

More detailed figures on assumed future migration streams between the world regions are discussed in Chapters 15 and 16.

References

Alonso, W., 1974, Policy-Oriented Interregional Demographic Accounting and Generalization of Population Flow Models, Working Paper 247, University of California, Institute of Urban and Regional Development, Berkeley, CA, USA.

Blanchard, O., Layard, R., Dornbusch, R., and Krugman, P., 1991, East-West Migration: The Alternatives – A Report of the Wider World Economy Group, Working Paper No. 101, Centre for Economic Performance, London, UK.

Böhning, W.R., 1981, Elements of a theory of international migration to industrial nations, in M. Kritz, C. Keely, and S. Tomasi, eds., *Global Trends in Migration: Theory and Research on International Population Movements*, Center for Migration Studies, Staten Island, NY, USA.

Dréze, J., and Sen, A., 1989, *Hunger and Public Action*, Clarendon Press, Oxford, UK.

Durning, A., 1989, *World Poverty*, Worldwatch Institute, Washington, DC, USA.

Fielding, A., 1993, Migrations, institutions and politics: The evolution of European migration policies, in R. King, ed., *Mass Migration in Europe: The Legacy and the Future*, Belhaven Press, London, UK.

Golini, A., Gerano, G., and Heins, F., 1991, South–North migration with special reference to Europe, in W.A. Dumon, ed., *Ninth IOM Seminar on Migration, South–North Migration*, International Organization for Migration, Geneva, Switzerland.

Green, A.G., 1976, *Immigration and the Post-War Canadian Economy*, Macmillan, New York, NY, USA.

Greenwood, M.J., and McDowell, J.M., 1992, The Macrodeterminants of International Migration, Paper presented at the Conference on Mass Migration in Europe, 5–7 March, Laxenburg, Austria.

Greenwood, M.J., and Trabka, E., 1991, Temporal and spatial patterns of geographically indirect immigration to the United States, *International Migration Review* **25**(1) (Spring).

Heyden, H., 1991, South–North migration, in W.A. Dumon, ed., *Ninth IOM Seminar on Migration, South–North Migration*, International Organization for Migration, Geneva, Switzerland.

Hoffman-Nowotny, J., 1981, A sociological approach toward a general theory of migration, in M. Kritz, C. Keely, and S. Tomasi, eds., *Global Trends in Migration: Theory and Research on International*

Population Movements, Center for Migration Studies, Staten Island, NY, USA.

Jasso, G., and Rosenzweig, M.R., 1986, Family reunification and the immigration multiplier: US immigration law, origin, country conditions, and the reproduction of immigrants. *Demography* **23**(3) (August).

Kelley, A.C., and Schmidt, R.M., 1979, Modeling the role of government policy in post-war Australian immigration, *Economic Record* **55**(2) (June).

Kryger, J.F., 1764, Svar på den af Kongl. Vetenskaps Academien för sistledit ar 1963, framstälde frågan: Hvad kan vara orsaken, at sådan myckenhet Svensk folk årligen flytter ur Landet? Och genom hvilka författningar kan det bäst före-kommas?

Lavasseur, E., 1885, Emigration in the nineteenth century, *Journal of the Statistical Society.*

Lee, E., 1966, A theory of migration, *Demography* **3**.

Lucas, R.E.B., 1981, International migration: Economic causes, consequences and evaluation, in M. Kritz, C. Keely, and S. Tomasi, eds., *Global Trends in Migration: Theory and Research on International Population Movements*, Center for Migration Studies, Staten Island, NY, USA.

Lutz, W., and Prinz, Ch., 1992, What Difference Do Alternative Immigration and Integration Levels Make to Western Europe, WP-92-29, International Institute for Applied Systems Analysis, Laxenburg, Austria.

MacPhee, C.R., and Hassan, M.K., 1990, Some economic determinants of Third World professional immigration to the United States: 1972–1987, *World Development* **18**(8) (August).

Montanari, A., and Cortese, A., 1993, Third World immigrants in Italy, in R. King, ed., *Mass Migration in Europe, the Legacy and the Future*, Belhaven Press, London, UK.

Öberg, S., and Boubnova, H., 1993, Poverty, ethnicity and migration potentials in Eastern Europe, in R. King, ed., *Mass Migration in Europe, the Legacy and the Future*, Belhaven Press, London, UK.

Öberg, S., and Wils, A.B., 1992, East-West migration in Europe, *POPNET* **22** (Winter):1–7.

Peoples, J., and Bailey, G., 1991, *Humanity*, West Publishing Company, St. Paul, MN, USA.

Quigley, J.M., 1972, An economic model of Swedish emigration, *Quarterly Journal of Economics* (February).

Rauchberg, H., 1893, Innere Wanderungen in Österreich, *Allgemeines Statistisches Archiv* **3**:183–208.

Ravenstein, E.G., 1885, The laws of migration, *Journal of the Statistical Society* **48**(2):167–227.

Reinans, S.A., and Hammar, T., 1993, *New Citizens by Birth and Natu-ralization*, CEIFO, Stockholm, Sweden.

Rogge, J.R., 1992, Refugee Migration: Changing Characteristics and Prospects, Working Paper ESD/P/ICPD.1994/EG.VI/19, United Nations, New York, NY, USA.

Sen, A., 1993, The economics of life and death, *Scientific American* (May).

Shah, N.M., 1992, Migration Between Asian Countries and Its Likely Future, Working Paper ESD/P/ICPD.1994/EG, VI/114, United Nations, New York, NY, USA.

Simon, J., 1993, The economic effect of immigration, *European Review* **1**(1).

Suhrke, A., 1993, *Pressure Points: Environmental Degradation, Migration and Conflict*, Number 3 of the Occasional Paper Series of the Project on Environmental Change and Acute Conflict, University of Toronto and the American Academy of Arts and Sciences (March), Washington, DC, USA.

Thomas, D.S., 1941, *Social and Economic Aspects of Swedish Population Movements*, Macmillan, New York, NY, USA.

UN, 1992, *World Population Monitoring, 1991*, United Nations, New York, NY, USA.

UN, 1993, *Population Distribution and Migration: The Emerging Issues*, United Nations, New York, NY, USA.

UNEP and UNDP, 1992, *World Resources*, Oxford University Press, Oxford, UK.

Vandermotten, C., and Vanlaer, J., 1993, Immigrants and the extreme-right vote in Europe and in Belgium, in R. King, ed., *Mass Migration in Europe, the Legacy and the Future*, Belhaven Press, London, UK.

Widgren, J., 1992, *Report for the Intergovernmental Consultations on Asylum, Refugees, and Migration Policies in Europe, North America, and Australia*, IC, Geneva, Switzerland.

Wilkinson, M., 1967, Evidence of long swings in the growth of Swedish population and related economic variables, 1860–1965, *Journal of Economic History* **27** (March).

Zelinsky, W., 1971, The hypothesis of the mobility transition, *Geographical Review* **61**:219–249.

Editor's Note for Part V

Chapter 13 gives the most complete account of intercontinental migration that can be composed with existing data. Even without illegal migration input, data on official or legal migration turn out to be fragmentary. In a discussion on the forces that will induce future migration, Chapter 14 shows that the traditionally studied pull and push factors of economic disparities are often submerged by the importance of legal and logistical restrictions on international migration. Short-term political changes as well as refugee movements spurred by war or famine can significantly impact on migration level. As in the past, international migration can be assumed to show great volatility in the future.

How can one derive from this information assumptions about the future? An informed guess would be to assume that the future maximum migration level will roughly equal the maximum that has been observed at certain times in the past. For such an exercise it is appropriate to make migration assumptions in absolute numbers, rather than rates, depending on population size. For some possible future migration streams, such as Asian migration into Siberia, there is no recent historical precedent for orientation, and numbers will have to be chosen rather freely. At the low extreme a convenient assumption is that of zero net-migration, namely, a balance of in-migration and out-migration. Such a scenario reflects the possible case of xenophobic policies, for example, in Europe, under which immigration would be reduced to an absolute minimum. The central scenario then gives the average of these two extreme scenarios; it should also be considered the most likely case. Specific numbers are given in Chapter 15.

Part VI

Projections

Chapter 15

The IIASA World Population Scenarios to 2030

Wolfgang Lutz, Christopher Prinz, and Jeannette Langgassner

This part presents the population projections that were carried out on the basis of the considerations given in Chapters 1 through 14. The part presents two different sets of projections. The first and foremost is the set of systematic permutation scenarios until 2030 presented in this chapter. Based on the considerations of experts in the previous chapters for each of the three components (fertility, mortality, and migration), two extreme paths (one high and one low) of future levels are assumed for each of the 12 world regions. This results in eight permutation scenarios, which serve the purpose of sensitivity analysis as discussed in Chapter 2. In these scenarios the three components are explicitly assumed to be independent. In addition the demand for one most likely projection for orientation is met by the central scenario, which results from the averaging of the high and low assumptions of all three components. For these scenarios, assumptions are only defined up to the year 2030 (see discussion of time horizon in Chapter 2). To illustrate some of the longer-term impacts of assumptions, results up to 2050 are presented in shaded areas of the figures for specific cases.

Chapter 16 presents some special scenarios for illustrative purposes until 2100. The presentation includes two sets of scenarios: three long-term extensions where the components are still essentially independent and a number of long-term scenarios that assume specific interdependencies between the components and feedbacks from the output parameters to fertility and mortality in the following periods. Because the number of possible interdependencies and feedbacks is almost infinite, the projections only illustrate selected possible mechanisms and results.

Chapters 15 and 16 also provide a comparison between the results for our world population scenarios and the world population projections published by the UN and the World Bank. In several respects, both parts – the systematic permutation scenarios until 2030 and the special scenarios until 2100 – go beyond other existing projections. Our scenarios also try to respond to a demand from scientists in the field of global environmental change. To facilitate the use of the results by others, an extensive set of tables is appended to the volume. A complete data set for all scenarios and all regions in five-year age groups and five-year time steps is also available on diskette from the authors.

15.1   Specification of Scenario Assumptions

In the following set of scenario projections for each of the three components (fertility, mortality, and migration), high and low values have been defined based on the substantive analysis of experts presented in Chapters 3 to 14. Since in general the experts did not come up with specific numerical information of changes in rates over time, a first necessary step lies in the operationalization of the views expressed by the experts.

The editor's notes at the end of each part of this book give brief statements on how the information given in the preceding chapters is used for defining specific assumptions. The full set of numerical assumptions presented in *Tables 15.1* to *15.3* resulted from a long and difficult discussion process that cannot be fully documented here. Reference is made to the preceding chapters of this volume and, concerning the industrialized countries, to the set of papers in Lutz (1991).

Table 15.1. Alternative fertility assumptions in the 12 world regions for 2030 (TFR).

| | 1990 | 2030 | | |
		Low	Central	High
North Africa	4.7	2.0	3.00	4.0
Sub-Saharan Africa	6.4	2.5	3.75	5.0
Central America & Caribbean	3.3	1.7	2.35	3.0
South America	2.9	1.7	2.35	3.0
West & Central Asia	4.2	1.7	2.35	3.0
South Asia	4.2	1.7	2.35	3.0
China/Hong Kong/Taiwan	2.2	1.5	2.25	3.0
Southeast Asia	3.2	1.7	2.35	3.0
North America	2.0	1.4	1.85	2.3
Japan/Australia	1.7	1.3	1.70	2.1
Eastern Europe	2.0	1.3	1.80	2.3
Western Europe	1.6	1.3	1.70	2.1

15.1.1 Future fertility

Assumptions about the future course of fertility may be derived from several sources of information. First, it is the analysis of past trends and the assessment of where individual countries and regions stand in the process of demographic transition. This assessment, presented for today's developing countries in Chapter 3, was a major guideline in making specific assumptions for the individual regions under the basic premise that the fertility transition that has started almost everywhere will essentially continue. While the low values assume a rapid pace in the continuation of the fertility transition, the high values assume a much slower pace – in some cases even a stagnation of the declining trend. In China it even implies increasing fertility.

For the near future the intentions expressed by women in representative surveys can be taken as an additional important piece of evidence. Chapter 4 analyzes this information for a selected number of countries. Sub-Saharan Africa has by far the highest fertility levels and the lowest levels of contraceptive prevalence, but in all countries the desired fertility rates, which have been derived from the surveys, are clearly lower than the actual ones – in Kenya by almost two children. This fact, together with indications of increasing contraceptive prevalence, leads to the expectation of significant fertility declines in the next decade, even in sub-Saharan Africa which has shown constant high fertility until recently.

In North Africa the fertility transition is already much further advanced, and more than one-third of the female population uses contraceptives. Desired fertility rates in this region indicate that further significant fertility declines are to be expected unless dramatic events, such as a rise in pronatalist fundamentalism, change the pattern. The three Asian countries considered here, Indonesia, Sri Lanka, and Thailand, already have total fertility levels below 3.0 with further declines expected. Latin America has an intermediate position comparable with that in North Africa. A specific feature about this region is that over the past decades fertility was rather stagnant at this intermediate level. But recent evidence indicates further decline.

In the longer run, without doubt it is general socioeconomic and cultural change that will determine fertility levels. But these trends are by no means easier to forecast than the direction of fertility change itself. One more specific aspect in this context is the role of government policies and family-planning programs. As pointed out in Chapter 5, experience with such programs over several decades has shown that they can have an important effect if they are well integrated into other government policies and, most importantly, if the socioeconomic development of the population has reached a point at which limitation of family size is considered a real option and advantageous by sizable segments of the population. Since many countries have been adopting such programs, they are likely to contribute in accelerating the fertility decline.

In terms of specific numerical assumptions, for all developing regions except South America and China, even the high value in 2030 was assumed to be lower than the current fertility level. This is because of the overwhelming evidence of a further continuation of the process of demographic transition in parts of the world that still have high fertility. For this reason no constant fertility scenario was specified. However, the high values (3.0 in all regions except Africa) do not assume a smooth fertility transition but an interruption or at least retardation of the process. This could be due to setbacks in socioeconomic development, cultural or religious movements such as a rise of fundamentalism, or strong heterogeneity with rather stable pre- and post-transitional populations living together in one region. The low values indicate a very rapid fertility decline that will not stop at 2.1 but continue to subreplacement fertility as it did in most industrialized countries. The resulting central values for 2030 are somewhat above replacement level in most regions, and significantly above in Africa. The fertility assumptions for China are based on the discussion in Chapter 6, and assume a low value of 1.5 as opposed to a high value of 3.0 in 2030.[1]

Making assumptions for today's industrialized countries is in one way more difficult and in another way easier than for today's high fertility countries. It is more difficult because even the sign of change is unclear: Will fertility increase or decrease? It is easier because the margin of uncertainty may be assumed to be smaller. For a modern urban society with increasing female economic activity, it is unlikely that fertility will be significantly above replacement level. But it seems equally unlikely that fertility will remain permanently below a level that is around half of replacement because, at an individual level, the desire for children seems to be deeply rooted in women and men and, at a societal level, rapid population aging would result in serious problems (see deliberations in Chapter 12).

Until a few years ago, the United Nations and other institutions preparing population forecasts assumed that fertility would increase to replacement level and that subreplacement fertility was only a transitory phenomenon. This assumption is theoretically supported by the above-discussed argument of homeostasis. In this view, fertility levels are not seen as the sum of individual behavior, but as one aspect of the evolution of a system where individual behavior is a function of the status of the system (see Vishnevsky, 1991). Under such a systems approach the assumption of replacement fertility in the longer run seems to be natural. For this reason we assumed a TFR between 2.1 and 2.3 in 2030 as the high-fertility assumption in the four industrialized regions.

It is difficult, however, to find many researchers that support this view. Too much evidence points toward low fertility. The return to replacement fertility has been criticized as an assumed magnetic force (Westoff, 1991) without empirical support. A large number of significant arguments support an assumption of further declining fertility levels. They range from the weakening of the family in terms of both declining marriage rates and high divorce rates, to the increasing independence and career orientation of women, and to a value change toward materialism and consumerism. These factors, together with increasing demands and personal expectations for attention, time, and also money to be given to children, are likely to result in fewer couples that have more than one or two children and an increasing number of childless women. Also, the proportion of unplanned pregnancies is still high, and some future improvements in contraceptive methods seem possible.

In conclusion one can say that the bulk of evidence points to the direction that fertility will remain low or even decline further. How far it can decline is not clear at this point. The expert group decided to settle for a TFR of 1.3 as the low value in the year 2030. This value is below the low-fertility assumptions in other projections, but it is far from being impossible. Actually several populations have already experienced such levels for extended periods. Taking into account the different ethnic composition in North America, the fertility range in this region was chosen to be slightly higher (1.4 to 2.3) than in Europe and Japan.

15.1.2   Future mortality

Mortality conditions at one point in time can be conveniently summarized by period life expectancy at birth, an indicator that results from a life table based on all age-specific mortality rates observed at that time. In the following discussion, this indicator is used to define mortality assumptions.[2]

The uncertainties about future improvements or possibly even declines in life expectancy are quite different in today's high- and low-mortality countries. The latter countries have seen impressive increases in life expectancy and their populations are approaching ages that used to be considered a biological upper limit to the human life span. Hence assumptions about future improvements crucially depend on whether such a limit exists and will soon be reached (see Chapter 12; Manton, 1991). In regions that still have much lower life expectancy, this question is irrelevant, and future mortality conditions will be determined by the efficiency of local health services, the spread of traditional (e.g., malaria) and new (AIDS) diseases, and the general level of subsistence.

Table 15.2. Alternative mortality assumptions in the 12 world regions (life expectancy at birth).

Region	Life expectancy 1990		Assumed change in years of life expectancy per decade		
	Male	Female	Low	Central	High
Developing regions					
North Africa	58.6	61.1	0.50	2.25	4.00
Sub-Saharan Africa	49.0	52.4	−3.00	0.00	3.00
Central America & Caribbean	65.7	71.3	1.00	2.00	3.00
South America	64.0	69.6	1.00	2.00	3.00
West & Central Asia	64.4	69.3	0.50	2.25	4.00
South Asia	58.1	58.4	0.00	2.00	4.00
China	68.6	71.8	1.00	2.00	3.00
Southeast Asia	61.2	65.3	0.00	2.00	4.00
Industrialized regions					
North America	72.2	79.0	1.00	2.00	3.00
Japan/Australia/New Zealand	75.3	81.1	1.00	2.00	3.00
Eastern Europe	65.9	74.7	0.50	2.25	4.00
Western Europe	73.0	79.4	1.00	2.00	3.00

At the moment, life expectancy at a national level is highest in Japan: 82.1 years for women and 76.1 years for men. Only 30 years ago in 1960–1964 female life expectancy was 71.7 and male life expectancy was 66.6, implying an average increase of 3.7 years per decade for women. Eastern Europe, on the other hand, had the same life expectancy as Japan during the early 1960s but has had almost no improvement since then, bringing it to only around 68 for men and 75 for women at present. During the 1970s most East European countries and the Soviet Union even experienced a decline in male life expectancy. Western Europe and North America took an intermediate position, where life expectancy increased steadily by about two to three years per decade. The recent trend clearly points toward further improvements, and the analysis of age- and cause-specific mortality trends do not give any indications of an imminent leveling off of improvements (Valkonen, 1991). Also studies on occupational mortality differentials in the Nordic countries – which are more homogeneous than countries in many other regions – still show significant inequalities, mostly by social class (Andersen,

1991), which may be taken as an indication of the possibility of further improvements if the higher-mortality groups change their lifestyles.

The considerations and high values outlined above made us assume future improvements that are much more significant than those assumed by most other national and international population projections. Assuming life expectancy to increase by three years per decade to 2030, however, we are still below recently observed improvements in Japan and parts of Western Europe. The resulting central variant of a two-year improvement per decade also seems plausible, as supported by Mesle (1993). A broader margin was chosen only for Eastern Europe because of greater uncertainties: 0.5 years was taken as the lower value assuming a continuation of the past slow improvements; 4.0 was taken as the upper value because there is a greater potential to catch up with the West if lifestyles should become similar to the Western pattern.

Health and mortality conditions in the developing regions have generally experienced very impressive improvements since World War II. Life expectancy in all developing countries has increased by more than 20 years since 1950–1955, when it was estimated to be around 40 years for both men and women. Some regions, such as East and West Asia, have seen especially rapid increases. Latin America, which already had higher life expectancies during the 1950s, has by now achieved lower mortality levels than Africa and Asia. In the Caribbean, the mortality decline is particularly impressive. These rapid improvements in mortality have led institutions that produce population projections to constantly change their assumptions. The UN had to move up the assumed life expectancy limit for men from 72.6 years, assumed in 1973, in steps to 82.5 years, assumed in 1988. Equal adjustments had to be made for women (see Chapter 7).

As with fertility, Africa seems to have the greatest uncertainties of all regions. In Chapter 8, Garenne concludes his survey of African mortality by stating that past trends in Africa have been induced by transfers of technology from the West, which affected virtually all countries in a short period of time. Public health, nutrition, economic development, and modern education were the key determinants of mortality decline. There are reasons for assuming that this declining trend of the past 30 years will not continue in Africa, and that differences between countries will prevail or even increase. This may be due to the spread of infectious diseases, especially the HIV virus, as well as problems of basic subsistence and food supply (see Chapter 10). In Chapter 9, Bongaarts presents a new calculation of the possible mortality impact of AIDS in Africa. Translated into life expectancies and projected further into the future, his calculations result in a considerable range of uncertainties. For sub-Saharan Africa, the values assumed for the scenario assumptions, which include not only AIDS but other uncertainties, are further increases of three years per decade in the best case and declines of three years per decade in the worst case. Consequently, the central value shows stagnation at the present level.

In the other developing regions, a general increase in life expectancy of between one and three years per decade has been assumed. In South Asia and Southeast Asia, which are more seriously affected by AIDS, the range was chosen to be greater assuming no improvements in the low case and 4 years per decade in the high case. For the Islamic regions of North Africa and West and Central Asia, a minimum increase of 0.5 years and a maximum increase of 4 years was chosen reflecting their somewhat greater potential for improvements.[3]

15.1.3 Future interregional migration

Of the three components of population change, international migration is the most difficult to examine for two reasons: less reliable and representative statistical information is available for assessing past and present migration levels; and migration patterns tend to show much less continuity with intensities, changing significantly within very short time periods depending on changing policies. Recent immigration trends in Western Europe clearly demonstrate the volatility of migration trends. During the early 1970s West Germany had an annual net migration gain of more than 300,000; five years later this had declined to only around 6,000 and even 3,000 during the early 1980s. During 1985–1989, however, the annual net gain increased sharply again to 378,000, 100 times that of the previous period. Few other countries have these extreme fluctuations, but the traditional immigration countries – USA, Canada, and Australia –

Table 15.3. Matrix of assumed high values of annual net migration flows, in thousands.

From	To North America	West Asia	Japan/ Australia	Western Europe	Eastern Europe	All
North Africa	90	15	20	275	75	475
Sub-Saharan Africa	115	5	40	275	75	510
Central America	550	0	10	45	45	650
South America	150	5	15	45	45	260
West Asia	25	0	10	10	20	65
South Asia	300	15	80	150	290	835
China	220	0	40	50	160	470
Southeast Asia	550	10	135	150	290	1,135
Total	2,000	50	350	1,000	1,000	4,400

show remarkable ups and downs. Annual net migration to Australia has declined from 112,000 in the early 1970s to 54,000 in the late 1970s. During the 1980s it increased again to over 100,000. For the United States and Canada only immigration figures are given, which for the USA shows a steady increase from around 280,000 per year during the early 1960s to around 800,000 during the early 1980s. In 1990–1991 the figures have declined to under 700,000.

Aside from the migration streams into Western Europe, North America, and Australia/New Zealand, labor migration within Asia has been remarkable over recent decades. For instance, during the late 1980s more than 430,000 workers left the Philippines annually, with around 280,000 of them going to the Middle East. The Republic of Korea lost an average of 170,000 workers per year during the early 1980s, India lost 240,000, and Pakistan lost 130,000 during the same period. The largest proportion of these workers went to the oil-rich countries in the Middle East. During the late 1980s these migratory streams within Asia have shown significant declines.

Due to the volatility of these trends, described systematically in Chapter 13, and the great role that short-term political changes play in both the receiving and sending countries, it is more difficult to speculate about the future of migratory streams than about future fertility and mortality trends. Furthermore, net migration always results from the combination of two partly independent migration streams, namely, that entering and that leaving a certain region for whatever reasons. These reasons are sometimes grouped into political (asylum seekers), economic (expected differentials in standard of living), and recently environmental factors. This last category remains rather vague because worsening environmental conditions often result from worsening economic conditions. As pointed out in Chapter 14, for all categories there seems to be great potential for further increases in interregional migration due to better communications between the regions, cheap mass transport facilities, and the persistent gap between the North, which is not only richer but also rapidly aging and most likely in need of young labor, and the South, which has many young people with low-income opportunities in their home countries.

The actual extent of future South–North migration streams depends not only on the pull and push factors, but also on the migrant acceptance policies in the receiving countries. If the European Union, for instance, decides to enforce a policy of virtually closed outside borders because of popular demand within the Union, this may well result in a situation of almost no net migration. Hence in the projections, zero was the low value chosen for net migration for all regions. This does not mean that borders will be entirely closed to migrants; it only assumes that the number of in-migrants approximately equals the number of out-migrants.

For the high-migration scenarios, annual net migration gains of 2 million in North America, 1 million in Western Europe, and 350,000 in Japan/Australia/New Zealand have been assumed. For Eastern Europe special assumptions were made for the period 1990–2030 with out-migration dominating the first decade, then a gradual replacement by immigration peaking at a surplus of 1 million in 2030. This also considers possible immigration from East Asia into Siberia.

The distribution of migrants from the assumed sending regions to the receiving regions and migration patterns among the less developed regions are based mostly on currently observed migratory streams. *Table 15.3* gives the assumed migration matrix in the high-migration case. In the low-migration case, all cells are zero; in the central scenario, values are half of those given in *Table 15.3*. Annual net migration loss is assumed to be 475,000 in North Africa, 510,000

in sub-Saharan Africa, 650,000 in Central America, 260,000 in South
America, 15,000 in West Asia, 835,000 in South Asia, 470,000 in
China, and 1,135,000 in Southeast Asia. Model migration schedules by Rogers and Castro (1981) were used to determine the age
patterns of migrants.

For Eastern Europe, net migration flows were assumed to change
significantly over time. The gain from developing regions was assumed to increase from 200,000 today to a net migration gain of 1
million (stated in *Table 15.3*) that is reached in 2030 and is assumed
to be largely a function of Asian migration into Siberia, which as
part of Russia belongs to Eastern Europe in this study. Simultaneously, Eastern Europe is assumed to experience a net loss to the
West of 500,000 annually, which would gradually decline to zero by
2010. The rationale behind this is an expected economic recovery
in Eastern Europe over the next two decades. In summary, the assumptions imply migration losses in the near future but significant
gains in the longer term.

15.2   Results from Alternative Population Projections until 2030

Taking 1990 as the starting year, the alternative scenario projections were carried out for the 12 world regions separately in five-year
steps, using MPOPS software for multistate population projections.
MPOPS, recently developed in collaboration with IIASA, uses age
distributions for all regions in 1990 based on UN (1993) data. As
described in Chapter 2, eight scenarios are defined by systematic
permutations of the high and low values assumed for fertility, mortality, and migration, and one central scenario combines the three
central, assumptions which in all cases are the means of the high
and low values.

The values chosen as the high, central, and low assumptions to
the year 2030 are presented in Section 15.1. In the case of fertility,
the values stated in *Table 15.1* only refer to the endpoint 2030. Fertility rates for the intermediate period have been derived from linear
interpolation between the present value and the value assumed for
2030. In today's industrialized countries the values given in *Table
15.1* are assumed to be reached by 2010. For mortality, the scenarios

have been defined in terms of improvement in life expectancy per decade. For migration the assumed levels of net migration are applied immediately and remain constant thereafter except for Eastern Europe, where a special path has been assumed.

Tables with results from all nine scenarios in all 12 regions as well as the world total and developing and industrialized countries together are given in the Appendices to the volume. These tables contain total population sizes, mean ages of the population, average annual growth rates, annual number of births, proportions of children aged 0–15, and proportions aged 60 years and over. Detailed age distributions are available on diskette.

15.2.1 Population size by region

Figures 15.1 and *15.2* give the results of the alternative scenario projections for the total world population and the population in today's industrialized regions from 1990 to 2030 and extended to 2050. As discussed above, scenarios have only been defined until 2030, but to illustrate some of the longer-term implications extensions to 2050 assuming constant rates beyond 2030 are given in the shaded area. The figure for today's developing countries is very similar to that of the world total and is therefore omitted.

Figure 15.1 clearly shows that further world population growth is certain. Unless an unpredictable, major disaster occurs, the world population will grow by at least another 50 percent to above 8 billion before the year 2030. It may also increase by 100 percent and reach close to 11 billion by the year 2030. All likely futures of world population growth lie within this range, i.e., between a 50 percent and 100 percent increase by 2030. The central scenario yields a total world population of 9.4 billion in 2030, corresponding to an increase of roughly 80 percent.

Extended beyond 2030, the high-fertility scenarios show further significant population growth, which in combination with low mortality would reach 15 billion by 2050. The central scenario extended beyond 2030 shows significant further growth to 11 billion by 2050, and even the scenario combining low fertility with low mortality results in further population growth mostly due to the momentum of population growth. Only low fertility combined with high mortality results in a clear leveling off and even a slight decline before 2050.

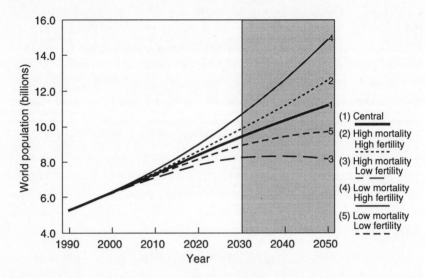

Figure 15.1. Alternative projected paths of world population size.

An astonishing feature of this figure is that mortality assumptions seem to make a much bigger difference than demographers tend to expect. Different mortality assumptions bring the high-fertility/low-mortality scenario more than halfway toward the central scenario. In 2020, for instance, the high-mortality/high-fertility scenario results in 200 million more people than the central scenario, but the low-mortality/high-fertility scenario results in 580 million more.

Compared over all scenarios, the total effect of mortality variation is about half that of the effect of fertility variation because of fertility's multiplicative effect. But this extent is still astonishing to demographers who tend to believe that fertility makes the biggest difference and look at curves that only differ by fertility. Of course, the relative impact of mortality depends on the degree of variation assumed in mortality, and this study assumes more variation than usual. In fact most projections, such as those published by the UN and the World Bank, do not assume any mortality variation. Naturally, their results only vary with fertility. A fair assessment of relative future effects needs to have a comparable degree of variability in all input parameters. In our scenario, definitions of low and high assumptions for fertility and mortality should by definition be

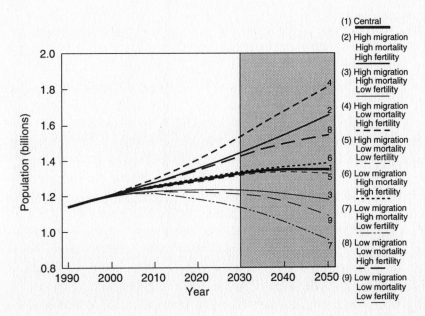

Figure 15.2. Alternative projected paths of population size in today's industrialized countries.

of comparable likelihood. They both follow a smooth path of adjustment. Hence it presents about as fair an assessment as one can assume given today's knowledge.

Trends in population growth are extremely divergent in different regions of the world. In Western Europe, the central scenario yields a mere 10 percent increase by 2030, but in sub-Saharan Africa it results in a tripling of the population. The central scenario results in a 35 percent increase in North America, a 75 percent increase in South America, and a 50 percent increase in China. Roughly a doubling of the population will occur in North Africa and South Asia as well as in Central America and the Caribbean.

High fertility combined with low mortality and low migration results in the highest world population growth of all scenarios. This scenario also gives the highest population growth in each developing region. Among others it results in a 3.6-fold increase of the sub-Saharan population and a 66 percent increase in the Chinese population. In the industrialized regions naturally the combination of high migration with high fertility and low mortality reaches higher population sizes, because migration streams are mostly assumed to flow into the industrialized countries. For all industrialized countries this increment due to migration is an extra 110 million people by 2030.

Figure 15.2 shows that in the industrialized countries, which in 1990 had 1.14 billion inhabitants, some further population increase is already preprogrammed and almost certain to take place until 2010, when the population will reach at least 1.21 billion, possibly even 1.3 billion. By 2030 some scenarios will have already resulted in a declining trend of population sizes. In the scenario that combines low fertility with high mortality and low migration, the population size of today's industrialized countries will be even lower in 2030 than it was in 1990. Compared over all scenarios, the range by 2030 is from a 1 percent decline in that scenario to a 35 percent increase in the case of high fertility, low mortality, and high migration. However, even within the industrialized countries, significant regional differences range between a 12 percent and 60 percent increase in North America, and between a 4 percent decline and a 25 percent increase in Western Europe.

The different paths of future population growth in different regions will inevitably lead to significant changes in the regional composition of the world's population. The lower part of *Table 15.4* illustrates these changes. *Table 15.5* gives the information for all industrialized and developing regions grouped together. The population of the industrialized countries in 1990 comprised 22 percent of the world's population. Under the central scenario, this proportion will decrease to a mere 14 percent by 2030. This decrease comes despite a 13 percent increase in population size. The population size of the developing countries is projected to increase by almost 100 percent, i.e., double, during the same time. The table indicates that this trend of changing regional weights in terms of population size is predetermined and practically inevitable. Under all scenarios the proportions of industrialized countries declines to between 13 percent and 15 percent by 2030, down from 22 percent in 1990. This is partly already embedded in today's age structure in both hemispheres, and also results from present fertility differentials and the assumption of only gradual changes. But even the assumption of

Table 15.4. Total population size and percentage distributions by region resulting from four selected scenarios by 2030.

	Population (millions) in 2030				
Region	1990	Central	High migr. High mort. Low fert.	Low migr. Low mort. High fert.	Low migr. Low mort. Low fert.
North Africa	140	330	276	388	312
Sub-Saharan Africa	502	1,496	1,199	1,825	1,424
North America	277	375	362	387	328
Central America & Caribbean	147	288	251	328	279
South America	294	515	463	572	488
West & Central Asia	197	442	397	487	419
South Asia	1,191	2,426	2,145	2,722	2,349
China & Hong Kong	1,159	1,722	1,538	1,927	1,610
Southeast Asia	518	934	814	1,059	909
Japan, Australia, & New Zealand	144	160	149	172	150
Eastern Europe	345	379	335	425	351
Western Europe	377	415	388	444	385
World total	5,291	9,482	8,317	10,736	9,004
	Percentage distribution in 2030				
Region	1990	Central	High migr. High mort. Low fert.	Low migr. Low mort. High fert.	Low migr. Low mort. Low fert.
North Africa	2.6	3.5	3.3	3.6	3.5
Sub-Saharan Africa	9.5	15.8	14.4	17.0	15.8
North America	5.2	4.0	4.4	3.6	3.6
Central America & Caribbean	2.8	3.0	3.0	3.1	3.1
South America	5.6	5.4	5.6	5.3	5.4
West & Central Asia	3.7	4.7	4.8	4.5	4.7
South Asia	22.5	25.6	25.8	25.4	26.1
China & Hong Kong	21.9	18.2	18.5	17.9	17.9
Southeast Asia	9.8	9.9	9.8	9.9	10.1
Japan, Australia, & New Zealand	2.7	1.7	1.8	1.6	1.7
Eastern Europe	6.5	4.0	4.0	4.0	3.9
Western Europe	7.1	4.3	4.7	4.1	4.3
World total	100.0	100.0	100.0	100.0	100.0

Table 15.5. Distribution of total population, births, children, and elderly in developing and industrialized countries, 1990 and 2030, according to selected scenarios.

		Developing countries		Industrialized countries	
		Absolute	Share	Absolute	Share
1990	Total population	4,149	78%	1,142	22%
	Births	115	88%	15	12%
	Children 0–14	1,477	86%	236	14%
	Elderly 60+	286	59%	198	41%
2030	Central scenario				
	Total population	8,167	86%	1,333	14%
	Births	165	92%	15	8%
	Children 0–14	2,270	90%	247	10%
	Elderly 60+	996	73%	373	27%
2030	Low migr./Low mort./High fert.				
	Total population	9,309	87%	1,427	13%
	Births	222	92%	19	8%
	Children 0–14	2,988	92%	275	8%
	Elderly 60+	1,210	75%	410	25%
2030	Low migr./Low mort./Low fert.				
	Total population	7,790	87%	1,159	13%
	Births	122	93%	9	7%
	Children 0–14	1,877	94%	115	6%
	Elderly 60+	1,082	72%	417	28%

instant replacement fertility would result in a decline to 17 percent (Lutz and Prinz, 1991).

No matter which scenario is chosen, Africa will expand its share in the world population most rapidly. It will increase from today's 12 percent to a projected 19 percent in 2030. In the face of this overwhelming increase in Africa, most other world regions will be stagnant in their shares or even lose percentages in the long run. China, which in 1990 had a share of 22 percent (equal to that of the industrialized world), is projected to decline under the central scenario to 18 percent in 2030. The most populous region in 1990, South Asia (which includes India), is likely to expand its share somewhat by 2030 and be home to more than a quarter of the world's population.

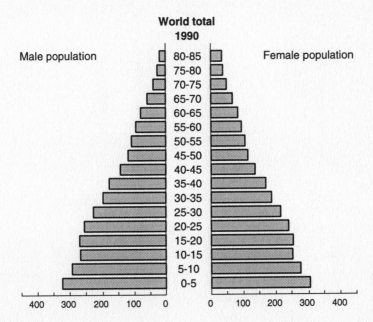

Figure 15.3a. Age pyramid for the world population in 1990, in thousands.

The changing distribution of people over the world regions also has an important age dimension. Because the growing populations are much younger, the regional distribution of children is changing more radically than that of the total population, while the proportion of all men and women above age 60 in today's industrialized countries will still be rather large in 2030, even under widely diverging scenario assumptions. Some of the relevant information is summarized in *Table 15.5*. Already in 1990, 88 percent of all children of the world were born in developing countries and a mere 12 percent in the industrialized regions, where still 41 percent of the world's elderly population (60 years and older) lives. Of the world population above age 75 more than half lives in the industrialized countries.

By the year 2030, this pattern will definitely change. It is amazing to see that even the most divergent scenarios produce very similar results in terms of the population distribution between industrialized and developing countries. This information, as shown in *Table 15.5*, indicates that the patterns for the future are very robust. It is

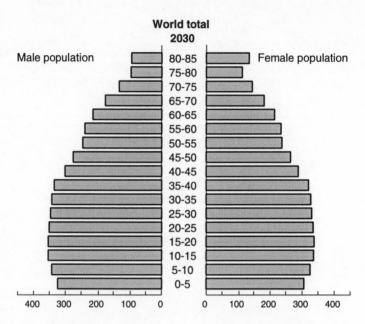

Figure 15.3b. Age pyramid for the world population in 2030 under the low-mortality/low-fertility scenario, in thousands.

practically certain that by 2030, between 92 percent and 93 percent of all births will be in today's developing countries, and only 7 percent or 8 percent in today's industrialized countries. For the time beyond 2030, this implies further changes in regional weights, as is discussed in the context of the very long-term projections in Chapter 16. Similarly the proportion of all children under age 15 living in developing countries will increase from 86 percent to between 90 percent and 94 percent. Because in today's developing countries larger cohorts will also survive to older ages, the proportion of the world's elderly population living in those regions will increase from 59 percent today to between 72 percent and 75 percent, again a statement that can be made with great certainty because all scenarios point in the same direction.

Finally, these considerations bring us to the more explicit analysis of future age structures. *Figure 15.3* graphically presents the consequences of alternative scenarios in the shape of age pyramids. *Figure 15.3a* presents the global male and female populations in 1990, the starting year of our projections. *Figures 15.3b* and *15.3c*

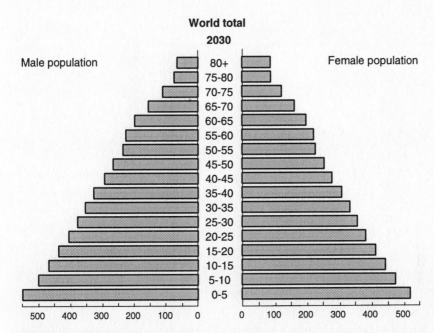

Figure 15.3c. Age pyramid for the world population in 2030 under the high-mortality/high-fertility scenario, in thousands.

give two age distributions projected for the year 2030 using the same scale, i.e., the lengths of the bars are comparable. *Figure 15.3b* presents the scenario resulting in the greatest degree of global population aging. It clearly illustrates the departure from the pyramid shape and the narrowing at the bottom, which is due to subreplacement fertility at the global level. Although total population size will be 56 percent larger (8.9 billion) than in 1990, under this scenario, the youngest age group 0–5 will have approximately the same size in 2030 as it had in 1990. Higher age groups increase most significantly. The age groups above age 50 will already have about twice their 1990 size. Above age 60, the increase is even greater. Above age 75, the number of women is clearly larger than the number of men – a phenomenon now only visible in the industrialized countries. *Figure 15.3c* contrasts this with the case of high fertility and high mortality. This is the *youngest* scenario, resulting almost in a doubling of the world population (9.9 billion) by 2030. The graph looks like a perfect pyramid with an almost linear slope that signals

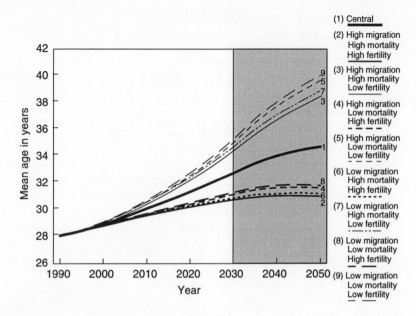

Figure 15.4. Alternative projected trends in the mean age of the world population.

continued population growth through ever-increasing cohort sizes at the bottom. These figures graphically demonstrate the fact that larger population growth means less aging and smaller population growth results in more aging.

15.2.2 Population aging

Population aging, a phenomenon that is already well recognized and a cause of concern in the industrialized countries, will also increasingly affect developing countries. In all regions, all scenarios result in aging, as measured by the mean age of the population or the proportion of the population above age 60. *Figure 15.4* shows that the mean age of the world population today is around 28 years. Only 9.2 percent of the world population is above age 60, while 32 percent are under age 15 (*Table 15.6*). Under all scenarios, the mean age and the proportion above age 60 will significantly increase over the next decades. This is another certainty in the future course of the world population. Even under the high-fertility and low-mortality

Table 15.6. Proportions of the population above age 60 resulting from selected scenarios by 2030.

Region	1990	Four scenarios in 2030			
		Central	High migr. High mort. Low fert.	Low migr. Low mort. High fert.	Low migr. Low mort. Low fert.
North Africa	5.6	8.4	8.6	7.9	9.8
Sub-Saharan Africa	4.6	4.8	5.1	4.5	5.8
North America	16.7	25.6	24.2	26.9	31.7
Central America & Caribbean	6.4	13.2	13.6	12.1	14.2
South America	7.6	14.8	15.8	14.1	16.5
West & Central Asia	6.6	11.1	11.2	11.1	12.9
South Asia	6.5	10.2	10.3	10.0	11.6
China & Hong Kong	8.8	20.9	22.2	20.0	24.0
Southeast Asia	6.3	13.5	13.6	13.2	15.3
Japan, Australia, & New Zealand	16.9	31.8	31.1	32.3	37.0
Eastern Europe	15.8	26.0	25.8	26.5	32.1
Western Europe	19.6	30.6	30.1	31.1	35.8
World total	9.2	14.3	15.0	13.9	16.6

scenario, which gives the lowest degree of population aging, the mean age of the world population will increase to 31 years by 2030. Under the low-fertility scenarios it will even reach 35 years, the present mean age of the North American population. With respect to the proportion above age 60 – an indicator that is more relevant for the old-age dependency burden of a society – the increase is even more rapid. By 2030 this proportion will increase from its present 9.2 percent to at least 12.7 percent under high fertility and high mortality, and at most 16.6 percent under low fertility and low mortality, i.e., an increase of between 40 percent and 80 percent. The central scenario yields a percentage of 14.3 percent above 60 by 2030.

Extended to 2050, the range of possible different speeds of aging is naturally much wider. In terms of mean age of the world population, which is currently 28 years, the high-fertility scenarios result in 31 years, the central scenario in 35 years, and the low-fertility scenarios in around 40 years by 2050. In terms of proportions above age 60, the range is from about 13 percent in the scenarios yielding very

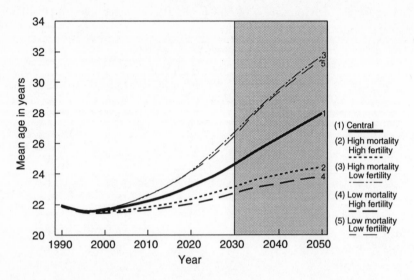

Figure 15.5. Alternative projected trends in the mean age in sub-Saharan Africa.

rapid population growth to 22 percent in the scenarios assuming rapid fertility declines. However, in various world regions ranges are much wider.

Figure 15.5 shows the projected future paths of the mean age of the population in sub-Saharan Africa – the region associated with the greatest uncertainties. Because of past high fertility, it is predetermined that the mean age will show a slight decline over the next few years. Thereafter, it is very likely to increase to between 23 and 26 years by 2030. A curbing of population growth that results *only* in somewhat more than a doubling of the population by 2050 will increase the mean age to around 32 years. This would mean serious problems in care for the elderly in societies that so far mostly rely on family support and have little government action in this field. Given the uncertainties about the future of AIDS, other infectious diseases, political instabilities, and civil wars possibly associated with famines, aging is probably not the most immediate concern in sub-Saharan Africa. In the context of the scenarios described here, the sections in Chapter 16 on feedbacks define severe

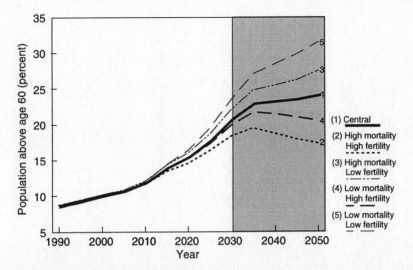

Figure 15.6. Alternative projected trends in the proportion of population above age 60 in China.

disaster scenarios for sub-Saharan Africa that result in significant temporary population losses due to excessive growth resulting in famines and wars.

China is one developing region where very rapid aging will certainly occur because fertility has already declined. *Figure 15.6* shows the increases in the proportions above age 60 under all different scenarios. This proportion will increase from a present 8.8 percent to around 20 percent by 2030 with a rather small range of uncertainty. Because this aging is already preprogrammed in the present age distribution, all scenarios show a similar increase. Hence in only 35 years China will have a higher old-age dependency burden than North America and about the same as Western Europe today. Given that Western Europe took more than a century to develop social-security schemes for the elderly and is confronted with serious problems today, China will have to make immediate intensive efforts to cope with this problem. China's authorities are well aware of this problem and are considering not pushing fertility too low in order to avoid too large imbalances in the age structure of the population.

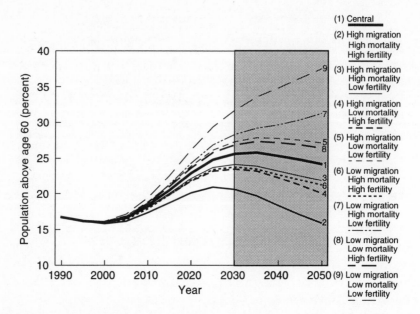

Figure 15.7. Alternative projected trends in the proportion of population above age 60 in North America.

Some of the other developing regions that recently experienced fertility declines are also certain to experience population aging. In Southeast Asia, the proportion above 60 will at least double by 2030. In South and Central America, the situation is very similar to Southeast Asia. In North Africa and West Asia, where fertility is still higher, aging is also certain but somewhat slower, at least until 2030; thereafter everything depends on the assumed future paths of fertility and to some degree also on mortality.

In the more developed regions, the proportion elderly is already rather high today, but further significant increases are inevitable due to the current age structure that reflects the low fertility and declining old-age mortality of the past decades. *Figure 15.7* gives the projected proportions above age 60 for North America. In 1990 this proportion was 16.7 percent. Over the next decade it is likely to even decline slightly due to the baby boom generation and their children that increase the population below age 60. In contrast, the mean age of the population already shows an increasing trend from 35 years today to around 37 years in 2010. After 2010 the baby boomers start to reach age 60, affecting the proportion above age 60, which will increase to between 21 percent and 32 percent by 2030, depending on fertility, mortality, and migration assumptions. The central scenario yields a proportion of 25.6 percent. Extensions to 2050 yield a further divergence of aging trends.

Western Europe is the world's oldest region in terms of its population. In 1990 it had a mean age of 38 years. Under all scenarios this mean age will increase to 40 years and higher by 2010. Under the scenario assuming low fertility, no net-migration gain, and increasing life expectancy, the mean age may even increase to 47 years by 2030. Extended to 2050 this scenario would result in an incredible 52 years as the average age of the population. In terms of proportions above age 60, Western Europe shows a clearly visible upward push after 2010, when the baby boomers come to retirement age. But in contrast to North America, the proportion elderly will significantly increase to around 23 percent before 2010. For 2030 the proportion elderly ranges from 26 percent to 36 percent. Extensions to 2050 yield a range from 23 percent to 43 percent of the population above age 60. It is hard to imagine today how such an aged society should function. But assuming further improvements in the health status of men and women above age 60 and productivity increases of the labor force, it is not entirely inconceivable.

One controversial issue that is being discussed more heatedly in Europe than in other regions is whether immigration can compensate for low fertility. The given scenario approach is an ideal setting to evaluate this question, which is discussed in detail in Lutz and Prinz (1993). The alternative scenario projections show for Western Europe that even very high constant annual net-migration gains of 1 million a year cannot fully compensate for the low fertility. In the short to medium run, immigration increases the labor force and therefore slightly dampens the increase in the proportion of the elderly. In the case of low fertility, low mortality, and no migration gain, this proportion would increase from 19.6 percent in 1990 to 35.8 percent in 2030. If one assumes an annual migration gain of 1 million – which is very high for a sustained level – this would only reduce the proportion by 2 percentage points to 33.6 percent in 2030. Extended to 2050 even the high-immigration scenario would result in 37 percent above age 60. But by 2050 Western Europe would have received more than 60 million immigrants, who together with their children would make up a large proportion of the population, something Europeans obviously fear. Hence the only way to avoid excessive aging in Europe in the long run is higher fertility. However, even the central scenario results in 31.3 percent above age 60 in 2050, and high fertility, low mortality, and no migration gain yield a proportion of 31.8 percent. Hence in all cases, Western Europe will have to adjust to significant aging. In Japan the situation is similar and even somewhat more extreme.

15.2.3   Population growth versus population aging

When comparing the information on projected aging to that on projected population growth, one very important feature becomes apparent. The scenarios that result in the highest population growth show only moderate population aging, while those showing a leveling off in population size imply very rapid population aging. Generally, very rapid population growth and very rapid aging are considered undesirable, but the scenario projections clearly show that one cannot avoid both. An intermediate path, such as that given by the central scenario, avoids extremes but still combines at the global level substantial population growth (a tripling of population size) with substantial aging (a doubling of the proportion above 60). Since the problems caused by and the possible solutions to rapid growth and rapid aging will substantiate at a regional level rather than at the global aggregate, this issue needs to be discussed within a more regional context. The epilogue to this volume takes up some of the policy issues related to the aging versus population growth dilemma.

15.2.4   Conclusion

The systematic permutation scenarios to 2030 described in this chapter show that three major certainties hold across all scenarios:

1. The world population will continue to grow. By 2030 it will have increased by between 50 percent and 100 percent.
2. The regional distribution of the world population will change significantly. Today's industrialized countries will present an ever-diminishing fraction of the world population whereas the

share of the African population will rapidly increase. In 2030 between 85 percent and 87 percent will live in developing countries.

3. The world population will become older. The mean age of the population will increase. In regions that already have low fertility, this aging process will be most pronounced.

15.3 Comparison with United Nations and World Bank World Population Projections until 2025

In Chapter 2 we exhaustively argue for the need of additional world population projections, supplementary to those prepared by the UN and the World Bank. In this chapter, we discuss the results that we obtained on the basis of our scenario assumptions, for the period 1990 to 2030. Are these results indeed so different from those prepared by other analysts and agencies? If the answer is yes, what are the main differences, and what are the reasons for those differences? To answer these questions, we compare the results of our own calculations with these global projections that are most often cited: the UN and the World Bank projections.

In this comparison, the nine systematic permutation scenarios are confronted with the high, medium, and low variants offered by the UN (1993) and the single projection offered by the World Bank (1992). The constant fertility variant prepared by the UN is not further considered, as it is only prepared "for analytical purposes" (UN, 1993:84). Two aspects are of particular importance: the "most likely" path offered and the connected range of uncertainty. Both estimates of population size and population aging are compared. *Table 15.7* gives the respective information for the year 2025.

By 2025, IIASA's central estimate gives a higher world population size and a lower overall proportion of elderly than the UN medium and the World Bank estimates, the latter two being quite similar. A major reason for this difference is the less rapid decline of fertility assumed in today's developing regions. The lower estimate of the population size in today's industrialized regions is largely due to a difference in the definition of regions: in the IIASA projections, the European republics of the former Soviet Union are included in the East European region, while the Asian republics are included in

Table 15.7. Comparison of IIASA results for the year 2025 with United Nations and World Bank projections.

Scenario	Total population size (in millions)			Share of population aged 60 and over (in %)		
	IIASA	UN	WB	IIASA	UN	WB
World total						
Central	8,955	8,472	8,345	13.2	14.1	14.5
Low	8,093	7,852	–	11.9	13.2	–
High	9,871	9,080	–	14.9	15.2	–
Developing regions						
Central	7,645	7,069	6,944	10.9	12.1	12.0
Low	6,857	6,562	–	9.8	11.3	–
High	8,483	7,577	–	12.3	13.0	–
Industrialized regions						
Central	1,311[a]	1,403	1,401	26.5	24.5	26.6
Low	1,154[a]	1,290	–	22.9	23.0	–
High	1,473[a]	1,503	–	31.0	26.5	–

[a]Does not include former Soviet Central Asian Republics.
IIASA projections consist of nine permutation scenarios; UN projections consist of three variants (constant fertility variant is not considered); and the World Bank projection has only one path.

the West and Central Asia region, and hence are counted as developing countries. The UN and the World Bank, on the other hand, summarize all former Soviet republics into the group of today's industrialized countries.

Independent of the difference in the regional divisions, the resulting range of uncertainty is significantly larger in the IIASA projections than in the UN projections. The resulting range of world population size is 1.8 billion in the IIASA scenarios versus 1.2 billion in the UN projections. The broader range in population size estimates is a consequence of both the mortality and the fertility uncertainties assumed; in the case of the industrialized region, however, migration assumptions play a significant role. The broader range in the proportion elderly is mostly a consequence of the mortality uncertainty assumed in the IIASA projections. The World Bank does not address the question of uncertainty.

Notes

[1] In all regions, 1990 age patterns of fertility were kept unchanged and scaled down (or up) according to the specification of the total fertility rate.

[2] UN model life tables (UN, 1982) corresponding to the respective region were used as input for 1990 to obtain age-specific mortality rates for today's developing regions. For the remaining regions, observed mortality rates were used.

[3] Future age-specific mortality patterns were derived from model life tables (UN, 1982; Coale and Guo, 1989). Coale-Guo "west tables" were extended up to life expectancies of 100 to provide mortality schedules for very high life expectancies.

References

Andersen, O., 1991, Occupational impacts on mortality declines in the Nordic countries, in W. Lutz, ed., *Future Demographic Trends in Europe and North America: What Can We Assume Today?* Academic Press, London, UK.

Coale, A., and Guo, G., 1989, Revised regional model life tables at very low levels of mortality, *Population Index* **55**(4):613–643.

Lutz, W., ed., 1991, *Future Demographic Trends in Europe and North America: What Can We Assume Today?* Academic Press, London, UK.

Lutz, W., and Prinz, Ch., 1991, Scenarios for the World Population in the Next Century: Excessive Growth or Extreme Aging, WP-91-22, International Institute for Applied Systems Analysis, Laxenburg, Austria.

Lutz, W., and Prinz, Ch., 1993, Modeling future immigration and integration in Western Europe, in R. King, ed., *The New Geography of European Migrations*, Belhaven Press, London, UK.

Manton, K.G., 1991, New biotechnologies and the limits to life expectancy, in W. Lutz, ed., *Future Demographic Trends in Europe and North America: What Can We Assume Today?* Academic Press, London, UK.

Mesle, F., 1993, The future of mortality, in R. Cliquet, ed., *The Future of Europe's Population: A Scenario Approach*, The Council of Europe, European Population Committee, Strasbourg, France.

Rogers, A., and Castro, L., 1981, *Model Migration Schedules*, RR-81-30, International Institute for Applied Systems Analysis, Laxenburg, Austria.

UN, 1982, *Model Life Tables for Developing Countries,* Population Studies, No. 77, Department of International Economic and Social Affairs, United Nations, New York, NY, USA.

UN, 1993, *World Population Prospects: The 1992 Revision,* Department for Economic and Social Information and Policy Analysis, United Nations, New York, NY, USA.

Valkonen, T., 1991, Assumptions about mortality trends in industrialized countries: A survey, in W. Lutz, ed., *Future Demographic Trends in Europe and North America: What Can We Assume Today?* Academic Press, London, UK.

Vishnevsky, A., 1991, Demographic revolution and the future of fertility: A systems approach, in W. Lutz, ed., *Future Demographic Trends in Europe and North America. What Can We Assume Today?* Academic Press, London, UK.

Westoff, C.F., 1991, The return to replacement fertility: A magnetic force? in W. Lutz, ed., *Future Demographic Trends in Europe and North America: What Can We Assume Today?* Academic Press, London, UK.

World Bank, 1992, *World Population Projections,* 1992–1993 Edition, Johns Hopkins University Press, Baltimore, MD, USA.

Chapter 16

Special World Population Scenarios to 2100

Wolfgang Lutz, Christopher Prinz, and Jeannette Langgassner

In Chapter 15, a systematic permutation approach is adopted to produce population projections to 2030. As described in Chapter 2, there is a demand for population projections with a longer time horizon. In this chapter we present such projections which extend the population scenarios to the year 2100. For such a long time horizon a different approach is required. Sensitivity issues, most relevant for the short and medium run, turn into problems of credibility and reliability. This chapter addresses the question of long-range extensions in two ways:

- One set of scenarios attempts to define plausible long-term extensions for all 12 world regions. A major assumption in the scenario design is that of a reasonable course of demographic transition, linking fertility and mortality. Three scenarios are specified for each region; parameter assumptions are made for the whole projection period.

- Another set of scenarios mainly serves to illustrate certain features of population dynamics. A number of possible interactions between demographic components and feedbacks from population size/density and aging on fertility and mortality are included. Only selected regions are considered.

16.1   Long-Term Extensions for All Regions

One possible systematic approach to long-range population projection would be an extension of all nine permutation scenarios. Some of those permutations, however, combine assumptions that seem implausible in the very long run, such as continued high mortality together with low fertility. While such a combination is possible for a couple of decades, it becomes implausible if continued indefinitely.   Also, the probability of extreme combinations decreases with increasing length of the projection.   Therefore, only less extreme assumptions (or rather combinations) are extended beyond the year 2030: the "most likely" central scenario, the high-fertility/high-mortality combination reflecting a slower completion of the demographic transition in today's developing regions, and the low-fertility/low-mortality combination mirroring a more rapid completion of the demographic transition. All three scenarios are combined with the medium migration assumption, both to simplify the interpretation of scenario results and because very little is known about long-term trends in migration.

16.1.1   Scenario assumptions

Choosing fertility levels in the very long run, at a point when all regions are assumed to have completed the fertility transition, comes close to a lottery within a certain range. For convenience, most long-range projections still choose replacement-level fertility as the ultimate level. But there is little justification for it aside from the very vague and unproven homeostasis concept. Here we suggest another rationale.   Ultimate fertility is assumed to be a function of region-specific population densities. Low densities are correlated with higher fertility, and vice versa. In our central scenario, fertility is assumed to ultimately reach a level between 1.7 and 2.1 children per woman by the year 2080, notably below replacement level in some regions. The projected density for 2030 (central scenario) is taken as a criterion. The least densely populated region – South America with 28 persons per km^2 projected for 2030 – is given the highest ultimate TFR (2.1), while beyond 300 persons per km^2 (only South Asia, with a density of 478 persons per km^2 by 2030) a TFR of 1.7 is assumed. For densities between 28 and

300, intermediate fertility levels are obtained through linear interpolation. The long-range low- and high-fertility assumptions are
set at 0.3 children below (and above) the value obtained for the
central scenario. *Table 16.1* gives, for each of the three scenarios,
(assumed) fertility and mortality levels for the years 2030 and 2100,
together with current 1990 values. Ultimate fertility in 2100 ranges
from 1.4 children per woman in South Asia under the low-fertility
assumption to 2.4 children in South America under the high-fertility
assumption.

Concerning mortality, in the long-range projections prepared by
the UN (1992), for each region one fixed path is assumed. An ultimate life expectancy at birth of 87.5 years for women and 82.5 years
for men is assumed, and improvements in life expectancy end once
the maximum figure is reached (between 2075 and 2150, depending
on the region). In sharp contrast, our mortality assumptions span
a very broad range in the very long term, reflecting the high uncertainty about possible ultimate mortality levels. In the low-mortality
case, almost no biological limit to life is assumed, mortality rate declines being extended to 2100 with a maximum life expectancy of 100
years. Life expectancy increases after 2030 are smaller than before
2030, with constant mortality under the high-mortality assumption,
a one-year increase per decade under the medium-mortality assumption, and a two-year increase per decade under the low-mortality
assumption. An ultimate life expectancy at birth of 100 years is
reached only in today's industrialized regions; the largest range of
uncertainty is found in sub-Saharan Africa (a difference of 38 years
between the low- and high-mortality assumptions by 2100).

The assumptions on fertility and mortality are combined to form
three plausible long-range world population extensions: central fertility with central mortality (central scenario extension), high fertility with high mortality (slow transition extension), and low fertility
with low mortality (rapid transition extension).

16.1.2 Population size and growth

No matter whether a medium, slow, or rapid course of demographic
transition for today's developing countries is assumed, world population size will surpass the 10 billion mark sometime in the middle
of the next century. If the demographic transition proceeds slowly,

Table 16.1. Ultimate fertility and mortality levels in three long-range assumptions by region: 2030 and 2100.

Region	Year	Fertility (TFR)			Mortality (female life expectancy at birth)		
		Low	Central	High	High[a]	Central	Low
North Africa	1990	4.66			61.1		
	2030	2.00	3.00	4.00	63.1	70.1	77.1
	2100	1.74	2.04	2.34	63.1	77.1	91.1
Sub-Saharan	1990	6.39			52.4		
Africa	2030	2.50	3.75	5.00	40.4	52.4	64.4
	2100	1.64	1.94	2.24	40.4	59.4	78.4
North America	1990	2.04			79.0		
	2030	1.40	1.85	2.30	83.0	87.0	91.0
	2100	1.79	2.09	2.39	83.0	94.0	100.0
Central America	1990	3.33			71.3		
& Caribbean	2030	1.70	2.35	3.00	75.3	79.3	83.3
	2100	1.63	1.93	2.23	75.3	86.3	97.3
South America	1990	2.91			69.6		
	2030	1.70	2.35	3.00	73.6	77.6	81.6
	2100	1.80	2.10	2.40	73.6	84.6	95.6
West &	1990	4.23			69.3		
Central Asia	2030	1.70	2.35	3.00	71.3	78.3	85.3
	2100	1.65	1.95	2.25	71.3	85.3	99.3
South Asia	1990	4.30			58.4		
	2030	1.70	2.35	3.00	58.4	66.4	74.4
	2100	1.40	1.70	2.00	58.4	73.4	88.4
China &	1990	2.20			71.8		
Hong Kong	2030	1.50	2.25	3.00	75.8	79.8	83.8
	2100	1.57	1.87	2.17	75.8	86.8	97.8
Southeast Asia	1990	3.19			65.3		
	2030	1.70	2.35	3.00	65.3	73.3	81.3
	2100	1.49	1.79	2.09	65.3	80.3	95.3
Japan, Australia,	1990	1.69			81.1		
& New Zealand	2030	1.30	1.70	2.10	85.1	89.1	93.1
	2100	1.44	1.74	2.04	85.1	96.1	100.0
Eastern Europe	1990	2.00			74.7		
	2030	1.30	1.80	2.30	76.7	83.7	90.7
	2100	1.75	2.05	2.35	76.7	90.7	100.0
Western Europe	1990	1.61			79.4		
	2030	1.30	1.70	2.10	83.4	87.4	91.4
	2100	1.59	1.89	2.19	83.4	94.4	100.0

[a]High mortality corresponds to lower life expectancies at birth.

Table 16.2. Alternative projected population sizes in developing and industrialized regions, in millions: 1990–2100.

Year	World total Central	Slow	Rapid	Developing regions Central	Slow	Rapid	Industrialized regions Central	Slow	Rapid
1990	5,291			4,149			1,142		
2010	7,352	7,427	7,271	6,097	6,154	6,033	1,255	1,273	1,238
2030	9,499	9,938	9,011	8,167	8,542	7,739	1,333	1,396	1,272
2050	11,238	12,452	9,913	9,859	10,923	8,653	1,378	1,528	1,261
2070	12,334	14,594	10,046	10,897	12,873	8,806	1,437	1,721	1,240
2100	12,562	16,090	9,126	10,980	13,994	7,885	1,582	2,096	1,241

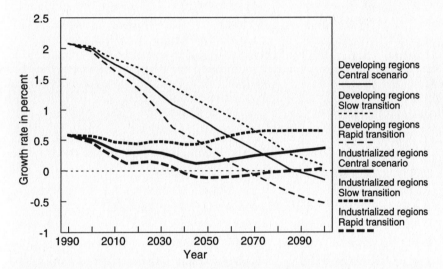

Figure 16.1. Alternative projected trends in average annual population growth rates.

total world population will even triple before starting to stabilize. Projected maximum population sizes are reached by 2090 in the central scenario (12.6 billion), by 2065 with rapid transition assumptions (10.1 billion), and by 2110 with slow transition assumptions (16.2 billion). Projected population sizes are given separately for developing and industrialized countries in *Table 16.2*. Region-specific results of the three long-range extensions are given in Appendix B.

Average annual growth rates, which start at 2.1 percent in today's developing and 0.6 percent in today's industrialized regions, are shown in *Figure 16.1*. Growth rates decline gradually

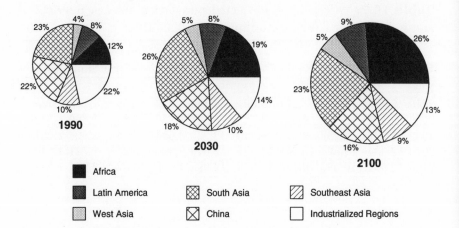

Figure 16.2. Regional distribution of world population projected under the central scenario: 1990, 2030, and 2100.

throughout the projection period in the former region, reaching negative values between around 2070 under the rapid transition and 2110 under the slow transition scenario. However, due to constantly positive net migration, growth rates decline only modestly in today's industrialized regions – a trend that is even reversed between 2040 and 2060. Under all three scenarios, in the very long run (late 21st century), population growth in these regions surpasses the respective growth in today's developing countries. This is due to both higher ultimate fertility in some of today's industrialized countries and continued immigration into these regions.

16.1.3   Regional distribution

During most of the 1990–2100 period, the population of today's developing countries and in particular of Africa – with a growth rate of still more than 1 percent annually by the year 2050 – grows very rapidly. Hence, as a consequence of both current differences and uneven future developments, the globe's regional distribution will change substantially. *Figure 16.2* gives the world's regional distribution in 1990 and the distribution projected with the central scenario for the years 2030 and 2100.

Africa will increase its share from 12 percent in 1990 to 19 percent by 2030 and even 26 percent by 2100. Today, Europe accommodates more people than Africa, but in the long run only a small fraction – or 7 percent – of the world population will live in European countries. Non-African developing countries will roughly maintain their current shares of world population, with the exception of China with a declining share under all three scenarios. Indeed, the future regional distribution – at least the direction of changes – is relatively insensitive to the course of the demographic transition assumed; it is largely determined by current demographic differentials in the 12 regions. Differences between scenarios are small.

16.1.4 Demographic transition

Scenarios have been defined in terms of age-specific fertility, mortality, and migration schedules. Crude birth and death rates, the two variables generally used to depict the process of demographic transition, are not input variables to the projections but rather result from a combination of the age-specific assumptions and the projected age distributions. Hence it is illuminating to compare their projected trends with respect to the future course of the demographic transition.

As an example, *Figure 16.3* focuses on South Asia (India and its neighbors), a region still early in the transition process. The crude birth rate in South Asia continues to decline rapidly under all scenarios. In contrast, the direction of change of the crude death rate is quite uncertain over the next 40 years, but it will certainly increase in the long run as a consequence of population aging. Much progress toward completion of the demographic transition is made during the coming decades. It will, however, most certainly not be completed before the middle or even the end of the 21st century under high-fertility assumptions, due to above-replacement fertility during the whole projection period.

16.1.5 Population aging

Substantial aging will be a major feature of future population trends in all regions of the world. While population aging is a recognized issue in today's industrialized countries, it is likely to occur even more rapidly in today's developing countries. One indicator of

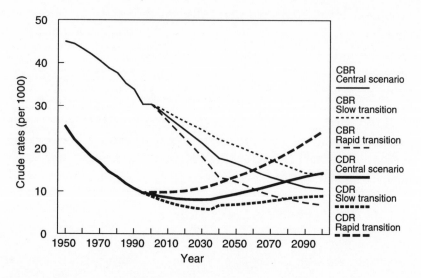

Figure 16.3. The demographic transition in South Asia, alternative projected crude birth and death rates.

Table 16.3. Projected mean ages, in years, of the populations in developing and industrialized regions: 1990–2100.

Year	World total			Developing regions			Industrialized regions		
	Central	Slow	Rapid	Central	Slow	Rapid	Central	Slow	Rapid
1990	28.1			25.9			36.1		
2010	30.2	29.7	30.7	28.4	28.0	28.8	39.0	38.2	40.0
2030	32.9	31.0	35.3	31.5	29.7	33.7	41.6	38.6	44.9
2050	35.5	31.8	40.5	34.5	31.0	39.3	42.5	37.5	48.4
2070	37.8	33.3	45.0	37.2	32.8	44.2	42.7	36.8	50.2
2100	41.3	36.5	50.0	41.1	36.5	49.8	43.0	36.8	51.1

aging which is strongly influenced by all three demographic components – fertility, mortality, and migration – is the mean age of the population. *Table 16.3*, distinguishing between developing and industrialized regions, shows an increase between 10 and 24 years in the projected mean age of today's developing regions. Aging in industrialized regions will be significantly more modest: under the high-fertility/high-mortality scenario, the mean age is projected to remain almost stable. As a consequence, age-structure differences between the two world regions are gradually reduced.

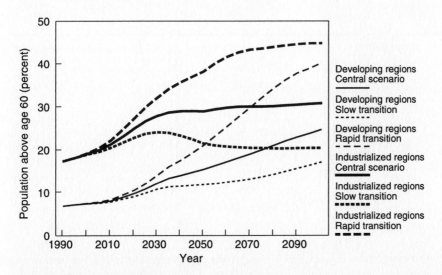

Figure 16.4. Alternative projected trends in the proportion of the population above age 60.

This convergence of age structures is also visible from *Figure 16.4*, which gives the proportion of the population aged 60 years and over, currently ranging from 4.6 percent in sub-Saharan Africa to 19.6 percent in Western Europe. The speed of aging will most likely be more rapid in today's developing countries, the more so under scenarios that limit population growth. Only further exponential growth of the population would keep the population young. The long-range calculations strongly support the point made for the systemic permutation scenarios until 2030 about the fundamental dilemma of future population trends in today's developing countries: either the population explodes in size or it ages to an unprecedented extent. None of these countries seems to be prepared for either development.

Figure 16.4 also shows the enormous uncertainty with regard to the future age structure. Taking today's industrialized regions as an example, a society with 20 percent elderly projected with the high-fertility/high-mortality scenario is totally different from a society with almost 45 percent elderly derived from the low-fertility/low-mortality scenario. While the range of uncertainty is equally broad in all regions, after around 2060 the proportion of elderly remains relatively stable in today's industrialized countries.

The dilemma between population growth and population aging and the trade-off between speed and extent of aging are discussed in some detail in the epilogue of this book.

16.2 Special Interaction Scenarios for Selected Regions

In this section we consider some specific scenarios assuming a higher degree of interaction between the three components and also allowing for feedback from output parameters, such as population size and age structure, to the components. First, we assume dependence between the three components themselves. Dependence between fertility and mortality is not further considered in this section since it is already taken into account in the specification of the three long-range extensions. Migration is, among many other things, a function of fertility, mortality, and in particular demographic differences between regions. However, it is also largely dependent on political measures; therefore we have decided not to adjust long-term migration levels. On the other hand, given the level of migration assumed in the long-range extensions, fertility levels might indeed be affected. The effect of an increase in overall fertility in today's industrialized regions from large inflows of migrants whose average fertility is significantly higher is investigated below.

Future fertility, mortality, and migration, to a largely unknown degree, may also be assumed to depend on other demographic variables, most prominently population size and age structure. As there is no consensus about how such a dependence might operate, explicit feedbacks from those demographic output variables to any one of the input components are usually not specified. Although there is full consensus that world population cannot grow indefinitely, no statement has been made in population projections about possible levels at which the world's capacity would be exhausted. Instead, one usually assumes long-term convergence to a stable population. At least for illustrative purposes, however, we should also investigate what would happen if humanity was not able to *naturally* find its way to stabilization. Or, what could happen if world population, or the population of any of its regions, continued to grow rapidly until reaching a threshold at which some sort of collapse, e.g., as a consequence of food constraints, seems unavoidable. Taking sub-Saharan Africa as an example, we show possible demographic effects of such an evolution given a certain population carrying capacity derived from agricultural data.

Similarly, persistent population aging might cause problems in society that trigger actions which in course may have an effect on some of the demographic components. Obviously, as the example of today's industrialized countries shows, populations can adapt to gradual changes in the age structure, at least up to a certain level. Very rapid aging, on the other hand, will certainly create structural problems. Again for illustrative reasons, one might think of a reaction to population aging in the form of a fertility increase. Society might increasingly consider the large number of elderly as a serious burden in many respects, which in turn might influence individual decision-making processes, especially if some very strong incentives for childbearing are introduced. Proportions of elderly beyond certain thresholds might therefore lead to a larger number of births. In the following sections, the three types of interactions suggested above are exemplified.

16.2.1 Higher fertility of immigrants affecting fertility in today's industrialized regions

To investigate the impact of high fertility among immigrants, the high-immigration/low-fertility regions (North America and Western Europe) are considered. The low-fertility/low-mortality extension is taken as an example. It is assumed that overall immigrant fertility is three children per woman, and that all first-generation immigrants maintain this higher fertility level throughout their lives. Second-generation immigrants, on the other hand, are assumed to immediately adapt to the country's low fertility level. Resulting fertility levels for the two regions, both with and without consideration of the higher fertility rates of immigrants, are given in *Table 16.4*. By 2100, the total fertility rate would be higher by 0.39 children in North America and by 0.27 children in Western Europe in the case of high fertility among immigrants (i.e., "adjusted" in *Table 16.4*).

Table 16.4. Total fertility rate and resulting population size (in millions) in North America and Western Europe under the special immigration–fertility interaction scenario.

	North America				Western Europe			
	TFR		Population		TFR		Population	
Year	Initial	Adjusted	Initial	Adjusted	Initial	Adjusted	Initial	Adjusted
1990	2.04		277		1.61		377	
2010	1.40	1.50	321	322	1.30	1.34	399	400
2030	1.40	1.58	356	362	1.30	1.39	400	403
2050	1.51	1.77	378	391	1.38	1.52	385	390
2070	1.62	1.94	404	429	1.47	1.66	365	373
2100	1.79	2.18	453	512	1.59	1.86	344	363

The difference is due to the higher level of immigration assumed into North America.

The effect on population size is very small, until around 2050 even negligible. By 2100, population size would be higher by 13 percent in North America and by 5.5 percent in Western Europe if the higher fertility rates of immigrants are considered (see *Table 16.4*). Similarly, effects on the population's age structures are also small, with the proportion elderly, for example, by 2100 being reduced from 39.3 percent to 36.2 percent in North America and from 49.7 to 47.2 percent in Western Europe. If first-generation immigrants adapt somewhat to the fertility level of their *new* country, these effects could even be smaller. The conclusion is that disregarding the question of fertility of immigrants does not introduce serious distortions in the short and medium term if immigration levels and fertility differentials are not too extreme.

16.2.2 Overshooting carrying capacity in sub-Saharan Africa

Obviously, *something* is going to happen if the population grows too rapidly or if the population density (in a certain region) passes a certain threshold. In the following, we attempt to define scenarios that explicitly assume feedbacks from population size or density on mortality. Sub-Saharan Africa is chosen as an example because it is the region that will probably experience the most rapid population growth. It is also the only region that might easily surpass

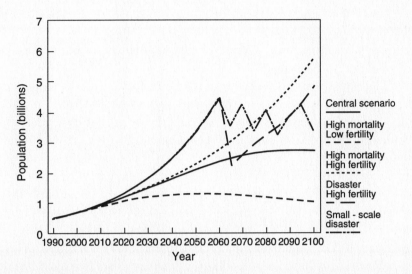

Figure 16.5. Projected population size in sub-Saharan Africa, with and without feedback on mortality.

the critical point of population size that was derived from a joint FAO/UNFPA/IIASA (1984) land-carrying capacity study. In this study, an agricultural carrying capacity of 4 billion people had been given for sub-Saharan Africa assuming medium agricultural inputs. The low input scenario resulted in sufficient agricultural production for only less than 1 billion.[1]

Figure 16.5 gives future population sizes in sub-Saharan Africa projected until 2100, including some feedback and disaster scenarios. The solid line gives the evolution derived from the central extension, with a gradual increase in population size over the next 80 years and a stabilization at around 2.7 billion people in the long run. All other lines reflect disastrous developments. Both the dotted line and the short dashed line (which begin in 1990) assume gradually increasing mortality (high-mortality or *unspectacular misery* scenarios). In these scenarios, like under the high-mortality permutation for that region, life expectancy decreases by three years per decade until 2030 and then remains constant. This reflects the possible condition of a slowly spreading mortality crisis which could be due to AIDS, deteriorating health systems, local famines, and regional conflicts. Fertility rates in these two scenarios are similar to the high- and low-fertility permutations until 2030, but are kept constant after 2030, with a TFR equal to 5.0 or to 2.5, respectively. In both cases mortality is very high, but the population could still grow exponentially if fertility rates also remain high.

The remaining scenario projects more fortunate developments in mortality: life expectancy increases three years per decade until 2030, when it reaches a level of 61 years for men and 64.4 years for women, and remains constant thereafter. Fertility, on the other hand, does not decline as rapidly. The TFR declines as in the high-fertility permutation until 2030, but remains at the level of 5.0 throughout the period because of the stagnation in mortality after 2030. Here, the demographic transition comes to a halt, and as a consequence the critical level of 4 billion people is reached in the year 2060 (long dashed line in *Figure 16.5*). At this point, *something* must happen; a feedback along the lines of a Malthusian "positive check" seems unavoidable. Two evolutions are envisaged, a more modest reaction and a very strong reaction, both in terms of feedback on mortality. In the first instance, 20 percent of the population (more children than adults) die through war, starvation, and disease. Only 10 years later, however, the magic 4 billion threshold will again be exceeded.[2] Assuming that no further improvements in agricultural production are made, the same negative mortality reaction occurs. In 2070, again, 20 percent of the population dies. The same kind of catastrophe is repeated in 2080 and in 2095 (dashed-dotted line in *Figure 16.5*). As long as fertility and mortality remain unchanged, a catastrophe would occur in 10- to 15-year cycles. The strong feedback assumption is in no way more desirable: it assumes that as a consequence of exceeding the 4 billion margin, half of the population is killed through war, starvation, and disease. In this very extreme case, another collapse would possibly occur 35 years later if fertility were to remain at its high level of 5 children per woman (long dashed line in *Figure 16.5*).

In terms of disaster scenarios, of course, all kinds of combinations of the continuous misery and spectacular collapse cases can be imagined at different population-size levels. The purpose of defining specific disaster scenarios and calculating the resulting population size and structures is mostly for illustrating population dynamics and for broadening our thinking about possible future population trends.

16.2.3 Social crisis from population aging causing fertility to increase

Unprecedented aging of populations might also cause reactions. If the mean age of the population or the proportion of elderly exceeds a certain threshold, a feedback to migration or fertility seems possible. Extremely high levels of aging could be disadvantageous for economic and/or social reasons. Economic handicaps might result in larger streams of immigration, which would only delay the process of aging. It is conceivable that reproductive behavior in such societies changes through a combination of individual reorientation and strong public incentives. To give an example, in the following discussion it is assumed that such a reaction indeed occurs. China and the Japan/Australia region are used as examples because they are particularly interesting as far as the speed of the mortality transition (China) and the level of life expectancy already reached (Japan/Australia) are concerned. To make an interesting case, the calculations are based on the rapid transition, long-range extension.

The underlying assumption is simple: as soon as a certain level of aging, measured in terms of the proportion above age 60 in the total population, is reached, fertility is assumed to switch from the low level to the central level for that particular region. If the aging level exceeds another – somewhat higher – threshold, fertility is even assumed to switch to the high level assumed for that region. The central and high fertility levels are, respectively, 0.3 and 0.6 children per woman, higher than the low level assumed in this low-fertility/low-mortality rapid transition extension. The aging levels at which fertility reactions are simulated are 20 and 25 percent elderly, respectively, in China and 25 and 33 percent in Japan/Australia. Results of such fertility feedbacks are given in *Table 16.5*, which contrasts total population sizes and proportions of elderly under three scenarios: the low-fertility/low-mortality rapid transition scenario without reactions, with only the first reaction, and with two reactions.

Table 16.5. Population size (in millions) and population above age 60 (in %) in China/Hong Kong and Japan/Australia/New Zealand under the special population aging–fertility feedback scenarios.

Year	China/Hong Kong			Japan/Australia/New Zealand		
	No reaction	One reaction	Two reactions	No reaction	One reaction	Two reactions
Population size						
1990	1,159			144		
2010	1,445	1,445	1,445	156	156	156
2030	1,604	1,637	1,637	154	161	161
2050	1,592	1,755	1,854	147	162	168
2070	1,461	1,804	2,081	137	163	177
2100	1,219	1,845	2,488	123	165	198
Proportion elderly						
1990	8.8			16.9		
2010	12.4	12.4	12.4	27.5	27.5	27.5
2030	24.1	23.6	23.6	35.9	34.4	34.4
2050	33.5	30.4	28.7	43.5	39.4	38.0
2070	41.8	33.9	29.4	50.0	42.2	38.8
2100	51.1	38.9	30.2	53.3	45.6	39.5

As a consequence of aging levels reached under the low-fertility/low-mortality scenario, the first fertility reaction occurs in 2025 in China and in 2010 in Japan/Australia, and the second reaction follows 10 and 20 years later, respectively. The consequence is of course substantial, in particular in the long run. The extent of aging would certainly be lower, but still – as one would expect – considerable aging would occur. In all instances, however, effects become visible only after 2050. By 2100, the proportion of elderly in China is lowered by 12 and 21 percentage points, depending on whether one or two fertility reactions are assumed. The respective figures for the Japan/Australia/New Zealand region are 8 and 14 percentage points. The effect is stronger in China because the fertility decline was more abrupt in that region and hence the population momentum has not yet fully worked through the age structure.

Effects on population size are perhaps even more pronounced. Instead of 1.2 billion Chinese by 2100, a figure only slightly above the 1990 figure, with two fertility reactions China would double its current size by the year 2100. Already with only one fertility feedback to the respective central fertility level, total population figures would be some 51 percent higher in China and some 34 percent higher in Japan in the very long run.

The main conclusion of this illustration is that impacts of feedbacks on fertility become effective only very slowly. However, in the long run, significant differences appear.

16.3 Comparisons with United Nations and World Bank Long-Range World Population Projections

Complementing the comparison between medium-range projections until 2025 in Chapter 15, in this section our three plausible long-range scenarios are confronted with the high, medium, low, medium/high, and medium/low long-range extensions offered by the UN (1992) and again the single projection offered by the World Bank (1992). As in Chapter 15, low, central, and high estimates of population size and population aging are discussed. *Table 16.6* gives the respective information for the year 2100.

Differences between the various projections are even more interesting in the long run. For both developing and industrialized regions, by 2100 UN medium estimates on population size are the lowest, and IIASA central estimates are the highest. World Bank estimates are closer to the UN estimate for developing countries, and closer to the IIASA estimate for industrialized countries. The higher estimates for the industrialized region are due to continued immigration streams and to significantly higher ultimate life expectancies in the IIASA extensions. Therefore, also the proportion of elderly in these countries is highest in the IIASA estimate. The larger population size and younger age structure for today's developing countries is still a consequence of the slower completion of the fertility transition assumed in the IIASA extensions.

The most striking difference concerns uncertainty ranges suggested by the UN and IIASA long-range extensions. According to the UN, by 2100 world population size ranges from 6 to 19 billion people, as a mere consequence of the speed of the fertility transition and with ultimate fertility levels of 1.7 and 2.5 in all regions. In contrast, the IIASA projections do not extend the systematic

Table 16.6. Comparison of IIASA results for the year 2100 with United Nations and World Bank projections.

Scenario	Total population size (in millions)			Share of population aged 65 and over (in %)		
	IIASA	UN	WB	IIASA	UN	WB
World total						
Central	12,562	11,186	11,651	19.6	21.6	22.3
Low	9,126	6,009	–	12.5	16.7	–
High	16,090	19,156	–	34.8	28.7	–
Developing regions						
Central	10,980	9,984	10,200	18.7	21.3	22.0
Low	7,885	5,314	–	12.0	16.4	–
High	13,994	17,168	–	34.0	28.2	–
Industrialized regions						
Central	1,582	1,202	1,452	25.9	24.9	24.6
Low	1,241	0,694	–	15.7	19.1	–
High	2,096	1,988	–	40.3	32.4	–

IIASA extensions consist of three scenarios; UN extensions consist of five variants (constant fertility and instant replacement variants are not considered); and the World Bank projection has only one path.

permutation scenarios beyond 2050, but instead somewhat more narrow long-term extensions are defined because of assumed likely interactions. Hence the resulting range of the world population is much smaller, between 9 and 16 billion people in 2100. The significantly higher minimum even with very low fertility is strongly determined by the assumed high gains in life expectancy, and in case of the industrialized regions also by continued immigration. This is also the reason why the high IIASA estimate for the industrialized region is even above the high UN estimate.

In contrast to population size, IIASA estimates report much larger uncertainty regarding the age structure. The proportion of elderly ranges from 12 to 34 percent in today's developing and even from 15 to 40 percent in today's industrialized regions. Due to the restrictive assumptions on mortality with only one future path, UN estimates on the proportion of elderly are in a much smaller range, right in the middle of the range suggested by IIASA estimates. UN estimates show a relatively high certainty about the extent and speed of aging to be expected in the future – which is simply a function of no assumed variation in mortality – while

IIASA estimates reveal a relatively higher certainty about future world population size.

The IIASA world population scenarios were only defined for 12 major world regions for reasons discussed in Chapter 2. Summary tables for each region for both the systematic permutations (Appendix A) and the long-range extensions (Appendix B) and for age structures for the central scenario (Appendix C) follow.

In another context the systematic permutation scenario approach until 2030 has been applied to 20 large European countries (see Prinz and Lutz, 1993). Other sets of individual country scenarios may follow in the future. All existing data are available on diskette from IIASA.

Notes

[1] This study has frequently been criticized for overestimating the agricultural potential of rain forests. Hence, without breakthroughs in agricultural production and with no massive imports of food it is feasible to assume a limit of 4 billion people for this region.

[2] Fertility and mortality rates are still kept constant at the same level that was already reached by 2030. This is also true in the "strong reaction" disaster scenario.

References

FAO/UNFPA/IIASA, 1984, *Potential Population Carrying Capacities in the Developing Countries,* Technical information to the project INT/75/P13, Food and Agriculture Organization, Rome, Italy.

Prinz, Ch., and Lutz, W., 1993, Alternative demographic scenarios for 20 large member states of the Council of Europe 1990–2050, in R. Cliquet, ed., *The Future of Europe's Population: A Scenario Approach,* The Council of Europe, European Population Committee, Strasbourg, France.

UN, 1991, *World Population Prospects 1990,* Population Studies, No. 120, Department of International Economic and Social Affairs, United Nations, New York, NY, USA.

UN, 1992, *Long-Range World Population Projections: Two Centuries of Population Growth: 1950–2150,* Department of International Economic and Social Affairs, United Nations, New York, NY, USA.

UN, 1993, *World Population Prospects: The 1992 Revision,* Department for Economic and Social Information and Policy Analysis, United Nations, New York, NY, USA.

World Bank, 1992, *World Population Projections,* 1992–1993 Edition, Johns Hopkins University Press, Baltimore, MD, USA.

Chapter 17

Epilogue

Wolfgang Lutz

This book serves two specific purposes: to respond to the demand for alternative population projections in the context of global environmental change and to advance the discussion on projection approaches within the demographic community. Beyond these two goals – which are in themselves ambitious enough – the book intentionally refrains from taking a position in other important and hotly debated issues, such as how many people should live on earth or should family-planning efforts be intensified. We believe that, at this point, by making a clearly defined contribution to an important but still limited issue, we can serve the highly confused discussion on future world population, development, and environment better than by considering all relevant issues at a necessarily more superficial level. Brief discussions of two, sometimes antagonistic, positions are presented in each of the following four sections. These help to clarify the specific contribution of this book to the discussion of population issues.

17.1 Possible versus Desirable Population Trends

This book tries to give the best possible answer to the question, what will be the size of the future world population, its regional distribution, and its age and sex structure. The book describes possibilities and likelihoods. But to ask which of the projected alternatives is desirable is a different question altogether. In the discussion of future world population growth, however, these two different questions are often mixed together which tends to result in confusion.

One controversial area where these two different questions tend to be confused is in the discussion of the world's carrying capacity. Chapter 10 of this book reviewed a large number of alternative estimates of how many people can live and be fed on earth; these estimates range from less than 1 billion to 1 trillion. Especially in recent years a number of estimates have been published that come up with figures below or only slightly above the present world population (e.g., Ehrlich *et al.*, 1993; Resources for the Future, 1984). If these estimates are meant in the sense of what is possible in terms of people living on earth, they are clearly wrong because more is possible (at least for the time being and most likely also in the future). To infer from such estimates that the quality of life will deteriorate after a certain threshold transcends the original ecological meaning of carrying capacity (how many people can live on earth?) and introduces welfare standards for those alive that are clearly part of the second question, namely, what kind of life is desirable.

What is the desirable quality of life for people, is a question far beyond the scope of this book. In this general form it may not even be possible to answer it. Great inequalities among people exist and are not likely to disappear soon. Therefore, it is impossible to apply a universal standard for quality of life, let alone define such a standard in the face of differing views on what is good. Population size is only indirectly related to the question of inequality, if it is relevant at all. In general it is not clear how even the average quality of life relates to total population size, although in specific case studies an association has been found.

Of course, statements of what is desirable cannot be completely detached from what is possible and likely. Calculations have been presented that the world population should only be 1 billion to assure an optimal quality of life.[1] But we know that the world population will almost certainly increase to at least 8 billion. The only response one can give is to ask "so what?"

Another recent public statement claimed more specifically that the world population must and can be reduced to 2 billion or less by 2100 to provide universal prosperity.[2] But only strong increases in death rates through intentional killing of people could decrease the population to such a low level by 2100 because even strict fertility control programs such as in China could never reduce fertility to a sufficiently low level. Such calculations that treat clearly impossible goals that may only be achieved through increasing mortality are not really useful in this discussion.

17.2   Unavoidable versus Avoidable Growth

It is a basic fact – which is also slowly being recognized outside the community of demographers – that population growth cannot simply be switched off through population policies. This is due to two factors: the reproductive behavior of large populations does not change radically over night and due to past high fertility ever-increasing numbers of young women are entering the reproductive ages (i.e., the so-called momentum of population growth). Of course, catastrophically high mortality or birth rates that, on average, are less than a third of today's level could always stop population growth, but this is extremely unlikely. In sub-Saharan Africa, for example, simulations show that fertility would have to decline to less than one child per woman overnight to prevent further population growth, which is an absurd scenario. This book gives estimates of what is possible in the real world based on our best present understanding of human behavior.

Within the limits of what is possible, alternatives exist. These alternatives have been numerically demonstrated in Chapters 15 and 16. For the year 2030 possible total world population sizes range from a minimum of 8.3 billion to a maximum of 10.7 billion. The long-range scenarios for 2100 give a minimum of 9.1 and a maximum of 16.1 billion based on assumptions as described in Chapter 16. One can interpret the minimum population growth resulting from the low fertility scenarios as realistically unavoidable further population growth. *Figure 17.1* gives this unavoidable growth until 2050 as the shaded area in the context of the five scenarios (disregarding migration) as defined in Chapter 15. It can be seen from

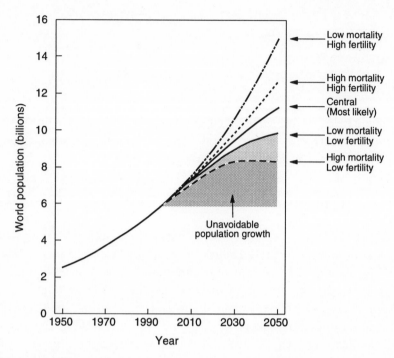

Figure 17.1. Unavoidable and possibly avoidable world population growth to 2050.

the figure that this realistically unavoidable growth adds 2.5 to 4.0 billion people (depending on the choice of mortality assumptions) to the world population, bringing it close to 10 billion by 2050 under the low-fertility and low-mortality scenario.

Figure 17.1 also shows that low fertility combined with high mortality would result in the lowest population growth (only 8.3 billion by 2050). Although this is a possible scenario, it is by no means a desirable one because the higher mortality would be associated with tremendous human suffering (e.g., in sub-Saharan Africa male life expectancy declines from 50 years presently to only 37 years in 2030). Hence, it can be assumed that any policy intending to increase the quality of life by averting avoidable population growth also aims at decreasing mortality. For this reason I chose the scenario combining low fertility with low mortality as the borderline between possibly avoidable and unavoidable growth.[3]

This decomposition into avoidable and unavoidable growth follows a somewhat different logic than the recent analysis by Bongaarts (1994) which estimates that of the likely 5.7 billion additional people in the developing world by 2100 (based on the World Bank projections), 2.8 billion are due to population momentum, 1.0 billion to high desired family size, and 1.9 billion to unwanted fertility. Aside from the issue of wanted and unwanted fertility, which is behind the assumptions of our scenarios but not a defining criterion, his decomposition is different in that it takes stable replacement-level fertility – a convenient but problematic concept as discussed in previous chapters – as the point of reference. All births below replacement fertility are considered momentum, all births above that level are considered avoidable through reduction in unwanted pregnancies and reduction in demand for large families. Alternative mortality trends are not considered in these calculations.

17.3   Population Growth versus Population Aging

Total population size – which tends to get almost exclusive attention in the discussion of future world population trends – is only one side of the coin. The other side is population aging. If population growth follows the unavoidable path, the mean age of the world population increases from 28.1 years currently to 35.0 in 2030 and even 39.7 years by 2050. The long-range scenario to 2100, which limits total population to 9.1 billion, even results in an increase of the mean age of the population to 50 years; the proportion of the population above age 60 would increase from the present 9.2 percent to an incredible 40.8 percent in 2100. For comparison, in the "oldest" region today, Western Europe, still only 20 percent of the population is above age 60. And today's developing countries seem to be hardly prepared to cope with the social challenges of massive aging.

The stated figures on projected population aging under different scenarios make it clear that when discussing possible and desired future population trends both sides of the coin – growth and aging – need to be taken into consideration. Alternative paths of aging are sometimes consciously disregarded with the argument that for an eventual stable situation the laws of population dynamics imply that at some point the higher mean age of the population resulting from stable low fertility and mortality patterns will be reached, no matter what the total population size. While this is certainly true in the very long run, the big difference for the coming decades lies in the speed of aging. A mean age of 36 years, which under the high growth scenario will only be reached in 2100, will already be reached around 2030 under the low-growth scenario. Hence the low-growth scenario will certainly put more stress on society to adapt to rapid and massive aging and develop support networks for the aged that can no longer count on traditional family support.

Mentioning the aging associated with a rapid curbing of population growth is not to say that both aspects are of equal importance. A weighting of the consequences of both aspects, again, is beyond the focus of this book and requires very different considerations. Asked for a first quick guess, I would assume that the benefits of rapidly declining fertility in terms of a lower child dependency ratio, less stress on infrastructure and life support systems, better educational opportunities for women, and a likely boost to productivity more than compensate the problems of aging, if sufficient attention is given to timely social policies.[4]

17.4   Population Policy versus Development

At least since the 1974 World Population Conference in Bucharest the question whether socioeconomic development will do the job of bringing fertility down or whether specific programs and incentive systems or even coercive measures are necessary has been at the top of international population agenda. Recently, increased environmental concerns and the emphasis of reproductive rights have added new fuel to the debate. This book has intentionally made only a very limited contribution to this issue because it is not a programmatic or political book.

What can this book contribute to the issue? Many chapters clearly show that there is room for population policy to influence the future paths of fertility, mortality, and migration and consequently the size, age structure, and regional distribution of the population. Some of the background chapters also demonstrate that policies did have an impact in the past and are likely to do so in the future. The fertility chapters further indicated that in many countries desired family sizes are smaller than actual ones, hence showing substantial demand for family planning and a need for better services and supply, and less necessity for incentives or even coercive measures. The empirical analysis in this book also shows that development and especially the social side of development with emphasis on women's education is a very important prerequisite for the decline of high fertility.

17.5   Conclusion

More concretely, the scenario approach described and applied in this book can also be useful in the specification of priorities for national population policies. A large number of international statements on population policies include language referring to the medium variant of the United Nations population projections as a goal, stating that efforts should be made to match the figures of that specific projection. I find this a regrettable abuse of projections that are intended to give the most likely future path rather than to be taken as a normative goal for policies. Such statements also imply that the UN medium projections are considered wrong in the sense that they no longer give the most likely path without the special efforts which the statement calls upon. The alternative scenario approach described and applied in this book together with the now easily available software could encourage those who define population policies to perform a number of alternative calculations, including scenarios that are considered desirable and realistically achievable. The simultaneous consideration of several alternative possible paths can also help to design more robust national development plans that should hold under somewhat different future population patterns. Finally, such scenario projection exercises contribute to the understanding that not only fertility but all three components – fertility, mortality, and migration – matter in the future size and structure of a region's population.

This book is a first attempt to simultaneously assemble the most relevant knowledge about past and future population trends, translate it into alternative projections, and try to meet the demand for information about the population variable in the context of global change. Many more steps by demographers and their colleagues in ecology and economics are necessary to integrate population aspects more specifically and correctly into the global discussion about sustainable development.

Notes

[1] See a paper by Paul Ehrlich *et al.*, in POPLINE, World Population News Service, January–February 1994.

[2] Cornell ecologist David Pimentel makes this claim according to POPLINE (World Population News Service, March–April 1994). He also claims that a population of 1 to 2 billion over the next century could be reached by limiting family size to 1.5 children. To check this claim we calculated the completely unrealistic scenario: starting in 1995, the total fertility rate decreases to 1.5 children in all world regions. But even in this case, world population would increase to 6.6 billion in 2025 and then decline to 3.5 in 2100. Even combining it with the worst case mortality assumptions (AIDS, starvation, etc.), the 2 billion mark is not reached by 2100. Under the still unrealistic scenario that fertility would decline to 1.5 everywhere within 20 years the total population in 2100 would be 4.7 billion.

[3] Alternatively the low-fertility/high-mortality scenario may be chosen as a reference if one prefers to consider high mortality as part of a strategy to avoid growth.

[4] This was found to be the case in a recent in-depth study on Mauritius (see Lutz, 1994).

References

Bongaarts, J., 1994, Population policy options in the developing world, *Science* **263**(February 11):771–776.

Ehrlich, P., Ehrlich, A., and Daily, G.C., 1993, Food security, population, and environment, *Population and Development Review* **19**(1):1–32.

Lutz, W, ed., 1994, *Population–Development–Environment: Understanding Their Interactions in Mauritius*, Springer-Verlag, Heidelberg, Germany.

Resources for the Future, 1984, Feeding a hungry world, *Resources* **76**:1–20.

Appendix A: Summary Results of Nine Systematic Permutation Scenarios to 2030

North Africa

Migration	Central	High	High	High	High	Low	Low	Low	Low
Mortality	Central	High	High	Low	Low	High	High	Low	Low
Fertility	Central	High	Low	High	Low	High	Low	High	Low
Total population size (in millions)									
1990	140	140	140	140	140	140	140	140	140
2000	179	179	178	180	178	179	178	180	178
2010	226	226	216	230	220	229	218	233	222
2020	278	281	250	293	261	290	259	302	269
2030	332	345	276	371	297	362	291	388	312
2050[a]	440	510	299	584	347	548	326	625	377
Mean age (in years)									
1990	23.6	23.6	23.6	23.6	23.6	23.6	23.6	23.6	23.6
2000	24.4	24.0	24.2	24.1	24.2	24.0	24.2	24.1	24.2
2010	25.4	24.6	25.5	24.7	25.6	24.6	25.5	24.7	25.6
2020	26.7	25.3	27.4	25.5	27.7	25.3	27.3	25.5	27.6
2030	28.4	26.0	29.8	26.5	30.5	25.9	29.7	26.5	30.4
2050[a]	31.6	26.8	34.7	27.8	36.1	26.8	34.5	27.7	35.8
Average annual growth rate (in %)									
1990	2.47	2.47	2.47	2.47	2.47	2.47	2.47	2.47	2.47
2000	2.41	2.34	2.02	2.46	2.14	2.46	2.15	2.58	2.27
2010	2.26	2.20	1.60	2.41	1.81	2.39	1.80	2.60	2.01
2020	2.00	2.09	1.13	2.38	1.43	2.25	1.31	2.53	1.60
2030	1.72	1.97	0.54	2.32	0.93	2.11	0.72	2.45	1.09
2050[a]	1.23	1.91	0.06	2.20	0.44	2.01	0.25	2.29	0.61
Annual number of births (in 1,000)									
1990	4,512	4,512	4,512	4,512	4,512	4,512	4,512	4,512	4,512
2000	5,600	5,679	5,369	5,685	5,375	5,679	5,369	5,685	5,375
2010	6,561	6,932	5,753	6,987	5,799	7,016	5,823	7,071	5,868
2020	7,266	8,271	5,744	8,449	5,866	8,529	5,926	8,709	6,050
2030	7,770	9,787	5,097	10,207	5,315	10,241	5,352	10,669	5,574
2050[a]	8,646	14,119	4,568	15,484	5,012	15,164	5,005	16,579	5,467
Proportion of population aged 0–14 years (in %)									
1990	41.5	41.5	41.5	41.5	41.5	41.5	41.5	41.5	41.5
2000	38.9	39.9	39.4	39.9	39.4	39.9	39.4	39.9	39.4
2010	37.0	39.1	36.2	39.1	36.2	39.0	36.1	39.1	36.2
2020	34.6	37.9	32.2	37.9	32.2	37.9	32.2	37.9	32.2
2030	31.7	36.8	27.5	36.6	27.3	36.8	27.6	36.6	27.4
2050[a]	27.2	35.7	21.6	35.3	21.1	35.7	21.8	35.3	21.3
Proportion of population aged 60 years and over (in %)									
1990	5.6	5.6	5.6	5.6	5.6	5.6	5.6	5.6	5.6
2000	5.6	5.5	5.6	5.6	5.6	5.5	5.6	5.6	5.6
2010	5.7	5.3	5.6	5.6	5.8	5.4	5.6	5.6	5.9
2020	7.0	6.2	7.0	6.7	7.6	6.2	7.0	6.7	7.5
2030	8.4	6.9	8.6	7.9	9.9	6.8	8.5	7.9	9.8
2050[a]	11.8	7.8	13.3	9.6	16.1	7.7	13.0	9.5	15.8

[a] Values beyond 2030 result from an extension of the scenarios, keeping all rates at their 2030 level.

Sub-Saharan Africa

Migration	Central	High	High	High	High	Low	Low	Low	Low
Mortality	Central	High	High	Low	Low	High	High	Low	Low
Fertility	Central	High	Low	High	Low	High	Low	High	Low
Total population size (in millions)									
1990	502	502	502	502	502	502	502	502	502
2000	690	690	684	695	689	690	684	695	689
2010	924	926	879	961	913	929	882	964	915
2020	1,201	1,209	1,067	1,325	1,165	1,219	1,075	1,335	1,174
2030	1,499	1,526	1,199	1,806	1,408	1,543	1,214	1,825	1,424
2050[a]	2,097	2,287	1,297	3,277	1,824	2,326	1,324	3,325	1,857
Mean age (in years)									
1990	21.8	21.8	21.8	21.8	21.8	21.8	21.8	21.8	21.8
2000	21.5	21.4	21.6	21.4	21.6	21.4	21.6	21.4	21.6
2010	22.1	21.7	22.5	21.6	22.5	21.7	22.5	21.6	22.5
2020	23.1	22.2	24.1	22.0	24.0	22.2	24.1	22.0	24.0
2030	24.5	23.0	26.6	22.7	26.3	23.0	26.6	22.7	26.3
2050[a]	27.8	24.3	31.7	23.7	31.3	24.3	31.6	23.8	31.3
Average annual growth rate (in %)									
1990	3.27	3.27	3.27	3.27	3.27	3.27	3.27	3.27	3.27
2000	3.09	2.98	2.64	3.23	2.89	3.01	2.67	3.27	2.92
2010	2.86	2.75	2.10	3.23	2.56	2.80	2.16	3.28	2.61
2020	2.53	2.42	1.37	3.13	2.04	2.46	1.41	3.16	2.08
2030	2.11	2.05	0.51	3.00	1.40	2.08	0.55	3.03	1.43
2050[a]	1.45	1.92	0.02	2.90	0.98	1.94	0.06	2.92	1.01
Annual number of births (in 1,000)									
1990	20,934	20,934	20,934	20,934	20,934	20,934	20,934	20,934	20,934
2000	27,555	28,145	26,697	28,190	26,740	28,145	26,697	28,190	26,740
2010	34,588	37,056	31,123	37,584	31,567	37,170	31,218	37,699	31,663
2020	41,325	47,063	33,028	49,436	34,675	47,406	33,273	49,784	34,925
2030	45,819	56,819	29,786	63,540	33,246	57,423	30,127	64,172	33,603
2050[a]	52,024	82,734	26,655	111,284	35,550	84,085	27,207	112,878	36,187
Proportion of population aged 0-14 years (in %)									
1990	46.0	46.0	46.0	46.0	46.0	46.0	46.0	46.0	46.0
2000	46.3	46.7	46.1	46.8	46.3	46.7	46.1	46.8	46.3
2010	43.6	44.8	41.9	45.5	42.6	44.8	41.9	45.5	42.6
2020	41.1	43.4	37.6	44.6	38.8	43.4	37.6	44.6	38.7
2030	37.8	41.4	31.8	43.1	33.4	41.4	31.8	43.1	33.4
2050[a]	31.8	39.4	24.6	41.5	26.3	39.4	24.7	41.5	26.4
Proportion of population aged 60 years and over (in %)									
1990	4.6	4.6	4.6	4.6	4.6	4.6	4.6	4.6	4.6
2000	4.2	4.1	4.2	4.2	4.2	4.1	4.2	4.2	4.2
2010	4.1	3.9	4.1	4.0	4.2	3.9	4.1	4.0	4.2
2020	4.3	3.8	4.3	4.1	4.7	3.8	4.3	4.2	4.7
2030	4.8	4.0	5.1	4.5	5.8	4.0	5.1	4.5	5.8
2050[a]	6.9	4.8	8.5	5.4	9.6	4.8	8.5	5.4	9.6

[a]Values beyond 2030 result from an extension of the scenarios, keeping all rates at their 2030 level.

North America

Migration Mortality Fertility	Central Central Central	High High High	High High Low	High Low High	High Low Low	Low High High	Low High Low	Low Low High	Low Low Low
Total population size (in millions)									
1990	277	277	277	277	277	277	277	277	277
2000	303	304	302	305	303	304	302	305	303
2010	325	335	322	339	326	325	312	329	316
2020	350	377	343	387	353	347	313	357	323
2030	375	424	362	443	381	368	309	387	328
2050[a]	410	534	388	568	421	400	272	433	305
Mean age (in years)									
1990	35.2	35.2	35.2	35.2	35.2	35.2	35.2	35.2	35.2
2000	35.5	35.4	35.6	35.5	35.7	35.4	35.6	35.5	35.7
2010	36.9	35.6	36.8	36.0	37.2	36.5	37.9	36.9	38.3
2020	38.2	35.3	37.9	36.2	38.8	37.6	40.7	38.5	41.6
2030	39.3	34.8	38.6	36.4	40.3	38.2	43.1	39.9	44.8
2050[a]	39.8	33.2	38.6	35.7	41.5	38.2	46.6	41.0	49.7
Average annual growth rate (in %)									
1990	1.00	1.00	1.00	1.00	1.00	1.00	1.00	1.00	1.00
2000	0.73	0.98	0.71	1.06	0.79	0.66	0.39	0.75	0.47
2010	0.69	1.16	0.64	1.29	0.78	0.61	0.03	0.75	0.19
2020	0.73	1.19	0.59	1.36	0.80	0.65	−0.04	0.86	0.21
2030	0.57	1.14	0.42	1.31	0.65	0.47	−0.40	0.70	−0.07
2050[a]	0.40	1.23	0.34	1.22	0.38	0.44	−0.85	0.48	−0.68
Annual number of births (in 1,000)									
1990	4,234	4,234	4,234	4,234	4,234	4,234	4,234	4,234	4,234
2000	4,202	4,466	3,949	4,478	3,960	2,295	3,949	4,478	3,957
2010	3,886	4,645	3,172	4,674	3,193	2,353	3,124	4,608	3,150
2020	4,376	5,693	3,261	5,751	3,298	2,809	3,117	5,529	3,214
2030	4,549	6,641	3,363	6,726	3,415	2,923	2,803	5,775	2,993
2050[a]	4,824	9,096	3,591	9,163	3,627	3,114	1,948	6,128	2,229
Proportion of population aged 0-14 years (in %)									
1990	21.5	21.5	21.5	21.5	21.5	21.5	21.5	21.5	21.5
2000	23.8	24.1	23.5	24.0	23.5	24.1	23.5	24.0	23.5
2010	22.3	25.1	22.0	24.9	21.8	22.8	19.5	22.6	19.3
2020	21.2	26.6	21.3	26.0	20.8	21.7	15.3	21.1	14.9
2030	21.3	27.6	21.6	26.5	20.6	22.1	14.5	21.1	13.8
2050[a]	20.5	27.9	21.0	26.4	19.4	21.5	11.8	20.0	10.6
Proportion of population aged 60 years and over (in %)									
1990	16.7	16.7	16.7	16.7	16.7	16.7	16.7	16.7	16.7
2000	16.0	15.9	16.0	16.0	16.1	15.9	16.0	16.0	16.1
2010	18.4	17.4	18.1	18.1	18.8	17.9	18.7	18.6	19.4
2020	22.9	20.2	22.2	21.8	23.9	21.9	24.3	23.7	26.1
2030	25.6	20.7	24.2	23.5	27.3	23.8	28.3	26.9	31.7
2050[a]	24.2	15.9	21.9	20.1	27.2	21.3	31.2	26.4	37.6

[a]Values beyond 2030 result from an extension of the scenarios, keeping all rates at their 2030 level.

Central America and the Caribbean

Migration Mortality Fertility	Central Central Central	High High High	High High Low	High Low High	High Low Low	Low High High	Low High Low	Low Low High	Low Low Low
Total population size (in millions)									
1990	147	147	147	147	147	147	147	147	147
2000	181	181	180	181	180	181	180	181	180
2010	219	218	210	220	212	222	214	223	215
2020	255	256	235	260	239	268	246	272	250
2030	289	297	251	306	259	318	271	328	279
2050[a]	342	382	254	407	274	429	292	456	312
Mean age (in years)									
1990	24.8	24.8	24.8	24.8	24.8	24.8	24.8	24.8	24.8
2000	26.6	26.2	26.3	26.2	26.3	26.2	26.3	26.2	26.3
2010	28.6	27.6	28.4	27.7	28.5	27.6	28.4	27.7	28.5
2020	30.8	29.2	31.1	29.3	31.2	29.1	30.9	29.2	31.1
2030	33.1	30.6	34.1	30.9	34.5	30.4	33.8	30.7	34.2
2050[a]	37.1	32.1	39.7	33.0	40.9	31.8	39.0	32.7	40.1
Average annual growth rate (in %)									
1990	2.11	2.11	2.11	2.11	2.11	2.11	2.11	2.11	2.11
2000	2.07	1.91	1.66	1.96	1.71	2.08	1.84	2.13	1.89
2010	1.80	1.65	1.21	1.73	1.29	1.94	1.51	2.02	1.59
2020	1.47	1.51	0.79	1.63	0.93	1.77	1.08	1.89	1.21
2030	1.18	1.35	0.29	1.54	0.50	1.59	0.58	1.77	0.78
2050[a]	0.64	1.16	−0.37	1.28	−0.19	1.37	−0.01	1.48	0.15
Annual number of births (in 1,000)									
1990	3,986	3,986	3,986	3,986	3,986	3,986	3,986	3,986	3,986
2000	4,797	4,825	4,591	4,826	4,591	4,825	4,591	4,826	4,591
2010	5,151	5,382	4,560	5,386	4,564	5,472	4,637	5,477	4,640
2020	5,250	5,896	4,273	5,915	4,286	6,169	4,475	6,188	4,488
2030	5,252	6,523	3,682	6,606	3,727	7,004	3,977	7,088	4,023
2050[a]	5,192	8,003	2,927	8,281	3,029	9,031	3,420	9,323	3,528
Proportion of population aged 0–14 years (in %)									
1990	37.6	37.6	37.6	37.6	37.6	37.6	37.6	37.6	37.6
2000	33.7	35.1	34.7	35.1	34.7	35.1	34.7	35.1	34.7
2010	30.9	33.3	30.9	33.4	31.0	33.3	30.9	33.4	31.0
2020	27.9	31.3	26.6	31.4	26.7	31.4	26.8	31.5	26.9
2030	25.1	29.9	22.4	29.8	22.4	30.0	22.7	30.0	22.7
2050[a]	21.2	28.6	17.1	28.3	16.8	28.8	17.6	28.6	17.3
Proportion of population aged 60 years and over (in %)									
1990	6.4	6.4	6.4	6.4	6.4	6.4	6.4	6.4	6.4
2000	6.9	6.7	6.8	6.8	6.8	6.7	6.8	6.8	6.8
2010	8.0	7.5	7.8	7.7	8.0	7.5	7.8	7.7	8.0
2020	9.9	9.0	9.8	9.5	10.3	9.0	9.7	9.4	10.2
2030	13.2	11.5	13.6	12.4	14.6	11.2	13.2	12.1	14.2
2050[a]	19.4	14.0	20.9	15.9	23.7	13.5	19.9	15.4	22.5

[a] Values beyond 2030 result from an extension of the scenarios, keeping all rates at their 2030 level.

South America

	Central	High	High	High	High	Low	Low	Low	Low
Migration	Central	High	High	High	High	Low	Low	Low	Low
Mortality	Central	High	High	Low	Low	High	High	Low	Low
Fertility	Central	High	Low	High	Low	High	Low	High	Low
Total population size (in millions)									
1990	294	294	294	294	294	294	294	294	294
2000	349	349	347	350	348	349	347	350	348
2010	407	411	397	415	400	412	398	416	402
2020	464	475	437	484	445	480	441	489	450
2030	516	544	463	564	480	552	471	572	488
2050^a	604	695	471	743	507	713	486	763	522
Mean age (in years)									
1990	26.6	26.6	26.6	26.6	26.6	26.6	26.6	26.6	26.6
2000	28.5	28.3	28.5	28.3	28.5	28.3	28.5	28.3	28.5
2010	30.2	29.7	30.5	29.8	30.6	29.7	30.5	29.8	30.6
2020	32.1	30.9	32.9	31.1	33.0	30.9	32.9	31.0	33.0
2030	33.8	31.9	35.5	32.3	35.9	31.9	35.4	32.2	35.8
2050^a	36.6	32.6	40.0	33.1	40.8	32.5	39.8	33.1	40.6
Average annual growth rate (in %)									
1990	1.73	1.73	1.73	1.73	1.73	1.73	1.73	1.73	1.73
2000	1.67	1.66	1.43	1.72	1.49	1.70	1.46	1.76	1.52
2010	1.50	1.50	1.06	1.58	1.14	1.56	1.12	1.64	1.21
2020	1.24	1.36	0.68	1.51	0.83	1.42	0.74	1.57	0.90
2030	1.01	1.30	0.28	1.48	0.48	1.35	0.35	1.53	0.54
2050^a	0.66	1.16	−0.26	1.29	−0.09	1.21	−0.18	1.34	−0.01
Annual number of births (in 1,000)									
1990	6,821	6,821	6,821	6,821	6,821	6,821	6,821	6,821	6,821
2000	7,908	8,098	7,654	8,101	7,657	8,098	7,654	8,101	7,657
2010	8,564	9,239	7,730	9,261	7,749	9,272	7,758	9,294	7,777
2020	8,719	10,093	7,179	10,160	7,226	10,197	7,254	10,265	7,302
2030	8,909	11,353	6,382	11,524	6,476	11,540	6,495	11,712	6,590
2050^a	9,327	14,288	5,378	14,892	5,602	14,692	5,574	15,304	5,802
Proportion of population aged 0-14 years (in %)									
1990	34.7	34.7	34.7	34.7	34.7	34.7	34.7	34.7	34.7
2000	30.7	31.2	30.7	31.2	30.7	31.2	30.7	31.2	30.7
2010	28.9	30.3	27.9	30.3	27.9	30.3	27.9	30.3	27.9
2020	26.7	29.2	24.5	29.3	24.6	29.3	24.6	29.3	24.7
2030	24.7	28.4	21.1	28.3	21.0	28.4	21.2	28.4	21.1
2050^a	22.3	28.2	17.1	28.1	17.0	28.3	17.3	28.2	17.1
Proportion of population aged 60 years and over (in %)									
1990	7.6	7.6	7.6	7.6	7.6	7.6	7.6	7.6	7.6
2000	8.4	8.3	8.4	8.3	8.4	8.3	8.4	8.3	8.4
2010	9.7	9.4	9.7	9.6	9.9	9.4	9.7	9.6	9.9
2020	12.2	11.4	12.4	11.7	12.7	11.4	12.3	11.6	12.7
2030	14.8	13.4	15.8	14.2	16.7	13.3	15.6	14.1	16.5
2050^a	19.2	15.0	22.1	16.3	23.9	14.8	21.8	16.2	23.6

^{a}Values beyond 2030 result from an extension of the scenarios, keeping all rates at their 2030 level.

West and Central Asia

Migration	Central	High	High	High	High	Low	Low	Low	Low
Mortality	Central	High	High	Low	Low	High	High	Low	Low
Fertility	Central	High	Low	High	Low	High	Low	High	Low
Total population size (in millions)									
1990	197	197	197	197	197	197	197	197	197
2000	251	251	249	252	250	251	249	252	250
2010	312	314	304	318	308	314	304	318	308
2020	378	386	357	397	367	386	357	397	368
2030	442	462	397	487	419	463	398	487	419
2050[a]	553	627	435	693	486	628	436	694	487
Mean age (in years)									
1990	24.9	24.9	24.9	24.9	24.9	24.9	24.9	24.9	24.9
2000	25.8	25.6	25.7	25.6	25.7	25.6	25.7	25.6	25.7
2010	27.1	26.6	27.3	26.7	27.4	26.6	27.3	26.7	27.4
2020	28.7	27.7	29.2	28.0	29.6	27.7	29.2	28.0	29.6
2030	30.7	28.9	31.9	29.5	32.6	28.9	31.9	29.5	32.6
2050[a]	34.9	31.0	37.5	32.3	39.2	31.0	37.5	32.3	39.2
Average annual growth rate (in %)									
1990	2.50	2.50	2.50	2.50	2.50	2.50	2.50	2.50	2.50
2000	2.37	2.29	2.08	2.38	2.17	2.29	2.08	2.38	2.18
2010	2.11	2.12	1.71	2.27	1.86	2.12	1.72	2.27	1.86
2020	1.84	1.88	1.22	2.09	1.43	1.89	1.22	2.09	1.43
2030	1.47	1.60	0.62	1.87	0.93	1.60	0.62	1.88	0.94
2050[a]	0.96	1.37	0.10	1.58	0.38	1.38	0.11	1.58	0.39
Annual number of births (in 1,000)									
1990	5,924	5,924	5,924	5,924	5,924	5,924	5,924	5,924	5,924
2000	7,212	7,281	6,978	7,284	6,980	7,281	6,978	7,284	6,980
2010	7,988	8,419	7,325	8,441	7,344	8,421	7,327	8,443	7,346
2020	8,546	9,702	7,336	9,776	7,391	9,708	7,340	9,781	7,395
2030	8,516	10,641	6,363	10,858	6,489	10,651	6,369	10,869	6,496
2050[a]	8,840	13,482	5,471	14,217	5,762	13,507	5,483	14,243	5,775
Proportion of population aged 0–14 years (in %)									
1990	38.7	38.7	38.7	38.7	38.7	38.7	38.7	38.7	38.7
2000	37.1	37.8	37.5	37.9	37.5	37.8	37.5	37.9	37.5
2010	34.4	35.6	33.6	35.7	33.7	35.6	33.6	35.7	33.7
2020	31.6	33.7	29.5	33.8	29.6	33.7	29.5	33.8	29.6
2030	28.3	31.6	24.8	31.6	24.8	31.6	24.8	31.6	24.8
2050[a]	23.3	29.1	18.4	28.6	17.9	29.1	18.4	28.6	18.0
Proportion of population aged 60 years and over (in %)									
1990	6.6	6.6	6.6	6.6	6.6	6.6	6.6	6.6	6.6
2000	7.2	7.1	7.1	7.2	7.2	7.1	7.1	7.2	7.2
2010	7.4	7.1	7.3	7.4	7.6	7.1	7.3	7.4	7.6
2020	9.0	8.2	8.9	8.9	9.7	8.2	8.9	8.9	9.7
2030	11.1	9.6	11.2	11.1	12.9	9.6	11.2	11.1	12.9
2050[a]	15.7	11.6	16.8	14.5	20.7	11.6	16.7	14.5	20.6

[a]Values beyond 2030 result from an extension of the scenarios, keeping all rates at their 2030 level.

South Asia

Migration	Central	High	High	High	High	Low	Low	Low	Low
Mortality	Central	High	High	Low	Low	High	High	Low	Low
Fertility	Central	High	Low	High	Low	High	Low	High	Low

Total population size (in millions)

1990	1,191	1,191	1,191	1,191	1,191	1,191	1,191	1,191	1,191
2000	1,487	1,488	1,480	1,494	1,486	1,488	1,480	1,494	1,486
2010	1,806	1,811	1,757	1,847	1,792	1,815	1,761	1,852	1,796
2020	2,130	2,149	1,993	2,250	2,086	2,163	2,006	2,263	2,098
2030	2,428	2,486	2,145	2,697	2,326	2,511	2,168	2,722	2,349
2050[a]	2,874	3,131	2,183	3,684	2,581	3,183	2,226	3,742	2,628

Mean age (in years)

1990	25.1	25.1	25.1	25.1	25.1	25.1	25.1	25.1	25.1
2000	25.8	25.7	25.9	25.8	25.9	25.7	25.9	25.8	25.9
2010	27.0	26.6	27.3	26.7	27.3	26.6	27.3	26.7	27.3
2020	28.6	27.7	29.3	27.9	29.5	27.7	29.2	27.9	29.5
2030	30.6	29.0	31.9	29.3	32.3	28.9	31.8	29.3	32.3
2050[a]	34.7	31.0	37.3	31.8	38.4	31.0	37.2	31.7	38.3

Average annual growth rate (in %)

1990	2.28	2.28	2.28	2.28	2.28	2.28	2.28	2.28	2.28
2000	2.15	2.03	1.82	2.17	1.96	2.05	1.84	2.19	1.98
2010	1.87	1.77	1.38	2.00	1.61	1.81	1.42	2.04	1.65
2020	1.57	1.53	0.88	1.86	1.21	1.57	0.92	1.90	1.25
2030	1.21	1.23	0.26	1.66	0.70	1.27	0.31	1.69	0.74
2050[a]	0.66	1.00	−0.29	1.39	0.15	1.03	−0.24	1.42	0.19

Annual number of births (in 1,000)

1990	36,132	36,132	36,132	36,132	36,132	36,132	36,132	36,132	36,132
2000	43,030	43,748	42,058	43,784	42,092	43,748	42,058	43,784	42,092
2010	46,542	49,236	43,033	49,560	43,316	49,354	43,136	49,678	43,420
2020	48,493	54,367	41,242	55,545	42,130	54,708	41,504	55,889	42,394
2030	47,298	57,753	34,701	60,595	36,386	58,322	35,062	61,173	36,753
2050[a]	45,225	67,768	27,709	76,363	31,154	68,949	28,300	77,611	31,775

Proportion of population aged 0-14 years (in %)

1990	37.9	37.9	37.9	37.9	37.9	37.9	37.9	37.9	37.9
2000	36.5	36.7	36.4	36.8	36.5	36.7	36.4	36.8	36.5
2010	34.1	35.1	33.1	35.4	33.4	35.1	33.1	35.4	33.4
2020	31.0	32.9	28.9	33.2	29.2	32.9	28.9	33.2	29.2
2030	27.7	30.9	24.2	31.2	24.4	30.9	24.2	31.2	24.5
2050[a]	22.5	28.3	18.0	28.5	18.0	28.4	18.0	28.5	18.0

Proportion of population aged 60 years and over (in %)

1990	6.5	6.5	6.5	6.5	6.5	6.5	6.5	6.5	6.5
2000	6.8	6.7	6.8	6.8	6.8	6.7	6.8	6.8	6.8
2010	7.1	6.8	7.0	7.1	7.3	6.8	7.0	7.1	7.3
2020	8.3	7.7	8.3	8.3	9.0	7.7	8.3	8.3	8.9
2030	10.2	8.9	10.3	10.1	11.7	8.9	10.3	10.0	11.6
2050[a]	14.3	10.8	15.5	12.9	18.4	10.8	15.4	12.9	18.3

[a]Values beyond 2030 result from an extension of the scenarios, keeping all rates at their 2030 level.

China and Hong Kong

Migration	Central	High	High	High	High	Low	Low	Low	Low
Mortality	Central	High	High	Low	Low	High	High	Low	Low
Fertility	Central	High	Low	High	Low	High	Low	High	Low
Total population size (in millions)									
1990	1,159	1,159	1,159	1,159	1,159	1,159	1,159	1,159	1,159
2000	1,328	1,332	1,322	1,334	1,324	1,332	1,322	1,334	1,324
2010	1,469	1,489	1,433	1,501	1,443	1,492	1,435	1,503	1,446
2020	1,605	1,663	1,513	1,693	1,540	1,670	1,519	1,700	1,547
2030	1,722	1,846	1,538	1,913	1,597	1,860	1,550	1,927	1,610
2050[a]	1,873	2,242	1,410	2,412	1,548	2,273	1,434	2,445	1,573
Mean age (in years)									
1990	28.9	28.9	28.9	28.9	28.9	28.9	28.9	28.9	28.9
2000	31.1	30.9	31.2	31.0	31.2	30.9	31.2	31.0	31.2
2010	33.8	33.1	34.2	33.2	34.3	33.1	34.2	33.2	34.3
2020	35.8	34.5	37.0	34.7	37.3	34.4	37.0	34.7	37.3
2030	37.6	35.1	39.9	35.8	40.6	35.1	39.8	35.8	40.6
2050[a]	39.7	34.0	43.9	35.7	45.9	34.0	43.7	35.6	45.8
Average annual growth rate (in %)									
1990	1.41	1.41	1.41	1.41	1.41	1.41	1.41	1.41	1.41
2000	1.32	1.16	0.90	1.21	0.95	1.17	0.91	1.23	0.97
2010	0.95	1.09	0.61	1.18	0.70	1.12	0.64	1.21	0.73
2020	0.86	1.08	0.29	1.23	0.45	1.11	0.32	1.26	0.48
2030	0.63	0.97	−0.20	1.23	0.12	1.01	−0.16	1.27	0.16
2050[a]	0.29	1.03	−0.81	1.09	−0.65	1.06	−0.76	1.12	−0.59
Annual number of births (in 1,000)									
1990	23,188	23,188	23,188	23,188	23,188	23,188	23,188	23,188	23,188
2000	24,728	25,693	23,570	25,697	23,574	25,693	23,570	25,697	23,574
2010	23,007	25,785	20,010	25,805	20,025	25,836	20,049	25,855	20,064
2020	25,147	30,692	19,530	30,761	19,572	30,849	19,632	30,918	19,674
2030	24,653	34,064	16,047	34,447	16,219	34,363	16,208	34,746	16,380
2050[a]	25,334	44,729	12,576	46,094	12,957	45,416	12,858	46,790	13,242
Proportion of population aged 0–14 years (in %)									
1990	27.4	27.4	27.4	27.4	27.4	27.4	27.4	27.4	27.4
2000	26.7	27.1	26.5	27.1	26.5	27.1	26.5	27.1	26.5
2010	23.2	24.8	21.8	24.8	21.8	24.8	21.8	24.8	21.8
2020	21.9	24.6	19.0	24.6	19.0	24.7	19.1	24.7	19.1
2030	21.3	25.6	16.9	25.4	16.7	25.6	17.0	25.4	16.8
2050[a]	19.9	27.4	13.8	26.6	13.1	27.4	13.9	26.7	13.2
Proportion of population aged 60 years and over (in %)									
1990	8.8	8.8	8.8	8.8	8.8	8.8	8.8	8.8	8.8
2000	10.2	10.1	10.2	10.2	10.3	10.1	10.2	10.2	10.3
2010	12.0	11.6	12.1	11.9	12.4	11.6	12.1	11.9	12.4
2020	15.6	14.6	16.1	15.4	16.9	14.6	16.1	15.3	16.8
2030	20.9	18.5	22.2	20.1	24.1	18.4	22.1	20.0	24.0
2050[a]	24.2	17.5	27.8	20.7	32.2	17.4	27.6	20.6	32.0

[a] Values beyond 2030 result from an extension of the scenarios, keeping all rates at their 2030 level.

Southeast Asia

Migration	Central	High	High	High	High	Low	Low	Low	Low
Mortality	Central	High	High	Low	Low	High	High	Low	Low
Fertility	Central	High	Low	High	Low	High	Low	High	Low
Total population size (in millions)									
1990	518	518	518	518	518	518	518	518	518
2000	624	624	620	626	622	622	618	626	622
2010	735	735	710	748	722	736	711	753	728
2020	841	844	778	878	810	854	786	897	827
2030	937	952	814	1,024	877	976	833	1,059	909
2050[a]	1,076	1,164	792	1,343	927	1,226	836	1,424	991
Mean age (in years)									
1990	25.6	25.6	25.6	25.6	25.6	25.6	25.6	25.6	25.6
2000	27.3	27.1	27.2	27.1	27.3	27.0	27.1	27.1	27.3
2010	29.2	28.6	29.4	28.7	29.5	28.3	29.1	28.7	29.5
2020	31.3	30.0	31.8	30.3	32.2	29.5	31.3	30.3	32.1
2030	33.3	31.1	34.5	31.8	35.3	30.4	33.7	31.7	35.1
2050[a]	36.7	32.1	39.1	33.5	40.9	31.2	38.0	33.3	40.5
Average annual growth rate (in %)									
1990	1.88	1.88	1.88	1.88	1.88	1.88	1.88	1.88	1.88
2000	1.85	1.70	1.47	1.82	1.59	1.74	1.51	1.90	1.67
2010	1.57	1.43	1.01	1.64	1.22	1.53	1.11	1.78	1.36
2020	1.28	1.25	0.58	1.55	0.88	1.37	0.69	1.68	1.02
2030	1.03	1.08	0.08	1.48	0.52	1.22	0.21	1.61	0.66
2050[a]	0.51	0.92	−0.51	1.22	−0.13	1.07	−0.31	1.33	0.05
Annual number of births (in 1,000)									
1990	13,232	13,232	13,232	13,232	13,232	13,232	13,232	13,232	13,232
2000	15,518	15,782	14,936	15,791	14,944	15,748	14,904	15,791	14,944
2010	16,322	17,302	14,584	17,379	14,650	17,310	14,591	17,525	14,773
2020	16,604	18,690	13,591	18,955	13,782	19,033	13,841	19,401	14,110
2030	16,706	20,487	11,813	21,149	12,189	21,250	12,281	21,931	12,673
2050[a]	16,146	24,305	9,444	26,475	10,277	26,024	10,279	28,199	11,130
Proportion of population aged 0–14 years (in %)									
1990	35.4	35.4	35.4	35.4	35.4	35.4	35.4	35.4	35.4
2000	32.4	33.0	32.6	33.0	32.6	33.3	32.8	33.0	32.6
2010	29.8	31.4	29.0	31.6	29.2	32.0	29.6	31.6	29.2
2020	27.1	29.7	25.2	29.8	25.3	30.3	25.8	29.8	25.4
2030	24.8	28.6	21.6	28.6	21.6	29.5	22.4	28.8	21.8
2050[a]	21.3	27.9	17.2	27.5	16.8	28.8	18.2	27.7	17.1
Proportion of population aged 60 years and over (in %)									
1990	6.3	6.3	6.3	6.3	6.3	6.3	6.3	6.3	6.3
2000	7.3	7.1	7.2	7.2	7.3	7.1	7.1	7.2	7.3
2010	8.1	7.7	7.9	8.0	8.3	7.5	7.8	8.0	8.3
2020	10.4	9.5	10.3	10.4	11.2	9.1	9.9	10.3	11.2
2030	13.5	11.7	13.6	13.4	15.6	10.9	12.8	13.2	15.3
2050[a]	18.3	13.2	19.4	16.5	23.9	12.1	17.7	16.1	23.2

[a] Values beyond 2030 result from an extension of the scenarios, keeping all rates at their 2030 level.

Japan, Australia, and New Zealand

Migration Mortality Fertility	Central Central Central	High High High	High High Low	High Low High	High Low Low	Low High High	Low High Low	Low Low High	Low Low Low
Total population size (in millions)									
1990	144	144	144	144	144	144	144	144	144
2000	152	152	151	153	152	152	151	153	152
2010	158	160	154	162	157	158	152	161	155
2020	159	165	152	171	158	160	147	166	153
2030	160	171	149	181	159	162	140	172	150
2050[a]	156	183	136	200	152	162	117	178	133
Mean age (in years)									
1990	36.9	36.9	36.9	36.9	36.9	36.9	36.9	36.9	36.9
2000	39.3	39.1	39.3	39.2	39.4	39.1	39.3	39.2	39.4
2010	41.4	40.3	41.6	40.7	42.1	40.7	42.0	41.1	42.5
2020	43.3	40.9	43.5	42.0	44.7	41.9	44.8	43.1	45.9
2030	44.5	40.7	44.7	42.6	46.7	42.3	46.7	44.3	48.7
2050[a]	45.8	39.5	45.9	42.6	49.3	42.3	50.2	45.5	53.6
Average annual growth rate (in %)									
1990	0.55	0.55	0.55	0.55	0.55	0.55	0.55	0.55	0.55
2000	0.44	0.58	0.32	0.67	0.41	0.47	0.20	0.56	0.30
2010	0.13	0.36	−0.08	0.54	0.12	0.14	−0.31	0.33	−0.11
2020	0.07	0.33	−0.18	0.54	0.06	0.11	−0.44	0.33	−0.18
2030	−0.03	0.35	−0.35	0.57	−0.05	0.05	−0.70	0.30	−0.37
2050[a]	−0.24	0.40	−0.54	0.46	−0.38	−0.02	−1.16	0.08	−0.90
Annual number of births (in 1,000)									
1990	1,685	1,685	1,685	1,685	1,685	1,685	1,685	1,685	1,685
2000	1,831	1,942	1,713	1,947	1,718	998	1,713	1,947	1,716
2010	1,626	1,926	1,324	1,942	1,336	984	1,317	1,931	1,323
2020	1,501	1,887	1,125	1,910	1,140	959	1,110	1,889	1,118
2030	1,574	2,168	1,120	2,200	1,140	1,054	1,049	2,083	1,060
2050[a]	1,392	2,378	923	2,400	936	1,002	679	1,972	682
Proportion of population aged 0–14 years (in %)									
1990	19.0	19.0	19.0	19.0	19.0	19.0	19.0	19.0	19.0
2000	18.1	18.4	17.8	18.4	17.8	18.4	17.8	18.4	17.8
2010	17.9	20.0	16.9	19.7	16.7	19.1	15.9	18.8	15.7
2020	16.0	19.7	14.9	19.1	14.4	17.6	12.5	17.1	12.0
2030	16.0	20.5	15.0	19.4	14.1	18.1	11.9	17.1	11.2
2050[a]	15.3	21.3	14.4	19.7	13.0	18.0	9.8	16.4	8.7
Proportion of population aged 60 years and over (in %)									
1990	16.9	16.9	16.9	16.9	16.9	16.9	16.9	16.9	16.9
2000	21.2	21.0	21.1	21.1	21.3	21.0	21.1	21.1	21.3
2010	26.6	25.4	26.4	26.4	27.4	25.7	26.7	26.6	27.7
2020	29.5	26.7	29.0	28.9	31.3	27.6	30.1	29.8	32.4
2030	31.8	27.1	31.1	30.6	34.9	28.6	33.1	32.3	37.0
2050[a]	34.0	25.0	33.6	30.5	39.9	28.4	39.2	34.2	45.8

[a]Values beyond 2030 result from an extension of the scenarios, keeping all rates at their 2030 level.

Eastern Europe

Migration Mortality Fertility	Central Central Central	High High High	High High Low	High Low High	High Low Low	Low High High	Low High Low	Low Low High	Low Low Low
Total population size (in millions)									
1990	345	345	345	345	345	345	345	345	345
2000	357	359	356	359	356	359	356	359	356
2010	368	375	357	383	364	373	354	380	361
2020	374	390	348	409	365	382	340	401	357
2030	379	408	335	442	368	390	319	425	351
2050[a]	376	455	299	519	356	406	257	469	312
Mean age (in years)									
1990	34.9	34.9	34.9	34.9	34.9	34.9	34.9	34.9	34.9
2000	37.0	36.9	37.2	36.9	37.2	36.9	37.2	36.9	37.2
2010	38.6	37.6	39.2	38.0	39.7	37.8	39.5	38.2	39.9
2020	40.0	37.5	40.9	38.6	42.1	38.1	41.7	39.3	42.9
2030	41.3	37.3	42.4	39.4	44.6	38.4	44.0	40.5	46.2
2050[a]	42.3	35.4	43.3	39.1	47.7	37.7	47.5	41.5	51.9
Average annual growth rate (in %)									
1990	0.43	0.43	0.43	0.43	0.43	0.43	0.43	0.43	0.43
2000	0.31	0.47	0.14	0.60	0.27	0.40	0.06	0.53	0.19
2010	0.21	0.44	−0.21	0.71	0.08	0.30	−0.37	0.57	−0.07
2020	0.12	0.42	−0.32	0.74	0.06	0.21	−0.57	0.54	−0.17
2030	0.12	0.54	−0.45	0.93	0.10	0.22	−0.85	0.66	−0.25
2050[a]	−0.13	0.67	−0.64	0.75	−0.40	0.25	−1.38	0.38	−0.98
Annual number of births (in 1,000)									
1990	4,823	4,823	4,823	4,823	4,823	4,823	4,823	4,823	4,823
2000	4,887	5,241	4,573	5,246	4,577	2,693	4,573	5,246	4,578
2010	4,746	5,771	3,736	5,834	3,778	2,955	3,722	5,814	3,787
2020	4,247	5,592	2,912	5,723	2,984	2,844	2,878	5,665	3,003
2030	4,122	6,074	2,560	6,299	2,667	2,968	2,400	5,998	2,584
2050[a]	3,918	7,264	2,124	7,508	2,209	3,178	1,596	6,421	1,788
Proportion of population aged 0–14 years (in %)									
1990	23.1	23.1	23.1	23.1	23.1	23.1	23.1	23.1	23.1
2000	20.1	20.4	19.7	20.4	19.8	20.4	19.7	20.4	19.8
2010	18.8	21.0	17.0	20.9	16.9	20.4	16.3	20.3	16.3
2020	18.3	22.5	15.6	22.0	15.2	21.2	14.0	20.7	13.6
2030	17.6	22.9	15.2	21.8	14.3	20.8	12.4	19.9	11.7
2050[a]	17.7	25.0	15.9	22.9	13.9	21.8	10.6	19.9	9.2
Proportion of population aged 60 years and over (in %)									
1990	15.8	15.8	15.8	15.8	15.8	15.8	15.8	15.8	15.8
2000	18.8	18.8	19.0	18.8	19.0	18.8	19.0	18.8	19.0
2010	19.6	18.7	19.7	19.7	20.7	18.9	19.8	19.8	20.8
2020	23.6	20.9	23.5	23.3	26.1	21.4	24.1	23.8	26.7
2030	26.0	21.2	25.8	25.4	30.6	22.1	27.1	26.5	32.1
2050[a]	29.0	19.5	29.6	26.2	38.2	21.8	34.6	29.0	43.6

[a] Values beyond 2030 result from an extension of the scenarios, keeping all rates at their 2030 level.

Western Europe

| Migration | Central | High | High | High | High | Low | Low | Low | Low |
| Mortality | Central | High | High | Low | Low | High | High | Low | Low |
Fertility	Central	High	Low	High	Low	High	Low	High	Low
Total population size (in millions)									
1990	377	377	377	377	377	377	377	377	377
2000	394	395	392	396	393	395	392	396	393
2010	404	412	397	416	401	407	392	411	396
2020	409	428	393	441	406	413	379	426	391
2030	415	446	388	471	411	420	362	444	385
2050[a]	407	482	357	525	399	420	302	462	343
Mean age (in years)									
1990	37.7	37.7	37.7	37.7	37.7	37.7	37.7	37.7	37.7
2000	38.6	38.4	38.7	38.5	38.8	38.4	38.7	38.5	38.8
2010	40.2	39.3	40.5	39.6	40.8	39.7	40.9	40.0	41.2
2020	41.8	39.6	42.2	40.5	43.1	40.7	43.5	41.7	44.5
2030	43.1	39.4	43.4	41.2	45.2	41.2	45.6	42.9	47.4
2050[a]	44.5	38.3	44.5	41.3	47.9	41.2	49.0	44.3	52.4
Average annual growth rate (in %)									
1990	0.44	0.44	0.44	0.44	0.44	0.44	0.44	0.44	0.44
2000	0.31	0.46	0.21	0.51	0.26	0.33	0.08	0.38	0.13
2010	0.10	0.38	−0.07	0.54	0.10	0.14	−0.33	0.31	−0.15
2020	0.17	0.41	−0.13	0.64	0.14	0.17	−0.42	0.42	−0.12
2030	0.07	0.42	−0.27	0.66	0.05	0.09	−0.65	0.37	−0.29
2050[a]	−0.25	0.43	−0.53	0.47	−0.39	−0.02	−1.21	0.06	−0.97
Annual number of births (in 1,000)									
1990	4,524	4,524	4,524	4,524	4,524	4,524	4,524	4,524	4,524
2000	4,560	4,848	4,258	4,862	4,270	2,491	4,258	4,862	4,268
2010	4,020	4,784	3,278	4,815	3,300	2,444	3,257	4,787	3,283
2020	4,158	5,255	3,109	5,324	3,153	2,662	3,060	5,251	3,137
2030	4,253	5,840	3,051	5,925	3,104	2,824	2,843	5,582	2,983
2050[a]	3,798	6,518	2,535	6,588	2,575	2,716	1,837	5,357	2,026
Proportion of population aged 0–14 years (in %)									
1990	18.5	18.5	18.5	18.5	18.5	18.5	18.5	18.5	18.5
2000	19.5	19.8	19.3	19.8	19.2	19.8	19.3	19.8	19.2
2010	18.6	20.6	17.6	20.5	17.5	19.6	16.6	19.5	16.5
2020	16.9	20.6	15.6	20.1	15.3	18.3	13.0	17.9	12.6
2030	17.0	21.6	15.9	20.6	15.0	18.9	12.6	18.0	11.9
2050[a]	16.0	22.2	15.2	20.5	13.7	18.6	10.3	17.1	9.1
Proportion of population aged 60 years and over (in %)									
1990	19.6	19.6	19.6	19.6	19.6	19.6	19.6	19.6	19.6
2000	21.0	20.9	21.0	21.0	21.2	20.9	21.0	21.0	21.2
2010	23.2	22.4	23.2	23.1	23.9	22.7	23.5	23.4	24.2
2020	26.4	24.0	26.1	25.9	28.1	24.9	27.2	26.9	29.2
2030	30.6	26.1	30.1	29.3	33.6	27.8	32.2	31.1	35.8
2050[a]	31.3	22.6	30.5	28.0	36.8	26.0	36.1	31.8	42.8

[a] Values beyond 2030 result from an extension of the scenarios, keeping all rates at their 2030 level.

Developing regions

Migration	Central	High	High	High	High	Low	Low	Low	Low
Mortality	Central	High	High	Low	Low	High	High	Low	Low
Fertility	Central	High	Low	High	Low	High	Low	High	Low

Total population size (in millions)

1990	4,149	4,149	4,149	4,149	4,149	4,149	4,149	4,149	4,149
2000	5,086	5,095	5,059	5,111	5,076	5,093	5,058	5,111	5,076
2010	6,085	6,130	5,906	6,239	6,010	6,148	5,923	6,263	6,033
2020	7,136	7,264	6,629	7,581	6,913	7,329	6,690	7,656	6,984
2030	8,153	8,459	7,084	9,167	7,664	8,585	7,194	9,309	7,790
2050[a]	9,958	11,037	7,142	13,144	8,495	11,326	7,359	13,473	8,748

Mean age (in years)

1990	25.9	25.9	25.9	25.9	25.9	25.9	25.9	25.9	25.9
2000	26.9	26.8	27.0	26.8	27.0	26.8	27.0	26.8	27.0
2010	28.3	27.8	28.7	27.9	28.7	27.8	28.7	27.9	28.7
2020	29.7	28.8	30.7	28.8	30.8	28.7	30.6	28.8	30.8
2030	31.3	29.6	33.3	29.8	33.5	29.5	33.1	29.7	33.5
2050[a]	33.7	30.3	38.0	30.6	38.7	30.2	37.7	30.6	38.6

Average annual growth rate (in %)

1990	2.08	2.08	2.08	2.08	2.08	2.08	2.08	2.08	2.08
2000	1.85	1.89	1.64	2.01	1.76	1.92	1.68	2.05	1.80
2010	1.65	1.73	1.26	1.95	1.47	1.79	1.32	2.02	1.54
2020	1.41	1.58	0.80	1.92	1.13	1.63	0.87	1.97	1.20
2030	1.10	1.37	0.22	1.85	0.69	1.43	0.28	1.90	0.76
2050[a]	0.81	1.27	−0.32	1.74	0.16	1.32	−0.24	1.78	0.23

Annual number of births (in 1,000)

1990	114,729	114,729	114,729	114,729	114,729	114,729	114,729	114,729	114,729
2000	135,690	139,253	131,853	139,358	131,953	139,219	131,821	139,358	131,953
2010	147,587	159,350	134,118	160,403	135,013	159,850	134,538	161,041	135,550
2020	160,868	184,774	131,922	188,997	134,929	186,599	133,246	190,934	136,337
2030	164,701	207,428	113,871	218,926	120,047	210,794	115,872	222,360	122,090
2050[a]	188,024	269,427	94,727	313,089	109,343	276,868	98,128	320,926	112,904

Proportion of population aged 0–14 years (in %)

1990	35.6	35.6	35.6	35.6	35.6	35.6	35.6	35.6	35.6
2000	34.6	34.8	34.4	34.9	34.4	34.9	34.4	34.9	34.4
2010	32.3	33.4	30.9	33.7	31.2	33.5	31.0	33.7	31.2
2020	30.3	32.3	27.4	32.8	27.8	32.4	27.5	32.8	27.9
2030	28.1	31.5	23.5	32.0	24.0	31.6	23.7	32.1	24.1
2050[a]	25.5	30.8	18.4	31.6	18.8	30.9	18.6	31.6	18.9

Proportion of population aged 60 years and over (in %)

1990	6.9	6.9	6.9	6.9	6.9	6.9	6.9	6.9	6.9
2000	7.4	7.4	7.4	7.4	7.5	7.4	7.4	7.4	7.5
2010	8.1	7.8	8.1	8.0	8.3	7.8	8.1	8.0	8.3
2020	9.7	9.1	10.0	9.6	10.5	9.0	9.9	9.6	10.5
2030	12.1	10.8	12.8	11.7	14.0	10.6	12.7	11.7	13.9
2050[a]	14.8	11.5	17.7	13.0	20.2	11.3	17.4	13.0	20.0

[a]Values beyond 2030 result from an extension of the scenarios, keeping all rates at their 2030 level.

Industrialized regions

	Central	High	High	High	High	Low	Low	Low	Low
Migration	Central	High	High	High	High	Low	Low	Low	Low
Mortality	Central	High	High	Low	Low	High	High	Low	Low
Fertility	Central	High	Low	High	Low	High	Low	High	Low
Total population size (in millions)									
1990	1,142	1,142	1,142	1,142	1,142	1,142	1,142	1,142	1,142
2000	1,207	1,210	1,201	1,213	1,204	1,210	1,201	1,213	1,204
2010	1,255	1,282	1,230	1,301	1,248	1,263	1,211	1,281	1,229
2020	1,292	1,360	1,236	1,408	1,283	1,301	1,178	1,349	1,224
2030	1,329	1,449	1,234	1,537	1,319	1,340	1,130	1,427	1,213
2050[a]	1,349	1,655	1,181	1,812	1,328	1,387	947	1,542	1,092
Mean age (in years)									
1990	36.1	36.1	36.1	36.1	36.1	36.1	36.1	36.1	36.1
2000	37.4	37.3	37.6	37.4	37.6	37.3	37.6	37.4	37.6
2010	39.0	38.0	39.3	38.3	39.7	38.4	39.9	38.8	40.2
2020	40.5	38.0	40.8	38.9	41.8	39.3	42.4	40.3	43.4
2030	41.7	37.6	41.9	39.5	43.8	39.7	44.6	41.5	46.5
2050[a]	42.6	36.0	42.4	39.1	46.0	39.4	48.1	42.7	51.6
Average annual growth rate (in %)									
1990	0.59	0.59	0.59	0.59	0.59	0.59	0.59	0.59	0.59
2000	0.43	0.61	0.33	0.70	0.42	0.45	0.17	0.54	0.26
2010	0.29	0.60	0.08	0.79	0.28	0.31	−0.24	0.51	−0.03
2020	0.30	0.62	0.02	0.86	0.29	0.30	−0.36	0.56	−0.06
2030	0.21	0.66	−0.12	0.92	0.23	0.23	−0.65	0.54	−0.23
2050[a]	−0.02	0.75	−0.27	0.79	−0.14	0.19	−1.14	0.28	−0.88
Annual number of births (in 1,000)									
1990	15,267	15,267	15,267	15,267	15,267	15,267	15,267	15,267	15,267
2000	15,480	16,497	14,493	16,533	14,524	8,477	14,493	16,533	14,519
2010	14,278	17,125	11,510	17,265	11,606	8,735	11,419	17,141	11,552
2020	14,281	18,428	10,407	18,707	10,574	9,274	10,165	18,334	10,494
2030	14,498	20,723	10,095	21,150	10,325	9,768	9,095	19,438	9,660
2050[a]	13,932	25,256	9,173	25,660	9,346	10,010	6,059	19,878	6,783
Proportion of population aged 0–14 years (in %)									
1990	20.7	20.7	20.7	20.7	20.7	20.7	20.7	20.7	20.7
2000	20.6	20.9	20.3	20.9	20.3	20.9	20.3	20.9	20.3
2010	19.5	21.8	18.5	21.6	18.3	20.6	17.2	20.5	17.0
2020	18.3	22.7	17.1	22.2	16.6	20.0	13.8	19.5	13.4
2030	18.2	23.6	17.2	22.5	16.3	20.2	13.0	19.3	12.3
2050[a]	17.7	24.7	17.2	23.0	15.5	20.3	10.7	18.7	9.5
Proportion of population aged 60 years and over (in %)									
1990	17.4	17.4	17.4	17.4	17.4	17.4	17.4	17.4	17.4
2000	19.1	19.0	19.1	19.1	19.3	19.0	19.1	19.1	19.3
2010	21.3	20.4	21.2	21.2	22.1	20.7	21.6	21.5	22.4
2020	25.0	22.4	24.6	24.4	26.8	23.4	25.9	25.5	28.1
2030	28.0	23.3	27.3	26.7	31.1	25.1	29.8	28.7	33.8
2050[a]	28.8	19.9	27.8	25.3	34.5	23.7	34.7	29.7	41.9

[a] Values beyond 2030 result from an extension of the scenarios, keeping all rates at their 2030 level.

World total

Migration	Central	High	High	High	High	Low	Low	Low	Low
Mortality	Central	High	High	Low	Low	High	High	Low	Low
Fertility	Central	High	Low	High	Low	High	Low	High	Low

Total population size (in millions)

1990	5,291	5,291	5,291	5,291	5,291	5,291	5,291	5,291	5,291
2000	6,293	6,305	6,261	6,324	6,280	6,304	6,259	6,324	6,280
2010	7,339	7,412	7,136	7,540	7,258	7,411	7,134	7,544	7,261
2020	8,428	8,624	7,866	8,989	8,195	8,630	7,868	9,005	8,208
2030	9,482	9,908	8,319	10,704	8,983	9,925	8,323	10,736	9,004
2050[a]	11,307	12,691	8,323	14,957	9,823	12,713	8,307	15,015	9,840

Mean age (in years)

1990	28.1	28.1	28.1	28.1	28.1	28.1	28.1	28.1	28.1
2000	28.9	28.8	29.0	28.9	29.0	28.8	29.0	28.9	29.0
2010	30.1	29.6	30.5	29.7	30.6	29.6	30.6	29.7	30.7
2020	31.4	30.2	32.3	30.4	32.6	30.3	32.4	30.5	32.7
2030	32.8	30.8	34.5	31.2	35.0	30.9	34.7	31.3	35.2
2050[a]	34.8	31.0	38.6	31.7	39.7	31.2	38.9	31.8	40.0

Average annual growth rate (in %)

1990	1.77	1.77	1.77	1.77	1.77	1.77	1.77	1.77	1.77
2000	1.58	1.65	1.40	1.77	1.51	1.65	1.39	1.77	1.51
2010	1.42	1.54	1.06	1.76	1.27	1.55	1.06	1.77	1.28
2020	1.24	1.43	0.68	1.75	1.00	1.44	0.69	1.77	1.02
2030	0.98	1.27	0.17	1.72	0.62	1.27	0.16	1.72	0.63
2050[a]	0.71	1.20	−0.32	1.63	0.12	1.20	−0.34	1.63	0.11

Annual number of births (in 1,000)

1990	129,996	129,996	129,996	129,996	129,996	129,996	129,996	129,996	129,996
2000	151,170	155,750	146,346	155,891	146,477	147,696	146,314	155,891	146,472
2010	161,865	176,475	145,628	177,668	146,619	168,585	145,957	178,182	147,102
2020	175,148	203,201	142,329	207,704	145,503	195,872	143,411	209,269	146,831
2030	179,198	228,151	123,965	240,076	130,372	220,563	124,967	241,798	131,750
2050[a]	201,956	294,684	103,900	338,749	118,688	286,879	104,187	340,804	119,687

Proportion of population aged 0–14 years (in %)

1990	32.3	32.3	32.3	32.3	32.3	32.3	32.3	32.3	32.3
2000	31.9	32.2	31.7	32.2	31.7	32.2	31.7	32.2	31.7
2010	30.1	31.4	28.8	31.6	29.0	31.3	28.6	31.5	28.8
2020	28.4	30.8	25.8	31.1	26.1	30.5	25.5	30.8	25.7
2030	26.7	30.3	22.6	30.7	22.9	30.0	22.2	30.4	22.5
2050[a]	24.6	30.0	18.2	30.5	18.3	29.7	17.7	30.3	17.8

Proportion of population aged 60 years and over (in %)

1990	9.2	9.2	9.2	9.2	9.2	9.2	9.2	9.2	9.2
2000	9.7	9.6	9.7	9.7	9.8	9.6	9.7	9.7	9.8
2010	10.3	10.0	10.4	10.3	10.7	10.0	10.4	10.3	10.7
2020	12.1	11.2	12.3	11.9	13.1	11.2	12.3	12.0	13.1
2030	14.3	12.6	15.0	13.9	16.5	12.6	15.0	13.9	16.6
2050[a]	16.4	12.6	19.1	14.5	22.1	12.6	19.3	14.7	22.4

[a] Values beyond 2030 result from an extension of the scenarios, keeping all rates at their 2030 level.

Appendix B: Summary Results of Three Long-range Extension Scenarios to 2100

North Africa				Sub-Saharan Africa			
Migration Mortality Fertility	Central Central Central	Central High High	Central Low Low	Migration Mortality Fertility	Central Central Central	Central High High	Central Low Low
Total population size (in millions)							
1990	140	140	140	1990	502	502	502
2010	226	229	222	2010	924	929	916
2030	332	356	307	2030	1,499	1,538	1,419
2050	440	515	364	2050	2,097	2,203	1,825
2070	529	674	392	2070	2,561	2,708	2,066
2100	595	827	379	2100	2,700	2,710	2,011
Mean age (in years)							
1990	23.6	23.6	23.6	1990	21.8	21.8	21.8
2010	25.4	24.9	25.9	2010	22.1	21.7	22.5
2030	28.4	26.3	30.9	2030	24.5	23.1	26.4
2050	31.6	27.8	37.0	2050	27.8	25.3	32.0
2070	34.7	30.0	42.4	2070	31.5	28.5	37.0
2100	38.9	34.2	48.3	2100	37.0	34.4	42.6
Average annual growth rate (in %)							
1990	2.47	2.47	2.47	1990	3.27	3.27	3.27
2010	2.26	2.40	2.10	2010	2.86	2.91	2.77
2030	1.72	2.10	1.27	2030	2.11	2.25	1.75
2050	1.23	1.66	0.70	2050	1.45	1.53	1.06
2070	0.75	1.14	0.19	2070	0.73	0.71	0.38
2100	0.19	0.46	−0.29	2100	−0.10	−0.35	−0.33
Annual number of births (in 1,000)							
1990	4,512	4,512	4,512	1990	20,934	20,934	20,934
2010	6,561	7,133	5,966	2010	34,588	37,316	31,787
2030	7,770	10,095	5,481	2030	45,819	57,274	33,498
2050	8,646	12,863	5,033	2050	52,024	69,684	32,236
2070	8,616	14,187	4,262	2070	48,788	66,498	27,332
2095	8,003	14,009	3,506	2095	39,077	49,757	21,181
2100	7,928	14,081	3,370	2100	37,804	47,550	20,242
Proportion of population aged 0–14 years (in %)							
1990	41.5	41.5	41.5	1990	46.0	46.0	46.0
2010	37.0	38.4	35.5	2010	43.6	44.7	42.4
2030	31.7	36.1	26.5	2030	37.8	41.2	33.2
2050	27.2	33.2	19.8	2050	31.8	36.3	24.8
2070	23.3	29.0	15.9	2070	26.0	29.9	19.7
2100	19.3	23.5	12.9	2100	19.4	21.5	15.3
Proportion of population aged 60 years and over (in %)							
1990	5.6	5.6	5.6	1990	4.6	4.6	4.6
2010	5.7	5.5	6.0	2010	4.1	3.9	4.3
2030	8.4	7.1	10.1	2030	4.8	4.0	5.8
2050	11.8	8.4	17.5	2050	6.9	5.1	10.1
2070	15.6	9.8	27.1	2070	10.3	7.1	17.3
2100	21.5	14.0	37.8	2100	16.6	12.2	26.5

North America				Central America and Caribbean			
Migration Mortality Fertility	Central Central Central	Central High High	Central Low Low	Migration Mortality Fertility	Central Central Central	Central High High	Central Low Low
Total population size (in millions)							
1990	277	277	277	1990	147	147	147
2010	325	330	321	2010	219	222	215
2030	376	397	356	2030	289	309	270
2050	420	470	378	2050	342	397	295
2070	475	570	404	2070	370	474	288
2100	577	757	453	2100	371	550	245
Mean age (in years)							
1990	35.2	35.2	35.2	1990	24.8	24.8	24.8
2010	36.9	36.1	37.7	2010	28.6	28.1	29.0
2030	39.2	36.4	42.2	2030	33.1	31.3	35.3
2050	39.7	35.2	44.8	2050	37.1	33.2	42.3
2070	40.3	35.2	46.5	2070	40.0	34.7	48.1
2100	41.2	35.6	47.8	2100	43.8	37.5	55.2
Average annual growth rate (in %)							
1990	1.00	1.00	1.00	1990	2.11	2.11	2.11
2010	0.68	0.82	0.53	2010	1.80	1.94	1.65
2030	0.69	0.89	0.48	2030	1.18	1.53	0.82
2050	0.54	0.89	0.26	2050	0.64	1.08	0.23
2070	0.65	0.99	0.37	2070	0.26	0.77	-0.26
2100	0.66	0.91	0.39	2100	-0.13	0.35	-0.72
Annual number of births (in 1,000)							
1990	4,234	4,234	4,234	1990	3,986	3,986	3,986
2010	3,757	4,427	3,086	2010	5,151	5,582	4,733
2030	4,520	5,950	3,243	2030	5,252	6,761	3,863
2050	5,109	7,447	3,286	2050	5,192	7,740	3,154
2070	5,819	9,070	3,512	2070	4,842	8,220	2,426
2095	6,895	11,520	3,938	2095	4,226	8,237	1,718
2100	7,114	12,058	4,013	2100	4,114	8,254	1,596
Proportion of population aged 0–14 years (in %)							
1990	21.5	21.5	21.5	1990	37.6	37.6	37.6
2010	22.3	24.0	20.5	2010	30.9	32.1	29.7
2030	21.5	25.1	17.9	2030	25.1	28.6	21.0
2050	21.0	25.5	16.6	2050	21.2	26.4	15.1
2070	20.9	25.2	16.5	2070	18.6	24.1	11.7
2100	20.5	24.7	16.4	2100	15.7	20.9	8.5
Proportion of population aged 60 years and over (in %)							
1990	16.7	16.7	16.7	1990	6.4	6.4	6.4
2010	18.4	17.6	19.1	2010	8.0	7.7	8.2
2030	25.5	22.1	29.2	2030	13.2	11.8	15.0
2050	24.4	18.1	31.9	2050	19.4	15.0	25.8
2070	26.5	18.4	37.1	2070	23.9	16.4	36.6
2100	28.1	19.0	39.3	2100	30.2	19.8	49.7

South America

West and Central Asia

Migration Mortality Fertility	Central Central Central	Central High High	Central Low Low	Migration Mortality Fertility	Central Central Central	Central High High	Central Low Low
Total population size (in millions)							
1990	294	294	294	1990	197	197	197
2010	407	412	402	2010	312	315	309
2030	516	549	485	2030	442	463	420
2050	604	695	523	2050	553	617	491
2070	667	840	526	2070	632	757	525
2100	727	1,033	495	2100	682	896	513
Mean age (in years)							
1990	26.6	26.6	26.6	1990	24.9	24.9	24.9
2010	30.2	29.8	30.7	2010	27.1	26.7	27.5
2030	33.8	32.1	36.1	2030	30.7	29.1	32.8
2050	36.6	33.0	41.4	2050	34.9	31.4	39.7
2070	38.4	33.9	45.7	2070	38.3	33.7	45.7
2100	40.5	35.8	49.8	2100	41.9	36.5	52.1
Average annual growth rate (in %)							
1990	1.73	1.73	1.73	1990	2.50	2.50	2.50
2010	1.50	1.62	1.37	2010	2.11	2.20	2.01
2030	1.01	1.35	0.70	2030	1.47	1.72	1.18
2050	0.66	1.07	0.25	2050	0.96	1.29	0.63
2070	0.38	0.87	-0.07	2070	0.52	0.87	0.19
2100	0.23	0.59	-0.27	2100	0.10	0.40	-0.21
Annual number of births (in 1,000)							
1990	6,821	6,821	6,821	1990	5,924	5,924	5,924
2010	8,564	9,314	7,812	2010	7,988	8,518	7,430
2030	8,909	11,448	6,531	2030	8,516	10,603	6,460
2050	9,327	13,583	5,778	2050	8,840	12,471	5,720
2070	9,446	15,256	5,033	2070	8,548	13,348	4,756
2095	9,389	16,649	4,360	2095	8,057	13,668	3,918
2100	9,395	16,966	4,239	2100	7,981	13,779	3,773
Proportion of population aged 0–14 years (in %)							
1990	34.7	34.7	34.7	1990	38.7	38.7	38.7
2010	28.9	30.1	27.6	2010	34.4	35.3	33.4
2030	24.7	28.1	20.7	2030	28.3	31.5	24.6
2050	22.3	27.1	16.6	2050	23.3	28.0	17.7
2070	20.7	25.6	14.3	2070	20.3	25.0	14.0
2100	19.0	23.2	12.8	2100	17.6	21.9	11.4
Proportion of population aged 60 years and over (in %)							
1990	7.6	7.6	7.6	1990	6.6	6.6	6.6
2010	9.7	9.4	9.9	2010	7.4	7.1	7.7
2030	14.8	13.5	16.7	2030	11.1	9.7	13.0
2050	19.2	15.3	25.1	2050	15.7	12.0	21.7
2070	21.9	15.7	33.3	2070	21.1	14.5	32.8
2100	25.5	18.0	41.3	2100	27.3	18.1	45.1

South Asia

Migration Mortality Fertility	Central Central Central	Central High High	Central Low Low
Total population size (in millions)			
1990	1,191	1,191	1,191
2010	1,806	1,815	1,796
2030	2,428	2,501	2,340
2050	2,874	3,097	2,595
2070	3,065	3,468	2,600
2100	2,855	3,440	2,212
Mean age (in years)			
1990	25.1	25.1	25.1
2010	27.0	26.7	27.4
2030	30.6	29.0	32.4
2050	34.7	31.6	38.6
2070	38.3	34.2	44.4
2100	42.4	37.8	51.0
Average annual growth rate (in %)			
1990	2.28	2.28	2.28
2010	1.87	1.92	1.81
2030	1.21	1.40	0.99
2050	0.66	0.89	0.34
2070	0.13	0.37	−0.18
2100	−0.43	−0.24	−0.74
Annual number of births (in 1,000)			
1990	36,132	36,132	36,132
2010	46,542	49,499	43,547
2030	47,298	58,120	36,613
2050	45,225	61,532	29,726
2070	38,971	57,680	22,318
2095	30,944	48,708	15,714
2100	29,701	47,303	14,658
Proportion of population aged 0–14 years (in %)			
1990	37.9	37.9	37.9
2010	34.1	35.0	33.3
2030	27.7	30.7	24.3
2050	22.5	26.8	17.5
2070	18.8	23.1	13.5
2100	15.5	19.1	10.4
Proportion of population aged 60 years and over (in %)			
1990	6.5	6.5	6.5
2010	7.1	6.8	7.3
2030	10.2	8.9	11.7
2050	14.3	11.1	18.7
2070	19.8	14.0	29.6
2100	26.2	18.4	42.0

China and Hong Kong

Migration Mortality Fertility	Central Central Central	Central High High	Central Low Low
1990	1,159	1,159	1,159
2010	1,469	1,491	1,445
2030	1,722	1,853	1,604
2050	1,873	2,220	1,592
2070	1,945	2,618	1,461
2100	1,968	3,132	1,219
1990	28.9	28.9	28.9
2010	33.8	33.2	34.3
2030	37.6	35.2	40.7
2050	39.7	34.6	46.6
2070	41.0	34.5	50.8
2100	43.9	37.0	55.5
1990	1.41	1.41	1.41
2010	0.95	1.09	0.78
2030	0.63	1.02	0.30
2050	0.29	0.84	−0.22
2070	0.17	0.79	−0.47
2100	−0.02	0.47	−0.63
1990	23,188	23,188	23,188
2010	23,007	25,892	20,107
2030	24,653	34,202	16,286
2050	25,334	41,203	13,215
2070	23,852	44,975	10,350
2095	21,379	45,986	7,788
2100	20,978	46,228	7,389
1990	27.4	27.4	27.4
2010	23.2	24.7	21.7
2030	21.3	25.5	16.6
2050	19.9	26.1	12.8
2070	18.4	24.8	10.8
2100	16.0	21.4	9.3
1990	8.8	8.8	8.8
2010	12.0	11.7	12.4
2030	20.9	18.5	24.1
2050	24.2	17.8	33.5
2070	25.9	16.4	41.8
2100	30.6	19.1	51.1

Southeast Asia				Japan, Australia, and New Zealand			
Migration Mortality Fertility	Central Central Central	Central High High	Central Low Low	Migration Mortality Fertility	Central Central Central	Central High High	Central Low Low
Total population size (in millions)							
1990	518	518	518	1990	144	144	144
2010	735	740	728	2010	158	159	156
2030	937	972	895	2030	160	166	154
2050	1,076	1,180	969	2050	158	172	147
2070	1,129	1,334	948	2070	154	180	137
2100	1,082	1,406	810	2100	151	195	123
Mean age (in years)							
1990	25.6	25.6	25.6	1990	36.9	36.9	36.9
2010	29.2	28.8	29.7	2010	41.4	40.5	42.3
2030	33.3	31.4	35.6	2030	44.5	41.5	47.6
2050	36.7	32.9	41.9	2050	46.1	40.9	51.6
2070	39.1	34.4	47.2	2070	46.7	40.2	54.3
2100	42.7	37.5	53.8	2100	47.8	40.5	56.2
Average annual growth rate (in %)							
1990	1.88	1.88	1.88	1990	0.55	0.55	0.55
2010	1.57	1.64	1.47	2010	0.27	0.36	0.16
2030	1.03	1.23	0.77	2030	0.05	0.21	−0.09
2050	0.51	0.81	0.20	2050	−0.11	0.16	−0.30
2070	0.11	0.49	−0.26	2070	−0.10	0.27	−0.33
2100	−0.31	0.00	−0.68	2100	−0.04	0.25	−0.36
Annual number of births (in 1,000)							
1990	13,232	13,232	13,232	1990	1,685	1,685	1,685
2010	16,322	17,641	14,936	2010	1,604	1,886	1,321
2030	16,706	20,937	12,455	2030	1,580	2,077	1,136
2050	16,146	22,831	10,272	2050	1,427	2,109	889
2070	14,512	22,680	7,849	2070	1,371	2,235	771
2095	12,152	20,625	5,573	2095	1,331	2,388	685
2100	11,761	20,295	5,199	2100	1,312	2,399	665
Proportion of population aged 0–14 years (in %)							
1990	35.4	35.4	35.4	1990	19.0	19.0	19.0
2010	29.8	30.9	28.6	2010	17.9	19.5	16.2
2030	24.8	28.1	21.0	2030	16.0	19.3	12.8
2050	21.3	26.1	15.6	2050	15.3	19.6	11.1
2070	18.7	23.5	12.3	2070	15.4	20.1	10.8
2100	15.9	19.9	9.3	2100	14.9	19.7	10.5
Proportion of population aged 60 years and over (in %)							
1990	6.3	6.3	6.3	1990	16.9	16.9	16.9
2010	8.1	7.8	8.4	2010	26.6	25.6	27.5
2030	13.5	11.8	15.7	2030	31.8	27.9	35.9
2050	18.3	13.8	25.3	2050	34.6	26.7	43.5
2070	22.0	15.1	35.2	2070	36.6	25.8	50.0
2100	27.5	18.8	47.2	2100	38.6	26.1	53.3

Eastern Europe				Western Europe			
Migration Mortality Fertility	Central Central Central	Central High High	Central Low Low	Migration Mortality Fertility	Central Central Central	Central High High	Central Low Low
Total population size (in millions)							
1990	345	345	345	1990	377	377	377
2010	368	374	363	2010	404	409	399
2030	380	400	362	2030	416	434	400
2050	385	433	351	2050	416	454	385
2070	392	485	333	2070	415	486	365
2100	427	592	322	2100	426	552	344
Mean age (in years)							
1990	34.9	34.9	34.9	1990	37.7	37.7	37.7
2010	38.6	37.7	39.8	2010	40.2	39.5	41.0
2030	41.2	37.8	45.2	2030	43.0	40.2	46.1
2050	41.9	36.4	49.3	2050	44.5	39.5	50.0
2070	41.7	35.4	51.1	2070	44.8	38.7	52.1
2100	41.5	35.3	51.2	2100	45.4	38.6	53.7
Average annual growth rate (in %)							
1990	0.43	0.43	0.43	1990	0.44	0.44	0.44
2010	0.27	0.39	0.12	2010	0.17	0.32	0.09
2030	0.15	0.35	0.00	2030	0.17	0.33	0.00
2050	0.04	0.44	−0.25	2050	−0.07	0.21	−0.27
2070	0.14	0.61	−0.26	2070	0.04	0.41	−0.23
2100	0.35	0.67	−0.04	2100	0.14	0.43	−0.18
Annual number of births (in 1,000)							
1990	4,823	4,823	4,823	1990	4,524	4,524	4,524
2010	4,684	5,650	3,749	2010	3,986	4,695	3,275
2030	4,211	5,860	2,799	2030	4,322	5,632	3,144
2050	4,305	6,715	2,461	2050	4,111	6,012	2,600
2070	4,615	7,825	2,415	2070	4,117	6,560	2,386
2095	5,065	9,316	2,495	2095	4,258	7,402	2,278
2100	5,151	9,627	2,510	2100	4,267	7,558	2,244
Proportion of population aged 0–14 years (in %)							
1990	23.1	23.1	23.1	1990	18.5	18.5	18.5
2010	18.8	20.8	16.6	2010	18.6	20.1	17.0
2030	17.9	21.9	13.6	2030	17.2	20.4	13.8
2050	18.5	23.7	12.8	2050	16.4	20.8	12.2
2070	19.2	24.3	13.1	2070	16.7	21.4	12.2
2100	19.5	24.2	14.0	2100	16.7	21.4	12.1
Proportion of population aged 60 years and over (in %)							
1990	15.8	15.8	15.8	1990	19.6	19.6	19.6
2010	19.6	18.8	20.7	2010	23.2	22.5	24.1
2030	25.9	21.6	31.1	2030	30.6	26.9	34.5
2050	28.9	20.5	40.8	2050	31.6	24.0	40.2
2070	28.3	18.0	44.8	2070	33.6	23.5	46.4
2100	28.2	17.9	45.0	2100	34.7	23.2	49.1

Developing regions **Industrialized regions**

Migration Mortality Fertility	Central Central Central	Central High High	Central Low Low	Migration Mortality Fertility	Central Central Central	Central High High	Central Low Low
Total population size (in millions)							
1990	4,149	4,149	4,149	1990	1,142	1,142	1,142
2010	6,097	6,154	6,033	2010	1,255	1,273	1,238
2030	8,167	8,542	7,739	2030	1,333	1,396	1,272
2050	9,859	10,923	8,653	2050	1,378	1,528	1,261
2070	10,897	12,873	8,806	2070	1,437	1,721	1,240
2100	10,980	13,994	7,885	2100	1,582	2,096	1,241
Mean age (in years)							
1990	25.9	25.9	25.9	1990	36.1	36.1	36.1
2010	28.4	28.0	28.8	2010	39.0	38.2	40.0
2030	31.5	29.7	33.7	2030	41.6	38.6	44.9
2050	34.5	31.0	39.3	2050	42.5	37.5	48.4
2070	37.2	32.8	44.2	2070	42.7	36.8	50.2
2100	41.1	36.5	49.8	2100	43.0	36.8	51.1
Average annual growth rate (in %)							
1990	2.08	2.08	2.08	1990	0.59	0.59	0.59
2010	1.74	1.83	1.64	2010	0.34	0.47	0.22
2030	1.24	1.49	0.95	2030	0.29	0.48	0.12
2050	0.78	1.07	0.39	2050	0.14	0.47	−0.11
2070	0.35	0.66	−0.07	2070	0.25	0.64	−0.06
2100	−0.14	0.08	−0.53	2100	0.37	0.65	0.04
Annual number of births (in 1,000)							
1990	114,729	114,729	114,729	1990	15,266	15,266	15,266
2010	148,722	160,893	136,318	2010	14,030	16,659	11,430
2030	164,921	209,439	121,184	2030	14,633	19,519	10,322
2050	170,735	241,906	105,134	2050	14,952	22,283	9,236
2070	157,574	242,844	84,326	2070	15,922	25,689	9,084
2095	133,226	217,640	63,758	2095	17,549	30,626	9,397
2100	129,661	214,456	60,464	2100	17,843	31,642	9,432
Proportion of population aged 0–14 years (in %)							
1990	35.6	35.6	35.6	1990	20.7	20.7	20.7
2010	32.1	33.2	30.9	2010	19.5	21.2	17.7
2030	27.8	31.2	23.7	2030	18.5	22.0	14.8
2050	24.1	28.9	18.0	2050	18.3	22.9	13.6
2070	20.8	25.6	14.5	2070	18.6	23.3	13.7
2100	17.2	21.0	11.6	2100	18.7	23.2	14.0
Proportion of population aged 60 years and over (in %)							
1990	6.9	6.9	6.9	1990	17.4	17.4	17.4
2010	8.1	7.8	8.4	2010	21.3	20.5	22.3
2030	12.2	10.8	14.1	2030	28.0	24.1	32.2
2050	15.5	11.9	21.1	2050	29.0	21.5	38.2
2070	19.0	13.2	29.9	2070	30.1	20.5	43.3
2100	24.7	17.2	40.2	2100	30.9	20.5	44.9

World

Migration Mortality Fertility	Central Central Central	Central High High	Central Low Low
Total population size (in millions)			
1990	5,291	5,291	5,291
2010	7,352	7,427	7,271
2030	9,499	9,938	9,011
2050	11,238	12,452	9,913
2070	12,334	14,594	10,046
2100	12,562	16,090	9,126
Mean age (in years)			
1990	28.1	28.1	28.1
2010	30.2	29.7	30.7
2030	32.9	31.0	35.3
2050	35.5	31.8	40.5
2070	37.8	33.3	45.0
2100	41.3	36.5	50.0
Average annual growth rate (in %)			
1990	1.76	1.76	1.76
2010	1.49	1.58	1.38
2030	1.10	1.34	0.83
2050	0.70	1.00	0.32
2070	0.33	0.65	−0.07
2100	−0.08	0.15	−0.45
Annual number of births (in 1,000)			
1990	129,995	129,995	129,995
2010	162,752	177,552	147,748
2030	179,554	228,958	131,506
2050	185,687	264,188	114,370
2070	173,496	268,533	93,409
2095	150,775	248,266	73,155
2100	147,504	246,098	69,896
Proportion of population aged 0–14 years (in %)			
1990	32.3	32.3	32.3
2010	29.9	31.1	28.7
2030	26.5	29.9	22.4
2050	23.3	28.1	17.4
2070	20.6	25.3	14.4
2100	17.4	21.3	11.9
Proportion of population aged 60 years and over (in %)			
1990	9.2	9.2	9.2
2010	10.4	10.0	10.7
2030	14.4	12.7	16.7
2050	17.2	13.1	23.3
2070	20.3	14.0	31.5
2100	25.5	17.6	40.8

Appendix C: Age Structures of the Central Scenario, 1990–2100, in millions.

	1990		2000		2010		2020		2030		2050		2100	
	F	M	F	M	F	M	F	M	F	M	F	M	F	M
North Africa														
0–4	10.6	11.0	12.6	13.3	14.9	15.7	16.6	17.5	17.8	18.9	20.0	21.2	18.5	19.5
5–9	9.6	10.1	11.2	11.8	13.5	14.3	15.5	16.5	17.1	18.1	19.5	20.6	18.6	19.6
10–14	8.3	8.7	10.2	10.7	12.2	12.9	14.5	15.4	16.3	17.3	18.7	19.9	18.6	19.7
15–19	7.1	7.4	9.5	9.9	11.0	11.7	13.4	14.1	15.4	16.3	17.9	19.0	18.3	19.5
20–24	6.3	6.6	8.2	8.5	10.1	10.5	12.1	12.8	14.4	15.2	17.5	18.5	19.0	20.2
25–29	5.4	5.6	6.9	7.2	9.3	9.7	10.9	11.4	13.2	13.9	16.8	17.8	19.4	20.5
30–34	4.8	4.9	6.1	6.4	8.0	8.3	9.9	10.3	11.9	12.5	16.0	16.9	19.6	20.8
35–39	4.0	4.0	5.2	5.4	6.7	7.0	9.0	9.4	10.7	11.2	15.1	15.9	19.6	20.8
40–44	3.0	2.9	4.6	4.7	5.9	6.1	7.7	8.0	9.6	10.0	14.0	14.7	19.6	20.7
45–49	2.4	2.3	3.7	3.7	4.9	5.0	6.4	6.7	8.7	9.0	12.7	13.2	19.3	20.4
50–54	2.2	2.0	2.8	2.6	4.3	4.3	5.5	5.6	7.3	7.5	11.2	11.6	18.8	19.7
55–59	1.8	1.7	2.2	2.0	3.4	3.3	4.5	4.5	6.0	6.0	9.7	9.9	17.9	18.6
60–64	1.5	1.4	1.9	1.6	2.4	2.2	3.8	3.6	4.9	4.8	8.4	8.2	16.6	16.8
65–69	1.1	1.0	1.5	1.2	1.7	1.5	2.8	2.5	3.8	3.5	7.0	6.7	14.8	14.4
70–74	0.8	0.7	1.1	0.9	1.3	1.1	1.8	1.4	2.8	2.5	5.2	4.6	12.8	12.0
75–79	0.5	0.4	0.6	0.5	0.9	0.6	1.1	0.8	1.8	1.4	3.4	2.9	10.0	8.9
80+	0.3	0.3	0.5	0.4	0.7	0.5	1.0	0.7	1.3	0.9	3.2	2.4	11.5	9.8
Total	70	71	89	91	111	115	136	141	163	169	216	224	293	302
Sub-Saharan Africa														
0–4	46.8	47.3	61.2	63.9	76.9	80.3	92.0	96.0	102.0	106.5	116.5	121.7	85.8	90.0
5–9	37.4	37.6	52.2	54.2	64.3	66.6	79.6	82.4	91.4	94.7	107.7	111.7	84.9	88.5
10–14	30.9	31.0	43.9	44.2	56.5	58.4	71.0	73.4	84.9	87.8	102.4	105.9	85.6	89.0
15–19	26.0	25.9	36.5	36.6	51.0	52.8	62.7	64.9	77.6	80.3	96.1	99.3	85.3	88.6
20–24	21.7	21.5	30.1	30.2	42.8	43.2	55.1	57.1	69.3	71.8	92.2	95.4	91.7	95.2
25–29	18.3	18.0	25.0	25.0	35.4	35.7	49.5	51.4	60.9	63.2	86.9	90.0	96.4	100.1
30–34	15.1	14.8	20.7	20.6	29.1	29.2	41.4	41.8	53.3	55.3	80.4	83.3	99.5	103.1
35–39	12.4	12.1	17.3	17.1	24.1	24.0	34.1	34.2	47.6	49.3	72.8	75.2	100.9	104.3
40–44	10.3	9.9	14.2	13.8	19.8	19.5	27.7	27.6	39.5	39.6	64.2	66.0	100.9	103.7
45–49	8.6	8.2	11.5	11.0	16.3	15.8	22.7	22.2	32.1	31.7	55.5	56.3	98.8	100.4
50–54	7.2	6.6	9.3	8.7	13.1	12.3	18.2	17.3	25.6	24.6	47.1	46.9	94.4	94.2
55–59	5.9	5.3	7.5	6.8	10.2	9.3	14.5	13.3	20.1	18.7	39.9	38.8	86.7	84.5
60–64	4.6	4.1	5.8	5.1	7.7	6.8	10.8	9.6	15.0	13.5	30.3	27.7	75.4	71.2
65–69	3.4	2.9	4.3	3.6	5.5	4.6	7.5	6.4	10.7	9.1	21.2	18.6	60.8	55.1
70–74	2.4	1.9	2.9	2.3	3.6	2.9	4.8	3.9	6.8	5.5	13.4	11.2	46.0	39.7
75–79	1.4	1.0	1.7	1.3	2.1	1.6	2.7	2.1	3.7	2.9	7.4	5.9	29.9	24.7
80+	0.9	0.6	1.2	0.9	1.5	1.2	1.9	1.5	2.5	2.0	4.9	4.0	24.5	20.6
Total	253	249	345	345	460	464	596	605	743	756	1,039	1,058	1,348	1,353
North America														
0–4	9.9	10.4	12.3	12.8	11.6	12.1	12.8	13.4	13.5	14.1	14.9	15.6	19.8	20.8
5–9	9.8	10.3	13.1	13.7	11.7	12.2	12.0	12.5	13.3	13.9	14.4	15.0	19.2	20.2
10–14	9.3	9.8	9.9	10.4	12.2	12.7	11.6	12.1	12.8	13.4	13.9	14.5	18.7	19.7
15–19	9.6	10.1	9.8	10.2	13.1	13.6	11.7	12.2	12.0	12.5	13.6	14.2	18.3	19.2
20–24	10.4	10.7	9.3	9.7	9.9	10.3	12.2	12.7	11.6	12.0	13.4	14.0	17.7	18.5
25–29	11.9	11.9	9.6	10.0	9.7	10.1	13.1	13.5	11.6	12.1	13.3	13.8	17.2	18.0
30–34	12.2	12.1	10.3	10.6	9.2	9.6	9.9	10.2	12.2	12.6	12.8	13.3	16.6	17.3
35–39	11.2	11.0	11.8	11.8	9.5	9.9	9.7	10.0	13.0	13.4	11.9	12.3	16.1	16.7
40–44	10.0	9.7	12.1	11.9	10.3	10.5	9.2	9.5	9.8	10.1	11.5	11.8	15.6	16.2
45–49	7.9	7.6	11.1	10.8	11.7	11.5	9.4	9.7	9.6	9.9	11.6	11.8	15.3	15.8
50–54	6.5	6.2	9.8	9.3	11.9	11.5	10.1	10.1	9.1	9.2	12.0	12.2	14.8	15.2
55–59	6.1	5.7	7.6	7.1	10.8	10.1	11.4	11.0	9.3	9.3	12.8	12.8	14.2	14.4
60–64	6.3	5.5	6.2	5.5	9.4	8.5	11.6	10.6	9.9	9.5	9.5	9.4	13.6	13.7
65–69	6.2	5.0	5.7	4.7	7.1	6.1	10.3	9.0	11.0	10.0	9.2	8.8	13.2	12.9
70–74	5.1	3.8	5.5	4.2	5.6	4.3	8.7	7.0	10.9	9.2	8.5	7.8	12.8	12.2
75–79	4.1	2.7	4.8	3.2	4.7	3.2	6.2	4.4	9.2	6.9	8.3	7.0	12.3	11.0
80+	5.2	2.5	5.9	2.9	7.2	3.7	8.1	4.2	12.6	6.8	21.4	12.5	36.6	23.9
Total	142	135	155	149	166	160	178	172	191	185	213	207	292	286

	1990		2000		2010		2020		2030		2050		2100	
	F	M	F	M	F	M	F	M	F	M	F	M	F	M
Central America and Caribbean														
0–4	9.8	10.2	10.6	11.1	11.5	12.1	11.8	12.4	11.9	12.4	11.8	12.4	9.2	9.7
5–9	9.0	9.4	9.7	10.1	11.1	11.6	11.6	12.1	11.9	12.4	11.9	12.4	9.4	10.0
10–14	8.3	8.6	9.6	9.9	10.5	10.9	11.4	11.9	11.8	12.2	11.8	12.4	9.7	10.2
15–19	8.3	8.5	9.0	9.3	9.7	10.1	11.0	11.5	11.6	12.1	11.7	12.2	9.8	10.4
20–24	7.3	7.4	8.3	8.5	9.6	9.9	10.4	10.9	11.3	11.9	11.8	12.3	10.2	10.8
25–29	6.2	6.1	8.3	8.4	9.0	9.2	9.6	10.0	11.0	11.5	11.8	12.3	10.5	11.1
30–34	5.0	4.8	7.3	7.2	8.2	8.4	9.6	9.8	10.4	10.8	11.7	12.1	10.9	11.4
35–39	4.1	4.0	6.1	6.0	8.2	8.3	8.9	9.1	9.6	9.9	11.5	12.0	11.1	11.6
40–44	3.4	3.3	4.9	4.7	7.2	7.1	8.2	8.3	9.5	9.7	11.2	11.7	11.3	11.7
45–49	2.8	2.7	4.0	3.8	6.1	5.9	8.1	8.1	8.8	9.0	10.8	11.2	11.4	11.9
50–54	2.3	2.2	3.3	3.1	4.8	4.5	7.0	6.9	8.0	8.0	10.1	10.4	11.5	11.8
55–59	2.0	1.9	2.7	2.5	3.9	3.6	5.8	5.5	7.8	7.7	9.2	9.3	11.5	11.6
60–64	1.6	1.5	2.1	1.9	3.1	2.8	4.5	4.0	6.6	6.2	8.9	8.7	11.3	11.1
65–69	1.2	1.1	1.8	1.5	2.3	2.0	3.5	2.9	5.3	4.6	7.9	7.4	10.9	10.4
70–74	0.9	0.8	1.3	1.0	1.7	1.4	2.5	2.0	3.8	3.0	6.7	5.8	10.6	9.6
75–79	0.6	0.5	0.8	0.7	1.2	0.9	1.7	1.3	2.6	1.9	5.8	4.5	9.8	8.2
80+	0.6	0.5	0.8	0.6	1.2	0.8	1.6	1.1	2.4	1.8	6.6	4.4	18.0	12.1
Total	74	73	91	91	109	109	127	128	144	145	171	171	187	184
South America														
0–4	17.3	17.8	18.4	19.3	20.1	21.1	20.5	21.5	21.2	22.1	22.3	23.2	22.5	23.8
5–9	17.2	17.5	17.1	17.8	19.2	20.1	20.2	21.1	20.9	21.6	22.0	22.9	22.4	23.7
10–14	16.0	16.3	17.0	17.4	18.2	18.9	19.8	20.7	20.4	21.3	21.7	22.6	22.4	23.6
15–19	14.5	14.7	17.0	17.3	17.0	17.7	19.1	19.9	20.1	21.0	21.3	22.0	22.2	23.5
20–24	13.6	13.8	15.9	16.1	16.9	17.2	18.1	18.8	19.8	20.6	21.1	21.8	22.4	23.6
25–29	12.8	12.9	14.4	14.4	16.9	17.0	16.9	17.4	19.0	19.7	20.7	21.3	22.4	23.5
30–34	11.0	11.0	13.4	13.4	15.7	15.7	16.8	16.9	18.0	18.5	20.2	20.9	22.4	23.5
35–39	9.5	9.4	12.6	12.5	14.2	14.1	16.7	16.7	16.7	17.1	19.9	20.5	22.2	23.0
40–44	7.7	7.6	10.8	10.6	13.2	13.0	15.5	15.3	16.6	16.6	19.5	20.0	22.1	22.8
45–49	6.1	6.0	9.2	8.9	12.3	12.0	13.9	13.6	16.4	16.2	18.6	19.0	21.9	22.3
50–54	5.3	5.1	7.4	7.1	10.4	10.0	12.8	12.4	15.0	14.7	17.4	17.5	21.6	21.8
55–59	4.5	4.3	5.8	5.5	8.7	8.2	11.7	11.1	13.3	12.7	15.9	15.8	21.1	21.0
60–64	3.9	3.6	4.8	4.4	6.8	6.2	9.7	8.9	11.9	11.1	15.3	14.5	20.5	20.0
65–69	3.1	2.7	3.9	3.4	5.1	4.5	7.7	6.8	10.4	9.4	14.5	13.2	19.5	18.3
70–74	2.2	1.9	3.0	2.6	3.8	3.2	5.5	4.7	8.0	6.8	12.2	10.5	18.4	16.4
75–79	1.6	1.2	2.1	1.6	2.7	2.1	3.7	2.9	5.5	4.5	9.2	7.4	16.4	13.3
80+	1.3	0.9	2.0	1.4	2.9	2.0	3.9	2.7	4.9	3.9	10.5	8.3	26.1	16.2
Total	147	147	175	174	204	203	232	231	258	258	302	301	367	360
West and Central Asia														
0–4	14.3	14.8	16.5	17.3	18.7	19.6	20.3	21.4	20.5	21.4	21.4	22.3	19.3	20.4
5–9	11.9	12.5	15.1	15.8	17.5	18.3	19.6	20.5	20.5	21.4	21.1	22.0	19.5	20.6
10–14	11.1	11.6	14.1	14.4	16.3	17.0	18.5	19.3	20.2	21.1	20.6	21.5	19.6	20.7
15–19	9.8	10.4	11.8	12.4	15.1	15.7	17.5	18.2	19.6	20.4	19.8	20.6	19.7	20.8
20–24	8.7	9.0	11.0	11.5	14.0	14.4	16.2	16.9	18.4	19.2	20.4	21.2	20.1	21.2
25–29	8.0	8.5	9.7	10.3	11.8	12.3	15.0	15.6	17.4	18.1	20.4	21.2	20.4	21.4
30–34	6.6	7.2	8.6	8.9	10.9	11.4	14.0	14.2	16.2	16.8	20.1	21.0	20.6	21.6
35–39	5.3	5.9	7.9	8.4	9.6	10.2	11.7	12.1	14.9	15.5	19.4	20.3	20.6	21.6
40–44	4.0	4.3	6.5	7.1	8.5	8.8	10.8	11.2	13.8	14.1	18.2	19.0	20.7	21.6
45–49	3.5	3.6	5.2	5.7	7.8	8.1	9.5	9.9	11.5	11.9	17.1	17.8	20.8	21.5
50–54	3.4	3.4	3.8	4.1	6.4	6.7	8.3	8.4	10.6	10.9	15.7	16.2	20.8	21.2
55–59	3.0	2.9	3.3	3.3	5.0	5.3	7.5	7.6	9.1	9.3	14.2	14.5	20.4	20.5
60–64	2.6	2.3	3.1	2.9	3.6	3.6	5.9	6.0	7.8	7.6	12.8	12.5	19.5	19.3
65–69	1.7	1.3	2.5	2.3	2.9	2.7	4.4	4.3	6.7	6.4	10.3	9.7	18.3	17.5
70–74	1.2	0.8	2.0	1.6	2.5	2.1	2.9	2.6	5.0	4.5	8.7	7.8	18.0	16.5
75–79	1.0	0.6	1.1	0.8	1.7	1.4	2.0	1.6	3.2	2.8	6.6	5.4	16.5	14.1
80+	0.9	0.5	1.1	0.6	1.6	1.1	2.4	1.7	2.9	2.3	7.4	5.7	27.3	19.4
Total	97	100	124	127	154	159	187	192	218	224	274	279	342	340

	1990		2000		2010		2020		2030		2050		2100	
	F	M	F	M	F	M	F	M	F	M	F	M	F	M
South Asia														
0–4	81.3	86.0	97.8	103.7	106.4	112.8	111.4	118.3	109.2	115.9	104.9	111.5	69.4	73.8
5–9	73.6	78.4	88.1	93.8	98.9	105.4	106.4	113.3	109.0	116.1	104.4	111.2	71.5	76.2
10–14	63.9	68.5	77.1	82.0	93.5	99.6	102.4	109.6	107.9	115.0	104.0	110.9	73.9	78.8
15–19	59.7	64.6	72.4	77.3	87.0	92.6	97.8	104.3	105.4	112.3	101.9	108.6	76.0	81.0
20–24	52.9	58.0	63.0	67.7	76.2	81.1	92.5	98.6	101.5	108.7	105.7	112.6	80.9	86.2
25–29	45.6	49.4	58.6	63.6	71.4	76.2	85.9	91.6	96.8	103.3	107.3	114.4	84.7	90.2
30–34	39.4	42.5	51.8	57.0	61.8	66.6	75.0	80.0	91.4	97.5	106.2	113.2	88.4	94.2
35–39	33.1	36.0	44.5	48.2	57.3	62.3	70.0	74.9	84.5	90.2	103.2	110.1	91.3	97.2
40–44	27.1	28.7	38.2	41.1	50.3	55.3	60.4	64.9	73.5	78.2	98.8	105.7	94.3	100.4
45–49	23.3	24.3	31.7	34.3	42.8	46.1	55.4	59.9	68.0	72.3	93.2	99.0	96.5	102.6
50–54	20.5	21.1	25.5	26.6	36.1	38.4	47.9	51.9	57.7	61.3	86.4	91.2	97.9	103.5
55–59	17.4	18.1	21.1	21.5	29.1	30.9	39.5	41.7	51.6	54.6	77.4	80.7	96.1	100.7
60–64	14.2	14.6	17.5	17.4	22.1	22.3	31.7	32.5	42.4	44.6	63.5	65.1	91.2	94.2
65–69	10.4	10.7	13.5	13.5	16.7	16.3	23.4	23.8	32.3	32.7	53.3	53.4	81.8	82.7
70–74	7.3	7.3	9.6	9.3	12.1	11.4	15.6	14.9	22.9	22.4	38.6	37.9	73.1	72.2
75–79	4.2	4.2	5.6	5.6	7.6	7.2	9.7	9.0	14.0	13.5	26.8	25.9	58.3	56.1
80+	2.5	2.5	4.2	4.4	6.0	6.0	8.1	7.9	11.0	10.7	23.7	23.7	70.3	69.2
Total	576	615	720	767	875	931	1,033	1,097	1,179	1,249	1,399	1,475	1,396	1,459
China and Hong Kong														
0–4	56.2	59.9	58.2	61.4	54.3	57.4	60.2	63.0	59.1	62.3	60.7	64.2	50.3	53.2
5–9	50.1	53.6	58.7	61.8	54.0	56.9	57.6	60.1	60.2	62.9	60.8	64.3	51.2	54.2
10–14	47.1	50.2	55.7	59.2	57.6	60.6	54.0	56.8	60.0	62.5	60.0	63.4	51.9	54.9
15–19	60.5	64.2	49.9	53.3	58.6	61.5	53.8	56.7	57.5	59.9	59.2	62.6	52.6	55.6
20–24	62.5	66.6	46.9	49.8	55.6	59.0	57.4	60.4	53.8	56.6	58.8	61.9	54.4	57.4
25–29	51.8	55.8	60.1	63.5	49.7	53.0	58.3	61.3	53.6	56.4	59.9	62.4	56.1	59.1
30–34	41.3	44.6	62.0	65.8	46.7	49.5	55.3	58.7	57.1	60.1	59.6	61.8	56.9	59.9
35–39	42.8	45.5	51.3	55.1	59.8	63.0	49.4	52.7	57.9	60.9	57.0	59.0	57.6	60.5
40–44	30.9	33.9	40.7	43.8	61.5	65.0	46.2	49.0	54.7	58.1	53.2	55.6	58.0	60.8
45–49	23.6	26.6	42.0	44.3	50.6	54.0	58.7	62.0	48.6	51.8	52.7	55.1	58.7	61.5
50–54	21.9	24.7	29.9	32.4	39.9	42.2	59.9	63.1	45.1	47.6	55.6	57.9	59.4	61.8
55–59	20.4	22.5	22.4	24.6	40.4	41.6	48.5	51.1	56.6	59.0	55.6	57.3	58.9	60.9
60–64	17.0	18.1	20.1	21.7	27.9	29.0	37.2	38.4	56.6	58.0	51.4	52.8	57.3	58.4
65–69	13.9	13.5	17.6	18.2	19.8	20.5	36.1	35.3	44.3	44.4	44.0	44.5	55.3	55.2
70–74	10.3	8.9	13.3	13.0	16.3	16.2	23.1	22.3	31.9	30.4	38.3	37.4	52.8	51.0
75–79	6.8	5.2	9.3	8.1	12.5	11.6	14.2	13.5	27.4	24.2	42.6	39.5	49.9	45.6
80+	5.2	2.9	8.2	6.1	12.6	10.6	15.3	15.1	22.0	20.1	57.1	46.5	95.6	81.7
Total	563	597	646	682	718	752	785	819	847	875	927	946	977	991
Southeast Asia														
0–4	31.8	33.1	35.1	36.9	37.1	39.0	37.9	39.9	38.2	40.3	37.0	39.1	27.1	28.6
5–9	30.1	31.2	32.4	34.1	35.6	37.3	36.9	38.7	37.6	39.5	37.3	39.2	27.9	29.3
10–14	28.1	29.1	31.1	32.2	34.3	35.8	36.4	38.1	37.3	39.1	37.4	39.3	28.7	30.0
15–19	28.0	28.8	29.8	30.9	32.2	33.8	35.5	37.0	36.7	38.4	37.3	39.2	29.3	30.6
20–24	25.6	26.1	27.8	28.8	30.9	32.0	34.1	35.5	36.3	37.9	37.7	39.5	30.9	32.1
25–29	22.5	22.4	27.7	28.4	29.6	30.5	32.0	33.5	35.3	36.7	37.4	39.1	32.0	33.3
30–34	19.9	19.4	25.2	25.6	27.6	28.4	30.6	31.6	33.9	35.2	37.1	38.7	33.2	34.5
35–39	15.6	15.2	22.1	21.9	27.3	27.9	29.3	30.1	31.8	33.1	36.4	37.9	34.0	35.4
40–44	12.1	11.8	19.4	18.8	24.8	25.0	27.2	27.8	30.3	31.1	35.8	37.1	34.9	36.3
45–49	10.4	9.9	15.1	14.5	21.5	21.1	26.8	27.0	28.8	29.3	34.6	35.6	35.4	37.0
50–54	9.5	8.9	11.5	10.9	18.7	17.7	24.0	23.7	26.5	26.6	32.9	33.4	35.4	36.9
55–59	8.1	7.4	9.7	8.8	14.2	13.2	20.4	19.3	25.5	25.0	30.1	30.2	35.1	36.3
60–64	6.4	5.6	8.4	7.4	10.3	9.3	17.0	15.3	22.1	20.8	27.6	26.6	34.1	34.5
65–69	4.7	3.9	6.7	5.6	8.1	6.8	12.1	10.4	17.7	15.6	24.5	22.6	32.3	31.6
70–74	3.2	2.5	4.6	3.6	6.3	5.0	7.9	6.5	13.4	10.9	20.0	17.4	29.9	27.5
75–79	2.1	1.5	2.9	2.1	4.2	3.1	5.3	4.0	8.2	6.2	15.9	12.9	25.2	21.4
80+	1.6	0.9	2.3	1.6	3.5	2.5	5.1	3.7	6.9	5.0	17.0	12.5	34.5	26.7
Total	260	258	312	312	366	368	419	422	467	471	536	540	540	542

	1990		2000		2010		2020		2030		2050		2100	
	F	M	F	M	F	M	F	M	F	M	F	M	F	M
Japan, Australia, and New Zealand														
0–4	4.1	4.3	4.8	5.0	4.3	4.5	4.1	4.3	4.3	4.5	3.9	4.1	3.6	3.8
5–9	4.4	4.6	4.6	4.8	4.7	4.9	4.0	4.3	4.2	4.4	3.9	4.1	3.7	3.8
10–14	4.9	5.1	4.1	4.3	4.7	5.0	4.3	4.5	4.1	4.3	4.0	4.2	3.7	3.9
15–19	5.7	6.0	4.4	4.6	4.6	4.8	4.7	4.9	4.0	4.2	4.1	4.4	3.8	3.9
20–24	5.2	5.4	4.9	5.1	4.1	4.3	4.7	5.0	4.3	4.5	4.3	4.5	3.7	3.9
25–29	4.9	5.0	5.7	6.0	4.4	4.5	4.6	4.8	4.7	4.9	4.2	4.4	3.7	3.9
30–34	4.7	4.8	5.2	5.4	4.9	5.1	4.0	4.2	4.7	4.9	4.0	4.2	3.8	3.9
35–39	5.3	5.3	4.8	5.0	5.7	5.9	4.3	4.5	4.6	4.7	4.0	4.2	3.8	4.0
40–44	6.0	6.1	4.7	4.7	5.1	5.3	4.8	5.0	4.0	4.2	4.3	4.5	3.9	4.1
45–49	5.1	5.1	5.2	5.2	4.8	4.9	5.6	5.8	4.3	4.5	4.6	4.8	3.9	4.1
50–54	4.6	4.5	5.9	5.9	4.6	4.6	5.1	5.2	4.8	4.9	4.7	4.8	3.9	4.0
55–59	4.4	4.2	5.0	4.8	5.1	5.0	4.7	4.7	5.6	5.7	4.5	4.6	3.8	4.0
60–64	3.9	3.7	4.4	4.1	5.8	5.5	4.5	4.3	5.0	5.0	3.9	4.0	3.9	4.0
65–69	3.3	2.6	4.1	3.7	4.8	4.4	4.9	4.6	4.6	4.4	4.2	4.1	4.0	4.1
70–74	2.6	1.8	3.5	3.0	4.1	3.5	5.4	4.8	4.3	3.9	4.5	4.3	4.1	4.0
75–79	2.1	1.3	2.7	1.8	3.6	2.8	4.2	3.4	4.5	3.7	5.1	4.5	3.9	3.7
80+	2.0	1.1	3.2	1.7	4.8	2.8	6.7	4.1	9.6	6.3	11.9	8.1	15.6	11.0
Total	73	71	77	75	80	78	81	78	81	79	80	78	77	74
Eastern Europe														
0–4	13.2	13.8	11.1	11.5	11.4	11.8	11.1	11.5	11.2	11.6	11.7	12.2	13.7	14.4
5–9	13.0	13.5	11.2	11.6	11.6	11.9	11.4	11.7	11.2	11.5	11.6	12.1	13.5	14.2
10–14	12.8	13.3	13.1	13.4	11.0	11.3	11.4	11.7	11.0	11.3	11.5	12.0	13.3	14.0
15–19	12.9	12.6	13.0	13.4	11.2	11.5	11.6	11.8	11.4	11.7	11.5	11.9	13.1	13.8
20–24	11.6	12.0	12.8	13.2	13.0	13.4	11.0	11.2	11.4	11.6	11.2	11.5	12.8	13.4
25–29	13.3	13.7	12.0	12.5	12.9	13.4	11.2	11.4	11.6	11.8	11.1	11.4	12.6	13.1
30–34	14.1	14.3	11.6	11.9	12.7	13.1	13.0	13.3	11.0	11.2	11.0	11.2	12.4	12.9
35–39	13.4	13.4	13.2	13.5	11.9	12.4	12.9	13.2	11.1	11.4	11.3	11.5	12.2	12.7
40–44	10.0	9.7	14.0	14.0	11.4	11.7	12.6	13.0	12.9	13.2	11.3	11.4	12.0	12.4
45–49	9.9	9.1	13.2	13.0	13.0	13.2	11.7	12.1	12.7	13.0	11.4	11.5	11.7	12.1
50–54	11.4	10.2	9.7	9.3	13.6	13.4	11.2	11.3	12.4	12.6	10.8	10.7	11.5	11.7
55–59	10.7	8.9	9.5	8.4	12.7	12.1	12.6	12.3	11.4	11.5	10.8	10.6	11.3	11.4
60–64	11.2	7.8	10.7	8.8	9.2	8.2	13.0	12.0	10.8	10.3	12.4	11.8	11.2	10.9
65–69	8.0	4.5	9.5	7.1	8.6	6.8	11.8	10.0	11.9	10.5	12.0	10.9	11.0	10.3
70–74	5.5	2.6	9.1	5.5	9.1	6.4	8.0	6.1	11.7	9.2	11.3	9.4	10.4	9.2
75–79	5.7	2.5	5.6	2.6	7.1	4.3	6.8	4.3	9.8	6.7	9.7	7.0	9.9	8.0
80+	5.0	1.8	6.0	2.3	8.4	3.9	10.8	5.5	11.5	6.1	18.2	8.8	26.6	13.0
Total	181	164	185	172	189	179	192	183	195	185	199	186	219	208
Western Europe														
0–4	10.9	11.5	13.3	13.7	11.5	12.1	11.3	11.9	11.7	12.3	11.2	11.8	11.6	12.2
5–9	11.3	11.9	13.6	14.1	12.0	12.5	10.9	11.4	11.8	12.4	11.0	11.6	11.6	12.2
10–14	11.8	12.4	10.9	11.4	13.2	13.7	11.5	12.1	11.3	11.9	11.1	11.6	11.6	12.2
15–19	13.2	13.8	11.2	11.8	13.6	14.1	12.0	12.5	10.9	11.4	11.3	11.9	11.6	12.2
20–24	14.8	15.4	11.7	12.3	10.8	11.4	13.2	13.6	11.5	12.0	11.7	12.3	11.5	12.0
25–29	15.0	15.5	13.1	13.7	11.2	11.8	13.5	14.0	12.0	12.4	11.8	12.3	11.3	11.8
30–34	13.8	14.0	14.8	15.3	11.7	12.3	10.8	11.3	13.2	13.5	11.3	11.8	11.2	11.7
35–39	13.0	13.2	14.9	15.4	13.0	13.6	11.2	11.6	13.5	13.8	10.8	11.3	11.3	11.8
40–44	12.6	12.7	13.6	13.9	14.7	15.2	11.6	12.1	10.8	11.1	11.4	11.8	11.3	11.8
45–49	11.5	11.5	12.9	13.0	14.8	15.1	12.9	13.4	11.1	11.5	11.9	12.2	11.3	11.7
50–54	11.3	11.1	12.3	12.3	13.4	13.5	14.5	14.7	11.5	11.8	13.0	13.1	11.1	11.5
55–59	10.7	10.1	11.1	10.9	12.6	12.4	14.5	14.4	12.7	12.9	13.2	13.2	10.9	11.1
60–64	10.5	9.2	10.7	10.0	11.8	11.4	13.0	12.6	14.1	13.9	10.5	10.4	10.8	11.0
65–69	10.1	7.7	9.9	8.6	10.5	9.5	12.0	11.1	14.0	13.2	10.6	10.3	11.0	10.9
70–74	7.1	4.9	9.2	7.1	9.7	8.0	11.0	9.6	12.3	10.9	10.8	10.1	11.2	10.8
75–79	7.4	4.4	8.0	5.1	8.2	5.9	9.1	7.0	10.8	8.7	11.4	9.8	10.9	10.0
80+	8.8	4.0	9.6	4.8	12.4	6.5	14.6	7.8	18.6	10.6	28.9	18.4	36.9	24.5
Total	194	184	201	193	205	199	208	201	212	204	212	204	217	209

	1990		2000		2010		2020		2030		2050		2100	
	F	M	F	M	F	M	F	M	F	M	F	M	F	M
Developing regions														
0–4	268.1	280.2	310.3	326.9	339.7	358.0	370.7	390.0	379.9	399.8	394.6	415.6	302.1	319.0
5–9	238.9	250.2	284.6	299.4	314.1	330.4	347.4	364.8	368.6	386.7	384.7	404.4	305.5	322.1
10–14	213.6	223.9	258.7	270.1	298.9	314.2	328.0	345.2	358.8	376.3	376.8	395.7	310.3	326.9
15–19	213.8	224.6	236.0	246.9	281.4	295.8	310.8	326.6	344.0	360.8	365.2	383.5	313.4	330.1
20–24	198.6	209.0	211.0	221.0	256.1	267.3	296.0	311.0	324.9	341.8	365.1	383.1	329.5	346.7
25–29	170.6	178.8	210.7	220.9	233.0	243.7	278.1	292.2	307.2	322.8	361.3	378.6	341.8	359.3
30–34	143.2	149.4	195.2	204.9	208.0	217.5	252.6	263.4	292.1	306.7	351.2	367.8	351.5	369.0
35–39	126.9	132.2	167.0	174.5	207.3	216.8	229.2	239.3	273.7	287.2	335.2	350.8	357.3	374.4
40–44	98.5	102.5	139.4	144.6	191.2	199.8	203.7	212.2	247.6	257.4	314.9	329.7	361.8	378.0
45–49	80.8	83.5	122.5	126.3	162.4	168.0	201.6	209.4	223.1	231.2	295.1	307.2	362.9	377.5
50–54	72.3	74.0	93.5	95.5	133.6	136.1	183.7	189.3	195.8	201.2	276.5	285.2	359.7	370.9
55–59	63.1	64.0	74.6	74.8	114.8	115.2	152.4	154.1	190.0	193.0	252.1	256.5	347.7	354.1
60–64	51.8	51.0	63.7	62.5	83.9	82.1	120.6	118.3	167.5	166.6	218.2	216.1	325.8	325.4
65–69	39.5	37.3	51.7	49.3	62.2	58.8	97.5	92.5	131.2	125.7	182.7	176.1	293.6	285.2
70–74	28.3	24.9	37.8	34.3	47.7	43.3	64.2	58.3	94.5	86.0	143.1	132.6	261.6	244.9
75–79	18.3	14.8	24.1	20.6	32.8	28.6	40.3	35.1	66.3	57.5	117.7	104.4	216.1	192.5
80+	13.3	9.0	20.4	15.9	29.9	24.7	39.3	34.4	53.9	46.6	130.3	107.5	307.9	255.6
Total	2,039	2,109	2,501	2,589	2,997	3,100	3,516	3,636	4,019	4,148	4,865	4,995	5,449	5,532
Industrialized regions														
0–4	38.1	39.9	41.4	43.0	38.9	40.6	39.3	41.0	40.7	42.5	41.7	43.7	48.8	51.2
5–9	38.4	40.3	42.5	44.1	40.0	41.4	38.3	39.9	40.5	42.2	40.8	42.8	48.0	50.4
10–14	38.8	40.6	37.9	39.5	41.3	42.6	38.8	40.3	39.2	40.9	40.4	42.3	47.4	49.7
15–19	40.5	42.5	38.4	40.1	42.4	44.0	40.0	41.3	38.3	39.8	40.5	42.3	46.8	49.1
20–24	42.0	43.6	38.7	40.4	37.8	39.3	41.2	42.4	38.7	40.2	40.6	42.3	45.8	47.9
25–29	45.1	46.1	40.3	42.2	38.2	39.8	42.3	43.7	39.9	41.1	40.4	41.9	44.8	46.8
30–34	44.8	45.2	41.8	43.2	38.5	40.0	37.7	39.0	41.1	42.1	39.1	40.5	44.0	45.9
35–39	43.0	43.0	44.8	45.6	40.1	41.8	38.1	39.4	42.2	43.3	38.1	39.3	43.4	45.2
40–44	38.6	38.3	44.4	44.5	41.5	42.6	38.3	39.6	37.5	38.6	38.5	39.6	42.8	44.5
45–49	34.4	33.4	42.4	41.9	44.3	44.7	39.8	41.0	37.8	38.8	39.6	40.3	42.2	43.7
50–54	33.8	31.9	37.8	36.8	43.6	42.9	40.0	41.3	37.8	38.6	40.5	40.8	41.3	42.4
55–59	31.8	28.9	33.2	31.2	41.2	39.5	43.3	42.4	39.0	39.3	41.3	41.2	40.2	40.9
60–64	32.0	26.3	32.0	28.5	36.1	33.6	42.0	39.5	39.7	38.6	36.3	35.6	39.5	39.5
65–69	27.6	19.8	29.1	24.1	31.0	26.8	39.0	34.7	41.5	38.1	36.0	34.2	39.2	38.2
70–74	20.2	13.1	27.4	19.7	28.4	22.2	33.1	27.4	39.2	33.2	35.1	31.5	38.5	36.2
75–79	19.2	10.9	21.2	12.7	23.5	16.2	26.4	19.2	34.2	26.0	34.4	28.4	36.9	32.7
80+	21.0	9.3	24.6	11.7	32.9	16.9	40.2	21.7	52.2	29.7	80.3	47.8	115.8	72.4
Total	589	553	618	589	640	615	658	634	679	653	704	675	805	777
World total														
0–4	306.2	320.1	351.7	369.9	378.6	398.5	410.0	431.0	420.6	442.4	436.3	459.3	350.8	370.2
5–9	277.3	290.5	327.1	343.6	354.1	371.9	385.7	404.7	409.1	429.0	425.5	447.2	353.5	372.6
10–14	252.4	264.5	296.6	309.6	340.2	356.8	366.8	385.5	398.0	417.2	417.2	438.0	357.7	376.7
15–19	254.3	267.1	274.3	287.0	323.9	339.8	350.8	368.0	382.2	400.6	405.7	425.8	360.2	379.2
20–24	240.6	252.6	249.7	261.4	293.9	306.5	337.2	353.4	363.6	382.0	405.6	425.4	375.2	394.6
25–29	215.7	224.9	251.0	263.1	271.3	283.5	320.4	335.9	347.1	363.9	401.7	420.5	386.6	406.1
30–34	188.0	194.6	236.9	248.1	246.5	257.6	290.2	302.4	333.2	348.8	390.3	408.3	395.5	414.9
35–39	169.8	175.2	211.8	220.1	247.4	258.6	267.2	278.7	315.9	330.5	373.3	390.1	400.7	419.5
40–44	137.1	140.8	183.8	189.1	232.7	242.4	241.9	251.8	285.0	295.9	353.4	369.3	404.6	422.5
45–49	115.2	116.9	164.9	168.2	206.7	212.7	241.4	250.4	260.8	270.1	334.7	347.5	405.1	421.1
50–54	106.1	106.0	131.3	132.4	177.2	179.1	224.6	230.7	233.6	239.8	317.0	326.0	400.9	413.3
55–59	95.0	92.9	107.8	106.1	155.9	154.8	195.7	196.5	229.0	232.3	293.4	297.8	387.9	394.9
60–64	83.8	77.2	95.7	91.0	120.0	115.7	162.6	157.8	207.2	205.2	254.5	251.7	365.4	364.9
65–69	67.1	57.1	80.8	73.4	93.2	85.7	136.5	127.2	172.7	163.8	218.7	210.2	332.8	323.4
70–74	48.5	38.0	65.2	54.0	76.0	65.6	97.3	85.8	133.7	119.2	178.3	164.1	300.1	281.1
75–79	37.4	25.7	45.3	33.3	56.3	44.8	66.6	54.3	100.5	83.5	152.1	132.8	253.1	225.2
80+	34.3	18.3	45.0	27.6	62.8	41.6	79.5	56.1	106.1	76.3	210.6	155.3	423.7	328.0
Total	2,629	2,662	3,119	3,178	3,637	3,715	4,174	4,270	4,698	4,801	5,568	5,669	6,254	6,308

Index

479